Unsung Hero of Gettysburg

Unsung Hero of
GETTYSBURG

The Story of Union General David McMurtrie Gregg

★ EDWARD G. LONGACRE ★

Potomac Books

AN IMPRINT OF THE UNIVERSITY OF NEBRASKA PRESS

Library of Congress Cataloging-in-Publication Data
Names: Longacre, Edward G., 1946– author.
Title: Unsung hero of Gettysburg: the story of Union General
David McMurtrie Gregg / Edward G. Longacre.
Description: [Lincoln, Nebraska]: Potomac Books, an imprint of
the University of Nebraska Press, [2021] | Includes bibliographical
references and index.
Identifiers: LCCN 2020038266
ISBN 9781640124295 (hardback)
ISBN 9781640124561 (epub)
ISBN 9781640124578 (mobi)
ISBN 9781640124585 (pdf)
Subjects: LCSH: Gregg, David McMurtrie, 1833–1916. |
Gettysburg Campaign, 1863. | United States. Army of the
Potomac. Cavalry Corps. Division, 2nd. | Generals—United
States—Biography. | United States. Army—Biography. |
Pennsylvania—Biography.
Classification: LCC E475.53 .L848 2021 |
DDC 355.0092 [B]—dc23
LC record available at https://lccn.loc.gov/2020038266

Set in Garamond Premier Pro by Laura Buis.

For Joe and Lucy Byers

CONTENTS

ILLUSTRATIONS

Maps

Photographs

Following page 122

ACKNOWLEDGMENTS

As when researching previous projects, numerous archivists, reference librarians, and research assistants provided materials without which I could not have completed my present work. Foremost among these are staff members of the institutions that house the two largest collections of David McMurtrie Gregg Papers: Lisa Adams, archival assistant at the Henry Janssen Library of the Berks History Center, Reading, Pennsylvania; and Chamisa Redmond, information and reference specialist at the Library of Congress. Additionally, Paul Harrison of the Archives I Reference Section of the National Archives and Records Administration provided access to myriad documents pertaining to Gregg's military career. Susan Lintlemann, manuscripts curator at the United States Military Academy Library, West Point, New York, and Victoria Russo of the reference staff of the Historical Society of Pennsylvania in Philadelphia also aided in my search for Gregg materials.

Fellow historians provided major support. Clark B. ("Bud") Hall and Theodore J. Zeman assisted my research into Gregg's participation, respectively, at Second Brandy Station and in the Bristoe Campaign. Robert F. O'Neill, Jr., shared his extensive research on Civil War cavalry operations during and prior to Gettysburg. John M. McNulty, past commander of the Pennsylvania Department, Sons of Union Veterans of the Civil War, helped track Gregg's postwar affiliation with the Grand Army of the Republic and the Military Order of the Loyal Legion of the United States. Gregg family historian David Fox provided helpful information on the general and his relations. As he has for so many of my previous titles, Paul Dangel supplied the excellent battle and campaign maps for the present study. My wife, Ann, provided material and moral support throughout my work. Last but certainly not least, I am indebted to Tom Swanson and his able staff at Potomac Books for taking on this project and seeing it through to publication.

INTRODUCTION

Gettysburg, in many respects the pivotal battle of the Civil War, had its share of heroes in both blue and gray. Many of these, whose deeds entitle them to recognition, honor, and perhaps even glory, never received the acclaim or the historical attention due them. One of the most neglected of these stalwarts is Gen. David McMurtrie Gregg, commander of the 2nd Division, Cavalry Corps, Army of the Potomac. Although his name has been largely forgotten today, Gregg was one of the most gifted and successful cavalry officers in U.S. military history.

Although his fame was won on many fields, it was at Gettysburg on July 3, 1863, that the thirty-year-old Pennsylvanian left a deep imprint on the nation's most important conflict. That day he had charge not only of his own, recently depleted division, fewer than 2,500 men, but also—strictly by happenstance—the 1,800-man brigade of Gen. George Armstrong Custer. With these troops Gregg engaged and held at bay a cavalry force of slightly lesser size under Gen. James Ewell Brown Stuart. Gregg's instinctive grasp of his situation, his coolheaded leadership throughout the struggle, and his inspired tactics prevented the Confederate chieftain from striking the right flank and rear of Gen. George Gordon Meade's Army of the Potomac at approximately the same time that Rebel infantry slammed into the Union center, an attack forever afterward known as Pickett's Charge.

Although it is not unusual that historians disagree when assigning priority to those aspects of the battle that decided its outcome, too many neglect to include Gregg's defense of the Union right as among the most consequential. Contemporary observers, however, especially those who served under Gregg at Gettysburg, were not reluctant to celebrate his contributions to victory. One of the most respected of these was Capt. James Harvey Kidd of the 6th Michigan. In his highly regarded postwar memoir of service in Custer's brigade, Kidd paid minute attention to the fighting on the third day at Gettysburg, drawing deeply not only from his own experience but also from the accounts of other participants. Kidd, who after Gettysburg would rise to colonel and command of his regiment, concluded:

> In the light of all the official reports put together link by link, so as to make one connected chain of evidence, we can see that the engagement which he [Gregg] fought on the right at Gettysburg on July 3, 1863, was from first to last, a well planned battle in which the different commands were maneuvered with the same sagacity displayed by a skillful chess player in moving the pawns upon a chessboard; in which every detail was the fruit of the brain of one man who, from the time when he turned Custer to the northward, until he sent the 1st Michigan thundering against the brigades of Hampton and Fitzhugh Lee, made not a single false move; who was distinguished not less for his intuitive foresight than for his quick perceptions at critical moments. That man was Gen. David McMurtrie Gregg.

Gregg's achievements encompassed much more than that critical three-day struggle midway through the war. At West Point (class of 1855) he demonstrated both classroom acumen and drill-ground proficiency of a high order. In the prewar army he established a solid record in both cavalry and dragoon service, winning commendation for his conduct in battle against the hostile Indian tribes of the Southwest and the Pacific coast. In one particularly sanguinary engagement against a confederation of tribes in the Washington Territory, his sage advice and calm decision-making enabled an outnumbered expeditionary force of all arms to escape an incipient massacre on a scale that would have overshadowed Custer's debacle at the Little Bighorn eighteen years later.

Not long after the Civil War broke out, Captain Gregg joined hundreds of regular army officers in accepting higher rank in the nation's volunteer force, being commissioned colonel of the 8th Pennsylvania

Cavalry. By imposing and enforcing a rigid drill program and weeding out incompetent subordinates, in a matter of weeks he transformed the underachieving outfit into one of the most proficient mounted units in the Army of the Potomac. He led it with marked ability during and following the Peninsula Campaign of spring–summer 1862, frequently demonstrating fitness for higher command. After the battle of Fredericksburg that December he was assigned command of a brigade of volunteer horse, and just before Gettysburg he was appointed to lead the 2nd Cavalry Division. At the head of this veteran command now-Brigadier General Gregg reached the zenith of his career, though celebrity would ever elude him.

Almost thirteen months after Gettysburg, following exemplary service under Meade and General-in-Chief Ulysses S. Grant during the Overland Campaign of 1864 (which included the Battle of the Wilderness, the major cavalry clashes at Todd's Tavern and Haw's Shop, and two large-scale raids under Meade's cavalry leader, Maj. Gen. Philip H. Sheridan), Gregg rose to lead every horse soldier involved in the siege of Petersburg. Although the assignment testified to the confidence Grant and Meade reposed in Gregg, the position appeared a hollow honor, two-thirds of the army's horsemen having accompanied Sheridan to a new theater of operations in Virginia's Shenandoah Valley. "Little Phil" and his troopers would remain in the valley for seven months, winning the publicity and glory denied to the troops engaged in the relatively static campaigning at Petersburg.

Nevertheless, Gregg served faithfully and well through the remainder of the siege, effectively commanding not only the 2nd Division but also the small cavalry division of the Army of the James, which supported Meade's operations. By the close of 1864 Gregg was a brevet major general and the senior mounted officer in the main theater of the war, universally praised by all who observed him in action. One high-ranking comrade, Maj. Gen. Winfield Scott Hancock, commander of Meade's II Corps, stated: "I have seen no officer whom I would prefer to have with me [in action]. . . . In battle, he is cool, tenacious, brave, and judicious."

His many accomplishments notwithstanding, Gregg's record is not without blemish or controversy. Present-day historians fault him for tactical mistakes during the battle of Second Brandy Station, June 9, 1863, which may have affected the outcome of this, the opening battle of the Gettysburg Campaign and at the time the largest mounted engagement of the war. Sixteen months later, during Grant's Overland Campaign, Gregg was held responsible at army headquarters for his failure to warn Meade of Robert E. Lee's attempt to turn his left flank and interpose between the Federals and Washington D C, the city Meade's army had been enjoined to protect at all costs. Even so, details of this supposed lapse remain obscure even at this late day and deserve careful analysis. Then, in early February 1865, less than two months before the climactic campaign of the war in the East got underway, Gregg abruptly resigned his commissions in both the regular and volunteer service, left the army, and returned to his adopted hometown of Reading, Pennsylvania. Because he never explained his untimely exit from the war, over the years historians have offered a variety of possible reasons, some of which strain credence.

His resignation cost the Army of the Potomac one of its most valuable soldiers and it may also have cost Gregg personally. It is possible his decision factored in his inability to fulfill his desire to return to the regular service after the war. The position he sought in the newly expanded army went, instead, to his cousin and wartime subordinate, Bvt. Brig. Gen. John Irvin Gregg, who had remained in the ranks through to Robert E. Lee's surrender in April 1865. Moreover, when a bill to provide Gregg with a pension moved through Congress in the early 1900s, political opponents delved into, and may have been swayed by, the circumstances of his departure from the conflict. Neither at the time, nor two years later when it was revived, did the bill pass.

Flaws and misadventures notwithstanding, David McMurtrie Gregg stands today as the *beau ideal* of Civil War cavalryman. Dignified, self-composed, and unflappable under pressure, he was unhesitatingly relied upon by his superiors, respected by his peers, and admired by his subordinates. Like all worthy officers, he was conscious of the image he projected to his men and his war-torn nation. Rejecting the behavior of publicity-seeking colleagues—so many of whom seemed to gravitate to the cavalry—Gregg held at arm's length the newspaper correspondents who tried to attach themselves to his command, restricting their access to his headquarters and refusing their requests to interview him.

Undoubtedly Gregg's modesty and disdain for self-promotion factored into his being overlooked by those who furthered the careers of Civil War commanders. For many reasons, not merely his contributions to victory on perhaps the most critical day in U.S. history, he does not deserve further neglect.

Unsung Hero of Gettysburg

1

The Man in the Invisible Circle

David McMurtrie Gregg was descended from military and political notables including David Gregg, who was born in Scotland in 1630 and served as a captain in the Roundhead army of Oliver Cromwell during the English Civil War. At age sixty, following distinguished service in the cause of Cromwell and Parliament, David Gregg's great-great-great-grandfather was killed, along with his twenty-five-year-old son, by vengeful Cavaliers. Two decades later the murdered son's two surviving sons and their sister emigrated to the New World, settling in Boston before spreading out to New Hampshire, New York, and Delaware. By 1724 one son, Andrew, along with his sister and their families, had settled in Lancaster County, Pennsylvania. The family participated fully in the Revolutionary War. James Potter of Huntingdon, Pennsylvania, an ancestor of David McMurtrie Gregg's grandmother Martha Potter, served as an officer in the Pennsylvania Line and fought staunchly at Trenton and Princeton before joining George Washington—whom he claimed as a personal friend—at Valley Forge. Meanwhile, Andrew Gregg's son, also named Andrew, served in the Delaware militia despite his youth.[1]

Once the United States won its independence, the Gregg family and its associated lines turned from affairs military to academic pursuits and then to public service. The younger Andrew Gregg taught at the University of Pennsylvania before winning a seat in the U.S. House of Representatives in 1791. He did so as a candidate of the Democratic-Republican Party of Thomas Jefferson and James Madison, opponents of the Federalists' vision of a strong central government. Andrew's political career flourished, if relatively briefly. In 1807 he was elected to the U.S. Senate, but his tenure was limited to a single term. From 1820 to 1823 he served as secretary of the Commonwealth of Pennsylvania and in the latter year ran unsuccessfully for governor. He then retired to his adopted hometown of Bellefonte, Centre County, one of the leading commercial and industrial centers between Pittsburgh and Harrisburg, and concentrated on mercantile and agricultural pursuits. Andrew died in Bellefonte in May 1835, three weeks short of his eightieth birthday.[2]

Andrew's son Matthew Duncan Gregg, born in 1804 in Penns Valley, Pennsylvania, the eighth of eleven children, married Ellen McMurtrie of Huntingdon County in 1828. The couple reared nine children, the third of whom—their second son, born in Huntingdon on April 10, 1833—they christened David McMurtrie. At that time David's father, a tall, imposing man with a dark beard and a penchant for elegant attire and fast horses, was practicing law, having been admitted to the bar in both Huntingdon and Centre Counties. It appears, however, that Matthew Gregg did not consider himself well suited to the profession. Over the next five years he, Ellen, and the children experienced a peripatetic existence, living successively in Huntingdon, Harrisburg, Hollidaysburg, and Pine Grove Mills before returning to the old family home at Bellefonte. There Matthew quit his law career and plunged into the burgeoning iron industry of the upper Juniata River valley, "a change," General Gregg's son, David McMurtrie Gregg, Jr., remarked years later, "which he had been considering for a long time."

The change of profession appears to have had a forceful effect on young David, who came to appreciate the larger-than-life image projected by the ironmasters of the day. As his son noted, "A successful furnace owner not only lived in a sumptuous manner in a large, well ordered mansion near his furnaces, but he was the overlord and patron of a small army of outside workers, all of whom were necessary to the successful operation of the plant. . . . Truly those men were Kings in their own right, and it is small wonder that an indelible impression of their importance was made on the mind of a boy who was bought up in the region where so many of the old furnaces were located." That impression may have started Matthew's son on a path to another field of endeavor where rank and authority prevailed and a high degree of order and efficiency was demanded of a large workforce.

The rapid growth of the local iron business, and the fierce competition it engendered, caused land values to skyrocket. The scarcity of suitable properties prompted Matthew Gregg to look beyond the Juniata valley to secure his and his family's future. In early 1845 he, his brother James, and their brother-in-law David Mitchell went into business in Loudoun County, Virginia, where they had purchased Potomac Furnace, one mile south of its namesake river on the road between Leesburg and Point of Rocks. In April the families of the three owners crowded inside the small manor house at the furnace.

At first all was well, and the new enterprise appeared a success, but an extremely hot summer spawned a yellow fever–like epidemic. The brothers were stricken with a form of the disease that proved fatal to both, Matthew dying in late July and James twelve days later. After burying her husband and brother-in-law and closing up their affairs, David's grief-stricken mother returned with her nine children to Hollidaysburg, the seat of Blair County, Pennsylvania, which had become a center of the Juniata iron industry and where her well-to-do brother Robert was then living.

Ellen never fully recovered from the shock of her family's fracture, which sapped her fragile health. Although their mother's condition constantly affected them to one degree or another, her children were relieved of some of their concern and sorrow through companionship with members of Ellen's extended family. The Greggs were related to nearly all the prominent families of their native region. No fewer than thirty first cousins lived in or near Centre County; they included Andrew Gregg Curtin, son of David's Aunt Jean Gregg Curtin of Bellefonte, who would become Pennsylvania's governor during and after the Civil War. The children rarely lacked companionship. The general's son related that "it was with particular pleasure that David recalled the visits made to the home of his father's first cousin, Mary Potter Wilson, at Potter's Mills, there being no less than six attractive daughters in that family, all of whom were so jolly and full of fun, that a stay under their hospitable roof was something to be looked forward to eagerly and long remembered."

David and his siblings sought comfort by throwing themselves into their studies in the local schools and, outside the classroom, into games both athletic and military in nature. In early youth both he and his older brother Andrew developed a fondness for horses and riding. Short-legged when he was young, David was at first unable to completely straddle a mount, "but as he was fearless, and seemed to take to horses instinctively, it was not long before he was able to ride comfortably any horse he found between his knees." One of his greatest pleasures was to visit a nearby hotel whose stable manager permitted him to exercise visitors' horses and water them at a local creek. At one point just before or shortly after the move to Virginia David was entrusted with an errand that required him to ride one of the family's horses a distance of sixty miles, a journey he completed without incident.

But the family's ordeal was not yet over. By the time she returned her family to Pennsylvania tuberculosis had begun to stalk Ellen Gregg. By 1847 the disease had progressed to the point that David's mother could no longer be ministered to adequately by local physicians. With the assistance of her brother, she was placed in an Allegheny Mountain spa at Bedford, thirty miles south of Hollidaysburg. The change of scenery had no effect, and Ellen succumbed to the wasting condition on August 17.

Their mother's enforced estrangement deeply affected David and his siblings, but the aftermath left an indelible imprint. On the night she died the children had gathered in a downstairs room of the Hollidaysburg house, adjacent to the Blair County courthouse. One of them happened to peer out the front window—and saw their mother standing outside. When the child cried out in shock and joy, at least some of the others looked out and saw the same vision. They rushed outdoors, expecting to find Ellen beckoning to them, only to find the yard empty. Wretchedly disappointed, the children returned to the house where, hours later, they received word of their mother's death at Bedford.[3]

As the general's son observed, "With the passing of their mother, life, as a united family, ended for the children, and they were taken into the homes of their Uncles and Aunts, who did everything in their power to make their lives happy and comfortable." Fourteen-year-old David and Andrew, two years his senior, were taken into the home of their uncle David McMurtrie and his wife Martha, a sturdy brick house in the center of Huntingdon. David would recall fondly the four years he spent in the McMurtrie fold. His uncle, who was well known for his generosity, spared no expense to make David and Andrew feel as much at home as possible; apparently he also helped support some of the other dispossessed children. Years later he would recall, "I took charge of this poor orphan family—My time and money has been freely spent in making them what they are this day."[4]

But the McMurtrie house was not a rest home or resort; David and his brother had to contend with hardships and adhere to a strict regimen. Because the large house was difficult to heat, the brothers spent frigid days in their upper-floor bedroom, where on winter mornings water would freeze in the wash basin. The McMurties were ardent Presbyterians, and the Sabbath was given over to church and Sunday school attendance, which David appears to have endured rather than embraced. Perhaps as a result of the strict upbringing thrust upon him, in later years he never made an open profession of religious convictions, although when he married he expressed a preference for the Presbyterian rite. At other points in his military career he attended Episcopal services and briefly took on the duties of a vestryman. Despite his lack of permanent religious affiliation, he was said to have considered Christianity "the foundation of society and the state."[5]

The grim fate that had beset the Gregg family since the summer of '45 proved relentless. Only four months after Ellen's passing, the youngest daughter, three-year-old Olitipa, whom David loved dearly, died of an undiagnosed illness. In 1851 the two oldest children—Martha, twenty-two and recently married, and twenty-year-old Andrew, David's companion in the McMurtrie home—succumbed to virulent diseases. In Andrew's case, the cause was tuberculosis, the same contagion as had taken their mother's life.

The grief and sorrow spawned by these multiple tragedies, especially the loss of the beloved older brother who died in his arms, must have had a devastating effect on the teenaged David, one that time failed to ameliorate. They turned his thoughts increasingly inward, and taught him to conceal his emotions and guard his privacy. Ever afterward he displayed a quiet and reserved demeanor and sometimes an abstracted aloofness that discouraged attempts at intimacy and held even long-time friends at arm's length. Those who attempted to define him spoke authoritatively of his character but less so of his personality. A typical description came from David McMurtrie Gregg, Jr.: affable and sometimes genial but not demonstrative, self-possessed to a remarkable degree, and with no tendency to exuberance. Gregg, Jr., quoted an unnamed observer: "Although always pleasant and courteous, he seemed to live within an invisible circle, ever the boundaries of which but few were allowed to trespass."[6]

David McMurtrie placed a high value on education, and he ensured that his nephews benefited accordingly. During his first two years in Huntingdon young David was educated at a private school run by a Mr. John Hall. Although the institution furnished its pupils with a "very excellent" educational foundation, Hall believed in punctuating his lessons with well-aimed blows from a rattan rod. One leg being shorter than the other, the teacher would rise stiffly on the longer limb to provide additional force to the thrashing he gave to those who could not or would not learn, thus producing an image that never faded from David's memory.

In the fall of 1849 the student escaped the rod when he entered Milnwood, one of Huntingdon County's leading academies. The following year he joined Andrew at the University of Lewisburg, forerunner of Bucknell University. It was during a semester break at Potter's Mills that tuberculosis claimed Andrew Gregg. His death left a permanent void in his brother's life.

One can suppose that after suffering this latest and most profound loss, college life held little allure for the young student. Even so, he continued his studies through the spring 1851 term. This would be the extent of his civilian educational career; before the year was out he learned he had received an appointment to the United States Military Academy. Exactly how this came about remains unknown, although it must have been set in motion by his uncle, and possibly by other family members as well. David's candidacy would have been enhanced by the family's well-known military heritage that dated at least to the Battle of the Boyne and included active campaigning against the hostile Indians of the northwestern U.S.[7]

He had been recommended for the position by Congressman Samuel Calvin, the first member of the House of Representatives from recently organized Blair County. Calvin never ceased to claim credit for helping launch the appointee's career in arms. Gregg's son noted that at this time Gregg was residing in Huntingdon County, a portion of which, along with a segment of the more westerly Bedford County, had helped create Blair. He points out, however, that his father could have claimed a "quasi-home" in Hollidaysburg, where an uncle and two aunts were then residing.

The recipient of Congressman Calvin's patronage displayed a somewhat apathetic attitude toward what another youth might have considered a coveted opportunity. His son wrote that "he accepted the idea of a military career but showed no great enthusiasm for it." Because West Point offered a finished education at minimal cost to the cadet and his family, it would have appealed to David as a means of lightening the burden that his uncle had undertaken in helping raise him and his brother. In fact this may have been his only incentive to accept the appointment. When growing up he likely indulged in military fantasies, like many children, but he had never seriously envisioned himself as a soldier; certainly he never entertained the idea of the military as a profession. Once he committed himself to a career in arms, he took his situation seriously and tried to live up to its highest standards. Yet he never lost his sense of balance, never allowed himself to be carried away by rank or position, and never strove for power and authority as so many fellow officers did in time of both war and peace.[8]

Matriculating at West Point meant a final severance of long-cherished family ties. The incoming cadet spent the last few months at home not only boning up on subjects integral to the academy's curriculum, including mathematics and French, but also bidding farewell to dozens of relatives and family friends, many of whom he would see rarely if at all over the next several years. Late in June, after a long handshake with his uncle and a warm embrace from his aunt, he boarded the southbound train at Huntingdon and set off for New York. The protracted journey, partly by stagecoach, partly by boat up the Hudson River from New York City, passed without incident, and he reached the wharf at West Point in the first week of June, almost a month before the class of 1855 entered upon its academic term.

The eighteen-year-old plebe was suitably impressed by the majestic, timber-fringed highlands that surrounded the reservation where he would spend his most formative years. Almost equally impressive was the campus itself, which included what another incoming cadet described as "the stately array of buildings away across the broadest and smoothest lawn I had ever seen. Half hidden by lofty elms, there was the immense gray stone barracks with towers and sallyport [entranceway], the academic building, the chapel, the library with a dome from which the flag was floating."[9]

David was quickly introduced to the decorum and discipline demanded of the profession he was about to enter, initially in the form of upperclassmen who shouted him to attention, then unleashed an unnerving barrage of questions and commands. Such behavior constituted his introduction to "deviling," the school's time-honored tradition of hazing. The assault on David's aplomb might have been even more severe had he not traveled from New York in the company of a much older plebe, George Henry Elliot of Massachusetts, whose heavy beard and out-of-fashion attire made him the immediate target of heavy-handed amusement. "Ah, sir," said an upperclassman upon greeting the New Englander, "I see that you have brought your son to the Point. Can I be of any service to you?"[10]

Perhaps Cadet Gregg's stoical aloofness served to disappoint those who attempted to discomfit him, for throughout his West Point career he would escape the more extreme efforts at hazing that regularly befell classmates such as the wizened Elliot. Relieved of this source of sometimes exquisite torment, he moved more or less smoothly through the world of the academy in the classroom, on the drill field, and in the barracks. In each of these venues he met and, despite his reserved demeanor, made friends of several fellow plebes. The class of 1855 was a large one, consisting at the outset of seventy-one members chosen from congressional districts in twenty-two states, plus seven presidential ("at large") appointments. The winnowing process, however, was severe and relentless; over the next four years the group would be reduced to thirty-four cadets who would graduate and receive commissions in the various combat and support branches of the army.[11]

The class consisted of several officers who would distinguish themselves in the war that, even in 1851, could be seen taking shape on the horizon of the troubled nation. Ten of Gregg's classmates would become general officers. Two of these hailed from New York: William Woods Averell, whose prewar and wartime career would consistently intertwine with Gregg's, and Alexander S. Webb, who, like Gregg, would win glory at Gettysburg but be denied fame. The others included Godfrey Weitzel and William B. Hazen of Ohio, Alfred T. A. Torbert of Delaware, and John W. Turner of Illinois. Louisiana-born Francis R. T. Nicholls and transplanted Indianan Francis H. Shoup would resign their commissions in the years following graduation in favor of law careers; in 1861 both would join the armies of the Confederacy, eventually rising to brigadier general. Two others who entered West Point with Gregg and would gain a star in the Union ranks, Francis L. Vinton of Maine and James W. Forsyth of Ohio, would be held back to graduate with the class of '56 because of academic deficiencies or an inordinate number of demerits. Forsyth would go on to a celebrated military career, and Vinton was considered one of the most brilliant members of his class, a man of literary, artistic, and scientific gifts as well as a model soldier.[12]

Yet another future general would gain his star only by brevet, a higher rank than an officer officially held, bestowed as a reward for gallant or meritorious conduct but lacking the authority, seniority, and at times the pay attached to the position. This was Cyrus Ballou Comstock of Massachusetts, who graduated at the head of Gregg's class for four years running. Blessed with a keen theoretical mind, a convivial spirit, and a knack for inspiring trust and confidence, Comstock would never gain a combat command but would finish the war as an aide and confidant to a list of renowned commanders that included Ulysses S. Grant and William T. Sherman.[13]

Cadet Gregg would maintain cordial relations with the majority of these future notables, as indeed he would with virtually every member of his class as well as with a few members of other classes. In time, however, each of his peers would become acquainted with his sensitivity to assaults on his privacy and composure. One incident stands out: when a jovial cadet slipped up behind him and slapped him on the back, he spun about and through gritted teeth said: "If you ever do that to me again I will knock you down." No one doubted he meant what he said.[14]

A number of Gregg's friends hailed from Southern states; when war came, they would resign from the U.S. Army and join Nicholls and Shoup in Confederate gray. During the conflict Gregg would seek opportunities to reestablish contact with some of these young men, whom he could never quite regard as enemies. One such was an upperclassman, John Randolph Chambliss, Jr., of Virginia, whose death in battle in August 1864 as a general officer of Rebel cavalry would come at the hands of one of Gregg's men. He was less close to another future Confederate cavalry leader, James Ewell Brown ("Jeb") Stuart, who would graduate one year ahead of him, but he cherished the company of the Virginian Fitzhugh Lee. The gregarious lowerclassman was the nephew of West Point's highly respected superintendent, Bvt. Col. Robert E. Lee. In the war that lay ahead Fitz Lee would become Stuart's most trusted subordinate, and at Gettysburg and on later fields one of Gregg's most combative opponents.

Perhaps the Pennsylvanian's closest friend at the Point was yet another Southerner, William Dorsey Pender of Edgecombe County, North Carolina, class of 1854. Although the two would appear to have had little in common beyond their shared educational experience, each cherished privacy and tended to speak only when he had something worth saying. Most cadets acquired nicknames, many of them laden with irony. The closed-mouth Pender would be known in the Corps of Cadets as "Poll," after the fabled chattering parrot, whereas Gregg would receive the less explicable moniker "Doctor Geeg." The bond that the two forged at West Point would be strengthened over the next four years through shared hardships and dangers on the western plains, particularly during an expedition against hostile Indians in the Northwest during which both officers came perilously close to a bloody death.[15]

Understandably, it took time to become acclimated to the cloistered, highly competitive, and regulation-driven world of the academy. From the first day of his existence as what was known as an "animal," David Gregg had to adjust to an environment decidedly alien to the one he had long known. His new world revolved around the subordination of individuality to the concept of a corporate body—the Corps of Cadets—while carefully inculcating such traits as self-command, dedication to duty, acceptance of discipline, and reverence for the nation's institutions.

Once shown to the barracks where, in a stroke of good fortune, he was to room with "Dad" Elliot, he found himself in a relatively modern habitation (new barracks had been constructed the previous year) but amid decidedly spartan surroundings. The chamber, which the two would subsequently share with as many as three other plebes, measured fourteen by twenty-two feet, with a single window that offered a panoramic view of the surrounding mountains. William Averell, who had been assigned a room of the same configuration in another wing of the barracks, offered a rather bleak description of the furnishings: "Within the room was a fire-place with an iron mantel, two alcoves at the inner end separated by a partition with hooks on each side of it for hanging clothing, and not an article of furniture of any description, and nothing but the window sill on which one might sit."

Only later would an iron bedstead be added, although mattresses would long be lacking because for the first two months of every academic year the cadets remained outdoors, housed in tents, during a period of near-constant drill and exertion known as the summer encampment. Coal-burning grates supposedly made the barracks habitable in winter but usually provided more light than heat. Candles and oil lamps also furnished light by which to read and study (gas lamps would not be available until three years after Gregg left the Point). Water was available via an old fashioned well with a wooden pump; it had to be carted into the room in a bucket.[16]

Gregg quickly encountered hardships other than bleak accommodations. When the first supper hour arrived he and Elliot were marched to the mess hall where they and other newcomers were pelted with a "perfect shower of bread crusts and baked potatoes," a welcoming ritual designed to test the victims' capacity to withstand embarrassment and discomfiture. David endured the experience without flinching or taking offense. His habitual equanimity would enable him to weather situations much more uncomfortable than this throughout his time on the Hudson. His son related that the food-spattered plebes "had no further troubles to face that day, and within a day or two their class was properly organized and the routine of life at the Point began for them."[17]

That first summer encampment was a time of both toil and tedium, but it would produce fond memories of experiences that promoted camaraderie and esprit de corps. The ever-nostalgic Averell remembered it as "arduous hours of drill through which we moved with the untiring regularity of the hands of a clock; the marches to and from the mess hall to the music of the drum and fife; the morning parade and guard mount . . . the soft illumination of the tent-lighted camp from which breathed forth the music of the violin and guitar, banjo and flute; and the murmur of voices in story and song until all were hushed after 'tattoo' and 'taps' into the silence of night when the quiet tread of sentinels tolled us to our dreams." Averell noted that by the close of August, when the camp was broken up and the cadets were ushered indoors, "we were physically in pretty good shape" and ready to tackle the challenges—and the terrors—of the classroom.[18]

By the early 1850s West Point had gained a well-deserved reputation as one of the world's most proficient institutions of military engineering, although it had yet to fully establish itself as a tactical training ground for future officers. Over the previous decade West Point officials had taken steps to broaden the institution's mission by adding emphasis to general military science, placing West Point on a footing with the elite military academies of Britain and France. The curriculum, however, remained top-heavy with highly technical subjects that underlay the engineering profession and demanded long and concentrated study. The primary emphasis was on higher mathematics (mainly algebra, plane and solid geometry, and trigonometry), instilled via daily recitation of subject material during a cadet's first two years of study.

Equally difficult to master were the courses in French, the international language of the military profession, as well as those in English grammar, geography, chemistry (including mineralogy and geology, subjects directly related to military technology), topographical drawing, natural and experimental philosophy (an amalgam of science-based courses including physics, mechanics, and astronomy), and ethics (a wide-ranging course that included rhetoric, political philosophy, moral science, and international law). Instruction in the tactics of the combat arms of the service and the six-lesson course in military and civil engineering known as "The Science of War" were reserved for a cadet's final year of study.[19]

The daunting course load took its toll on cadets who had failed to establish a basic proficiency in most of these subjects prior to matriculation. From the start, however, Gregg experienced little difficulty maintaining a desirable academic ranking. Having been well prepared for extended study and effective recitation by Mr. Hall and the other teachers who had tutored him at Huntingdon and Lewisburg, he closed out his first year at the Point ranking eighth in his class of fifty-three, having demonstrated admirable proficiency in his English studies and almost as much in mathematics. His standing slipped a bit during his second year at West Point, at the end of which he ranked thirteenth out of forty-three classmates in order of general merit. Again, he did well in his math-based courses while gaining acceptable grades in French.[20]

He fared poorly, however, at one of the academy's most distinctive courses, military drawing. Understandably, the highest grade in that subject went to James Abbott McNeill Whistler of Massachusetts, who would become one of the most celebrated U.S. artists of his era. Whistler's heart was not in his military studies, however, and he failed to gain the stature he might have secured had he been more proficient in chemistry ("if silicon were a gas," he later remarked with feigned regret, "I would have been a major general").[21]

At the end of his third year at the academy (June 1854), Cadet Gregg again finished thirteenth in his class, although because of the class's depleted size the ranking was proportionally lower than the year before. He bore down in his final year at the academy. He finished near the top in each of the several subjects that composed the final year's curriculum, including the tactical courses. Ironically, considering his future posting to the mounted arm, he placed higher in infantry tactics than in cavalry tactics. His relative proficiency in the school of the infantryman and also of the artilleryman would stand him in good stead when he served closely with units of both arms during wartime, especially on those occasions when they came under his provisional command.[22]

A cadet's class standing was directly affected by the number and severity of his offenses against the school's hefty, arcane, and sometimes capricious body of regulations. The punishments that such offenses incurred included suspension, banishment to prison barracks, and "walking extras," hours-long tours of guard duty on weekends when most cadets were free from routine chores. More than a few cadets washed out of the Point because of their personal conduct as much as or more than their academic failings. Studied self-control meant that transgressions of this sort never affected Gregg's standing. He steered well clear of the number of demerits—200 in a single year—that could trigger instant dismissal.

He accumulated seventeen black marks during his first academic year, fifty-four the following year, and sixteen during 1853–54, almost all for minor offenses such as being tardy for class, roll call, and drill. In his senior year he picked up forty demerits, relatively few considering that with graduation imminent most cadets felt confident enough to stray from the path of rectitude with greater frequency than before. However, the peace of mind of many truants was shaken when Secretary of War Jefferson Davis announced in March 1855 that any cadet who had accumulated more than a hundred demerits as of January 1 would be suspended from the academy for three months. This was the cause of Cadet Vinton's failure to graduate with the class of '55.[23]

His ambivalence about a military career notwithstanding, Gregg worked hard to make a success of his years at the Point, eventually attaining the rank of cadet lieutenant. At first it was something of an uphill climb, at least physically. Although he would eventually grow to slightly above six feet, a thin frame made him look even taller. Because his musculature was undeveloped, he found it hard to lift, let alone wield, the heavy saber (sometimes known as the "wrist-breaker") that was issued to him for cavalry practice. Thanks to the riding he had done since early childhood, however, he was known to be a good equestrian, so much so that he was regularly assigned "Old Bumper," a fractious steed that many other cadets avoided. His seat was not always perfect; as Cyrus Comstock recorded, during an equitation lesson midway through his second year, Gregg was "thrown off his horse falling flat."[24]

Though usually quiet and reserved, Doctor Gregg partook fully of the social scene of the cadet corps. Neither prig nor prude, he was open to socializing and on at least one occasion fled school bounds in pursuit of entertainment and paid a steep price for his offense. Although it is not known if he ever accompanied thirsty classmates to nearby Buttermilk Falls to visit the fabled mecca of cadet dissipation known as Benny Havens's Tavern, he did imbibe "whiskey punch" and other alcoholic beverages, at least during the holiday season—at times to the point of being visibly "mellow." Occasionally he even presided over "jollifications" held in his room to celebrate an end to the most recent in a seemingly unending round of examinations—alcohol likely flowed freely on such occasions. According to Cadet Comstock, forbidden libations were routinely smuggled into the barracks by George D. ("Tub") Ruggles of New York, who was generous enough to share his stash with his buddies. During his wartime career Ruggles would be the soul of rectitude as senior staff officer to army commanders including George B. McClellan, John Pope, and George Gordon Meade. At the Point, however, the portly party animal was known to have "whiskey or brandy in his clothes bag nearly all the time." On one occasion Comstock found him hiding "about three demijohn's & two or three bottles empty, up the chimney" of his room.[25]

Gregg appears to have preferred to do his infrequent carousing on Christmas Day, one of only two officially sanctioned holidays in the academic year (the other being New Year's). On December 25, 1853, he got into an altercation with Alfred Torbert, who would later become one of his closest friends as well as, eleven years later, a fellow cavalry division commander in the Army of the Potomac. When the drunken Torbert made a snide remark about Gregg's character, the latter took offense and apparently intended to physically rebut the criticism. He was prevented from doing so by the equally tipsy George Elliot, who threatened to thrash Torbert and force him to retract the slur. He, too, was restrained by cadets, including William Averell; Averell was then rooming with Gregg and Elliot. It is not known whether punches were thrown, but the confrontation ended without Gregg becoming involved. Presumably the would-be antagonists, once they sobered up, buried the hatchet.

A more serious incident occurred exactly one year later, Gregg's last Christmas at the academy. "Running the limits" of the installation while restricted to barracks was considered a major transgression, meriting severe punishment. Having been duly present and accounted for during the daily inspection, seven first-classmen (i.e., cadets in their fourth year) including Gregg, Elliot, and Weitzel, slipped out of their rooms late that afternoon or early in the evening and thus were absent when a second, unannounced inspection took place. More than an hour later the truants straggled back to the barracks to find themselves "hived" by the inspecting officer and under arrest. Subsequently Gregg and four of the others, all cadet officers, were reduced to the ranks, and the remaining delinquents were sentenced to walk six weekends' worth of extras.

In some circles the punishment was considered unduly harsh, especially in view of previous incidents of a more violent nature in which those involved had gotten off lightly. The previous March two fistfights had broken out between upperclassmen Jeb Stuart and John L. Grattan of New Hampshire, who, as Cyrus Comstock noted in his diary "d[id] not like each other very well." Stuart threw the first punch, but he and Grattan were immediately separated. Shortly afterward the two went at it again and this time the New Englander "hit Stuart once & fairly floored him" before the fight was broken up. Both men were placed under arrest and Stuart lost his cadet sergeant's stripes. Five days later, however, Colonel Lee released the antagonists as well as two others who had involved themselves in the fracas, and Stuart, widely regarded as one of the superintendent's pets, regained his lost rank. Comstock called the result "rather queer justice but then a 1st Sergts chevrons do not come off easily." Even so, Comstock believed that Stuart should have been suspended. It is not known if Gregg received the same dispensation, but there are no later references to him with the rank of lieutenant.[26]

One indication of Gregg's popularity among his peers and the reputation he gained for erudition was his election in May 1854 as president of the West Point Dialectic Society. One of very few extracurricular organizations of the period, the society was a literary and debating club in which first-classmen predominated. It met on Saturday nights to read and critique members' papers on such topics as "Should Capital Punishment Be Abolished?" and "Should Nations Go to War to Preserve the Balance of Power?" Although some faculty members believed that the organization unduly distracted its members from their studies, it flourished because it gave the cadets a rare social outlet while helping hone their literary and oratorical skills.[27]

Although flattered by the honor, Gregg proved too shy to give the address customarily delivered by the society's president at the start of the academic year. On this occasion it was to be given before a large audience that included such distinguished guests as the stepson of George Washington and family members of former president and Mexican War hero Zachary Taylor. When Gregg dropped out the honor fell to Averell, who never forgot "the utter terror, the shivering fright that I experienced when seated on the platform while the audience assembled." He got through the evening without disgracing himself but it is doubtful whether he forgave his roommate for subjecting him to the ordeal.[28]

Gregg handled another honorific speaking engagement without trepidation, gaining much praise. As part of the traditional July 4 ceremonies during his senior year he was chosen as second orator of the day. The proceedings began with the corps and its officers forming in front of Colonel Lee's quarters, then marching en masse to the chapel. There before the assembled throng Gregg read aloud the Declaration of Independence. According to his friend Comstock, he did "very well." In fact, the New Englander preferred Gregg's performance to that of the principal speaker, Francis Nicholls, whose discourse on the importance of the occasion lacked "reality and earnestness."[29]

Gregg's occasional reticence did not prevent him from enjoying other occasions on which he and his classmates entertained visitors to the academy, especially when they included young women. In contrast to the insular atmosphere that the institution normally exuded, balls and other social engagements were held every year that Gregg was a member of the corps, especially during the summer encampment in his final year. The guest list ranged from military, political, and diplomatic dignitaries, including War Department officials and New York

Governor Horatio Seymour, to the families and friends of academy personnel. William Averell, the floor manager at some of these functions, pointed out that "as many as four hundred guests sometimes attended our balls." They included, on more than one occasion, Commanding General and Mrs. Winfield Scott and their youngest daughter, Cornelia. Averell considered Cornelia, the wife of an officer who had served on her father's staff in Mexico, "one of the loveliest women I ever saw." Orchestral music and convivial conversation overflowed the auditorium, and dancing continued until midnight. These breaks in the too-often dreary routine of academic life were relished by the cadets and fondly remembered.[30]

Regardless of how many pretty girls David Gregg escorted to the dance floor, all paled in comparison to one he met at another official function, the commencement exercises of 1854. In attendance that day was seventeen-year-old Ellen Frances ("Ellie") Sheaff of Reading, Pennsylvania, then visiting the area in the company of her aunt and uncle. Spurred by their family's rich military history, Judge J. Pringle Jones and his wife had interrupted their travels to Niagara Falls and the White Mountains to witness the academy ceremony. Although David and Ellen had not previously met, they were linked by family associations that included high political office. Another of Ellen's uncles had married a first cousin of the cadet. Furthermore, she was the great-granddaughter of Joseph Hiester, Pennsylvania's governor from 1820 to 1823; David's paternal grandfather, Senator Andrew Gregg of Bellefonte, had served as Secretary of the Commonwealth in the Hiester administration. Another notable ancestor of Ellen's was Frederick Augustus Muhlenberg, first Speaker of the U.S. House of Representatives.

Ellen had moved from Reading to Philadelphia at age ten. The daughter of an upper-middle-class family, she lived in comparable wealth after her father's death and her mother's remarriage to James Murray Rush in January 1847. Her mother's death in December 1849, however, seems to have left Ellen adrift; she spent her teen years in a series of boarding schools before attending a finishing school on Maryland's Eastern Shore. Since her older sister Catharine's marriage in 1854, Ellen had been residing in Philadelphia with "Kate" and her husband, naval admiral's clerk A. Murray Stewart.[31]

According to the family's chroniclers, the newly christened upper classman and his distant relative were instantly attracted to each other and a romance began to blossom. Eight years later, following a courtship made uncomfortably long by David's military service far from the home of his beloved, they would become husband and wife. Thus it was that the U.S. Military Academy not only furnished David McMurtrie Gregg with the theoretical and practical foundation for a successful career in the army, but also provided the chance encounter that brought about a long, happy, and fruitful marriage.

2

Lieutenant Gregg's Frontier

Thanks to his achievements in the recitation room and on the drill plain and his standing on the roll of general merit, David McMurtrie Gregg ranked eighth when he and his thirty-three classmates were graduated on July 1, 1855, and commissioned into the army. His impressions upon leaving the institution at which he had spent four seminal years may well have approximated those of his classmate William Averell, who recorded them two decades later as "the realization of hope, the sweet triumph of graduation, the sad rending of a pleasing network of friendships, the dispersion of comrades forever."[1]

The sudden separation from so many friends and close acquaintances might well have been the most lasting sensation. Despite the ever-growing threat of national disunion, academy officials had worked diligently to minimize sectional discord and foster nationalistic sentiments, thus buttressing cadet solidarity. A few years before Gregg arrived on the Hudson, the superintendent's office, for the first and only time, had vetoed a subject that the Dialectic Society intended to debate: whether a state "under any circumstances [has] the right to nullify an act of Congress"—a then-potent political issue that anticipated the secession crisis of a decade later.[2]

One event that sparked a degree of discord at the academy, as it did nationally, was the 1846–48 war with Mexico, which facilitated the expansion of slavery in some of the conquered territories. Not for another three or four years after Gregg's class graduated, however, would sectional passions approach dangerous proportions. One of the flashpoints was the October 1859 raid by abolitionist John Brown and a small army of followers on the federal armory and arsenal at Harpers Ferry, Virginia, with the goal of igniting a slave insurrection. Little more than a year later, the election of Abraham Lincoln would complete the shattering of the corps by those political, economic, and cultural divisions that, sadly, could not be resolved short of civil war.

Spared such distractions, Gregg upon leaving West Point could look with pride at his accomplishments and survey the unforeseeable but undeniably bright future that they had secured for him. His period of anticipation began back home in Hollidaysburg, where he spent most of the sixty-day furlough granted him prior to reporting for active duty. He also visited relatives in Bellefonte and Huntingdon.[3]

At one of the family venues he received word of his initial unit assignment. Graduating in the top one-quarter of one's class was an achievement of note. It failed, however, to secure Gregg a berth in the elite branch of the army, its topographical and construction engineer corps. That honor was reserved for Cyrus Comstock and Godfrey Weitzel, the top two names on the list of general merit. The outcome, however, was agreeable to Gregg, whose lifelong love of horses ideally fitted him for the regiment he was assigned to, the 2nd U.S. Dragoons.

Since its creation in 1836 the 2nd Dragoons had distinguished itself in action on fields as far apart as the Florida Everglades, the Texas plains, and the mountains and swamps of Mexico under such luminaries as Lt. Col. Philip St. George Cooke and Capt. Charles A. May. In wartime and peace it had served in distinctive fashion. Like its older sister, the 1st Dragoons, the 2nd was a cross between traditional horse-bound cavalry and mounted infantry, in that its men were trained and equipped to fight both in the saddle and on foot as conditions warranted.[4]

This tactical flexibility owed to the ingenuity (or the parsimony) of the U.S. Congress, which saw in the dragoons a means of combining two branches of the service for the price—in arms, equipment, and upkeep—of one. Yet, as is so often the case when attempting to combine tactical functions, too often the result was, as one historian has put it, an "unhappy form of compromise" in that the typical dragoon appeared neither fish nor fowl. Still, until the year of Gregg's graduation the dragoons constituted the only mounted units in service (two regiments designated as cavalry had begun recruiting early in 1855).

Moreover, the functional distinctions meant little to the young Pennsylvanian. Dragoons, like cavalrymen, rode to the battlefield no matter how they fought when they got there, and the means of transportation were what mattered to him.[5]

Gregg's posting to the 2nd Dragoons was a provisional action. Like every graduate of the Class of '55, he had been commissioned a brevet second lieutenant. The brevet allocated him to the army at large, not to a specific regiment or corps, and it would remain in effect only until a permanent place was found for him. Unit manpower numbers were capped by regulations; a newly commissioned officer could be assigned at his full rank only when a vacancy occurred. Because the army had yet to devise a pension system, openings almost always depended on a senior officer's death or his retirement because of age, wounds, or disability.[6]

Opportunities for promotion might be few and slow to emerge, but positions in the mounted arm, where hard campaigning took a toll of officers and men alike, opened up with a fair degree of regularity. Gregg remained in his quasi-limbo status only until his furlough ended. On or about September 1 he was notified of his elevation to the full rank of second lieutenant in the 1st U.S. Dragoons, the oldest mounted organization in the army. Formed at Jefferson Barracks, Missouri, in the summer of 1834, the 1st had accumulated a record of service at least as distinguished as that of its younger sibling, having seen action against hostile Indian tribes in various states and territories. Its original mission had been to guard the routes of expansion as far west as the Rocky Mountains and as far south as the Red River. It had also played a conspicuous role in the capture and occupation of Upper California during the conflict with Mexico.

As the first unit of its kind to take the field since 1815, the 1st had established the pattern, both administrative and operational, that all horse regiments adhered to—not only the 2nd Dragoons but also the Regiment of Mounted Riflemen, another fusion of cavalry and infantry functions that had been organized during the war with Mexico. The 1st Dragoons boasted its own array of notables, including Cols. Stephen Watts Kearny and Richard B. Mason and Lt. Cols. Benjamin L. ("Old Ben") Beall and Edwin Vose Sumner. Among those junior officers who would gain prominence, though not always in the field, was Lt. Jefferson Davis, who after graduating from West Point in 1828 had risen to the highly responsible post of regimental adjutant before resigning from the army to take up planting in Mississippi, lead volunteer troops in Mexico, and seek political office.[7]

The dragoons' awkward mixture of tactical missions owed much to its assigned weaponry. In contrast to the long-range riles wielded by infantrymen, the typical dragoon of the mid-1850s was armed with a smoothbore carbine (also known as a musketoon), a lightweight, short-barreled small arm that could be more easily fired and reloaded on horseback. Many models were breechloaders, which further simplified their use in the saddle. The drawback was that, because the early carbine lacked rifling, it was effective at shorter range and less accurate than the infantry's weapon of choice. In addition to this less-than-formidable firearm (in the main, the 52-caliber Model-1843 Hall carbine of "North's improved pattern"), the dragoon carried a European-style saber heavy enough to have reminded Gregg of the troubles he had hefting such weapons at West Point. He also toted either a single-shot percussion pistol or a 44-caliber Colt "Hartford Dragoon" revolver.[8]

The tactical instruction the dragoons received at this stage of their development could not meet the many and onerous demands of mounted service. From the time of its organization, the 1st Regiment had been scattered across nine hundred miles of territory. During the first two years of its existence only three of its eight (later ten) companies were stationed at regimental headquarters in Missouri; the other units served in such far-off venues as Louisville, Cincinnati, and New York City. Because the outfit was never consolidated, it never trained as a unified force. Over time its primary mission evolved into that of a frontier police force. As a result, the dragoons never developed a coherent code of cavalry tactics, a glaring impediment to operational fulfillment.

This undesirable situation worsened when the companies served under infantry commanders, as often happened at their far-flung stations in the West and South. Such officers employed the dragoons primarily if not exclusively as foot troops. Fortunately, strong leadership gave hope of being able to overcome such roadblocks to success. As one historian of frontier troops and weaponry notes, "In many instances it remained for younger men to gain [experience] in the hard school of actual fighting before any real headway could be made" in the evolution of cavalry tactics. David Gregg would be one of these change-makers.[9]

At the time Gregg left home to join his regiment, the 1st Dragoons was headquartered at Fort Union along the Santa Fe Trail in the New Mexico Territory. He would not have to travel that far, however, to begin to learn the ropes of his chosen profession. To help offset the limitations placed on development of the mounted arm, the army had established at Jefferson Barracks a cavalry school, a post-graduate institution where officers, including recent West Point graduates, received additional training before reporting to their assigned units. As William Averell put it, "The seclusion of the Military Academy had been so complete that we soon found that there was a vast deal for us to learn immediately." The Cavalry School enabled the new officers to gain practical experience in the instruction and management of enlisted recruits who were collected there from time to time before being sent to their duty stations. Once the officers were deemed ready to join their regiments, these detachments would serve as officers' escorts through territory inhabited by Indians.[10]

Late in September Gregg left Pennsylvania for the third time in four years (he had received a single furlough midway through his West Point career) and entrained for points west. By September 28, at the end of a tortuous 650-mile journey, he was in St. Louis, where he took a room in the Planters House, one of the city's most notable hostelries. There he found himself in familiar company: Cornelius Van Camp and Lewis Merrill, who had graduated, respectively, third and twentieth in his West Point class. Like Gregg, the young men were bound for Jefferson Barracks prior to joining their regiments—in Van Camp's case the newly established 1st Cavalry, and in Merrill's the 1st Dragoons. On September 29, one day before they were due at the Cavalry School, the trio was reunited with three other members of their class heading for the same destination. These were Albert V. Colburn, newly assigned to the 2nd Cavalry, and John V. DuBois and William Averell, who were to join the Regiment of Mounted Riflemen.[11]

Averell was easily the most conspicuous member of the group. The scion of an upper-middle-class family from western New York, he gave the impression of having come from even greater wealth; his nickname at West Point had been "The Swell." He had a personality to match his supposed origins. Cyrus Comstock described him this way: "You cannot name a subject with which he is not acquainted or tell a story he cannot double, with an *air*, too." Averell would prove to be an officer of ability but also a first-class opportunist, willing to go to almost any length to further or embellish his career. His ambition and talent for self-promotion ensured that over time he would outstrip his modest, less demonstrative colleague from Pennsylvania in the areas of promotion and command preference.[12]

On the last day of the month the six classmates checked out of their rooms and made the eleven-mile trip to Jefferson Barracks by carriage. As soon as escorted onto the installation, they reported to Charles A. May, now a colonel, commander of the Cavalry School as well as of the 2nd Dragoons. From the first the young officers were highly impressed by the memorably tall and long-bearded May, who had achieved national distinction during the fighting below the Rio Grande. He was particularly known for having led a column of fours (i.e., four troopers riding abreast) in a thunderous charge that overran an enemy battery, captured a Mexican general, and supposedly helped Zachary Taylor win the battle of Resaca de la Palma. May was an imposing figure; Averell described him as "an emotional man and quick to anger—perhaps with a temper a trifle dangerous." The colonel would exert a great influence on the numerous pupils assigned to Jefferson Barracks, many of whom regarded him their *beau ideal* as an officer of horse.

Daily routine at the Cavalry School was both rigid and rigorous. Drill in mounted and dismounted tactics consumed five and a half hours each day, and the schedule rarely changed. Averell recalled that "the great plain outside the Post presented the most attractive and animated spectacle during drill hours. Nearly a thousand mounted men were instructed there daily in all the schools—from that of a trooper mounted, to that of the squadron [a grouping of two companies that constituted a basic tactical formation of every cavalry outfit], and finally of the regiment. . . . Within sixty days over eight hundred men and horses had been broken in and formed into coherent troops and squadrons. . . . It tested the qualification of every officer to the utmost."

In addition to unit training, Lieutenant Gregg's day was given over to stable call, during which he and each of his comrades oversaw the watering, feeding, and grooming of some thirty horses. The newcomers had the evenings pretty much to themselves. When not on duty as officer of the day or officer of the guard they often galloped off to St. Louis, where they dined, visited the theater, and attended social engagements regularly offered to the local military community.[13]

Averell and most of the other recent West Point graduates were fated to remain at the Barracks for several months (in November the Cavalry School would be transferred to Carlisle Barracks, Pennsylvania). Gregg's tenure, however, was limited to two weeks, barely enough time to learn the basic tenets of mounted service. In mid-October he was unexpectedly faced with retracing his long journey from the East Coast, having been ordered to carry official dispatches to Fort Columbus, New York, home of the army's general recruiting service.

Why he was chosen for this mundane errand, especially so soon after traversing half the country, is not known, but he dutifully set out for the East. Details of the trip are lacking, but his son tells of an incident en route that sheds some light on the young officer's "character and kindness of heart." Not far from his destination, while riding at night in an unheated coach on the Erie Railroad, he lent his army overcoat to a young, recently married woman whom he found suffering from cold. Gregg himself took a seat in the smoking car where he spent the night trying, unsuccessfully, to keep warm in his officer's tunic.[14]

When he finally reached his destination on Governor's Island, he found his peripatetic existence far from over. Within three weeks of his arrival he would receive orders to report to his regiment, then headquartered at Fort Union, New Mexico. The only happy feature of his brief layover in New York Harbor was the opportunity to renew acquaintances with friends from the U.S. Military Academy, Fort Columbus being the closest major army post to West Point and as such, a staging area for staff members and recent graduates preparing, like Gregg, to join their regiments in the field. He left there on November 6 in a

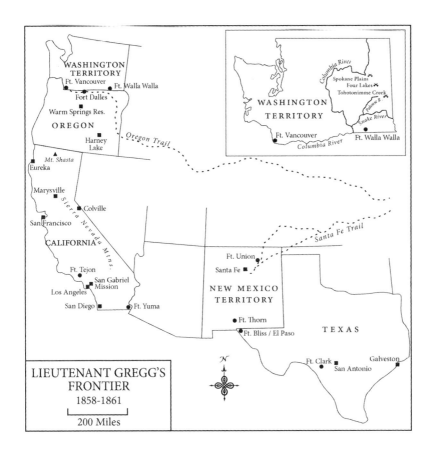

Map 1. Lieutenant Gregg's frontier, 1858–61. Created by Paul Dangel.

column of officers and enlisted men that included dozens of recruits bound for various posts in the South and West.[15]

Although the caravan's route is not known with specificity, it likely traveled down the Mississippi River to Galveston, Texas, and then overland to San Antonio. At the latter stop Gregg joined a wagon train and set out for Fort Clark, 120 miles to the west. Upon reaching Clark he fell in with a column of foot soldiers bound for Fort Bliss, near El Paso, led by Col. Benjamin L. E. Bonneville of the 3rd U.S. Infantry. The 1,000-man force set out in late November and reached the fort, at the end of a 350-mile trek through a wild, broken, and lightly populated swath of Texas, in the later part of January 1856. It had been a grueling march, the ordeal worsened by the effects of a "norther" that struck without warning and left everyone in the party wet, cold, and miserable.

During one leg of the journey Gregg further risked his physical well-being by taking a shortcut to the proposed camping site for the night. Traveling alone by horseback through a sea of chaparral, he came suddenly upon a sinister-looking figure in buckskin, standing by the side of the winding trail, rifle in hand. Though startled and more than a little alarmed to find a white man in such an inhospitable venue, Gregg rode up to him, nodded in greeting, and continued past, half expecting to topple from his saddle with a ball cartridge in his back. When beyond rifle range he dared glance back to discover that the man had not changed his position one iota; "arms resting on his rifle as before," he gazed intently after the rider.

At Fort Bliss, Gregg, body and nerves intact, joined two other officers and three orderlies assigned to Fort Union, and started north by horseback and wagon for Santa Fe. Though forced to cut its way through the prairie wilderness, the little band made good time, completing the 275-mile ride in under a week. The travelers spent the next three days in that territorial capital, headquarters of the Military Department of New Mexico, before starting on the final leg of the journey—a memorable ordeal thanks to a desert blizzard that struck just before Fort Union was reached. On February 2, weary, bedraggled, and almost numb from cold, the six soldiers straggled into the reservation on the Mountain Branch of the Santa Fe Trail, and a relieved Gregg reported to the post commander. The long, wayward, arduous, and perilous excursion to his first semi-permanent duty station was finally at an end.[16]

Once recovered from the rigors of the journey he found himself assigned to Company H of the 1st Dragoons. He spent the next six months handling a multiplicity of responsibilities, most of the time while in command of his unit, its other officers being on detached duty elsewhere. This was a common situation in a far-flung area of operations such as the Military Department of New Mexico, upon which many demands were made, chiefly by settlers who appeared to believe that the relatively small garrison should be everywhere, cheerfully providing security and logistical support. Considering that Gregg had no prior experience with many of the duties thrust upon him almost from the moment of his arrival, and that he was called on to tend to the daily needs of upward of a hundred troopers and their mounts, one can readily believe his son's comment that his weeks at Fort Union were "busy ones for him." One compensation was the ability to divide his workload with fellow officers, including the close friend from West Point whose presence at Fort Union helped make life at that isolated outpost bearable, Lieutenant William D. Pender of Company I.[17]

In August regimental headquarters and three of the 1st's companies—Gregg's and Pender's as well as Company F under a West Pointer one class ahead of Gregg, Lieutenant John T. Mercer—were ordered transferred to Fort Tejon, California, near the village of Los Angeles. Soon another desert journey—this one covering more than a thousand miles—was underway. The column, commanded by Maj. George A. H. Blake and Bvt. Maj. William E. ("Old Billy") Grier, Mexican War veterans who would play conspicuous roles in the early months of the larger war that lay ahead, was primarily composed of what Gregg called "re-enlisted men, that is, having seen five, ten, and some a greater number of years of service." In a present-tense sketch of his frontier service he described the mounted portion of the column as professionalism at its finest, "each horse perfectly groomed, equipments in the best possible condition, sabre and musketoon without spot or tarnish, overcoat and blanket in regulation roll at the pommel, and valises at the cantle—not an article not allowed by regulations anywhere to be seen—

the old trooper so accustomed to the saddle, that horse and rider are seemingly one. A good company indeed, and one you need not fear to travel with."

The spit-and-polish command wended its way southwest to Fort Thorn. It reached that post, on the west bank of the Rio Grande some seventy miles north of El Paso, in mid-September. It lay over there for two weeks collecting supplies for the rest of the march and before month's end was pushing on through the southern corridor of New Mexico. David Gregg, Jr., noted that the route ran through the Peloncillo Mountain range via the valley of Stein's Pass. From there the column tried to follow a wagon trail laid out by Lieutenant Colonel Cooke when leading a force composed of dragoons, artillery, and infantry including five companies of Mormon volunteers on a four-month, 1,100-mile march to San Diego during the war with Mexico. This proved no mean feat. As Gregg noted, "In many places the trail is so nearly obliterated that it is deemed necessary to take a guide."[18]

To call the conditions of the march through the Arizona Territory grueling would be an understatement. As Gregg recalled, the vast expanse was "quite unexplored and its only inhabitants [were] Apache and other Indians, save at one point, Tucson, where numerous Mexicans resided.... The surface of the country [was] very rough and broke[n], the soil sterile." Water holes being scarce, men and horses were constantly parched. Then, when the column was in bivouac along the San Pedro River, a sudden grass fire cost Gregg an eyelash and some of the whiskers he had begun to cultivate as soon as he joined his regiment (at this time the dragoons were the only soldiers permitted to wear long hair and beards).[19]

The march to California proved so wracking to mind and body that at least one enlisted man shot himself, considering suicide preferable to further travel under a blazing sun through clouds of dust, across a wasteland at the same time barren and overpopulated by wolves and rattlesnakes. By the first week in November the column, no matter which direction it took, was traversing snake-infested ground. At the end of an especially enervating march a physically exhausted Gregg was in the process of dismounting when his first sergeant called out to him: "What do you think of that fellow, Lieutenant?" Gregg looked down at "the largest & most dangerous looking rattlesnake that I have yet seen, within a few feet of my horse." The sergeant had killed it with his pistol seconds before Gregg's boots touched the ground. "At the sight of the enormous reptile," wrote Gregg's son, "he fell into a dead faint at his sergeant's feet." Here was the first manifestation of an undiagnosed medical condition from which Gregg would never be free—fainting attacks would recur throughout his life.[20]

Despite the inhospitable conditions, the column made almost twenty miles a day on the march even when forcing a passage of the rugged San Fernando Mountains. The trip was relieved only by brief stopovers at Fort Yuma, at the confluence of the Gila and Colorado Rivers, and the settlement that had grown up around the historic San Gabriel Mission, reached on December 6. Gregg's latest ramble through the Southwestern wilderness finally ended in the last days of December. At Fort Tejon, almost 1,200 miles from Fort Union, he and his comrades became members of a garrison whose primary mission was to protect settlers from attacks by Paiutes, Mojaves, and other tribes as well as by discontented pre-statehood residents known as Californios, while also protecting those friendly (or less aggressive) Indians who during the previous year had been settled on local reservation lands.[21]

Gregg and his comrades in Companies H and I spent seven months at Tejon while other units of the 1st Dragoons established themselves at smaller installations in the Oregon and Washington Territories. Gregg had plenty of time to study the local fauna and flora. He appears to have been especially interested in the habits of the grizzly bear although whether he came into close contact with the beast is unknown; there is no record of his having hunted one during his stay in middle California.

His most vivid memory of service at Tejon occurred within weeks of reaching the post. In late January an earthquake later estimated to have struck on a scale rivaling that of the San Francisco quake of almost fifty years later—shook the local countryside, nearly destroying the fort and its dependencies. Although the epicenter of the seismic event lay almost 100 miles from Tejon, the damage done there was greater than elsewhere in the sparsely inhabited area. Gregg would never forget "the mutterings of the subterranean thunder, undulatory motion of the earth toppling over houses, and causing giant oaks to be swayed about like straws and in many instances uprooted; the fright of the herds of horses and mules; the disappearance of springs, and the gushing forth of water at new points; the large fissure in the earth [that] traced a distance of more than a hundred miles." In fact, the quake caused a rupture in the San Andreas Fault 220 miles long.[22]

In August 1857 yet another tortuous march began when Gregg's company was transferred to the Washington Territory to garrison Fort Walla Walla. The post had been established the previous fall by Bvt. Lt. Col. Edward J. Steptoe, 9th U.S. Infantry, to control the hostile Indians of that valley region and protect the routes of transportation and exploration. The journey would include a winter-long layover at Fort Vancouver on the Columbia River, 800 miles from Tejon and 200 from the dragoons' final destination. The route led up the valley of the Sacramento River, down the Willamette, through the gold fields and iron works near Marysville and Eureka, California, and around the Cascades near Mount Shasta.

Unlike the trek from New Mexico, this journey was conducted "in comparative comfort" thanks to a well-marked trail, numerous sources of water, and the availability of daily forage. These and other advantages placed Gregg in a pleasant frame of mind; he would fondly recall some incidents of the trip, even one that made him the butt of comrades' humor. When the column was about to cross King's River in the Sierra Nevada Mountains some 150 miles out of Fort Tejon, Gregg, that day acting as quartermaster of the expedition, determined to reach the designated evening campsite in advance of the main body so that "suitable arrangements might be made about forage for the animals." Wishing to spare his nearly winded horse, he took the advice of the master of the column's supply train to ride "a capital saddle mule, rather small to be sure, but very fleet and well broken."

When Gregg mounted the animal his boots almost touched the ground, but he suppressed any misgivings and took to the road. "The lope of the animal was short," he wrote, "but not disagreeable, and he held to it with wonderful endurance" until the river was reached. Suddenly consumed by thirst, the mule plunged into the stream, forcing his rider to draw up his knees until his heels were resting on the mount's rump. Thus postured, Gregg could not prevent the mule from drinking long and deep—so long that he was still at it an hour later when the rest of the column appeared in the distance. Aware of the embarrassment to come, Gregg begged and pleaded, but "to all remonstrances and entreaties the mule turned a long deaf ear." Thus, when the company reached the stream "stern discipline required that those old troopers should not laugh aloud." Even so, Gregg imagined that many of them "shook in their boots." The denouement was threefold. The stubborn mount refused to cross the river until the rest of the herd had done so. This cost Gregg the time he needed to procure forage. As a result, "never afterwards could he be persuaded to mount a fine saddle mule."[23]

Fort Vancouver was reached in October. Company H did duty there until the following spring. Life at the fort, as at all frontier outposts, had its disadvantages and inconveniences—the following spring, rain fell for ninety consecutive days—but the local vista, especially perennially ice-covered Mount Hood, which rose 15,000 feet above the stockade, Gregg considered "worth a trip across the continent to see." One gathers that he would have enjoyed gazing at these sights far longer than he was permitted to do so.

In March 1858 Gregg's column resumed its journey to Fort Walla Walla, which it reached without difficulty late the following month. Soon after arriving the lieutenant learned that an expedition was being fitted out to confront fractious Mormons and the Palouse Indians. The former were accused of encouraging unrest among the various tribes that also included the Spokanes and Coeur d'Alenes. The Palouses stood accused of having rustled army stock and killed miners en route to the gold mines of Colville in east-central California. To an objective observer, the tribes' behavior was an understandable response to a series of treaties that army officers and political officials had persuaded them to sign, the terms of which had been violated with impunity.[24]

Colonel Steptoe led the force that left Walla Walla on the morning of May 6; it consisted of Gregg, five other officers, and 158 men. The soldiers, drawn from three companies of the 1st Dragoons and some infantry units, were accompanied by a pack train and two 12-pounder mountain howitzers, compact guns that could be disassembled for easy maneuvering over rough terrain. Later that year eight companies of the 1st would be issued state-of-the-art shoulder arms. Only ten fifty-four-caliber Sharps carbines had found their way into Steptoe's column, however, because the breech loader was viewed as an experimental weapon. Most of the soldiers had to rely on the short-range, often unreliable "Yeager" musket.[25]

During its first days on the journey Steptoe's understrength column proceeded eastward on the Oregon Trail, crossed the Snake River, and headed for the valley of the Palouse River. Early on May 16, having crossed Tohotonimme Creek, the soldiers were suddenly confronted by upward of a thousand warriors from all three of the local tribes as well as from others not suspected of being hostile. Steptoe halted and parlayed with their leaders. He declared his intentions to be peaceful but the warriors refused to disband, and the colonel had no recourse but to retreat.

When the column, which carried only about forty rounds of musket and pistol ammunition per man, attempted to turn back to Walla Walla on May 17, the tribes attacked its rear and flanks. Soon the soldiers found themselves surrounded; they were forced to dismount, dig in atop a hillock, and fight for their lives. To reach that position they had to run a gauntlet of musket fire, arrows, and lances. When a group of warriors attempted to circle around the defenders and cut them off, Steptoe had Gregg remount his men and attempt to intercept the enemy before too late. The race, "though close," was won by the dragoons. Finding themselves outdistanced, the Indians seized another hill that commanded Steptoe's new position. Gregg determined to attack, and the charge he led temporarily cleared the strategic elevation. At once, however, he saw that it could not be held, and so Company H fought its way back to the main body, where its men vowed to sell their lives as dearly as possible.[26]

Outnumbered and outpositioned, their howitzers capable of slowing but not stopping an extended series of mounted and dismounted attacks, several of Steptoe's men fell. Leadership was compromised when two well-respected officers, Capt. Oliver Hazard Perry Taylor and Lt. William Gaston, fell mortally wounded. In all, the soldiers lost six killed and twice as many wounded before darkness and a coming rain halted the incipient massacre. Two of the dead had come from Gregg's company; one had been shot out of his saddle while riding directly behind the lieutenant.

Now down to three rounds per man, Colonel Steptoe, according to the most reliable historian of the expedition, was of a mind to remain on the exposed elevation throughout the night "and die like brave men," if necessary, in the morning. Steptoe's senior subordinate, Capt. Charles W. Winder of the 9th Infantry, accompanied by Gregg, attempted to dissuade him from this course but initially failed. Late at night the two officers tried again and this time persuaded the colonel to permit the column to try to cut its way out. A furtive reconnaissance had identified a seam in the Indians' perimeter, and the darkness and rain would facilitate the escape attempt.[27]

Gregg, who was now the senior mounted officer of the command, was assigned the task of organizing the column for the breakout as well as supervising a band of skirmishers to serve as a rear guard. The effort began as soon as both the dead and the howitzers had been buried, men, horses, and wagons moving off with equipment muffled and in response to whispered commands. To the surprise of virtually everyone involved, the operation succeeded. The column slipped down the hillside, around a sleeping enemy who apparently failed to establish sentinels, and, eventually, across the Palouse River. Spared a close pursuit, on May 19 Steptoe was met by a relief force from Walla Walla that had been contacted by a friendly Nez Perce sent to summon help before the fighting became general. Three days later the decimated column straggled back to the starting point of the expedition.[28]

The Steptoe Disaster, as it became known throughout the army, galvanized the army into action. Upon learning of the expedition's fate, Bvt. Brig. Gen. Newman S. Clarke, commander of the Military Department of the Pacific, organized such a strike. From Fort Vancouver in mid-June Clarke notified the local tribes that those Indians who had led the attack on Steptoe must be surrendered to the army and executed. When, as expected, his demands were rebuffed, Clarke dispatched two columns to move against the tribes from different directions. The larger force, under Col. George Wright of the 9th Infantry, marched northward from Walla Walla on August 27, following Steptoe's route though the Palouse Mountain range. The six-hundred-man command included two companies of Wright's regiment, four companies of artillerymen serving as infantry, a pair of mountain howitzers, and one battalion (two squadrons) of the 1st Dragoons that included Gregg's and Pender's companies.

Wright had been ordered to "attack all hostile Indians with vigor; make their punishment severe, and persevere until the submission of all [wa]s complete." Targets included the warriors who had murdered the Colville miners as well as those responsible for attacking Steptoe. The colonel was also directed to recover the howitzers that Steptoe had been forced to leave behind when he retreated. Wright believed that he had the means to avenge the recent loss of men, guns, and prestige, and his confidence was not misplaced. His men had been thoroughly trained in Indian-style tactics and were eager to even old scores. Unlike Steptoe's command, Wright's had an ample supply of ammunition, stored in several of the wagons that made up the column's four-hundred-mule supply train. Moreover, most of his men were armed with the new Model-1855 Springfield rifle-musket, capable of downing an enemy more than a thousand yards away.

Wright's only concern was that the Indians might run rather than fight. This was proved groundless on September 1 when contact was made with a sizable group of Indians on the northern reaches of the vast plain that stretched toward the Spokane River. Around a grouping of four watercourses the Indians who had ambushed Steptoe—Wright estimated their number as between four hundred and five hundred—offered battle. Riding back and forth on their bedecked-for-war ponies, they were easy targets for Wright's Springfield-wielding infantrymen and were cut down by the dozens. With his stunned and bleeding enemy visibly reeling, Wright sent in Major Grier at the head of the dragoon battalion to end what became known as the Battle of Four Lakes. "Charge the rascals!" shouted "Old Billy," and Gregg and his comrades slammed into the demoralized warriors. In minutes dismounted tribesmen were being ridden down, shot, and sabered while those still mounted were scattering in every direction, defiant and combative no longer.[29]

Gregg would never forget his adventures this day. Riding at the head of his company, he found himself singled out by a warrior whose musket failed to discharge. Before the man could resort to the bow and arrow, the lieutenant raised his once-unmanageable saber and brought it down on the assailant's head, splitting his skull. First Sergeant Edward Ball, riding behind Gregg, halted, dismounted, scooped up the Indian's bow and quiver, and presented them to Gregg, who would cherish them as mementos of his service on the plains.[30]

Grier ordered a pursuit but the survivors' ponies outdistanced the dragoons' worn-out mounts. Wright halted his command, pitched camp, and rested his command for the next three days. On September 5 he resumed his offensive across the tree-fringed and ravine-infested Spokane Plain. That day he caught up with his adversaries, many of whom had assumed defensive positions in the concealing timber. Wright pried them loose with well-directed volleys of rifle- and howitzer-fire. This day Gregg's company, assigned to defend the little guns, saw much less action than it had four days earlier. The other dragoon companies, however, charged into the thick of it. Lieutenant Pender killed two of the enemy at close range; when his pistol misfired, he grabbed a third opponent and threw him from his saddle, to be dispatched by a soldier riding behind.[31]

Company H's support enabled the howitzers to do severe damage. At one point they brought a tree limb down on one of the chiefs, disabling him and demoralizing his men. Meanwhile, Wright's infantry drove the Indians for four miles, inflicting unsustainable casualties. The survivors finally scattered, and this time Grier's horsemen, carbines blazing, pursued them relentlessly. The running fight covered twenty miles, at the end of which no able-bodied Indian was in sight.

The twin victories at Four Lakes and Spokane Plain ended concentrated Indian resistance in the area, and the defeated leaders soon made peace overtures. Wright persuaded them to hand over those accused of inciting the attack on Steptoe and of depredations against white civilians. Fifteen warriors were subsequently hanged; others were clapped in irons. Along with more than a few comrades, Gregg came to believe that Wright had treated the defeated foe with "unnecessary severity," especially when some individuals not proven to have played a significant role in the Steptoe Massacre were summarily executed. Another example of the extremes to which Wright went to demonstrate his dominance was the slaughter of hundreds of Indian ponies. These had been captured on September 8 by Major Grier at the head of Gregg's and Pender's companies following a skirmish with Indians who had regrouped after their defeat on Spokane Plain.

While surrender negotiations were ongoing, some of the dragoons returned to the Steptoe battlefield, where they recovered the bodies of Captain Taylor and Lieutenant Gaston as well as the abandoned howitzers. Initially the officers were buried at Walla Walla; in 1861 their remains were reinterred, side by side, in the cadet cemetery at West Point. In later years Gregg visited their graves whenever opportunity arose.[32]

Savoring his triumph, Wright turned south and on October 5 marched into Fort Walla Walla, captives and spoils in tow. He was greeted warmly by a high-level delegation from Washington including members of the Inspector General's office. The following day garrison troops and distinguished visitors joined in wining and dining the heroes who by chastising Steptoe's assailants had redeemed the good name of the Army of the Pacific.[33]

It appears that Lieutenants Gregg and Pender had applied for leaves of absence prior to the Steptoe expedition; both were granted shortly after Wright's column returned to Walla Walla. In a matter of days the friends were traveling by steamer down the coast and then, either via the mouth of the Columbia River or the port of San Francisco, on a 1,100-mile journey to the Isthmus of Panama, then the only accessible link between the Atlantic and Pacific coasts. The six-week-long journey through a section of Central America overrun by dense vegetation and battered by extremes of weather was tedious and disagreeable, but at journey's end it may have seemed worth the suffering. Upon returning to Pennsylvania Gregg was able not only to reunite with his family in Huntingdon and Hollidaysburg but also to reestablish contact with Ellen Sheaff, to whom he had been writing regularly from a series of depressingly distant points.

Gregg's respite from service both dreary and dangerous might well have ended almost as soon as it had begun, but early in December his leave was extended through the following spring. Even so, when it ended on May 1, 1859, he must have deeply regretted the necessity of tearing himself from family and friends and, in company with Lieutenant Pender via the same body- and mind-numbing trip to San Francisco, returning to his assigned duty station. At Walla Walla he was welcomed not only by his brother officers and the enlisted men of his command but also by a certain "faithful companion and friend." An Irish terrier named Tarry had become attached to the lieutenant during the latter's service at Fort Union, had accompanied him on the long march to Walla Walla, and had pined for his return every day of his seven-month absence in the East. Tarry was a fighter; Gregg's son notes that the canine, who slept every night at the foot of his master's cot, "feared nothing on two legs or four," not even a captive grizzly bear that he bit and clawed.[34]

In the fall of 1859 both Pender and Tarry accompanied Gregg to his newest posting, Fort Dalles, which was 140 miles southwest of Walla Walla in the newly established state of Oregon. At that recently renovated installation on the left bank of the Columbia, site of a trading post of some renown, Gregg spent the next two years. For much of that period he was assigned to supervise operations at the Warm Springs Indian Reservation, 50 miles from the fort. At other times he joined scouting expeditions through Snake Indian Country (the Snakes were a confederation of three local tribes, the most notable being the Northern Paiutes). In May 1860, under Maj. Enoch Steen of the 1st Dragoons, Gregg took part in a skirmish at Harney Lake in the southeastern section of Oregon.[35]

When not on field duty, Gregg found daily routine at the Dalles enervating and tedious. He filled the dreary hours by writing to his siblings, aunts and uncles, and, of course, Miss Sheaff. He resisted the temptation to find solace in drinking, the primary off-duty vice of officers stranded on the ragged edge of civilization. Although not a prig, Gregg steadily refused to be one of the garrison's habitual cardsharps. He also stayed aloof, when possible, from less socially acceptable pursuits. The combination of alcohol and gambling sometimes produced friction within the officer corps as well as in the enlisted force. Gregg tried to avoid involvement in personal disputes, but on one occasion he was called out, along with a close friend, when the latter was accused of insulting a hot-tempered fellow officer. Though opposed to dueling in principle, Gregg accepted the challenge in support of his colleague. Fortunately, the disagreement blew over without resort to violence.

Violence of another sort reared its head when, in the wake of the John Brown raid, the sectional crisis infiltrated even the most distant outposts of the army. Tensions ran high with the receipt by telegraph or outdated newspaper of the latest round of political acrimony, whether in the halls of Congress or on the plains of border states such as "Bleeding Kansas." Rivalries sparked by officers' deep-seated allegiance to their home region or the national union may have set in motion the duel in which Gregg, through no fault of his own, was nearly involved.

The sectional debate and the evident approach of open conflict threatened to create rifts in long-time friendships. Gregg's son wrote of "a warm friend of David's, a Southerner of the fiery dramatic type, [who] worked himself up to a fine frenzy over the question of the right of secession." Perhaps in the aftermath of a drinking session, the officer announced that once war broke out he would resign his commission, return to his native state, and take his stand, sword upraised, in defense of all he held dear. Supposedly the man's friend good-naturedly replied that "when so standing, he would find himself toe to toe with Lieutenant Gregg, also armed with a sabre, ready to hold the northern side of the line."

Gregg spent the winter of 1860–61 at the Warm Springs reservation, where he displayed interest in the welfare of its occupants. When opportunity arose he counseled his charges against the "jealousies and enmities" that were creating dissention among the several tribes. During this period he also appears to have contributed, as liberally as his army pay would permit, to the construction of a church in one of the local villages whose potential congregation included professional gamblers and saloon keepers, an element he considered in great need of the benefits of organized religion.[36]

Early in '61 Gregg received orders to return to one of his old outposts, Fort Tejon. Because the local superintendent of Indian affairs feared that dissident Snakes might attack Warm Springs, for a time Gregg was retained at the reservation, but eventually he bade farewell to the breathtaking beauty of the Columbia River country and made the long return trip to California. Soon after arriving he learned of his promotion to first lieutenant, to date from March 21. On April 12 he was assigned as adjutant of his regiment. Over the next two months he efficiently handled the myriad of administrative duties that the position entailed.[37]

April 12, 1861, was a fateful day in the life of not only Lieutenant Gregg of the 1st Dragoons but also of his divided nation. Shortly after four o'clock that morning South Carolina cannons and mortars began to fire on the U.S. Army garrison inside Fort Sumter in Charleston harbor. The following day, thirty-four hours after the bombardment began, the garrison surrendered, ensuring that open warfare was imminent. Years of overheated rhetoric about the right of secession and the necessity of sectional and national defense had come to an all-too-predictable climax.

3

From the Pacific to the Potomac

T he outbreak of war meant yet another transcontinental journey for a young officer, though it would not take place for four
months. The prospect may have been daunting, but Gregg
would make the trip at a higher rank than on any of his previous out-
ings. On May 14, 1861, less than a month after being elevated to first
lieutenant in his regiment, he was no longer a dragoon, having been
promoted to captain in the newly authorized 3rd U.S. Cavalry. The
outfit's formation, prompted by a need for professional leadership in
wartime, indicated that the army had taken favorable note of Gregg's
career. The companies of the 3rd (twelve of them, in contrast to the
ten-company structure of every other mounted regiment) were to be
staffed by young officers of polish and promise. These included such
future luminaries as Capts. August V. Kautz, John H. Taylor, and James
Russell Lowell, and Gregg's first cousin, John Irvin Gregg of Bellefonte.[1]

The latter, though not a West Pointer, had received a commission
from civil life. A veteran of the war with Mexico in which he had risen
from private soldier in a Pennsylvania volunteer outfit to captain of
infantry, he had left the army at war's end to engage, like so many
other members of his family, in the iron trade. John Irvin Gregg's distinguished record in combat had recommended him for a posting to
the cavalry, his service preference, and his cousin was gladdened by the
prospect of serving with him.[2]

Less pleasing, perhaps, was the prospect of soldiering alongside a
certain academy classmate. Scanning the list of new appointments,
David would have noticed among the lieutenants the name of Wil-

liam "Swell" Averell. The New Yorker had made a creditable record in the mounted rifles. Still, it seemed fitting that, having graduated eighteen places below Gregg on the academic roll, he should gain a lesser rank in the outfit in which they would both serve.

Military organization continued to be a work in progress. Three months after being assigned to his newly authorized outfit, Gregg found himself an officer in the 6th U.S. Cavalry. On August 3, 1861, Congress decreed that every mounted regiment would henceforth be designated as cavalry, their numerical order to be based on their original dates of formation. Thus the 1st Dragoons became the 1st Cavalry and the 2nd Dragoons the 2nd Cavalry. The Regiment of Mounted Riflemen was now the 3rd Cavalry, and the most recent organizations—the 1st, 2nd, and 3rd Cavalry—were designated the 4th, 5th, and 6th Cavalry. The renumbering may have promoted consistency but, given the importance the army ascribed to heraldry, it had a detrimental effect on those officers and men who felt that their regiments had lost some of the honor attached to their old names.[3]

Colonel Wright of the 9th Infantry was reluctant to allow Gregg and certain other officers to depart the posts at which he had placed them. Finally, on August 9, the colonel notified department headquarters: "I have permitted Captain Gregg, Third Cavalry [*sic*], to obey the orders he has received from the War Department." Gregg would join a growing exodus of officers and men from the Pacific Coast to Washington DC and northern Virginia where the war's first effects had already been felt on the field of battle. Only now was news filtering back to Oregon and California—via telegraph, the Pony Express, and the press—of the first major confrontation, which had taken place on July 21 near a rail depot, Manassas Junction, and a stream called Bull Run, less than thirty miles southwest of the nation's capital.[4]

In that clash of pea-green armies, the Confederates had had the advantage of fighting on the defensive against a hastily trained Union force laden with volunteer officers and civilian soldiers who lacked the ability to attack with any degree of effectiveness. The predictable result was that the Rebels under Gens. Joseph E. Johnston, Gustave Toutant Beauregard, and Thomas Jonathan Jackson (who at the height of the battle had received the enduring nickname "Stonewall") parried every thrust delivered by their primary antagonist, Brig. Gen. Irvin McDowell. Late on that sweltering Sunday, after the Federals had exhausted themselves in piecemeal assaults, their enemy cobbled together a counterattack that swept them from the field and into a disorganized retreat via Centreville and Fairfax Court House to their camps around Washington. It may have been the opening salvo of a long conflict, but the rout of McDowell's larger but less tenacious command suggested the need in the eastern theater of regular-army expertise. Captain Gregg was anxious to add his share of professionalism while the Union was still salvageable.

It was late in the month before Gregg could close out his duties at Warm Springs, where he would be relieved by a "reliable sergeant" until an officer was assigned to replace him on a permanent basis. His departure commenced at Fort Tejon, where he bade farewell to colleagues, friends, and his Irish terrier and joined numerous officers heading east from nearby installations including the little village of Los Angeles (population 4,385). At that post he made the acquaintance of Capt. Winfield Scott Hancock, chief quartermaster of the Southern Military District of California, then traveling to Washington with his comely and utterly charming wife, Almira. Gregg's close association with Hancock, a soldier of great ability and charisma, would endure throughout the war and for decades afterward. Gregg cemented the relationship at the outset by offering the couple the stateroom he had secured on the ship that carried them down the coast prior to the grueling six-week passage to New York and Washington via Panama.

When the heterogeneous group of soldiers, dependents, and other civilians reached Manhattan, several passengers, including Gregg and the Hancocks, dined at one of Manhattan's many seafood restaurants. Famished for the sort of delicacies denied them at their distant outposts, Gregg and some of the others stuffed themselves with a specialty of the house, oysters on the half-shell. Evidently they did not know when to cease feasting, because within a few hours the captain and several of his comrades were violently ill. Put to bed at the Astor House hotel under a physician's care, they were forced to linger in the city until fully recovered. Supposedly those who had escaped the worst effects of the meal, including Hancock, could not resist adding insult to gastric injury: "Well, goodbye old fellows, we are off for Washington. This little fight will last only a couple of weeks, and we will be in it, reaping glory and laurels, whilst you will be lying here in bed." If the anecdote is accurate, Hancock had a rather malicious sense of humor, especially considering the favor Gregg had done him on the long and disagreeable ocean voyage.[5]

It is not known how long the overindulgent diners remained in their sickbeds, but assuredly they missed the date on which they were to report to their respective units. Gregg's belated journey to the War Department was further extended by a side-trip to Philadelphia during which he spent time in the company of Miss Sheaff, then staying with her sister and brother-in-law at a hotel in the city. During the visit he began to press his suit with "that delightful young lady." He must have been persuasive, for he seems to have left for Washington in high hopes that she would accept his proposal.[6]

Reporting at last to the office of the adjutant general of the army, he was ordered to join the soon-to-be-christened 6th Cavalry at its Pittsburgh, Pennsylvania, recruiting rendezvous, which he did on August 21, 1861. He remained in his native state for only three weeks before the regiment, its organization already well underway, was transferred to Bladensburg, Maryland, six miles northeast of the nation's capital.

In the Washington suburbs he reconnected with his cousin Irvin Gregg, who had been training with the 6th since late June. He discovered, however, that Lieutenant Averell would not be serving alongside them. Two days after Gregg reported at Pittsburgh the New Yorker had been granted a leave from his regular army duties to accept a commission as colonel of a regiment of volunteers (an outfit recruited by state authorities from among the civilian population for wartime service, in contrast to the professional soldiers of the regular army). The plum position he gained in the soon-to-be-distinguished 3rd Pennsylvania Cavalry, which drew its manpower from the streets of Philadelphia and the countryside outside the city, had been tendered by Gregg's first cousin, Governor Andrew Gregg Curtin. The officers of Averell's new command appear to have welcomed him with open arms; as one later remarked, the newcomer was "a fine soldier, and his appointment to its [the regiment's] command was its making."[7]

Whether or not his classmate was worthy of the promotion, David Gregg must have been surprised and more than a little chagrined to learn that one of his contemporaries—one, perhaps, of lesser attainments—had gotten a jump on him in the quest for rank and authority. A growing number of professional soldiers had transferred to the volunteers at a higher grade than they had held in the regulars, but Averell's promotion had come about in an unorthodox manner, largely as the result of his participation in the fighting along Bull Run. Having been stationed in the East upon war's outbreak he had been in a more fortuitous position than Gregg to exploit opportunities such as the one that had opened up to him.

In addition to fortunate timing, Averell profited from his close association with a superior who had risen to high station early in the conflict, Capt. Andrew Porter, formerly of the Regiment of Mounted Riflemen. When Porter played military and political connections to rise to the rank of colonel at war's outbreak and then to the rank of brigadier general in the volunteers, he attached Averell to the staff of his 2nd Brigade, 2nd Division, in General McDowell's Army of Northeastern Virginia. By July 21 Averell had become Porter's most trusted subordinate. Thus, when the 2nd Division leader, Brig. Gen. David Hunter (former colonel of the 6th U.S. Cavalry) was wounded early in the battle, his senior subordinate, Porter, succeeded him. Upon moving up the chain of command, Porter called on Averell to "look after this brigade yourself." In one of the most unusual arrangements in military history, through the rest of the day a twenty-eight-year-old first lieutenant of regulars directed the operations of three New York regiments—one of volunteers, the others of militia—each of which was commanded by an officer who outranked him.

The anomalous brigadier did not win fame and glory on July 21. Most of the maneuvers he ordered foundered on the inexperience or incompetence of his subordinates. In fact, blundering on an army-wide scale cost McDowell not only a chance for victory but also his exalted position. On July 27 he was officially replaced in command of the newly renamed Army of the Potomac by thirty-four-year-old Maj. Gen. George Brinton McClellan, whose minor but well-publicized campaigning in western Virginia had gained him the nickname "Young

Napoleon." In contrast to McDowell, William Averell emerged from the defeat with his reputation not only intact but burnished. His ability, and his unquestioned authority, to command some 2,500 officers and men in combat marked him as an officer worthy of greater responsibility than that of a company commander of horse.[8]

Although perhaps disappointed with his own rather lowly station, Captain Gregg embraced the responsibilities incumbent on a subaltern in the 6th Cavalry. The raw material at his disposal was in need of instruction in every duty from mounting a saber charge to properly cleaning the hooves and hides of their mounts, but the men had to be brought along slowly and carefully enough to ensure their ability to absorb both the basics and the nuances of their chosen branch. A literate young recruit, Sidney M. Davis, would write that Gregg and the other officers "began moderately with us, first instructing us as to the proper mode of saddling and bridling up, rolling up and strapping on the pommel and cantle of our saddles our overcoats and blankets, and carrying forage and rations on horseback."[9]

Within a few weeks the instructional regimen suddenly became more demanding. A fellow officer in the 6th noted that he drilled the men of his company "both in arms and also in *real* discipline. My whole time has been occupied in study and practice." In late September the program speeded up with the receipt of orders to participate in a grand review of the mounted arm of McClellan's vast command. Thereafter, as Davis recalled, "we were hurried along into company and division [i.e., larger-unit] drills with an energy of purpose commendable, perhaps, in the officers, but severe on the men and horses."[10]

The review, which took place on September 24, was attended by a bevy of high-ranking officials including President Lincoln, General McClellan, his chief of cavalry, Brig. Gen. George Stoneman, Col. (later Brig. Gen.) Philip St. George Cooke (the Mexican War hero who commanded the army's regular cavalry), and observers from various foreign armies. Although at this point not every member of the 6th Cavalry had been mounted, at least two thousand horsemen in full panoply paraded past the reviewing stand. In their midst rumbled seven batteries of horse (or "flying") artillery, each of whose gunners rode horseback rather than on the ammunition boxes atop their limbers and caissons as did those cannoneers who served with infantry units.[11]

Presumably the honored guests were suitably impressed by this, one of the earliest displays of mounted strength in the eastern theater of the war, although their reactions were not publicized. Only three weeks before the review, however, General Stoneman, a fifteen-year veteran of dragoon and cavalry service, complained that the men under his command were "poorly cared for, badly instructed, and a good deal dissatisfied." Three weeks later his opinion had not improved; as he informed McClellan's chief of staff, there was "an almost total want of knowledge on the part of both officers and men [of the volunteers], of what constitute[d] a cavalry soldier." One nagging concern was the ongoing conflict between state and federal regulations regarding the relative rank of regulars and citizen-soldiers. The disconnect, Stoneman wrote, had "given rise to an endless amount of contention and quarreling which [would] continue until something like uniformity [could] be established."[12]

Not until early October was the 6th Cavalry fully mounted, equipped, and deemed ready to move toward the seat of war. Yet it was not ready to forgo instruction in the "school of the trooper." In its new camp just east of the U.S. Capitol drill resumed in full force. In less than a week, however, Captain Gregg abruptly departed the field, having contracted a highly communicable strain of a disease that had begun to ravage McClellan's army: typhoid fever. The insidious bacterial infection, the product of army camps lacking adequate sanitation and hygiene, landed him for the second time in three months flat on his back in a sick bed, this time wracked by fever, body aches, vomiting, and diarrhea.

Because the 6th's camp's lacked the facilities required to treat his condition, Gregg was removed to a general hospital in Washington. His symptoms, which would persist for three or four weeks, were severe enough to cause him great anxiety. His state of mind was further shaken when, only a few days into his recuperation and almost helplessly weak, he awoke one night to the glow of flames and the stench of smoke. He was unable to rise from his cot to summon help; fortunately, a hospital steward was asleep nearby and after repeated efforts Gregg roused him. Peering out the nearest window, the man initially reported that the fire appeared to issue from a building across the street. Assuring the patient there was no cause for alarm, he attempted to go back to sleep. Only when Gregg loudly ordered him to inspect the other rooms of the building did the orderly investigate—before rushing back to report the entire hospital on fire.

The immobile Gregg was greatly relieved when the orderly offered to wrap him in a blanket and carry him from the building piggyback fashion. This he did even as other patients and staff members made their way as best they could through the smoke-filled corridors. Once outside and at a safe distance from the building, Gregg's rescuer deposited him gently on the curb, then rushed back into the building to recover the captain's personal belongings.

At this point, as he had on an unknown number of prior occasions, Gregg fainted away. Some hours later he awoke in a strange bedroom, ministered to by a troupe of chorus girls, the residents of a theatrical boarding house across the street from the hospital. Gregg's son relates that his father never forgot his charming attendants and their evident concern for his welfare. From the boarding house he was subsequently transported to another hospital, where his recuperation continued. When far enough along he was permitted to complete his convalescence in Philadelphia, although whether he did so in a military hospital or at the home of relatives remains unknown. If the latter, it seems likely that the woman he fondly called "Nell" would have been at his side at some point to see him through the last stages of his recovery.

The leave Gregg had been granted was sufficient to enable him to travel to New York, where he took a room at the Astor House, site of his recent dietary misadventures. He appears to have gone there to visit one of his cousins, former congressman and Manhattan man-about-town James X. McLanahan, and his wife, Ann. While in the city Gregg took advantage of an invitation to a formal reception hosted by a friend of the McLanahans, a society matron he had never met. "Swell" Averell might have been at ease in such a gathering of metropolitan fashion plates, but not the unpretentious Gregg. Adrift in a sea of strangers, he was rescued from his unease by Cousin James, who introduced him not only to the hostess but to "several charming young ladies who were not averse to entertaining an interesting young officer from the front."

He spent the remainder of his leave back in Philadelphia. It is unlikely that he informed Ellen (then residing at the home of Kate and Alexander Stewart) of those "charming young ladies" with whom he spent the evening. Instead he summoned up the fortitude to propose marriage, and she accepted. Gregg, Jr., notes that the culmination to the lengthy courtship "must have gone a long way towards reconciling him to the return to camp life and Virginia mud."[13]

The transition from affairs of the heart to military affairs occurred on the last day of 1861, when Gregg reported to the rendezvous of his regiment in the Washington suburbs. Perhaps with a sigh of resignation, he resumed the task of making cavalrymen out of recruits as raw as uncured leather and as ignorant of war's demands as any youngster weaned on the martial glories of Walter Scott and Thomas Mallory. Thanks largely to the solicitude of William Averell, however, his resumption of company-level duties would be brief. Early in November, only two months after assuming command of the 3rd Pennsylvania, the well-connected Averell was selected to lead the first brigade of volunteer cavalry formed during the war. It consisted of his own regiment and another recruited in and near Philadelphia, the 8th Pennsylvania, otherwise known as "Chorman's Mounted Rifle Rangers."

Averell considered the 8th "a most promising body of officers and men with the exception of the Colonel." Ernest G. Chorman may have been a maven of Quaker City society, but his sole claim to military experience was a brief stint as a noncommissioned officer in a volunteer infantry regiment during the Mexican War. Averell soon found a convenient way of ridding himself of Chorman's less-than-inspired leadership. A board charged with examining the qualifications of volunteer officers had been set up in Washington and Averell was detailed as one of its members. The panel, which convened once a week, had the power to recommend the dismissal of unworthy candidates, and Averell almost always conducted the examinations. In mid-December Brig. Gen. Fitz John Porter, commander of the division to which the 3rd Pennsylvania was attached, called Chorman before the board. At

intervals over the next month the former foot soldier was closely inter-
rogated as to his knowledge of military affairs in general and, in particular, cavalry organization, tactics, and missions. Found deficient, he
was persuaded to resign his commission as of January 15.

Two days after Chorman's departure, he was succeeded in command
of the 8th Pennsylvania, then stationed at Arlington Heights, Virginia, by Col. David McMurtrie Gregg, who thereby joined the U.S.
Volunteers. In an act of well-reasoned nepotism—and in response to
a petition of several of the regiment's officers—Governor Curtin had
recommended the promotion of his cousin to rehabilitate an outfit
that had gone to seed in Chorman's hands while sadly neglected by
army headquarters. Because the Republican governor was a powerful
supporter of the Lincoln administration, his efforts on behalf of his
relative prompted the War Department to speedily grant Gregg the
extended leave required by an officer of regulars transitioning to the
volunteer service.[14]

Upon reporting to his new command, based near Fort Corcoran at
the Virginia end of the Arlington aqueduct, he saw that "Camp Leslie"
was in need of a complete overhaul. Too many of its officers appeared
lazy and apathetic as well as poorly schooled in cavalry organization and
operations. There were exceptions—a number of subalterns appeared
eager to learn and serve even if barely keeping one lesson ahead of the
troopers they were charged with training. These men were pleased
by the change of command; in a letter published in the *Philadelphia
Inquirer* one expressed his approval of "the appointment of the gallant and accomplished Capt. D. M. Gregg. . . . With such a leader the
country [might] expect to hear a good account of the 8th Pennsylvania if an opportunity should ever occur."[15]

Gregg's enlisted force was composed of promising material, but
thanks to incompetent leadership it had become frustrated and demoralized. Although occasionally sent forth to reconnoiter the disputed
territory between Washington and the Rebels still encamped on the
Bull Run battlefield, for the most part the regiment had been consigned
to training camp, much like the recruit-heavy 6th U.S Cavalry. Three
weeks before Gregg arrived, an enlisted man had complained in a letter home of "getting tired of this inactive life." Comrades agreed that

camp life had become "dreary" and "particularly dull" because "the spirit of a soldier['s] life [was] to be constantly moving."[16]

Undisciplined, disgruntled, and lacking a guiding hand, more than a few men had turned to drink when and where they could get it, which could inspire horseplay with unintended consequences. Cpl. Robert Cummings wrote his sister that he had been stabbed in the knee with a large carving fork while "playing the fool around the camp fire." Shenanigans of this sort had an immediate impact on regimental readiness.[17]

The corporate morale had not been improved by the recent weather, which had turned Camp Leslie into a bottomless lagoon. "The mud is about ass deep," an enlisted man complained. "It rains nearly every day . . . and it don't look like clearing for six months. This is a God forsaken country and I wish I was out of it." The general unhealthiness of the local area made some believe the 8th would have to relocate, perhaps closer to the enemy's lines. "I think we wont [*sic*] stay here all winter," the complainant added. Rumor suggested an early movement against the Confederate capital; as Corporal Cummings wrote, "The cry is on to Richmond but we will have hot work before we get there." Cummings had begun to doubt that the outfit was equal to the task.[18]

One of the most serious defects of the 8th Pennsylvania was a general shortage of arms and equipment. With the assistance of Averell and presumably also of General Porter, Gregg rectified this deficiency as quickly as possible. Within weeks of his assumption of command, a contemporary historian has noted, "new and complete [sets of] camp and garrison equipage with a full outfit of arms and accoutrements were obtained." The colonel also upgraded the instructional program, replacing incompetent drillmasters with those familiar with the lessons set forth in the tactics manuals furnished by the War Department.[19]

The first efforts at drill under Gregg's supervision revealed how poorly the task had been attended to before his coming. Many, perhaps most, of the would-be-cavaliers, being city dwellers, had little or no prior experience with horses except as the motive power behind streetcars and dray wagons. Consequently, troopers and horses, rather than acting as a team, too often went their separate ways, a situation that usually ended with riders no longer in the saddle but stretched out on the hard ground. This could leave the recruit terrified of his required mode of transportation. One veteran recalled that many of his comrades "showed much more fear of their horses than they ever did afterward of the enemy." Some barely made it into the saddle. During an early drill Gregg found one recruit so burdened with superfluous equipment that his horse could barely move. He told the man: "About the only thing you have neglected to provide yourself with is step ladder" on which to climb aboard.[20]

Slowly but steadily, conditions at Camp Leslie improved. Gregg fortified regimental morale as well as proficiency by acquiring (after some initial difficulty) effective weaponry, including the highly sought-after Sharps repeating carbine, as well as enough horses to fully mount the regiment. To encourage esprit de corps, he continued a practice that predated him, the issuance of mounts to the various units by color: blacks to Company C, sorrels to Company E, dark bays to Company G, light bays to Company H, and so on. The allocation process had a practical application; it enabled Gregg to differentiate one unit from another at a distance. The color-coding would cease once large numbers of remounts arrived from the government's horse depots. Then, too, horses of various hues were seized from nearby farms by dismounted troopers who did not care to wait for a replacement. It was said that to avoid detection a stolen horse was often disguised to the point that "his own dam would not [have known] him."[21]

Perhaps Gregg's most effective reform was ridding the 8th of incompetent or lax subordinates, many of them political appointees, whom he hauled before the examining board. He had reached an agreement with Averell that anyone sent to the latter for examination deserved to be removed from his position—and in fact all who appeared before the panel were rejected. As a result, within two months of Gregg's commissioning no fewer than eleven officers—three captains and eight lieutenants, including an assistant surgeon and the regiment's chief quartermaster—joined Colonel Chorman in the ranks of the unemployed either through resignation or summary discharge. The purge continued into the summer, when several other subalterns found themselves returned to civilian life thanks to Gregg's unswerving efforts to separate wheat from chaff.[22]

His efforts to improve regimental efficiency quickly won the support of Averell, who admitted to some embarrassment that a West Point classmate was serving under him but who greatly appreciated Gregg's willingness to make the relationship work. As he recalled after the war, "although Gregg had been my senior in our class rank, he served with me during that time as faithfully and subordinately as he could have served had he been of a younger class. He not only divided the general duties with me but brought that comradeship which is a welcome comfort to a hardworking Colonel of cavalry."[23]

His workload left Gregg little time for interests outside the narrow, and often stifling, confines of camp. He found it difficult to stay in touch with relatives, friends and even Ellen, who had returned to her native Reading to stay with her aunt and uncle, Judge and Mrs. Jones. The couple had set a date for their wedding, to take place at the Jones residence on February 27. The timing of the ceremony was a matter of careful consideration, Gregg believing that it would predate the assumption of active campaigning. The "On to Richmond" cry had been taken up by the newspapers just as it had prior to Bull Run, and the White House was anxious that a full-scale offensive be deferred no longer than the coming of spring, when Virginia's roads would be free of mud and snow. However, McClellan was not McDowell, able to be influenced by public opinion and political pressure to take the field before his troops were fully organized and trained. The end of February seemed like a safe bet for the granting of leave, one that would accommodate a honeymoon of suitable duration.[24]

Meanwhile, the prospective bridegroom gloried in his regiment's revitalization. On the last day of January he took time from his multiplicity of duties to write his cousin Maria C. Hiester of Milmont, Franklin County, Pennsylvania, whom he had last seen at the Hotel Continental in Philadelphia near the end of his sick leave. After apologizing for his delay in answering her most recent letter, he lightheartedly surveyed his present situation ("here I am, Colonel of the 8th Pa. Cavalry, sinking with my Regiment beneath a sea of Virginia mud"). He then imparted good news: "I was told [before assuming command of it] that I would be so much disgusted with the condition of my Regiment, that I would have but one wish . . . that I had never seen a Volunteer Regiment; now the friends who saw so much unhappiness in store for me, will be agreeably surprised to learn that I am quite cheerful and hopeful. The material of my Regiment is excellent." He went on to note "if the officers c[ould] only be brought to do their duty," he would soon have a most creditable outfit.

Gregg's promotion had not gone unnoticed among his military and civilian acquaintances. To Maria he rather sarcastically addressed his sudden popularity, which may have owed to the favors the new colonel might be in a position to grant: "A new light has dawned upon me since my advancement to my present position. Before I was well pleased in the thought that I had a few tried friends, but only now is it discovered to me that always I had hosts of friends who now ask only slight rewards for so much unobtrusive friendship. Oh! The world!" Though he did not mention it in his letter, his elevation had also garnered favorable attention in the public press. Early in February the *Inquirer* described him as a strict disciplinarian but also "an accomplished gentleman and a thorough soldier."

The balance of Gregg's missive included opinions he shared with officers and men throughout the ranks: "There can be no advance of this Army for some considerable time owing to the condition of the roads. Camp life just now is very disagreeable—there is a general suspension of practical instruction and attention is only given to ditching, draining, &c." He added that he had recently heard from Ellen in Reading; she and Kate appeared to be enjoying the premarital visit, which "will be protracted to a very great length."

This last comment seems to have been based on misinformation, as his cousin learned upon receiving a letter from Ellen a few weeks later. Although Reading appeared the most logical setting for the forthcoming nuptials, the bride-to-be was finding the town "quite a change" from Philadelphia, because in the Jones household she and her sister "can't do exactly as we want." Furthermore, "there is nothing going on here, *except the perfect quiet* which generally reigns in this jumping off place."

Ellen confided her wedding plans to Maria, whom she hoped to have as one of her bridesmaids. Everything depended on her fiancé gaining the requisite leave. In that event, she wrote, "We will be married here in the evening & *every* one will be invited." Given the number of family members she shared with her beloved, the ceremony promised to be well attended indeed.[25]

But it was not to be. Apparently presaging an early resort to full-scale operations, by mid-February the 8th Pennsylvania had begun to play a more active role in the operations of McClellan's army. On February 18 a portion of the regiment made a reconnaissance to Vienna, Virginia, a between-the-lines hamlet twelve miles west of the capital where the Rebels had an advance outpost. Four days later the detachment returned to Vienna while also scouting southward toward Flint Hill, another of the enemy's regular haunts. By February 16 Gregg was writing Maria Hiester: "It is at present altogether out of the question for me to obtain a leave of absence." Having not been to Washington for a month, he had lacked the opportunity to petition the War Department for the desired favor. He was anxious that the wedding should take place as soon as possible even if he was "only be able to obtain leave for a very few days. . . . A day or two away and then back to my camp." He expected marching orders as soon as the weather cleared although he noted: "Yesterday we had a fall of several inches of snow, today a thaw."[26]

Unable to leave his regiment even briefly, Gregg must have chafed at the subsequent delay in taking the field, which extended through the middle of March. His frame of mind marginally improved when late in the month a third regiment was added to Averell's brigade, one with which Gregg was quite familiar, the 1st U.S. Cavalry. He was pleased to reunite with its commander, "Old Billy" Grier, although the reunion caused some unavoidable embarrassment. The venerable dragoon who had been Gregg's superior during the 1858 campaign in the Washington Territory had since been promoted to lieutenant colonel, one grade below Gregg's rank. Thus, whenever the 8th Pennsylvania and 1st U.S. operated in tandem the spanking-new volunteer officer, not the experienced regular, would command the combined force.[27]

A partial offensive by the Army of the Potomac took place on March 6, when it was learned that the Confederates under Joseph E. Johnston had begun to vacate their winter quarters between Centreville and

Manassas. The unexpected move—based on Johnston's belief that his army must occupy more defensible ground below the Rappahannock River, thirty miles closer to Richmond—caught his adversary by surprise. There followed a belated pursuit, apparently at the express direction of McClellan. Averell's cavalry took the lead in a twenty-six-mile slog through roads clogged with mud and barricaded with the debris of the retreating enemy.

The operation involved little more than long-range skirmishing with the Rebel rear guard. The pursuers were content to hasten their adversaries on their way and to scavenge among their abandoned camps for anything worth appropriating. In a letter to his family, however, Averell described Johnston's retreat as "one of the greatest victories of the war." By turning and running the Confederates had "ruined their cause in Europe [where they enjoyed moral and material support], demoralized their army at home and lost millions of dollars in materials. All this ha[d] been achieved for us by McClellan without a battle."[28]

Despite published reports that awarded the honor to other elements of the army, the 3rd and 8th Pennsylvania were the first units to occupy Manassas after Johnston left. When efforts to make this clear began to circulate, only Averell's own regiment reaped the credit. Gregg, displaying a determination to gain the recognition due him and his men, complained in a letter to his West Point classmate, Lt. Col. Albert V. Colburn, aide-de-camp at army headquarters, that the 8th was being denied acknowledgment of its achievements. "An official recognition of the service is not asked for my regiment," he added, "but since I was personally instructed by the Commander-in-Chief [i.e., McClellan] to perform a certain duty, it would be gratifying to myself and regiment to know that he was informed that the duty had been successfully performed."[29]

Following the march to Manassas Averell's command fell back to Fairfax Court House—according to its leader, in order to be closer to the army's newly established advance supply depot. The brigade camped there for less than two weeks before it was ordered to stand ready to be transferred, along with the rest of an army that had swollen to some 105,000 officers and men, to the wharves of Alexandria, Virginia. From there McClellan's giant host would be transported via steamboat and other water craft to Fort Monroe at the tip of the Virginia Peninsula, between the James and York Rivers.[30]

Fed up with McClellan's studied inactivity, Lincoln had demanded that he get moving in the direction of the enemy capital. "Little Mac" had complied, but slowly. His initial plan, hammered out at a series of conferences with the commanders of the army's divisions (soon to be enlarged into corps), was predicated on descending Chesapeake Bay by troopships as far as Urbanna on the Rappahannock, forty-seven miles northeast of Richmond. Such a movement, if made with requisite speed and stealth, promised to turn Johnston's flank, cutting off his army at Manassas. Once the Confederates evacuated their eight-month-old campsite, however, the plan—to which Lincoln had assented only grudgingly—gave way to an advance on Richmond from the south via the Peninsula. Even before the president approved the new concept, McClellan predicted: "We are now on the eve of the success for which we have been so long preparing."[31]

The Army of the Potomac began moving out on March 17. Two weeks later, Gregg's outfit, along with numerous other units, was still awaiting transportation from Alexandria, the result of a "recent blow off Fort Monroe [that] has doubtless prevented the transports from coming." Thanks to a recent reorganization of the army's mounted forces, the 8th was no longer part of William Averell's command. On March 24 the regiment had joined a division-size force under Philip St. George Cooke known as the Cavalry Reserve. One of Cooke's two brigades, commanded by Col. George A. H. Blake (who had led the column that included Gregg's regiment from Fort Union to Fort Tejon in late 1856), comprised the 8th Pennsylvania, 1st U.S., and two squadrons of volunteers from Illinois and New York. Yet organization continued to be fluid. During the campaign that lay ahead Gregg's regiment would frequently serve apart from Blake's command; by late April it would be attached to another of Cooke's brigades, led by Brig. Gen. William H. Emory.[32]

In the last week of March or the first days of April, the 8th Pennsylvania disembarked from the steamer conveying it down the coast and moved inland from Fort Monroe. On April 4, with almost 70,000 troops on solid ground, McClellan's long-awaited offensive got under-

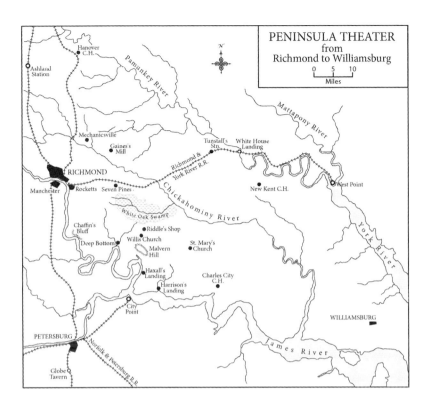

Map 2. Peninsula theater, from Richmond to Williamsburg. Created by Paul Dangel.

way. Extended columns of men, horses, guns, and wagons moved simultaneously up both sides of the Peninsula toward Yorktown, where a small army under Brig. Gen. John Bankhead Magruder lay in wait. Magruder's main line extended west from the port city as far as the meandering Warwick River. At this time Johnston's larger command was still on the Rappahannock near Fredericksburg, but within days it would be hastening to Magruder's assistance.

In accord with well-defined roles and missions, McClellan's horsemen paved the way for his foot soldiers and artillerists. Averell, who had temporarily returned to command of the 3rd Pennsylvania, marched in front of Brig. Gen. Samuel P. Heintzelman's right wing on the direct road to Yorktown. Although some accounts have suggested that the 8th Pennsylvania had the advance of Brig. Gen. Erasmus D. Keyes's IV Corps three miles to the north, moving via Young's Mill and Warwick Court House, this cannot be established. The record suggests that the 5th U.S. Cavalry took the lead, with Gregg's men somewhat farther to the rear, probing the woods and byroads for lurking Rebels.[33]

The first day of the march went well, and by evening both columns were halfway to their initial objectives. Magruder had elected not to sacrifice detachments of his 14,500-man force to detain the Yankees except at a few points where skirmishes broke out and quickly ended. Alert to the prospect of ambushes, Gregg's regiment took great pains to clear the road of fallen trees and other roadblocks. The slow work forced the infantry and artillery to move in stop-start fashion, but the pace was preferable to that of the next day, when a several-hour downpour turned the Peninsula into a vast quagmire. The gummy clay beneath the region's topsoil was so thick that horses and riders could not move with any degree of haste.

When progress was made at a few points, the enemy responded violently. In front of Yorktown Magruder's advance guard brought Averell and Heintzelman to a dead halt. Having acquired a working knowledge of this sector of the local defenses, McClellan had expected as much. But because he lacked accurate information on the western end of Magruder's line he was floored when thousands of Confederates opened on Keyes's column from behind long, deep earthworks. A single cavalry regiment could do little to improve the situation; Gregg's men gave way as foot soldiers and guns pushed forward as quickly as the mud would permit. Taking up positions in the rear and on the flanks of the advancing column, the 8th Pennsylvania saw little action during the remainder of the day, which ended with the Army of the Potomac virtually immobilized.

The situation did not improve over the next several days. In addition to being held at bay, McClellan was dazzled by the tricks Magruder played on him. The theatrically minded Virginian divided his force into small segments, which he marched back and forth within sight of Union binoculars. As one of his soldiers would write, this was done "with no other view than to show ourselves to the enemy at as many different points of the line as possible." By giving the impression of a continuous flow of troops and guns, Magruder convinced his opponent that he could not successfully assault Yorktown—he would have to besiege it.[34]

The operation, which featured the slow and cumbersome placement of dozens of cannons and mortars ferried from Washington to command the enemy's line, would consume an entire month. The ground being unfavorable for mounted operations, the 8th Pennsylvania would see little activity of strategic consequence during this period of preparation and maneuvering. In fact, the situation would not change materially throughout the unfolding campaign.

4

Subordinate to Averell and Pleasonton

George McClellan's preparations to level Yorktown were complete by May 4, but before he could unleash his massive array of weaponry, Joe Johnston, who had joined forces with John Bankhead Magruder a month earlier, evacuated the Peninsula in favor of newly enhanced fortifications around Richmond. The Union commander was caught off guard by his enemy's proactive strategy, just as he had been when stymied by Magruder on the Warwick River. Belatedly he ordered a pursuit by as much of his army as he could get together on short notice. Cavalry and horse artillery led the way, dogging the Rebels' heels on the road to Williamsburg.[1]

Shortly before Johnston's exodus another reorganization had shaken up the Union mounted arm. One result was that the 8th Pennsylvania changed commands yet again. No longer an element of Philip St. George Cooke's reserve force, it had been brigaded with another volunteer regiment, the 6th Pennsylvania. Known as "Rush's Lancers" for the unique and antiquated weapon its enlisted men toted, the 6th had been recruited among the social, financial, and athletic elite of Philadelphia. Its blueblood commander, Col. Richard H. Rush, appears not to have favored the alliance with Gregg, probably because, given Gregg's regular-army experience, the latter commanded both regiments when they served side by side. Rush was said to be jealous of his colleague, who commanded the trust and respect of his men. In contrast, according to a member of the 6th, Rush and his subordinates were "a set of Aristocrattic [sic] Fops, and have no more feelling [sic] for the men in the Ranks than so many dogs." Be that as it might, the regiment had an elite reputation that made it attractive to aspiring young officers. In November family members would pull strings to secure a lieutenant's commission in the 6th for twenty-year-old Thomas Jackson Gregg. In the spring of 1863 David, by then a general officer, would have his youngest brother transferred to his staff, to ride beside him on every field of battle. In later months another of David's brothers, William Henry Harrison ("Harry") Gregg, would also serve under him as an officer in the 13th Pennsylvania Cavalry.[2]

If Colonel Rush was vexed by Gregg's presence, William Averell regretted his absence. In a letter home late in April Gregg's classmate noted that in place of the 8th Pennsylvania his command now included the 1st New Jersey Cavalry, led by a flamboyant British soldier-of-fortune, Col. Sir Percy Wyndham. "It is not so good a regiment as Gregg's," Averell opined, "but is tolerable."[3]

In fact, the 8th Pennsylvania, although it had made great strides in discipline, deportment, and tactical proficiency, had far to go to prove itself an effective force in combat. It had had no opportunity to do so upon Yorktown's evacuation, having been left in the rear along with most of the army's horsemen while General Cooke led the pursuit. On May 4, 1862, one day before the forward elements of McClellan's army tangled with Johnston south of Williamsburg, the cavalry under Cooke overtook the Rebel rear guard and skirmished with it. Among the combatants in this spirited but indecisive clash was Brig. Gen. James Ewell Brown Stuart of Virginia, Johnston's senior mounted leader—and the son-in-law of General Cooke. Stuart would battle his relative more than a few times before the campaign ended, just as he would engage David Gregg on many fields over the next two years.

The fighting outside Virginia's colonial capital had repercussions, positive and negative, for the horsemen of the Army of the Potomac. The battle displayed the grit and aggressiveness of which the regulars were capable despite their diminished condition, which hasty recruiting had failed to improve. Cooke had suffered thirty-five casualties but he had inflicted almost as many on Stuart's vaunted cavaliers—in fact, the regulars had done well merely by catching up to the Virginian, given his six-hour head start from Yorktown. Numerous officers had comported themselves ably and courageously; Gregg was proud to learn that many hailed from the 6th Cavalry. They included John Irvin Gregg, whose heroics this day heralded his subsequent rise to high rank in the volunteer service.[4]

Another effect of the recent fighting presented problems for McClellan's cavalry, which immediately afterward was reduced to small detachments for field service. In the months ahead it would be fragmented time and again, often on an infantry general's whim, its pieces—companies, squadrons, and battalions—remanded to menial tasks. Brig. Gen. William H. Emory would complain that his brigade was "practically neutralized by this assignment of duties." Another result of the wholesale detaching was a pernicious experiment in decentralized authority. For reasons of his own, General Stoneman, McClellan's cavalry leader, had assumed control of the fighting on May 4, superseding Cooke. The arrangement continued after the battle, Cooke being demoted to the command of Emory's brigade and the latter, despite his volunteer rank, reduced to leading the 6th U.S. Cavalry. The structural changes would hamper the cavalry for months to come, prompting Emory to transfer to an infantry command.[5]

Only occasionally did a mounted unit see action above the small-unit level. When the 8th Pennsylvania did so for the first time, it was said to have faltered disastrously. On May 14 the regiment, which had been ordered to scout communication lines that Johnston had recently abandoned, took part in a skirmish with units of all arms near New Kent Court House, halfway between Williamsburg and Richmond. At some point the regiment came under a blistering cannonade that would have shaken many a regular regiment, let alone a group of citizen-soldiers under artillery fire for the first time. Supposedly the shelling caused the men of the 8th—some of them, at least—to panic and skedaddle, but the circumstances are a matter of contention. The only criticism of the regiment's performance came from a member of the 1st New York Cavalry, who claimed that Gregg's outfit "gained an unenviable reputation for the speed it made in getting away from the enemy" prior to rampaging through the ranks of some infantry units, breaking their formations as well. The 1st New York, however, was not a part of Brig. Gen. Erasmus D. Keyes's corps and as far as can be determined was not present at New Kent and thus in no position to critique the fighting.[6]

In his report of the skirmish, General Keyes noted that the 8th, which had been sent to picket the main road to Richmond miles in advance of the rest of its corps, had been "annoyed by the enemy's shell[ing]." It seems likely that Keyes would have faulted the 8th had it acted as the New Yorker charged. Moreover, two weeks after the fight, by which time the 8th had been detached from the IV Corps, Keyes petitioned army headquarters "to have Colonel Gregg and his regiment permanently assigned to my command." He would not have requested the reattachment of a unit that had disgraced itself under fire.[7]

Nor would Keyes have continued to assign the regiment scouting missions of obvious importance. On May 19 he sent Gregg's men, along with an infantry brigade and two batteries, to cover the surveying of the countryside around Bottom's Bridge on the Chickahominy River, the Peninsula's most imposing watercourse, a dozen miles east of Richmond. The mission, which involved the army's chief engineer officer, Brig. Gen. John G. Barnard, accompanied by Gregg's West Point classmate Lt. Cyrus Comstock, was successfully accomplished. So too was a second reconnaissance of the same venue the following day, involving only the 8th Pennsylvania.[8]

Late on May 20 McClellan's troops began to cross the meandering, sluggish, but deceptively deep river. Because Bottom's Bridge had been partially dismantled by the retreating Confederates, as had a bridge on the Richmond and York River Railroad three-quarters of a mile upriver, elements of Keyes's corps waded the stream, which they did without opposition. On May 25 Keyes advanced to a point about seven miles from Richmond known as Seven Pines. That same day Heintzelman's III Corps crossed, thus placing 30,000 troops south of the stream while leaving some 70,000 comrades on the north bank. Engineers and fatigue parties quickly rebuilt Bottom's Bridge and the railroad trestle while laying two more spans over the Chickahominy, one of them christened Grapevine Bridge for the twisting channels of the river in that vicinity.[9]

On May 23 General Keyes dispatched eight companies of the 8th, along with two infantry regiments, to scout Richmond Road. The mission marked the first time that Gregg, by virtue of seniority, commanded a brigade-size force, an assignment that indicated the trust he had inspired in his superiors. Under his supervision the three units made—as he reported to Colburn, his friend at headquarters—"a thorough examination of the country to the front and between the main road and the railroad." He "examined all the roads to the right and left," duly noting their course and condition. In so doing he encountered and chased away two Confederate detachments, the second of which—estimated to consist of an infantry regiment and 400 cavalry—was gouged out of its wooded shelter and prodded into a hasty retreat. According to a newspaper correspondent on the scene, the enemy fled for more than half a mile. At this point Gregg ran hard aground against a much larger force that made further progress toward Richmond inadvisable. Having penetrated "3 miles from the Chickahominy and 10 miles from Richmond," the more than 1,500 troopers and foot soldiers under his command returned safely to their encampments near Bottom's Bridge.[10]

Despite the mission's accomplishments, one of Keyes's subordinates, Brig. Gen. Henry M. Naglee, believed that Gregg's command had been too small to make sufficient headway toward Richmond. The following morning, May 24, Naglee led a much larger force—five infantry regiments, two batteries, and the 8th Pennsylvania—along the road between Williamsburg and the enemy capital. Early that rainy afternoon the advance guard, including Gregg's horsemen, encountered an enemy force about a mile and a half out. It comprised at least as many foot soldiers and cannoneers as Naglee was leading plus a large contingent of Stuart's cavalry. Naglee hastily deployed to meet it, extending his column across the tracks of the Richmond and York River Railroad and covering both sides of the Williamsburg Road.

Against moderate pressure Naglee pressed ahead as far as the depot of Savage's Station, where resistance stiffened. Attempts to outflank the Rebels, who were under Stuart's overall command, proved ineffective largely because of the latter's well-placed artillery. Naglee concentrated the fire of his own guns and that of a phalanx of sharpshooters against the batteries, and late in the afternoon the Rebels began to give way. Naglee, to exploit what he called the "unsteadiness in the ranks

of the enemy," called up the 8th Pennsylvania, supported it with portions of three infantry regiments as well as four cannons, and ordered
Gregg to attack.

Surveying the heavily wooded ground, the colonel of the 8th Pennsylvania must have wondered what a mounted charge could accomplish.
Whether he communicated his misgivings to his superior, however,
is unknown. What is known is that Gregg saluted smartly, aligned
his ranks, ordered the men draw sabers, and had his bugler sound the
charge. Away went the Pennsylvanians over the rough and broken terrain, the rear ranks attempting mightily to keep pace with those in front,
horses neighing madly under the thunder of artillery and the rattle of
rifle fire. For three hundred yards the horsemen maintained enough
cohesion to suggest they would strike the target with maximum force,
but then a body of skirmishers, concealed in a roadside thicket, laced
the right flank of the mounted column with a sustained volley. As his
horses recoiled, rearing and bunching up in the road, Gregg ordered a
halt. Shouting above the din, he called on the men to dismount, sheath
their swords, and return fire with carbines and pistols.

A well-directed fusillade from the 8th quickly silenced the ambush-
ers, who beat a precipitate retreat, whereupon Gregg searched for a
better vantage point to continue the fight. Discovering what Naglee
described as a "depression in the ground"—apparently one of considerable depth and width—he wheeled the regiment into it, sheltering
men and mounts from further harm. Naglee wrote that he "was preparing to follow [Gregg's assault] with skirmishers, and to order a second cavalry charge," when one of Keyes's aides conveyed an order that
no further advance be made. This effectively ended the day's action;
the enemy having drawn off, the Federals "slept on the wet ground"
through the night.

It would appear that General Naglee did not appreciate the efforts
of the 8th Pennsylvania this day. In his after-action report he commended each of his infantry subordinates but conspicuously omitted
mention of Gregg. If he had expected more of the single mounted regiment at his disposal he should not have directed that it charge infantry and artillery holding defensive positions that could not be reached
by mounted men. At this stage of the war the high command of the

Army of the Potomac lacked an appreciation of how cavalry should be used in support of the other arms of the service in offensive operations. Until McClellan and his infantry commanders gained a better understanding of its roles and missions, the cavalry would not be an effective tool in the fight to take Richmond, dismantle the Confederate government, and save the Union.[11]

Joseph E. Johnston, normally the sole of caution, realized that he must do something daring, if not desperate, to save Richmond from overwhelming attack or devastating siege. Though outnumbered nearly two to one, on the morning of Saturday, May 31, he launched a preemptive strike against the IV Corps near Seven Pines and the rail depot of Fair Oaks Station. The plan was just audacious enough to succeed, for the Yankees were not expecting a blow from that side of the rainswollen Chickahominy. But from the start the attack went awry, the result of poor staff work, high-level miscommunication, and a failure to carry out assigned missions on the part of such talented subordinates as Maj. Gens. James Longstreet and D. H. Hill. In the end the furious but belated and mismanaged offensive was beaten back by Keyes's men with help from Heintzelman, whose corps rushed up from the east via the Williamsburg Road. Critical support also came from elements of Maj. Gen. Edwin V. Sumer's II Corps, which made a daring eleventh-hour crossing of rickety Grapevine Bridge, every other span on the river having been washed away by a thunderous downpour the previous night.

By day's end the Union line south of the Chickahominy had been stabilized. A follow-up assault on June 1 did not alter the situation except that near its conclusion Johnston was seriously wounded by a shell fragment. Carried to the rear, he was succeeded in command of what had become known as the Army of Northern Virginia by Robert E. Lee, who for the past three months had been serving as military advisor to Confederate president Jefferson Davis.[12]

Gregg and his regiment took part in the fighting of May 31–June 1, but the nature and extent of their participation is a matter of conjecture. Some of Gregg's colleagues, perhaps jealous of his rise to high rank in the volunteers, would claim that the 8th saw no action at all on either day. One such critic was Maj. William H. Medill of the 8th Illinois Cavalry, brother of Joseph Medill, fiery editor of the *Chicago Tribune*, a Republican organ that staunchly supported the Lincoln administration. Writing to his sister almost a year after the battle, Medill revealed his disgruntlement at failing to gain the rank and notability that the politically conservative Gregg had attained, which by then included a star on his shoulder straps: "Promotions are made without reference to merit . . . Col Gregg, of the 8th Pennsylvania Cavalry is an instance. He is made a Brigadier for gallant and meritorious conduct at Fair Oaks, when he and his regiment were not near that fight. . . . His regiment certainly is the poorest in the army."[13]

At least one postwar source notes that the 8th was in fact engaged at Seven Pines but offers no clue to the nature of its involvement: "The ground being unfavorable for manoeuvring [*sic*], only detachments were engaged." Contemporary accounts also offer sparse information. From the reports of General Naglee and other IV Corps commanders it would appear that when fighting began on May 31 the 8th Pennsylvania was in bivouac on the far left flank of Naglee's brigade line, which stretched north for about two miles from Seven Pines to the Nine Mile Road, another thoroughfare to Richmond. The brigade had taken up this position on May 27, three days after the reconnaissance that culminated in the aborted charge by the 8th.[14]

The most detailed account of the regiment's role in the fight, brief though it is, comes from a letter written by Trooper Cummings almost three weeks afterward. According to the enlisted man, when the fighting commenced on May 31 the 8th was stationed close by Naglee's 104th Pennsylvania, whose position was overrun by D. H. Hill with the loss of more than 200 casualties. The semiliterate Cummings claimed that the 8th nearly shared the fate of its infantry comrades: "The rebels threw shells into our camp so thick that we had to get out of that [place] pretty quick leaving a great many thing[s] behind."

After abandoning its camp the 8th re-formed and took on a mission more appropriate to cavalry in such a crisis. "We were formed in line of battle in the rear to keep straglers [*sic*] from running back," Robert Cummings wrote. "Our situation was not a pleasant one for the shells flew around us pretty thick and wounded men came to the rear by hundreds."

Although still under the enemy's guns "we remained their [*sic*] until darkness closed the scene." The following day, according to Cummings, "we where [*sic*] ordered in another direction and did not see any of the fight on Sunday." In fact, only Company M of the 8th saw action of any consequence on June 1—skirmisher and picket duty, which it performed "very efficiently until relieved by order of General Keyes on the 3rd."

In the fighting of May 31 the 8th suffered only four casualties—two enlisted men wounded, two others missing and presumed captured—an indication that although holding precarious positions throughout the day Gregg kept the men sufficiently sheltered from harm. On the evening of June 2, according to Robert Cummings, the regiment was returned to its bivouac on the battlefield. "Such a sight," he wrote, "I never beheld before. Dead men and horses lay in every direction.... In the morning when I awoke I found that I had been sleeping on a grave and the poor fellow had not been buried but a few inches under ground."[15]

However much or little it contributed to Union fortunes at Seven Pines, the 8th saw hard service at intervals over the next month in response to competing demands on it. On June 2 part of Brig. Gen. Joseph Hooker's division of the III Corps, supported closely by Gregg's troopers, recovered and held the ground lost on May 31—perhaps not a major accomplishment, as Lee had withdrawn the Army of Northern Virginia to the Richmond defenses. On June 3, still operating with Hooker, a squadron of the 8th reconnoitered other parts of the battlefield without encountering hostile forces.[16]

Less than a week later, Gregg's outfit was again fragmented. While seven of its companies remained attached to Hooker's command, four were sent to serve at the headquarters of General Edwin Sumner, and the twelfth company (Company A) was designated as unattached— that is, available for service whenever and wherever required, and on short notice. On June 10 the units assigned to Hooker reconnoitered to Haxall's Landing on the James River. Four days later two of the other companies were sent to scout the area around the White Oak Swamp bridge. There they overran a picket post, capturing some of its occupants and a small quantity of weapons and equipment.[17]

By mid-June the 24 officers and 619 men of the 8th Pennsylvania were experiencing the worst of times both in terms of exposure to enemy bullets and lack of basic comforts. That day Trooper Cummings wrote his nephew: "The rebels mean to make a desperate stand here. I might say that the battle is going on every day for the last three weeks for there is not an hour in the day but what you can hear the roar of the cannon and can hear the sharp crack of the rifle as they aim the deadly bullet at each others [*sic*] hearts." At this same time Capt. Peter Keenan, one of Gregg's ablest subordinates, wrote home: "Since we left Yorktown we have not had even the common camp comforts; we now sleep in our blankets in all kinds of weather—of this we do not complain but I tell you it tells heavy on some constitutions and will make old men of us all."[18]

Conditions appeared unlikely to improve any time soon. On June 17 Colonel Gregg was ordered to report—presumably with his entire regiment—to Brig. Gen. Silas Casey's brigade of Keyes's corps. The colonel pleaded an inability to comply, citing the 8th's dual assignment to Hooker and Sumner. In fact, two of his companies were now serving a third master, the IV Corps brigade of Brig. Gen. Darius N. Couch. Too much was being asked of the regiment, especially in view of its declining physical state, the result of arduous campaigning in Virginia's malaria-infested lowlands. "The strength of the regiment being considerably reduced by sickness," Gregg informed IV Corps headquarters, "it will be difficult to meet any further demands for service from my regiment." He petitioned for the outfit's assignment to a single corps—preferably Keyes's—but his request was not granted nor was his workload reduced.

Immediately after Gregg made his request the 8th was sent on long-distance reconnaissance in the direction of Charles City Court House, one of Stuart's stopovers during a recent raid. On this mission it recaptured numerous horses and mules that the Confederate leader had been unable to carry off. On at least one occasion around this time elements of the 8th operated on yet another front, that held by Brig. Gen. Philip Kearny's division of the III Corps. Spread thin to comply with orders from so many commanders, it was not surprising that by the third week of June the 8th Pennsylvania was nearing total exhaustion.[19]

If its casualty count suggests limited action at Seven Pines, the fact that the 8th reported no losses during the balance of the campaign demonstrates rather conclusively that Gregg and his men were spared direct participation in the Seven Days Battles of June 25–July 1. These clashes—all but the first, at least—represented Robert E. Lee's reaction to signs that McClellan had moved close enough to Richmond to guarantee the city's destruction or starvation.

The week-long fighting was put in motion by J. E. B. Stuart, who on June 12 set out to obey his new superior's directive to study the positions of the various segments of the Union army. Only one of these, Fitz John Porter's newly formed V Corps, remained north of the Chickahominy. After certifying that the right flank of Porter's command was "in the air"—connected to neither a supporting force nor a natural anchor—Stuart exceeded his orders by making a complete circuit of the Army of the Potomac, in the process foiling a mismanaged pursuit by General Cooke and contributing to his father-in-law's relief from command of the Cavalry Reserve on July 5.[20]

Returning in triumph to his army on June 15, Stuart helped persuade General Lee to launch a series of attacks that would sweep their overconfident enemy from the gates of Richmond. On June 26, one day after McClellan made a reconnaissance in force of the Confederate right flank at Oak Grove, Lee struck Porter's troops near the northeastern suburb of Mechanicsville. The audacity that would become a hallmark of "Marse Robert" was reflected in his decision to leave 25,000 troops between Richmond and the Chickahominy and attack above the river with 47,000 others. The savage but relatively brief (six-hour) battle ended in Confederate defeat, mainly because a cooperating force of 18,000 called in from the Shenandoah Valley under Stonewall Jackson unaccountably failed to assault McClellan from the rear while the main force struck his exposed flank.

The power of the unexpected offensive defeated McClellan mentally if not materially. That night he began a headlong retreat toward Malvern Hill, fourteen miles from Richmond and seven and a half miles from Harrison's Landing on the James River, the army's ultimate destination. Lee was not content to let him go. Retreaters and pursuers collided at Gaines's Mill on June 27, near Garnett's (Golding's) Farm on June 28, at Savage's Station the following day, at White Oak Swamp and Allen's Farm on June 30, and finally along the slopes of Malvern Hill. The last-named action finally checked the Army of Northern Virginia, which on July 1 lost more than 5,300 killed, wounded, and captured in a series of uphill attacks against deeply held positions stiffened by as many as 250 cannons.[21]

Information on the 8th Pennsylvania's operations—even its location—during the Seven Days Battles is exceedingly sparse, although sporadic glimpses can be gleaned from a few extant sources. Supposedly the regiment was employed in screening the retreat from Mechanicsville, which seems a logical enough assumption, though no details are available. It is known, however, that for two days after the battle of June 26 the regiment scouted along the left (east) bank of the Chickahominy, conducting what General Keyes called a "spirited reconnaissance."[22]

On June 28 Gregg was assigned a mission dictated by McClellan's recent decision to transfer his base of operations and supply from the York River to the James River. That day the 8th swam its horses—all 731 of them—across the Chickahominy at Long Bridge, six miles downstream from Bottom's Bridge, passing its arms and ammunition over the winding stream on rafts. Once on the west bank the outfit rejoined Keyes's corps, which had begun to cross the river at some fords and the few intact bridges. The day ended without loss of man or beast, a tribute to Gregg's supervision of a complex and risky operation.[23]

On June 29 the IV Corps began its trek to the James, where Union gunboats would protect the army's shoreline refuge. According to General Keyes the move was made easier by "the assistance of scouting parties from the Eighth Illinois and Eighth Pennsylvania Cavalry" whose scouts acquainted him with every accessible road, trail, and path to the river. To maximize their support Keyes split up the two regiments, sending the Pennsylvanians "along an obscure road through the woods" that had been brought to his attention by Captain Keenan, whom he called "as skillful as an Indian in woodcraft." The 8th led the way along the winding, sometimes barely discernible roads and through dense woods "all night silently 6 miles." By the morning of June 30 the corps was encamped, "with all its artillery and baggage in good order, on the banks of the James River." Here was yet another accomplishment of which Gregg and his officers and men could be justifiably proud.[24]

According to William Averell, writing after the war, in the wake of the fighting at Malvern Hill the 8th Pennsylvania picketed the army's right flank and center, "an extremely important service," but Averell supplied no particulars. Because Gregg failed to file an official report of his regiment's activities during this period (or if he did, it has been lost to history), nothing is known about the 8th during the climactic stage of the Peninsula Campaign. In the aftermath of the Seven Days Battles, however, its movements and services are somewhat better accounted for.[25]

The day after Malvern Hill Brig. Gen. Randolph B. Marcy, McClellan's chief of staff (and father-in-law) ordered not only that the 8th Pennsylvania should continue to serve General Keyes, whose corps was on the back end of the retreat column, but that "all the cavalry that can be collected . . . [must] assist in covering the rear of [the] column and in bringing up artillery and troops," the latter a reference to the hundreds of stragglers who lined the roadsides during every extended march. In pursuit of this mission the 8th joined some infantry units and a four-gun battery in escorting a section of the army's ponderous but precious supply train. Confederate forces pursued more or less closely on the road to Harrison's Landing, but aided by what General Keyes called "a few 100-pounders" fired by one of the gunboats in the James, they were kept at arm's reach. That same day, July 2, Gregg detached two dozen men, supplied with axes by Keyes's quartermasters, and sent them to demolish one of the Chickahominy bridges as soon as the rear guard crossed it. The assignment was completed efficiently and in timely fashion.[26]

By the morning of July 2 the Army of the Potomac, now 90,000 strong (25,000 of its men had been rendered *hors de combat* during the recent fighting) had squeezed itself into a narrow corridor astride Berkeley Hundred, one of Virginia's most historic plantations. The withdrawal from Malvern Hill had been swift and shrouded in darkness. For a time Lee did not know where his opponent had gone, but he did not believe him gone for good; the uncertainty concerned him.

One historian of the campaign claims that Lee "continued to credit his opponent with a certain degree of military acumen and a fighting spirit; he did not yet understand that some days since, the Young Napoleon had lost his nerve and thrown over his campaign and thought now of nothing but escape."[27]

Content to remain in his safe haven under the guns of the navy, over the next month McClellan made no serious attempt to reengage Lee, who slowly closed in on Harrison's Landing. The extent of Little Mac's response to his defeat within sight of Richmond's spires and steeples was to wire Washington for 50,000 reinforcements to "retrieve our fortunes." This demand was the most recent expression of McClellan's unswerving belief that Lincoln had failed to provide him with enough troops to counter an enemy whose numbers he grossly overestimated. More than once Washington had withheld troops earmarked for the Peninsula but only because of Jackson's distracting advances in the Shenandoah and the president's concern that McClellan had left behind too few troops to safeguard the capital.[28]

Only Little Mac's horsemen appeared prepared to carry on the war. On July 6 Gregg was ordered by cavalry headquarters to scout the Charles City Road north and northeast of General Keyes's camps, a mission made more than a little difficult by an enemy who had obstructed every approach to the area with felled trees. Pressing ahead, Gregg sent a squadron across a creek that led to the recently destroyed Turkey Island Bridge. One mile from the bridge he ran into a considerable number of infantry and cavalry pickets. He returned to base after successfully avoided a bruising confrontation, but the nature of his findings remains unknown.[29]

Soon after leading his regiment back to the starting-point of its latest reconnaissance, Gregg suddenly and surprisingly was detached from command of the 8th. On July 8 General Stoneman grouped several of his regiments into a division. The reorganization, apparently a response to the recent departures of Generals Cooke and Emory, produced two small brigades, the first commanded by Averell and consisting of the 1st New York and 4th Pennsylvania. The second brigade, composed of the 8th Pennsylvania, the 8th Illinois, and two squadrons of the 6th New York, was assigned to Gregg. Squadron-size units of horsemen were parceled out to the five corps of the army. The general order announcing the assignments spelled out the duties of Averell and Gregg. The former was to "keep the country in front of the right wing of the army and on its right thoroughly scouted over and patrolled by strong parties," and would "make a daily report to . . . headquarters of the results of the operations of his brigade for the information of the general commanding the Army of the Potomac." Similar instructions governed Gregg's activities in covering the left flank of the army.

The reorganization meant a major increase in Gregg's authority and responsibilities. Although the shakeup reaffirmed his status as subordinate to his West Point classmate (he would transmit his daily reports to Stoneman through Averell), it removed him from the New Yorker's shadow at least to a degree. Gregg was further heartened when one day after the order was published his old regiment, the 6th Regulars, under Capt. August Valentine Kautz, was detailed to his command.[30]

Gregg's advancement lasted less than a month. Early in August he was superseded by a newcomer to high command whose ambitions included even higher rank and authority. This was Alfred Pleasonton of the 2nd U.S. Cavalry, a brigadier general of volunteers since July 18. A West Pointer (Class of '44) and a veteran of the Mexican War, Pleasonton was at least as ambitious as William Averell and he enjoyed better connections, including McClellan himself and his chief of staff.[31]

Even more so than William Averell, Pleasonton ingratiated himself with his superiors, to whom he often dispensed unsolicited advice. A few days after inheriting Gregg's erstwhile command the brand-new brigadier wrote Marcy "as a friend" seeking to convince McClellan that Lee's army was much smaller than the commanding general believed. Fewer than 40,000 Confederates, Pleasonton claimed, stood between Harrison's Landing and Richmond. The opportunity existed to land "a crushing blow" that would prove "invaluable to disconcert the troops of the enemy to the north of us. . . . I shall willingly carry out the general's orders, be they what they may, but I think he has an opportunity at this time few men ever attain."[32]

Pleasonton had a point, properly presented or not. Lee's army had been seriously weakened by the fighting from Yorktown to Malvern Hill, having suffered 5,000 more casualties than its much stronger adversary. McClellan, however, was in no mood to consider anything like a major offensive. A week before Pleasonton wrote, Little Mac had made a final, convulsive effort to regain the advantage before Lincoln's newly appointed general-in-chief, Maj. Gen. Henry Wager Halleck, could order the Army of the Potomac to abandon the Peninsula for a more advantageous theater of operations. On August 5 McClellan formed a 17,000-man expeditionary force under General Hooker and sent it to retake Malvern Hill, which the Confederates had occupied following the battle of July 1. It was at best a half-hearted gesture, for as soon as Lee responded aggressively Little Mac called it off and returned the bewildered troops to Harrison's Landing.[33]

Though quite willing to abandon the mission once it proved difficult, McClellan had been considering a return to Malvern Hill for at least two weeks before attempting it. On July 23 Gregg had led a detachment of his brigade including Captain Keenan's squadron and a contingent of IV Corps infantry to reconnoiter the approaches to the hill via the Charles City, Long Bridge, and Quaker Roads. Gray-clad pickets were encountered at various points but they were easily driven off, enabling Gregg to ascertain that only three companies of cavalry occupied the slopes and summit. The paucity of defenders was probably the main reason McClellan decided to try to reclaim the position.[34]

The 8th Pennsylvania also accompanied Hooker's August 5 expedition, but its participation was limited to a brief pursuit of the Rebels driven from the heights; its casualty count was a single horse killed. Even so, Pleasonton in his report of the operation was generous with his praise, citing all who took part, including Gregg and his executive officer, Maj. Pennock Huey. The brigade leader's flair for hyperbole is reflected in his reference to "the happy results of this successful movement by Major General Hooker in the recapture of Malvern Hill."[35]

A far less pleasant operation closely followed the abortive attempt to regain the high ground. General Halleck, having determined that McClellan could accomplish nothing of lasting value in his present position, ordered him to evacuate the Peninsula. The withdrawal from the James River to Williamsburg and Yorktown and from there to Alexandria and the Potomac River supply base at Aquia Creek began on August 7. That day Stoneman extended his picket lines, shielding

McClellan's battle-weary but still-confident army as it pulled up stakes and cleared out.

The last infantry unit departed the riverbank on August 16, whereupon the cavalry withdrew to Charles City Court House and Barrett's Ferry at the mouth of the Chickahominy. Three days later Pleasonton's brigade marched into Yorktown to await transports to carry them north. One of his men described the retreat as "well managed not a man lost or a single cent of Property fell into their [the enemy's] hands. It was a clean thing." The 1st Brigade seems to have had a rougher time of it. William Averell, already physically unwell, described his role in the evacuation as a "disagreeable duty," one that threatened him with "a general break down." Diagnosing his condition as "malarial fever," he went on sick leave as soon as he reached Washington. David Gregg would soon follow.[36]

At the outset of the Seven Days Battles, a second Union army in the Old Dominion (named the Army of Virginia), commanded by Maj. Gen. John Pope, had begun to operate east of the Blue Ridge Mountains with the missions of protecting Washington, clearing the Shenandoah Valley, and threatening Richmond in support of the Army of the Potomac. Now stationed in the Culpeper–Orange Court House area, Pope's command, 50,000 strong, was targeting Richmond's communications. It got off to a fast start; by July 24 the Army of Virginia had already launched several reconnaissances of and raids on Gordonsville, where the enemy maintained a major supply base.[37]

Official Washington, though heartened by Pope's progress, suspected that Lee, having beaten McClellan into submission, would turn west to counter the new opponent. Little Mac was ordered to hasten reinforcements to Culpeper before Lee could defeat his second enemy army in less than two months. But in addition to being reluctant to evacuate the Peninsula and thus admit the failure of his grandly conceived and massively mounted campaign against Richmond, McClellan was in no hurry to reinforce Pope, whom he personally detested. Like many another politically conservative member of his officer corps, he considered Pope, who had won some small-scale victories in the western theater, not only an interloper but also an incompetent, a loudmouth, and a bully in his dealings with Southern civilians. Perhaps worse, Pope, who had adopted Republican principles, was viewed by McClellan and his lieutenants as a toady to the Lincoln administration. Thus Little Mac took his time heading north. Not until August 14 did he dispatch elements of the III and V Corps to Pope's area of operations. This would be the extent of his support before time ran out for the Army of Virginia.[38]

Validating Washington's concern, less than two weeks after Malvern Hill Lee detached a force under Jackson, eventually totaling 24,000, and hurled it at Pope. In a meeting engagement on August 9 at Cedar Mountain near Culpeper Court House, Stonewall defeated Pope's advance echelon, halting its movements toward Orange Court House. Once McClellan's abandonment of the Peninsula was fully in motion, Lee hastened west to unite Longstreet with Jackson. Over the next three weeks the triumvirate of Confederate leaders thoroughly outwitted and befuddled Pope before bringing him to battle on the fringes of the Bull Run battlefield. Mesmerized by Jackson's maneuvering, Pope's army went under, its left flank crushed by Longstreet on August 30. Having suffered more than 16,000 casualties to his enemy's 9,200, Pope led his remaining troops in headlong flight to the Washington defenses. They barely managed to avoid being cut off in a rain-soaked rear-guard action at Chantilly, Virginia, on September 1, one day after Pleasonton and Gregg returned to Washington from the wharves at Alexandria.[39]

In the immediate aftermath of the collapse of his drive on Richmond, McClellan's career went on hold. Following the Pope debacle, however, Lincoln, Halleck, and Secretary of War Edwin M. Stanton believed they had no choice but to retain Little Mac in command of an army that, having absorbed Pope's survivors, now numbered 102,000. The Union authorities could not permit a command vacuum. Only four days after the battle known as Second Bull Run, Lee, bubbling with confidence and hopeful of a dramatic victory on Northern soil, began to cross the upper Potomac near Leesburg into Maryland. McClellan was ordered to pursue and bring the invasion to a speedy conclusion.

Thus opened, on the heels of two botched campaigns, an opportunity for the Union high command to salvage a victory on its own ground. The result was the Antietam Campaign, named for the river that flowed around the village of Sharpsburg in the northwest corner of the Old Line State. There on September 17 invader and pursuer would combine to produce the bloodiest day in U.S. history, with a combined total of almost 23,000 combatants killed, wounded, or captured.[40]

David McMurtrie Gregg saw no field service during this period, missing both the climactic battle and the lead-up to it for reasons both distressing and pleasant. As soon as Pleasonton's brigade reached Washington, Gregg was ordered to report at Upton's Hill, five miles west of the capital, where Brig. Gen. Jacob D. Cox was monitoring Lee's movement toward Leesburg. Upon reaching that eminence where, nine months earlier, Julia Ward Howe had been inspired to compose the "Battle Hymn of the Republic," Gregg was dispatched to reconnoiter fourteen miles upstream, establishing an observation post at Great Falls on the right bank of the Potomac. He moved out immediately. Once in position he scrutinized every avenue of approach and recorded all enemy activity of any note whatsoever. His reports went simultaneously to army headquarters and the War Department, both entities being extremely anxious to track Lee's invasion route, especially should his troops veer off in different directions.[41]

At Great Falls Gregg was no longer a member of the 2nd Brigade of Stoneman's command. On September 10 McClellan had overseen yet another reorganization of his mounted arm. Having become disenchanted with Stoneman's leadership as he had with General Cooke's, Little Mac replaced the former with Brig. Gen. John Buford, a hard-bitten old campaigner and a leading light of the 2nd Dragoons. Perhaps because he had been wounded at Second Bull Run, Buford was assigned to a desk job rather than a field command. Operational control passed to Alfred Pleasonton, thus fulfilling a major goal of that ambitious officer. His elevation, however, would be relatively short-lived. Within five months, Stoneman, who upon losing his position accepted command of an infantry division in the III Corps, would reappear at the head of the army's cavalry.

Pleasonton reveled in his new authority while it lasted. In quick order his division-size force grew to comprise five brigades, including the erstwhile Cavalry Reserve, now made up of only the 5th and 6th U.S. Cavalry The remainder of his command was composed of volunteers, including a brigade entrusted to Col. John Franklin Farnsworth of the 8th Illinois, a friend of Pleasonton and a close acquaintance and avid supporter of Abraham Lincoln. Farnsworth, whose promotion was based on the date of his commission (which predated Gregg's in the volunteer ranks), received command of four regiments, including the 8th Pennsylvania.[42]

It is not known how long Gregg remained on the upper Potomac. It must have been no more than a fortnight, because he fell ill circa mid-September and was sent to Washington for medical attention. His condition was initially described as remittent fever, a vague diagnostic term indicative of no particular disease and whose primary symptom was a widely fluctuating body temperature. The ailment was probably akin to the "Chickahominy fever" that had forced Averell to take sick leave and from which he had only recently recovered. By September 27, with McClellan's army resting in southern Maryland following the bloodletting at Antietam, Gregg was reported by the headquarters of the Department of Washington to be "slowly recovering" at the Kirkwood House. His stay at that hotel on Pennsylvania Avenue indicates that he had already been released from an army hospital. Only a few weeks later, however, he suffered a relapse. His condition was now diagnosed as intermittent fever, a localized infection malarial in nature.[43]

Gregg refused to allow poor health to disrupt the plans that he and Ellen had made. Given his disability and the fact that McClellan seemed disinclined to reengage Lee in the foreseeable future, early in October the colonel was able to secure a short leave of absence. On October 4 Ellen wrote to her Uncle Joseph: "We have concluded not to delay our marriage any longer." The following Monday they would be quietly wed at White Marsh Township near The Highlands, the home of the bride's maternal grandmother, fifty-five miles north of Philadelphia. The new venue had replaced Reading, Pennsylvania, so recently that Ellen was uncertain if all invited would make it to St. Thomas's Episcopal Church, the Sheaff family's house of worship over the past half-century. She and David had discarded their earlier preference for multiple bridesmaids and groomsmen. In this time of crisis and sacrifice, she wrote, "neither of us want[ed] to make any fuss."

Colonel Gregg's son notes that the wedding day "dawned very brightly and nothing occurred to mar the joy of the occasion" presided over by the Reverend Francis D. Egan, chaplain of the 8th Pennsylvania. Gregg, Jr., adds that upon exiting the church the happy couple passed a double line of Sunday School children in the care of Ellen's aunts. As they climbed into a carriage that would take them to the reception site they were serenaded by a band provided by Uncle John Sheaff.

That evening, festivities complete, the newlyweds took the train to New York. They spent a week at the stylish Metropolitan Hotel on Broadway, glorying in the sights of the great metropolis. At honeymoon's close Ellen would come home to her sister's family in Philadelphia and David would return to his regiment. Although uncertain when they would meet again, they could take comfort in having embarked on a journey of love and happiness in the midst of a land awash in conflict and suffering.[44]

5

Brigadier General of Volunteers

During Gregg's absence Jeb Stuart and his born-to-the-saddle troopers had made a second circuit of the Army of the Potomac, one that, like its predecessor, had long-range repercussions. This time his target was southern Pennsylvania, where supply depots and transportation lines almost forty miles in George McClellan's rear appeared ripe for pillage and destruction. From October 10 to 13 Stuart (a.k.a. the "Beau Sabreur of the Confederacy") and his 1,800 riders terrorized towns and villages as far north as Mercersburg and Chambersburg, wrecking bridges and railroad track; rounding up horses, mules, and wagons; and confiscating a wealth of clothing, equipment, and foodstuffs for his command.

Pursued at some distance by forces loosely coordinated by George Stoneman and led by Alfred Pleasonton and William Averell (the latter's health having "much improved" during his recent leave), the Yankees achieved no greater success in curtailing Stuart now than they had four months earlier. Pleasonton would blame the outcome on a late start, mud-caked roads, and poor maps. Thus hampered, he failed to track Stuart's successive positions or even determine at which point the latter crossed the Potomac into Maryland. Averell, through illogical maneuvering, ensured that the half-dozen regiments at his disposal came nowhere near the rampaging Rebels.[1]

Such a performance, had it come at an earlier date, might have crippled Averell's career; two weeks before Stuart began his raid, however, Gregg's classmate had been elevated to the rank of brigadier general of volunteers. His promotion did not sit well with some of his colleagues, including Bvt. Maj. John Baille McIntosh of the 5th U.S. Cavalry, who two months hence would succeed Averell in command of the 3rd Pennsylvania. In a letter to his wife written during Stuart's raid, McIntosh declared that "the idea of his [Averell's] promotion for distinguished conduct . . . is perfectly ridiculous. His promotion was gotten by favoritism & political influence combined." This was an opinion that David Gregg probably shared.[2]

Apparently only a small number of Gregg's men accompanied either Averell or Pleasonton on the pursuit. As the latter reported on October 11, "The 8th Pennsylvania has not yet been able to obtain horses to replace the old ones of the Peninsula now used up." Thus the regiment as a whole had been spared the indignity of failing to overtake the defilers of its home state, whose route had taken them far afield from the scene of recent campaigning. One of their ports of call had been the Mercersburg-area home of Ellen's uncle, Dr. Joseph Hiester, on whose property they had camped and fed their horses.[3]

The so-called Chambersburg Raid, which stoked the ire of the rank-and-file of the Army of the Potomac as well and that of editors and politicians across the North, hastened the demise of George B. McClellan. The general sealed his fate by ignoring War Department prodding to cross into Virginia until October 26, more than a month after Lee had done so; moreover, the movement, when finally made, took several days. His lethargy, apparent apathy, and inability to secure the flanks and rear of his army prompted Lincoln to fire him on November 7.

His ouster was long overdue, but Lincoln, who had made the mistake of giving high command to both McClellan and John Pope, erred again—in a sense, more egregiously—by replacing Little Mac with Maj. Gen. Ambrose E. Burnside. The erstwhile leader of the army's IX Corps had twice rejected the president's overtures while admitting his incapacity for army command. This was as honest a self-evaluation as any Union general ever offered, but Lincoln refused to accept it at face value. Now the army and the nation would have to live with his long-shot gamble.[4]

A few days after Stuart's return to Virginia the newlywed Colonel Gregg rejoined his regiment to the congratulations and best wishes of officers and men alike. His return coincided with the onset of a month's worth of maneuvering, reconnoitering, and fighting by McClellan's and then Burnside's cavalry. He continued to serve under Pleasonton, but, perhaps as a result of the latter's inability to overtake Stuart, the erstwhile division leader had been reduced to command of a brigade that included, in addition to Gregg's regiment, the 6th U.S., 8th Illinois, 3rd Indiana, and 8th New York.[5]

In advance of McClellan's movement, on October 26 Pleasonton led his troopers across the Potomac at Berlin, Maryland, and entered the fecund valley between the Blue Ridge and the Catoctin Mountains. He was soon reinforced by Averell's brigade as well as by several regiments under Brig. Gen. George Dashiell Bayard, formerly a member of Pope's army and more recently leader of most of the horsemen assigned to the defense forces of Washington. Bayard, a highly experienced and well respected veteran of the 1st U.S. Cavalry, had been one class behind Gregg at West Point, where the two had become closely acquainted. Although Bayard was yet another example of a younger officer who had risen more quickly in the volunteer ranks than his classmate, Gregg had a high opinion of him both as an officer and as a man. As the near future would reveal, Bayard thought just as highly of his fellow West Pointer.[6]

Almost as soon as he crossed the river, Pleasonton tangled with Stuart's pickets, who were guarding their army's current sanctuary in the northern Shenandoah Valley. In response to McClellan's belated advance, Stuart would soon be screening James Longstreet's movements through the Blue Ridge gaps toward the Culpeper Court House vicinity. At this point most of Pleasonton's attention was directed to locating the various elements of the Army of Northern Virginia. Over the next five days his patrols reconnoitered southward into the Loudoun Valley, making visits to such enemy haunts as Purcellville, Middleburg, and, five miles south of the former and six miles north of the latter, the sleepy village of Philomont.

November 1 inaugurated ten days of sustained fighting between the cavalries during which the 8th Pennsylvania was more or less heavily engaged at every turn. That day Gregg, commanding not only his own regiment but also the 3rd Indiana, led the way into Philomont just as a large body of Stuart's men, accompanied by some foot soldiers, prepared to depart. To overtake the Rebels Gregg sent a squadron of the 8th along the southwest-running road to Union. Short of that ironically named Confederate bastion, the squadron met and engaged the enemy for an indefinite period but was eventually compelled to retire. The colonel hastened to its side with the rest of the 8th, and the fighting quickly escalated.

The outcome hung in the balance for perhaps an hour, but at that point Gregg's facility for fighting his men both afoot and in the saddle turned the tide. When dismounted skirmishers from both of his regiments advanced, covered by mounted comrades, the enemy was "handsomely driven" from a sheltering wood. In gaining this result Gregg had been closely supported by Battery M, 2nd U.S. Artillery, under Lt. Alexander C. M. Pennington, one of the ablest "flying" batteries in Union service. This appears to have been the first occasion on which Gregg and Pennington united to thwart an enemy advance. They would connect again with great effect on many a future field.[7]

In a hastily scrawled communiqué near day's end General Pleasonton informed army headquarters that "we have had some skirmishing with Stuart. He outnumbers us & has infantry & drove my advance back with some loss, but my guns have punished him severely. . . . Col. Gregg & Maj. Keenan of the 8th Penn. did good service today skirmishing with a superior force of the enemy." The brigade leader reported, as proof of his commitment to the fight, twenty-one casualties. Gregg's demi-brigade had suffered half of the losses but no fatalities: one officer, eleven men, and four horses had been wounded.[8]

On November 3 Pleasonton pursued the Rebels who had fallen back to Union. The better part of Gregg's command saw little action, spending the day supporting Pennington's and other batteries. Meanwhile, several companies of the 8th Pennsylvania under Gregg's second-in-command, Lt. Col. Amos E. Griffiths, swept through Bloomfield in the Blue Ridge foothills, driving out what Gregg called a "strong picket of the enemy," taking prisoners, confiscating horses and equipment, and freeing a high-ranking staff officer who had been captured hours earlier.[9]

On the same day Averell's brigade, which had been lingering on the Potomac near Williamsport, Maryland, caught up with Pleasonton and took the advance. Gregg's classmate proceeded southwest through the Loudoun Valley to Upperville and Piedmont, both of which he occupied after sending defenders scurrying toward Ashby's Gap in the Blue Ridge. Next day, when Averell moved against Rebel-occupied Markham, Gregg was detached to support him, the first time he had served under the New Yorker in seven months. The reunion, however, was brief; upon reaching the field Gregg found the fighting over and the town in Averell's possession. Markham's occupation would enable the Federals to keep an eye on Manassas Gap, only twenty-two miles northeast of the village. This defile, the lowest crossing of the Blue Ridge Mountains in Virginia, was a likely avenue of egress by Stonewall Jackson once he left his position in the upper Shenandoah Valley to join Robert E. Lee and James Longstreet at Culpeper.

Gregg was not the only cavalryman who arrived too late to see action November 4. Circumstances had prevented Jeb Stuart from being on the scene, compelling others to command in his absence. He was back in action the next day, however, leading the North and South Carolina brigade of his senior subordinate, Brig. Gen. Wade Hampton, and the Virginia brigade of Col. Thomas L. Rosser south toward Barbee's Cross Roads, where he took up a position across Pleasonton's path.[10]

On November 5 Gregg was back with Pleasonton during one of the earliest engagements of the Fredericksburg Campaign. That morning Pleasonton advanced in force to Barbee's, a strategic junction east of Sugar Loaf Mountain, two of whose roads led to the north side of the Rappahannock River. He was heading there to better cover Manassas Gap in response to one of the last orders McClellan would issue before he got the ax. As expected, Pleasonton almost immediately encountered Stuart's force, which he estimated at three thousand men and four guns. The result was one of the war's first large-scale clashes between forces almost exclusively composed of cavalry and horse artillery. Uninfluenced by infantry involvement, the proceedings would make an unambiguous statement about the relative strength, savvy, and tenacity of the antagonists.

Even before reaching the crossroads the Federals drew fire from a section of artillery commanding the road to Chester Gap as well as from dismounted cavalry to the left of the road. Pleasonton replied with two of Pennington's guns while sending Gregg's regiments to the left "to occupy some woods to the front and turn their flank." One of Pennington's sections unlimbered to the front and right of Pleasonton's line, supported by the 8th New York Cavalry of Col. Benjamin F. ("Grimes") Davis, a steel-nerved old dragoon from Mississippi. Meanwhile, John Farnsworth's Illinois and Indiana brigade moved up the road to the front. As Pleasonton noted in his report of the action, "Gregg, with great skill and activity, soon outflanked the rebel lines and caused them to withdraw their guns. They attempted to charge him, but did not succeed."

For his part Gregg reported that "my dispositions were quickly made, and three squadrons—two of the Eighth Pennsylvania and one of the Sixth Regulars . . . dismounted and deployed as skirmishers and gallantly advanced, ascending a slope of clear ground to attack the enemy in the wood, and, if possible, capture the section . . . [which] poured load after load upon the line, without checking it." At length the skirmishers protecting the gunners gave way, enabling Gregg to attempt to take the two cannons from the rear and cut them off from Stuart's force. To do so he advanced two columns of dismounted men. One moved up so boldly, however, that it persuaded the section to limber up and withdraw too quickly to be captured.

The second column, having lost contact with the first amid the heavily wooded terrain that separated them, was itself nearly cut off when counterattacked by two regiments of horsemen. Its mounts "completely exhausted" by their quick advance, the column seemed ripe for capture, especially because, as Pleasonton estimated, half of Stuart's force was now arrayed against it. It was permitted to disengage and walk its blown horses to the rear thanks to a supporting attack by Davis's New Yorkers. The dramatic charge, during which the colonel was shot out of his saddle, swept the field of most of Stuart's men. By displaying so much speed, power, and panache, Davis's men drew applause from every onlooker, including an on-scene representative of the army headquarters staff, Capt. George Armstrong Custer, formerly of the 5th U.S. Cavalry.[11]

The Beau Sabreur neither expected nor accepted the outcome. In a dispatch to his army's headquarters Stuart described the fight as a victory. In case some participants or observers failed to agree, he blamed the outcome on the poor general health of his horses, which threatened the readiness of the entire command. But Pleasonton, Gregg, Davis, and their men knew better. Throughout the day they had held the upper hand, had demonstrated more aggressiveness and skill than their opponent, and had thoroughly outfought a force of cavalry and artillery whose strength was comparable to their own. The outcome boded well for the future of the Union mounted arm and its leaders.[12]

Pleasonton continued to joust with Stuart over the next two weeks, but the 8th Pennsylvania saw little action. The single exception occurred at Amissville near the south bank of Hedgeman's River (the local name of the North Fork of the Rappahannock), to which Pleasonton moved on November 7, having left behind enough men to secure the scene of the fighting on November 5. There Gregg's regiment, supported by Grimes Davis's New Yorkers and a section of Pennington's battery, the entire force under Gregg's command, collided with a sizable reconnaissance force of all arms. Unfazed, the colonel threw out skirmishers who "handsomely resisted the advance of infantry and cavalry, and, when joined by the other regiments of the brigade, still occupied the front line, and successfully held their positions against the superior force of the enemy." In the end Stuart was driven from Amissville and neighboring Jeffersonton at the cost of two artillery pieces and thirteen officers and men captured. Some of the fugitives headed for army headquarters at Culpeper Court House, others down the north bank of the Rappahannock in the direction of Falmouth, directly across from Fredericksburg.[13]

The following day Pleasonton's troopers fanned out below Hedgeman's River, skirmishing with Stuart outside the village of Newby's Cross Roads and the hamlet of Washington. In so doing they covered the approaches from Culpeper as well as those from Chester and Thornton Gaps in the Blue Ridge while also screening the main army at and around Warrenton, twenty miles north of Lee's headquarters. On November 10 Stuart, with Fitz Lee's horsemen and two brigades of infantry, launched a reconnaissance-in-force from Culpeper, compelling Pleasonton to meet it with his entire force near Amissville. No details of Gregg's participation have been uncovered; apparently the encounter was relatively brief and the Rebels, bent on monitoring Pleasonton's dispositions, were "repulsed late in the afternoon with severe loss."[14]

For seven days following the most recent fight at Amissville, Pleasonton was content to keep his main body well north of Culpeper, though he pushed detachments to within six miles of the place. On November 17, however, the cavalry's field of operations suddenly shifted downriver toward Falmouth. For this dramatic break in the status quo Pleasonton could thank Ambrose E. Burnside.

In the days prior to McClellan's relief there seemed little pattern to the army's activities, but once Burnside took over the operational picture became clear. The new commander was no tactician. He had proven as much at Antietam, where for five hours his corps had failed to cross the creek and overwhelm a small but resolute force of sharpshooters along the Rebel right flank. Had he acted with promptitude, he might have handed McClellan a decisive victory that would have kept him in power. His deficiencies aside, however, Burnside, did know something of strategy, and he developed a seemingly viable plan to advance on Richmond via Fredericksburg before Lee could stop him. In the end logistical foul-ups and a failure to secure crossing sites in timely fashion would prevent Burnside from getting any closer than Falmouth, but for two weeks after McClellan's departure the Army of the Potomac appeared to have an opportunity to steal a march on its opponent.

While awaiting Lincoln's approval of his blueprint of operations Burnside revised the structure of his army with a view to centralizing authority. On November 14, having received the go-ahead from Washington, he published a general order that announced the formation of three so-called grand divisions. The new entities would be commanded by his senior subordinates, Maj. Gen. Edwin Sumner (the Right Grand Division, consisting of the II and IX Corps), Maj. Gen. Joseph Hooker (the Center Grand Division, consisting of the III and V Corps), and Maj. Gen. William Buel Franklin, whose Left Grand Division united the I and VI Corps. Two months later a Reserve Grand Division, composed of the XI and XII Corps, would be added. Burnside believed the grouping of corps would facilitate control of his

130,000-man army; in fact the extra layer of organization would prove an unwieldy impediment.[15]

It would take a week for the assignment of cavalry units to be announced, but the delay did not prevent their commanders from carrying out the tasks usually delegated to them. By November 15 the army was in motion and its horsemen were out in full force, leading the way and blocking the infantry from enemy view. Assigned to support Hooker's grand division, Pleasonton kept his riders "well out, along the Rappahannock," picketing the fords along the twelve-mile stretch of riverbank between Waterloo and Rappahannock Station. At the rail depot he made contact with Bayard's brigade. The latter's imminent incorporation into the Army of the Potomac would give Burnside approximately 11,500 horse soldiers equipped for field service exclusive of units lost to all manner of detached duty.[16]

On November 22 Gregg and the 8th Pennsylvania reached Falmouth, where they lingered briefly before moving to King George Court House, twenty-some miles to the southeast, there to establish a more permanent presence. Over the next week the regiment performed the usual round of picket and reconnaissance duty while waiting for the rest of the army to assemble in the new area of operations. The Rebels were already on the scene. Longstreet's men had arrived on November 19, and they appeared to have free access to Burnside's position. Before daylight on December 2 a squadron of the 8th Pennsylvania on detached duty at Leeds's Ferry twenty miles below King George Court House was attacked by a ninety-man detachment of Stuart's 9th Virginia Cavalry. The Rebels had crossed the river by boat before concealing themselves in a wood. As Pleasonton reported, "Resistance was made, but unsuccessfully; 1 officer and about 50 [of our] men were taken, and removed at once across the river."

The attack came as an embarrassment to Gregg, especially as the river was nearly a mile wide at the ferry and the crossing should have been detectable even in the dark. Another inconvenient fact was the ferry's well-known status as a haven for parties engaged in an illicit trade between Richmond and Baltimore, something the 8th Pennsylvania had been ordered to curtail. Pleasonton attempted to exonerate Gregg of the charge of neglect of duty by declaring that the open landscape

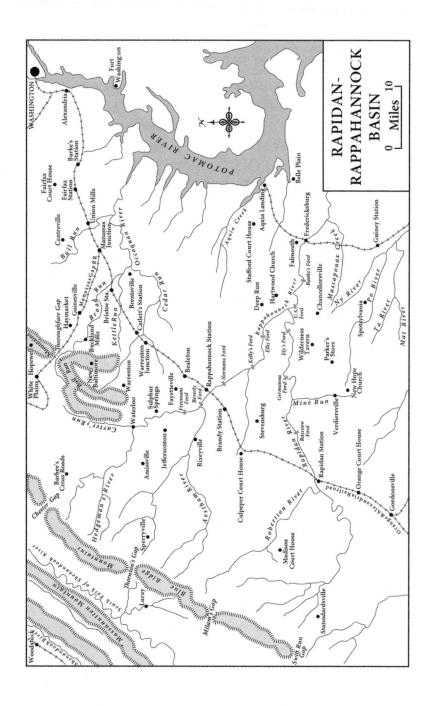

Map 3. Rapidan-Rappahannock Basin. Created by Paul Dangel.

around the ferry "made it liable for a small force to be cut off at any time." He noted that Gregg's additional duties, which included supporting an artillery unit on the river seven miles below King George Court House, prevented the colonel from stationing a large force at Leeds's Ferry.

Reports of the squadron's capture reached army headquarters and the next day Burnside's adjutant general, Brig. Gen. Seth Williams, made a personal investigation. As a result, Pleasonton reinforced Gregg with eight hundred members of the 8th New York and 3rd Indiana, ordered the colonel to withdraw all detachments from the most exposed locations, and enjoined him "to be vigilant in patrolling the country." Lasting blame did not accrue to Gregg, who had been placed in a difficult situation beyond his control, one he would not have chosen given the obvious hazards. Yet the enemy crowed over the daring exploit, Stuart calling Lee's attention to "the perils attending such an expedition, the boldness of its inception . . . [and] its brilliant execution."[17]

Gregg rebounded quickly. On December 3–4, despite being unable to coordinate closely with the U.S. Navy, he sank or otherwise destroyed several flatboats on the shores of the Rappahannock. Confederates had used them to cross at Port Royal, eighteen miles southwest of Falmouth, as well as at Port Conway on the opposite bank, in order to attack the cavalry's outposts and harass the navy's gunboats with sharpshooter fire. On December 8 Gregg won Pleasonton's praise when his pickets nabbed two Rebel officers, one a signal corpsman carrying dispatches from Richmond. The capture of the other, a captain in the regiment that had ambushed the squadron at Leeds's Ferry, appeared a stroke of poetic justice.[18]

Through the first weeks of December the army waited for its commander to complete his preparations to cross the river, occupy Fredericksburg, and march on Richmond. The now-bridgeless Rappahannock could only be crossed on pontoons, a cumbersome and time-consuming process at best. Two trains, each consisting of forty wagons, each wagon carrying a boat and the floor boards to be attached to it, had been assembled at Washington. One was to have been ferried down the Potomac to Aquia Creek, ten miles northeast of Falmouth, the other to be hauled overland to Burnside's headquarters. Due to one of the bureaucratic foul-ups all too common in the Army of the Potomac, it was never impressed on the engineer officer in charge of the overland train that it was to be dispatched as expeditiously as possible.[19]

The lack of emphasis on urgency, added to the effort involved in forming so extensive a train and the terrible condition of the roads between Washington and Falmouth, resulted in the pontoons arriving on November 25, nineteen days after Burnside had ordered them. Additional delays prevented them from being laid until the second week in December. By then Robert E. Lee, who had foreseen a movement toward Fredericksburg as early as November 12, had moved into position to oppose a crossing. The Army of Northern Virginia, 75,000 strong upon the recent return of Jackson's corps from the Shenandoah, was arrayed along the heights west and south of Fredericksburg, occupying sturdy breastworks and rifle pits protected by banks of artillery.[20]

The drastically altered situation should have given Burnside pause and prodded him to plan anew. It did not; the stubborn commander clung to his faith in giving battle to an enemy he could defeat strictly through numerical superiority. But as December approached, he began to display uncertainty and confusion, especially with regard to his cavalry. On November 21 the army's horsemen had finally been informed of their place in the new table of organization. Pleasonton's brigade had been attached to Sumner's grand division, Averell's to Hooker's command, and Bayard's to Franklin's. The cavalry would see action at maximum strength. The order announcing the assignments directed that "all detachments of cavalry serving with corps, divisions, brigades, &c., . . . at once rejoin their respective commands."

Burnside, however, had no definite plan for employing his troopers in the fight to come. On December 9, two days before the pontoons were finally laid at six locations across and downriver from Fredericksburg, the army leader called a conference of his senior subordinates, including Pleasonton, Averell, and Bayard. For some hours he discussed in detail the army's forthcoming operations, but devoted almost the entire briefing to its infantry. As Averell later explained the overall concept, "The right grand division was to cross at Fredericksburg, the left below, and the centre [*sic*] grand division to follow the right." He added, however, that Burnside was "still unsettled as to what should be done with the cavalry." In the end it was decided that each of its brigades should "follow its [grand] division as it moved across the river."[21]

As it happened, once the army crossed and gave battle few horsemen were committed to the fight. Not so the infantry, which underwent a horrific bloodletting. At about 8:30 on the fog-shrouded morning of December 13 Franklin's grand division began its attack on the Union left, followed almost three hours later by Sumner's command on the upper flank and much later still by Hooker's troops, whose belated entrance was the result of their commander failing to persuade Burnside to call off the fight. By the middle of the afternoon the offensive had bogged down against sharpshooter and cannon fire that tore gaping holes in the attacking columns. The criminally stubborn Burnside refused to quit; piecemeal, uncoordinated assaults continued until almost dark. By then some 13,000 Federals had fallen dead or wounded as against 5,300 Confederates, and McClellan's successor had been forced to concede abject defeat.[22]

As Burnside must have foreseen, the battlefield offered his horsemen almost no maneuvering terrain. Small wonder that few took part beyond observing from a safe distance, where, as a Massachusetts officer later assigned to Gregg's command noted, they "did not see an enemy or hear the whir-r-r of a single shot." Of the principal officers, only Pleasonton left a report of his activities—a brief and inadequate one. Yet he had a greater responsibility to detail his operations than either Averell or Bayard, because shortly before the battle Burnside had elevated him once again to division command, giving him twice as many regiments to report on as his subordinates. When Pleasonton moved up, Gregg took command of a brigade consisting of his own outfit plus the 6th U.S. and the 6th New York. He himself left no report of the battle; Pleasonton mentioned only the regulars, whom Gregg had "posted above and to the rear of Falmouth, in support of batteries."[23]

Disastrous as it was, the combat at Fredericksburg had a major effect on David Gregg's career. Early in the fighting on the lower flank, George Bayard, while attending an open-air council of war at Franklin's headquarters, was struck by a shell that mutilated his right thigh and, twenty-four hours later, took his life. The news left Gregg profoundly sad not only because of his regard for the mortally wounded brigadier but because Bayard had been forced by an unfolding campaign to forgo a leave during which he had intended to marry his longtime sweetheart. The tragedy also affected Gregg professionally, because as senior colonel of cavalry in the army he appeared the logical choice to replace Bayard. The dying man felt the same way. One of Bayard's aides recalled the last words he spoke to his staff: "Give my compliments to General Burnside, and say that I desire Colonel Dave Gregg to command my cavalry."[24]

The appointment was duly made, apparently in a matter of hours. When it took effect Gregg inherited five of the best-appointed regiments of horse in the entire army. Their reputation for dependable service and hard fighting would only enhance his own. Of perhaps more importance, the assignment gave him a command indisputably his own, whose fortunes would rise and fall in cadence with his. No longer would he be directly subordinate to Pleasonton or Averell, except on those occasions when his command was attached to theirs.

The regiments that Gregg inherited—the 1st Maine, 1st New Jersey, 2nd and 10th New York, and 1st Pennsylvania, plus an independent company of District of Columbia volunteers—had fought ably under Bayard, whose loss shocked and saddened them. From the first, however, the new man made a good impression. Soon after he took over a correspondent with the *New York Herald* wrote: "[Gregg] seems to give universal satisfaction, and to fill the place of the lamented Bayard as well, perhaps, as any officer that could have been selected." He would retain the brigade for only two months before moving up to a position of even greater authority, yet all but two of those outfits would accompany him to his new command and remain with him for the duration of his war career. In the long run the great majority of those who had followed Bayard through the Shenandoah Valley, at Second Bull Run, and before Fredericksburg would come to regard Gregg as a worthy successor, one entitled to the same respect and trust as their esteemed first leader.[25]

But they would not long address him as Colonel Gregg. On January 17, 1863, he wrote the Adjutant General's Office formally accepting the appointment of brigadier general of volunteers that had been conferred on him the previous November 29. Most present-day sources confuse the timing of the promotion, dating it from January 17 but noting that it was backdated to November 29 for seniority purposes. Official records, however, indicate that the appointment was not backdated.[26]

By any standard of measure the appointment, which raised Gregg from the crowded ranks of colonels commanding regiments of cavalry in the Army of the Potomac, was richly merited. Officially it owed to his exemplary service as leader of the 8th Pennsylvania as well as his occasional stints in brigade command. Several superiors had recommended him for promotion; so had at least one political figure who had already helped advance his career. Five weeks before Lincoln made the appointment Governor Andrew Gregg Curtin had written the president, strongly urging it. Aware that his recommendation carried the scent of nepotism, Curtin was forthright in explaining the family connection, and there is no reason to believe that Lincoln acted merely to gratify an influential supporter of his administration. Curtin never believed so, and as far as can be determined the appointment did not generate charges of favoritism or cries of protest from anyone inside or outside the army regardless of political orientation.[27]

Less than two weeks after his beaten and bleeding troops returned to the north bank of the Rappahannock, Burnside began to envision a means of rehabilitating his reputation and proving his army capable of retaking the field with undiminished spirit and energy. Instead of repeating the mistake he had made by thrusting his army into the midst of the enemy, he now decided to cross the river miles downstream. To mask his intentions, detachments including a large body of cavalry would feign attacks at the fords upstream from Fredericksburg.

The plan had its strengths, but Lincoln, who had not been informed of it in advance, halted it before it got underway. The president had been tipped off by a couple of disaffected generals who, while on leave in Washington, warned him that the army had lost confidence in its leader and was about to be sacrificed again. After belatedly conferring with Burnside, Lincoln agreed to a revised offensive aimed at crossing well upstream from Lee's left flank.[28]

The operation got off to a promising start in unseasonably warm weather on January 20, 1863, but within twenty-four hours a terrific storm showered the marching troops with rain and snow, trapping them, their horses, and their supply vehicles in a sea of ice-coated mud. An officer in the 1st New Jersey, stationed four miles south of Falmouth on the Richmond, Fredericksburg and Potomac Railroad, messaged Gregg: "The rebels evidently know of our movement. . . . About an hour before sundown yesterday afternoon, great cheering was heard opposite our upper reserve post, and shortly afterwards a [sign] was shown to our pickets with *Burnside stuck in the mud* painted on it in large letters." The officer had learned that trains carrying Rebel troops were heading toward the reported position of Burnside's crippled army: "Some cheering was also heard in the direction of the depot."[29]

With the army immobilized by what one of Gregg's troopers called "almost fathomless mire," Lee shifted his forces to the threatened sector, and by late on January 23 Burnside was forced to call off his "Mud March." The ill-fated attempt to restore the army's morale, coming as it did on the heels of a major debacle, ended his unhappy tenure in command. On January 26 Lincoln relieved him in favor of General Hooker, one of the ousted man's severest critics but a relatively discreet one. Clever, talented, and highly ambitious, "Fighting Joe" had striven to undermine his superior largely through the use of surrogates, thus masking his machinations from Lincoln, Edwin Stanton, and Henry Halleck.[30]

In many ways Joe Hooker and David McMurtrie Gregg were polar opposites, but the former's assumption of army command redounded to the latter's benefit as well as to that of all branches of the army. Unwilling to throw his troops blindly into battle, Hooker spent three months instituting and appraising a series of programs calculated to improve everyone's physical and psychological health. He saw to it that the army, in its camps at and around Falmouth, received better and more frequently issued rations, improved medical and hospital care, upgraded sanitation, and a more regular distribution of arms, ammunition, and equipment. Morale-building efforts included the regular granting of ten-day leaves and the issuance of corps badges that not only facilitated unit identification but instilled pride in one's organization. Hooker also streamlined administrative and command functioning, such as by eliminating Burnside's cumbersome grand divisions.[31]

In Gregg's eyes one of the most effective and far-reaching reforms was the issuance of General Orders No. 4, dated February 12, which reorganized the mounted branch. It created for the first time a full-sized corps of cavalry, three divisions strong, and placed it on a level with the highest echelons of the infantry. Hooker's choice to lead the corps was something of a surprise. George Stoneman, whom McClellan had virtually driven out of the army, returned to the cavalry. Rumor had it that Hooker had placed Stoneman on notice that, backed by a body of horsemen almost 12,000 strong and supported by some of the finest artillery units in the army, he must produce visible results. Through the first two years of war Jeb Stuart had outmaneuvered and outfought his widely scattered and seemingly impotent adversaries, literally running circles around them. Hooker would accept none of the excuses for failure offered to his predecessors. The cavalry would have to perform on a level that validated the care and attention he had devoted to it.

Assignment of Stoneman's ranking subordinates was made strictly on the basis of seniority. Pleasonton took the 1st Division, consisting of seven regiments including the 8th Pennsylvania and a single independent squadron. Averell's 2nd Division also contained seven regiments, one being the 16th Pennsylvania, led by John Irvin Gregg (now a colonel). David Gregg, next in the line of succession, headed the 3rd Division, embracing the same five regiments and one squadron he had led since Fredericksburg plus the 1st Maryland, recently transferred from the defenses of the upper Potomac. Later the 12th Illinois, then also on detached duty on the Potomac, would be added to his command, giving him enough units to form two brigades. On February 16 command of those brigades was assigned to Cols. H. Judson Kilpatrick of the 2nd New York and Eugene von Kielmansegge, 1st Maryland. The latter would soon be replaced by Col. Percy Wyndham, the Briton who had led the 1st New Jersey to war.[32]

From his first days in division command Gregg clapped a firm hand on his officers and men and fixed an observant eye on their well-being. As had been the case with the 8th Pennsylvania, many of his troopers were worn down by hard service, performing extensive picket and scouting duty on the Rappahannock while also guarding the supply depots at Aquia Creek, Belle Plain, and Potomac Creek. A typical regiment in the division, the 1st Pennsylvania, during the five weeks preceding December 31 had made more than a hundred marches, not including numerous recons and expeditions; moreover, it had devoted at least a portion of its strength to picket duty almost every day during that period. As a result the outfit had become the smallest component of the 3rd Division, sometimes numbering fewer than 350 officers and men present for duty.[33]

Other units had suffered as much, and some even more severely. In early February it was reported that Gregg's old regiment, now led by Lieutenant Colonel Griffiths, had been so long exposed to the numbing cold and the several snow and ice storms that twenty-four of its men "had their hands and feet badly frozen, but still stuck to their saddles in the greatest agony imaginable." Suffering was widespread. At the end of one particularly harsh day a sergeant in the 1st Maine noted in his diary that "the snow was blowing, the wind howling, and we were all hovering over our little fires and not in a very admiring mood of army life. We failed to see the romance of it, and thought it tough amusement." To a man, Gregg's division yearned for warm food and comfortable beds—the sort of pleasures obtainable when one's turn to go home on leave came around.[34]

To combat the elements officers and men often dosed themselves with alcohol either confiscated from local civilians or purchased from sutlers, civilian merchants who were licensed to travel with and sell to the army. Gregg sympathized with his troops' plight, but when too many began to suffer more from the effects of alcohol than from the weather he discontinued the sale of whiskey to officers without his express approval—prohibiting it entirely when they were on duty—and took steps to limit the availability of applejack and "white lightning" to the enlisted force. At the same time, along with other commanders, Gregg attempted to reverse the corps's increasing desertion rate—a direct consequence of such severe, unending duty—through surveillance, arrests, and court-martials.[35]

The troopers were not the only victims of the miserable climate; so too were the cavalry's horses, most of which were kept saddled and bridled twenty-four hours a day. In late February General Stoneman complained directly to Hooker: "[The corps's picket line] is but little less than 100 miles. One-third on duty at one time gives 40 men to the mile on post at one time. . . . Considering the condition of the roads, it is a good day's march to get out to the line and another to return, so that actually the horses are out one-half the time or more . . . [thus] little more than one-third of the time is allowed the horses in which to recruit." In addition to being overworked the animals went for long periods without sufficient grain, oats, and hay. Col. Rufus Ingalls, chief quartermaster of the army, admitted in a memorandum to army headquarters: "Numerous complaints have been made of late by commanders of batteries and cavalry regiments that their animals have suffered at different times for want of a sufficient supply of forage." Ingalls claimed that "every exertion had been made by them to obtain it" and that adequate amounts of forage were available "at the principal depots," but distribution remained a problem.[36]

Despite Gregg's best efforts to limit his men's and mounts' exposure to weather and excessive duty, the workload grew incrementally. By mid-February, while Hooker's infantry rested and recuperated, the cavalry was busier than ever. On February 15 the army's picket area was expanded and divided into four sectors assigned to the men under Pleasonton, Averell, Gregg, and John Buford, who upon Stoneman's ascension had taken over a reconstituted reserve consisting of the regulars of the corps as well as the erstwhile lancers of the 6th Pennsylvania. Gregg's division, whose right flank touched Buford's left, was assigned to guard a ten-mile stretch of the Northern Neck, the rugged, thinly settled peninsula between the Rappahannock and the Potomac. The heavily wooded country provided a sanctuary for regular Confederates, guerrillas, and bushwhackers who, easily evading detection, singled out exposed outposts and struck them without warning or mercy.[37]

The cavalry's dire situation appeared to lack any hope of improvement—but change was on the horizon. Warmer weather was weeks away as was the start of a several-month period during which the entire corps, instead of spending countless hours in the saddle on picket, would get to do some fighting—in fact, a great deal of it.

6

A Failed Raid, a Drawn Battle

General officers as well as the rank and file could avail themselves of Joseph Hooker's liberal leave policy. By late February, William Averell had just returned from ten days off duty and both Alfred Pleasonton and David Gregg were eligible to follow suit. Because Pleasonton had not taken leave in many months his application received priority, but apparently the unmarried officer withdrew it so that David and Ellen might be together for the first time since their wedding. It is possible that Gregg spent at least a portion of his furlough, which began about March 5, visiting family and friends in Huntingdon and Hollidaysburg.[1]

His leave came on the heels of a much-publicized debacle. On February 25 Fitz Lee, with 400 picked men, crossed the Rappahannock undetected and attacked the far right flank of the Union picket line. The target area, patrolled by the troopers of Lee's West Point friend Averell, was anchored at Hartwood Church, eight miles upriver from Falmouth. The raiders struck with such stealth that 186 pickets became casualties, 150 of them as captives. One of the regiments caught in Lee's path was John Irvin Gregg's 16th Pennsylvania, whose men, when flooded over by Rebels, broke and "ran like sheep."[2]

The incident, which embarrassed the entire corps, infuriated Hooker, who demanded a retaliatory strike in order to save face and restore morale. Generals Stoneman and Averell immediately assented and on March 17 the latter led 2,100 cavalrymen and a light battery across the river at Kelly's Ford, thirty miles upriver from Falmouth. Advancing toward Culpeper Court House, Averell swarmed over the camps and outposts of the Rebels who had routed his pickets. During the five-hour struggle that followed the cavalry of the Army of the Potomac for the first time fought a large (though still heavily outnumbered) force of enemy horsemen to a standstill while driving at least one regiment of Virginians into ignominious flight. Attempts to counterattack failed thanks to the tenacity of regiments fighting to redeem their reputations, including the 16th Pennsylvania. His triumph complete, Averell withdrew, having incurred 78 losses compared to 170 for the enemy including the mortal wounding of Stuart's young artillery chief, Maj. John Pelham. The victory brought Averell much favorable publicity and restored, at least for a time, Hooker's faith in his improved cavalry. By the time Gregg returned from leave enthusiasm was running high throughout the corps.[3]

The corporate morale was buoyed again on April 6 when President Lincoln, during a visit to the army to consult with its new commander and study the effects of his reforms, reviewed Hooker's cavalry near Belle Plain, inside Gregg's picket lines. The occasion was a major event in the life of the corps, which turned out in spit-and-polish array. The men's carbines, pistols, and sabers gleamed in the sunlight from repeated polishing, their horses had been studiously groomed, and a several-piece band awaited the cue to make music. It should have been a gala day for Gregg and the 3rd Cavalry Division, but an unanticipated event made it, instead, a memorable ordeal. The night before, the general had purchased from an officer in the 1st Maine a warhorse described as a "splendid blood bay, over 16 hands high, clean limbed, beautifully formed, fine carriage and evidently high spirited" but with, as Gregg later discovered, "a mouth of iron." On the morning of the review he rode his new steed to the head of his command, where, after waiting some hours for Lincoln to inspect the other divisions, he was joined by the president, accompanied by a two-hundred-man escort that included Hooker and Stoneman. Lincoln, Gregg observed, was mounted "on a horse that seemed rather undersized for one of his proportions." When the ungainly rider extended a greeting, Gregg saluted, shook the outstretched hand and gazed into "the anxious, careworn, deeply impressive face of Abraham Lincoln."

Trailed by Lincoln's star-studded escort, the two started off side by side along the first rank of troopers. As they trotted along the band began to play, accompanied by the collective rasp of hundreds of sabers unsheathed more or less simultaneously. Spooked by the sounds, Gregg's horse took off like a gazelle across ground broken by drainage ditches filled with unmelted ice. Gregg tried mightily to rein it in but the "old fashioned dragoon bit" in its mouth was not strong enough to produce results. Gregg's situation was bad enough, but then he saw that the president's horse was trying to keep pace, causing his awkward rider to call out: "General Gregg, I beg of you that you will not ride quite so fast!"

Within minutes the pair had outdistanced the president's party and Lincoln was displaying shock and anxiety. Gregg finally brought his mount to a halt by pulling on one of the reins with all his strength, "not, however, without having described a wide curve beyond the left of the line." By now Lincoln was "considerably shaken up and gave evidence of mingled excitement and fatigue—his tall silk hat had fallen on the back of his head and his knees had risen well towards the pommel of his saddle." Gregg suddenly realized that the president believed they had been riding at a typical cavalry gait; having recovered his composure, he remarked, "General, what a furious and exciting ride we have had." Relieved that he had not maimed or killed his commander-in-chief, Gregg kept a firm grip on the reins through the rest of the day, which concluded without further incident. He would ride the horse, who proved to have "many fine qualities," including a remarkably calm demeanor under fire, for almost two years, but never without a highly restrictive bit in its mouth.[4]

One of Gregg's subordinates believed that a gala review "forebode[d] a great battle," and in this case, at least, he was right. By April 12 Hooker had developed the plan that would return his rejuvenated army to the south side of the Rappahannock, where it would retrieve the honor it had lost at the hands of his predecessor. Adopting some features of Burnside's strategy, he would cross most of his men over the Rapidan River at Germanna, Ely's, and U.S. Mine Fords before leading them around Robert E. Lee's left flank and into his army's rear. A diversionary attack against the heights of Fredericksburg under Maj. Gen.

John Sedgwick would hold Hooker's antagonist in place, preventing him from detecting and responding to the turning movement until too late to stop it.

The main offensive would be set in motion in the last days of the month, but to increase its prospects the army's horsemen would cross at or near Kelly's Ford two weeks in advance of the general movement and raid far behind enemy lines, ideally as far as Richmond. Stoneman was assigned a variety of targets: railroad track, bridges, culverts, canals, and other elements of infrastructure, as well as provisions of all kinds. Hooker hoped that an unnerved and harassed Lee would fall back upon the defenses of Richmond even before he was attacked. As the army's adjutant general, Seth Williams, put it in his April 12 letter of instructions, Stoneman's objectives were "turning the enemy's position on his left . . . throwing your command between him and Richmond, and isolating him from his supplies, checking his retreat, and inflicting on him every possible injury" that would lead "to his discomfiture and defeat." A major goal was the destruction of the Richmond, Fredericksburg and Potomac (RF & P) Railroad, "the shortest [route] for the enemy to retire on" when forced from his present position. Stoneman was also to engage and defeat forces stationed along the Orange and Alexandria (O & A) Railroad at Culpeper and Gordonsville while, if practicable, sending a force to raid the supply depot at lightly defended Charlottesville.[5]

Stoneman, eager to show what a sizable force of well-mounted, well-equipped, and highly motivated cavalry could do, set off in timely fashion. On April 13, having left a single brigade under Pleasonton to provide Hooker with reconnaissance and combat support, the corps commander led 10,000 horsemen and 400 horse artillerists out of winter quarters around Falmouth and started for Rappahannock Station on the O & A, eight miles upstream from Averell's crossing site of March 17. As he departed Belle Plain at mission's commencement Gregg issued a circular announcing the first movement in force by the 2,905 officers and men of the 3rd Cavalry Division, "thoroughly and effectually prepared for operations in the field."[6]

On April 15, after wasting a day sparring with elements of Stuart's command on the south side of the river, Stoneman prepared to force a crossing. But it was too late, thanks to the onset of the same foul weather that had stymied Burnside's Mud Marchers, this time in the form of thirty-six hours of rain and hail. Before the storm reached its height Stoneman pushed across a single brigade under Grimes Davis (detached from Pleasonton's division), but he elected to keep everyone else on the north bank till the skies cleared.

This did not happen, and the river did not recede adequately, for two weeks, during which the immobilized troopers grew restless and surly. Gregg, seeking higher ground for his men, spent the period transferring his camps from the Rappahannock up the railroad to Bealton Station, then northwest to Sulphur (or Warrenton) Springs on the north fork of the Rappahannock (known locally as Hedgeman's River), and finally to Warrenton Junction. A frustrated Hooker bombarded Stoneman with demands to get moving while Lincoln, who was closely monitoring the situation by telegraph, fretted that "General S. is not moving rapidly enough to make the expedition come to anything. . . . I greatly fear it is another failure already."[7]

Stoneman was finally able to cross late on April 29, two days after the troops in Hooker's flanking column left Falmouth to open the campaign. Predictably, infantry and cavalry bunched up at the Rappahannock fords, impeding the progress of both. Then came further delay, Stoneman poring over new orders he had received the previous day from Hooker's headquarters. They called for his force to be broken into two columns, one to mask the operations of the other. The main force was to operate against the resources of the Virginia Central Railroad and the RF&P while the more westerly wing under Averell contained those Confederates known to be holding points on the O&A below the Rapidan, before striking toward the rail junction and supply cache at Gordonsville. At some point the columns were to unite; Hooker suggested the junction take place on the Pamunkey River.[8]

Having briefed his subordinates on the new plan, Stoneman sent Averell—his division enlarged to 3,400 men by the addition of Grimes Davis's troopers—on his way down the O&A toward Brandy Station and from there to the Rapidan. Almost from the start, this phase of the operation was a disaster. Averell never reached the point at which he was to communicate with Stoneman and thus failed to receive updated instructions on what to do next, including rendezvousing with the main force on the South Anna River. In obedience to previously received orders, on the second day out Averell occupied Culpeper Court House, capturing a few defenders and confiscating foodstuffs before encountering small bodies of cavalry under Fitz Lee and his cousin Brig. Gen. W. H. F. ("Rooney") Lee. Although instructed to keep the enemy occupied, Averell permitted the cousins to break contact, Fitz heading east—presumably to join Stuart near Fredericksburg—and Rooney pounding south toward Rapidan Station.

Averell tailed the latter, slowly, to the north bank of the river, where he heard reports of Confederate movements in the area, including Gordonsville, which had been occupied by 25,000 troops under Stonewall Jackson. Afraid to proceed farther, he spent the rest of April 30 and all of May 1 confronting "strong and skillfully constructed" defenses across the stream. He was still there on the morning of May 2 when peremptorily ordered to report in person to Hooker, who wanted to know "what you are doing at Rapidan Station." One imagines that Averell made the trip in an uneasy frame of mind.[9]

After parting with Averell, Stoneman and the main column, supported by a horse artillery battery and preceded at a distance by a brigade-size force of skirmishers under John Buford, crossed the Rappahannock at Kelly's Ford early on April 29 and the Rapidan at Raccoon Ford the next day. Throughout the first day of May the command plodded down the Orange Plank Road, bedeviled by a new round of rain storms and heavy fog. At a crossroads the column angled south toward the health spa of Orange Springs where it surprised and scattered some enemy cavalry and confiscated a "quantity of public stores."

En route to his next stopover, Louisa Court House, seventeen miles distant, Stoneman learned that Stuart, who supposedly held the surrounding area in some force, had recently departed for points unknown, quite possibly Robert E. Lee's headquarters. The news was unsettling to everyone involved in the expedition, especially its leader. Engaging Stuart and preventing him from linking with the forces opposing Hooker had been one of Stoneman's objectives.

Believing Louisa Court House to be strongly held, at daybreak on May 2 Stoneman had Gregg divide Judson Kilpatrick's brigade, which

had the advance, into three parties to strike the town itself as well as
above and below it. Stoneman must have been at least a little embarrassed when Kilpatrick's men went galloping through the place "yelling like demons" only to discover it defenseless. Thus unhindered, a
pioneer corps attached to the column destroyed five miles' worth of
track as well as a water tank and other structures along the right-of-
way while comrades waylaid commissary and ordnance stores.

From Louisa Court House Stoneman led the column southeast as
far as Thompson's Cross Roads on the lower bank of the South Anna.
Here the corps commander called together his senior subordinates.
As he later wrote, "I gave them to understand that we had dropped in
that region of country like a shell, and that I intended to burst it in
every direction . . . and thus magnify our small force into overwhelming numbers." In pursuit of the new strategy he ordered detachments,
none larger than two regiments, to strike multiple targets. Accordingly, on May 3 Gregg led his 1st Maine and 10th New York and a two-
gun section of artillery—preceded and followed by parties of regulars
including one under Capt. Wesley Merritt of Stoneman's staff—to way-
lay transportation facilities farther down the South Anna.

Gregg faithfully and ably carried out his orders, according to one
chronicler of the raid doing "more damage than expected." His men
tore up railroad track, burned storehouses, and destroyed at least two
foot-and-railroad bridges, including commodious Ground Squirrel
Bridge. Another target, the South Anna Bridge, was found to be too
well defended to be seized and demolished by a detachment of the 1st
Maine. On May 4 Gregg returned to Thompson's Cross Roads before
being sent to neighboring Yanceyville, where the next day he crossed
the South Anna, afterward burning the span there as well. In his after-
action report he noted that those who had accompanied him to the
South Anna "marched a distance of 106 miles in thirty-eight hours."[10]

In accord with Stoneman's bursting-shell strategy, other elements of
the 3rd Cavalry Division had been sent in various directions to search
and destroy. Sir Percy Wyndham, accompanied by the 1st New Jersey
and 1st Maryland, galloped southwestward to Columbia, at the confluence of the James and Rivanna Rivers, to damage a canal and level
an aqueduct. The 12th Illinois of Lt. Col. Hasbrouck Davis, an officer

with a history of daring exploits, was sent to destroy portions of the RF&P at Ashland, fifteen miles north of Richmond, and via Hanover Junction, parts of the Virginia Central. Meanwhile, Judson Kilpatrick, at the head of his 2nd New York, galloped off under vaguely worded orders to "operate in the direction of Richmond." Stoneman, with five hundred of John Buford's men, would remain at Thompson's Cross Roads until the raiding parties rejoined him.

Gregg's detachments inflicted extensive damage to enemy property but none of a lasting nature. Wyndham destroyed a bridge on the James and took an ax to canal locks and boats but failed to blow up the aqueduct because he lacked "the proper materials." The 12th Illinois burned depot buildings, trestles, and military supplies but tore up only "half a dozen rails" on the railroads it struck. At Ashland Station Davis performed his most memorable capture: a train carrying 250 sick and wounded Confederates, whom he paroled and released. Turning north, he burned a trestle near Hanover Junction, but a train hauling infantry and three guns prevented him from damaging a third railroad, the Richmond and York River. On the verge of being surrounded, Davis fled down the Peninsula to the Union lines around Yorktown.[11]

Kilpatrick's feats, though dramatically achieved, were hardly the stuff of military lore. After tearing up track and torching depot facilities on the RF&P the ambitious and aggressive but not always level-headed colonel descended on a city he intended to frighten from afar. A few miles from Richmond he encountered pickets armed with artillery, whom he charged and drove toward the capital's inner defenses. But when pursuers closed in he ended his feint and withdrew, like Davis, to Yorktown, on the way burning a bridge on the Chickahominy and running a train into the river.[12]

With the exception of Kilpatrick and Davis the leaders of the various parties returned to Thompson's Cross Roads by May 5 and within a few hours were following Stoneman northward. Gregg made good time despite his many played-out horses. He recrossed the Rapidan on the morning of May 7 and the Rappahannock the following day. On May 11 he went into camp near Deep Run on Hedgeman's River.[13]

Stoneman made his return march in high spirits, believing his mission fully accomplished and expecting a warm welcome home. On

May 7 he was shocked to learn that while he was away Hooker had been defeated by Lee in the Wilderness, a seventy-square-mile jungle of scrub oak, second-growth pine, and tangled thicket south of the Rapidan, and had returned to Falmouth. Stoneman suspected that this, the latest in a series of bungled offenses in the Virginia theater, would have long-lasting repercussions, but he had no idea of their magnitude or the effect they would have on his career.

Many of Stoneman's troopers and their supporters in the main army pronounced the expedition a sweeping success. Shortly before the raiders recrossed the Rappahannock, Captain Custer of Hooker's staff, who had not participated in the operation, wrote a political supporter: "Stoneman stands very high in the estimation of the entire Army and his raid is considered to surpass any that Stuart ever made." Another who based his opinion on hearsay, Maj. Gen. George Gordon Meade, commanding Hooker's V Corps, informed his wife: "Stoneman's success was very complete, and his whole operation brilliant in the extreme." Gregg himself believed that the expedition had convinced the Cavalry Corps of "its ability to do whatever might thereafter be required when employed in its proper sphere." Over time, however, the impression that Stoneman had achieved something tangible and sustainable underwent a major reassessment.[14]

In the aftermath of Hooker's defeat it became painfully obvious that the cavalry had done nothing to influence the campaign in his favor. Averell's and Gregg's columns, and especially the small parties Stoneman had dispatched from Thompson's Cross Roads, had struck somewhat randomly at isolated targets whose destruction or disabling would have little impact on the operations of the Army of Northern Virginia. Moreover, the damage done, extensive though it appeared in some places, would be repaired by work parties within seventy-two hours of Stoneman's retreat. Hooker complained in a May 10 communiqué to Secretary Stanton that rail traffic between Fredericksburg and Richmond had been interrupted for only a day: "The bridges of importance appear to have remained untouched. With the exception of Kilpatrick's operations, the raid does not appear to have amounted to much." To many observers the main feature of the raid was the thousand broken down or otherwise unserviceable horses that failed to accompany their riders home.[15]

One reason why the effects on Confederate infrastructure were not longer lasting was Stoneman's failure to supply his men with the proper tools, such as levers and claw crowbars; for lack of explosives, Wyndham had been unable to destroy the James River aqueduct. Then, too, operational intelligence had been lacking, causing Gregg to strike the Virginia Central where no bridges existed and to grandly attack an undefended depot. Stoneman lacked excuses for his poor performance. There had been no concerted effort to pursue or harass his troopers, which should have enabled them to accomplish more than they had.

The raid's most glaring deficiency was Stoneman's failure to coordinate operations with Hooker's main body, largely the result of his inability to cross the Rappahannock before the storm hit (as Gregg put it in his post-mission report, one day earlier "the water could be crossed at a step"). Had Stoneman started on time it is possible that all or most of his men would have returned to the main army before the turning movement began. As it was, with only a single brigade of horsemen to rely on Hooker had stumbled into battle inside the visibility-limiting, movement-hindering tangle of trees and underbrush below the Rapidan.[16]

Lee knew what to do with the opportunity granted him. Realizing that the attack at Fredericksburg was secondary to the main Union effort, he left a small force to contain Sedgwick while confronting Hooker at nearly full strength in an area that would neutralize the latter's numerical superiority. His plans suddenly askew, Hooker went over to the defensive. Lee took advantage—and a great gamble—by splitting his army yet again on May 2, sending Jackson on a twelve-mile march across the his enemy's front, then around its right flank and into its rear, causing a ruinous stampede. Though mortally wounded by his own men in the early evening aftermath of the assault, Jackson had effectively unhinged both the Army of the Potomac and its leader. The following day Jeb Stuart, enabled to assume infantry corps command thanks to the impotent threat posed by Stoneman, succeeded his close friend Jackson. On May 3 Stuart's command, along with other forces, smashed head-on into the reeling Federals, causing further destruction and prompting Hooker, knocked insensible by a shell burst, to order a full-scale retreat once he regained consciousness.[17]

The fallout from the Stoneman Raid was more severe and of greater duration than any damage the raiders had done in the enemy's rear. On May 3 Hooker relieved Averell from command on the grounds that he had not carried out his orders, being led stray and bamboozled by small bands of Rebels; the brigadier was directed to report to the War Department for possible reassignment. Some of Averell's colleagues considered him a scapegoat for Hooker's blundering. Justified or not, the New Yorker's relief forever ended his association with the Army of the Potomac. It is not known whether Gregg had contact with him during the remainder of the war.[18]

Hooker was not done seeking victims. Two weeks after his return Stoneman became the target of his superior's unrelenting wrath. On May 22, reeling from Hooker's public disparagement of him and exhausted by his recent exertions, he applied for medical leave. Hooker approved the request, but he had no intention of recalling Stoneman to active duty. He was replaced by Alfred Pleasonton, who had only recently been promoted to command both his own and Averell's divisions.[19]

It appears that when he went raiding Stoneman had left Pleasonton behind for considerations not strictly military. Stoneman did not trust his pushy subordinate, whom he probably suspected was after his job. Reduced to brigade command, Pleasonton seemed unlikely to accomplish much in Stoneman's absence; moreover, he would be denied a share of the honors sure to accrue from a well-delivered strike deep inside enemy lines. But Stoneman guessed wrong; Pleasonton did a competent job of screening the army's crossing of two rivers while preventing Rebel cavalry from impeding the movement of Hooker's columns through the Wilderness. Hooker took note.

This was not all. Late on May 2, in the wake of Jackson's assault, Pleasonton found himself in a fortunate place at an opportune time. To stop the stream of fugitives from the front he supposedly ordered one of the three regiments at his disposal—it happened to be Gregg's old 8th Pennsylvania, now under Major Pennock Huey—to charge the pursuers and disrupt their formations. The forlorn-hope effort cost the Pennsylvanians more than a hundred casualties, including the death of the able Peter Keenan, and its success was marginal at best. Pleasonton, however, reaped credit not only for slowing the enemy's advance but for shoring up a defensive position near the seventy-acre clearing known as Chancellorsville. His later claim to having prevented a disaster on the Union right flank was never verified but his superior accepted it as fact. The next time Lincoln visited the army, Hooker introduced Pleasonton to the president as the man "who saved the Army of the Potomac the other night."[20]

Pleasonton's elevation to corps command—and, it was assumed, the quick acquisition of a major generalship—did not elicit universal approval. John McIntosh reacted to the news by claiming: "I never had such a disgust in me before." He considered resigning rather than serving under such a schemer as Pleasonton. One of McIntosh's subordinates wrote: "This being under Pleasanton [*sic*] is very demoralizing." He hoped the man would be promoted even higher, to the point "that we [might] be rid of him." A cavalry surgeon described Pleasonton as being "about as fit" for his new position "as any 2nd Lieutenant in the command." Capt. Charles F. Adams, Jr., of the 1st Massachusetts dismissed the new commander as "pure and simple a newspaper humbug."[21]

No surviving comments reveal David Gregg's reaction to Pleasonton's promotion. He was aware of the well-entrenched rumor that the man played army politics to maximum effect. In fact, the new corps leader would not receive his second star until he enlisted the active support of a former subordinate, Congressman John F. Farnsworth of Illinois. One way in which Pleasonton persuaded the highly influential Republican to "talk this [his promotion] into the President" was to offer the legislator's favorite nephew, Capt. Elon Farnsworth of the 8th Illinois, a position on the corps staff and an opportunity to gain a star of his own. Gregg may have entertained reservations about Pleasonton's swift climb to the top and how he achieved it, but given that he himself had twice profited from the support of a powerful relative, he could hardly have condemned his superior for playing political connections for career gain.[22]

Pleasonton's rise and Averell's fall opened up two positions near the top of the chain of command. Although technically still Pleasonton's, command of the 1st Cavalry Division effectively passed to John Buford, who had served effectively, albeit quietly, on the recent raid. Averell's erstwhile division went to an unlikely candidate, Col. Alfred N. Duffié of the 1st Rhode Island. Although of limited ability and rigid military mind, the flamboyant Frenchman had made a name for himself at Kelly's Ford, while his (possibly forged) credentials as a graduate of the military academy at Saint Cyr impressed Pleasonton. The colonel's acquired subordinates were a talented lot; they included John Irvin Gregg, leader of his 2nd Brigade. Duffié's position in the new order was something of an anomaly in that he commanded the 2nd Division while David Gregg, his senior, retained the 3rd Division. On several occasions, however, Gregg would lead Duffié's division as well as his own.

On the day he assumed command Pleasonton learned what his superior expected of him. He had proposed that Gregg be assigned to picket the Rappahannock fords as well as the O & A, the army's lifeline of supply to Washington, with headquarters at Catlett's Station. He recommended that the rest of the corps guard the other end of the army's front, from near Brooke's Station on the RF&P to Dumfries. But Hooker found fault with Pleasonton's ideas; he believed that a single division should picket the Rappahannock and that the stations his subordinate proposed lay too far from the main army. Adjutant General Williams explained that "the main body of the cavalry must be nearer, and held well in hand and in readiness to spring at a moment's notice, in case of an enemy's raid or of an advance movement." In closing, Williams added some stern advice: "Spare no labor to place the cavalry arm of the service in a high state of efficiency at the earliest practicable moment . . . this arm has been greatly impaired from want of system, organization, and judicious employment."[23]

One assumes that Pleasonton paid heed to Hooker's instructions, but he focused his attention on the "judicious employment" of his new command. Aware that the corps's image had suffered at Stoneman's hands, he searched for an opportunity to prove that under his stewardship the cavalry was capable of great things. To make his point he needed the proper resources in sufficient quantity. The day Pleasonton broached his suggestions to Hooker, Gregg, who had been assigned to the railroad mission, requisitioned a thousand remounts from Washington, explaining that the great number of dismounted men in his camps represented "the most serious inconvenience and much impair[ed] the efficiency of the command." He also mentioned the continuing absence of Kilpatrick's 2nd New York and Hasbrouck Davis's 12th Illinois, which had yet to secure transportation from Yorktown. Their loss left the division with fewer than two thousand men available for service, "drawn out like a thread over a line of about 40 miles" to patrol a railroad, a river with numerous fords, and a country infested with guerrillas and bushwhackers. The latter represented a species of warrior not previously encountered in large numbers but which had become a growing menace. Gregg specifically pointed to the region around Rappahannock Bridge; lacking supports, he would be unable to prevent an enemy from crossing below that point. His concerns were quickly addressed. Pleasonton bolstered him—despite Hooker's injunction against too many horsemen on the railroad—with Duffié's command. For the first time, Gregg effectively commanded two full-size divisions.[24]

On May 23 Gregg from his headquarters at Bealton Station on the O & A relayed to Pleasonton a piece of news that, although unremarkable on the surface, set in motion a series of events that would lead to the largest mounted battle of the war to date. A deserter from one of Stuart's regiments had confirmed rumors of a cavalry buildup at Culpeper Court House, seventeen miles southwest of Bealton, although the man did not know the reason for it and was ignorant of future operations. Five days later Gregg reported that Rebel cavalry had grouped near Warrenton. The spate of activity convinced Hooker that Lee was up to something and that Stuart would play a large role in it. This Hooker wished to forestall; as he told the Secretary of War, "If Stoneman had not almost destroyed one-half of my serviceable cavalry force, I would pitch into him in his camps."[25]

The reports tallied with intelligence gathered by the operatives of the army's Bureau of Military Information and passed on to Hooker on May 27 indicating that all three of Stuart's brigades had recently moved from Fredericksburg to Culpeper in preparation for a raid northward.

Gregg himself on May 28 informed Pleasonton that his scouts had found Stuart's cavalry camped within a few miles of Culpeper. At about the same time Union spies in Richmond learned of a conference involving Lee and his military and political superiors at which a "forward movement" by the Army of Northern Virginia had been agreed upon. Then, early in June, Hooker's signal officers detected the movement of Confederate units away from Fredericksburg—to points unknown.[26]

In fact, more than a cavalry raid was afoot. On June 3 Lee, emboldened by his success at Chancellorsville and convinced that Hooker would remain inactive, began to shift his army toward the Shenandoah Valley. His objective was the country north of the Mason-Dixon Line where a decisive victory might permanently tip the balance of the war, ensuring the Confederacy's survival. By June 8 two-thirds of his infantry—the corps of James Longstreet and Lt. Gen. Richard S. Ewell, Jackson's successor—had already reached Culpeper, leaving behind only A. P. Hill's corps, which was scheduled to follow in short order.

Upon arriving at the courthouse Longstreet and Ewell joined Stuart's division, which thanks to recent additions from North Carolina and the Shenandoah numbered close to ten thousand officers and men. Stuart had shown off his enlarged command in a series of reviews that had attracted high-level visitors from Richmond. Afterward he moved six miles east to bivouac in the fields around Brandy Station. The depot lay within easy reach of the Rappahannock, which Stuart, leading the invasion march, planned to cross early on June 9.[27]

Hooker yearned to know what Stuart was up to, where his forces lay, and whether infantry was nearby. He decided to have Pleasonton pitch into him, demonstrating the newly forged power of the Cavalry Corps. Hit hard enough, the gray horsemen would not be going anywhere any time soon. Pleasonton, while welcoming the chance to show what he and his reorganized and rejuvenated troopers could do, would later claim that he had been sent to Culpeper on a "reconnaissance in force."

He intended to reconnoiter by fording the river in two columns, to unite at Brandy Station for the push west. He ordered Gregg, still commanding both his and Duffié's divisions, to cross at Kelly's Ford while Buford splashed across at Beverly Ford, eight miles upstream, beginning at around 4 a.m. on June 9. To stiffen the cavalry's thrusts,

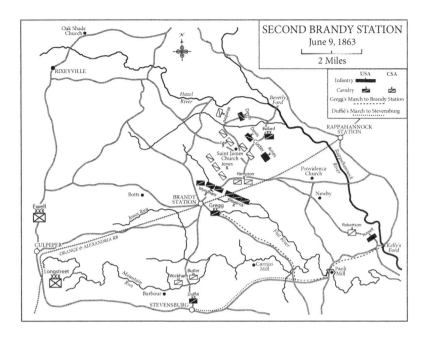

Map 4. Second Brandy Station, June 9, 1863. Created by Paul Dangel.

Hooker would provide Pleasonton with infantry support. One brigade of Meade's corps would cross the river in rear of each column, guarding its flanks and rear and keeping open a retreat route if needed. Its inclusion should have told Pleasonton that Hooker expected him to fight but the cavalryman still supposed he was being sent merely to locate Stuart and ascertain his intentions.[28]

The march to the river opposite Brandy Station was made with commendable stealth—if Pleasonton was ignorant of Stuart's whereabouts, the latter had no inkling the former was coming. When Buford's column—the brigades of Grimes Davis and Col. Thomas C. Devin, to which had been attached the five regiments of regulars under Maj. Charles J. Whiting—forded the fog-shrouded river about 4:30 a.m., the advantage appeared to lie with the Federals. Startled pickets gave way before the blue horde, and Stuart's horse artillery, grouped in a vulnerable position near St. James Church, almost fell to the enemy as a body. Awakened by the shooting, Stuart frantically ordered up the brigades of Wade Hampton and Brig. Gen. William E. ("Grumble") Jones, with Rooney Lee's troopers not far behind, and suddenly Buford's push was slowed to a crawl.[29]

With the enemy's attention directed upriver, Gregg had an opportunity to cross at Kelly's Ford, pass Stuart's embattled right flank, and gain the rear, possibly producing a stampede. He failed to capitalize, however, through a litany of errors that anyone who appreciated Gregg's acumen and levelheadedness would hardly believe him capable of. His first mistake was failing to cross in unison with Buford to take maximum advantage of Stuart's predicament. Most historians fault Colonel Duffié, whose division was assigned to cross in advance of Gregg's, for delaying the operation until 6 a.m. Supposedly this happened because, having camped well back from the river to avoid detection, the Frenchman lost his way to the ford and had to countermarch. In fact, Gregg had been instructed to cross first; he changed the order of advance almost at the last minute without informing Pleasonton. The belated decision left Duffié little time to put his troopers and artillery on the road to Kelly's Ford.

Gregg's supervision of Duffié was lacking in two other respects. He either overrode his instructions from Pleasonton, which were based on Hooker's desires, or Pleasonton had not clearly conveyed them to him. Pleasonton's plan of operations called for Duffié, once across the stream, to proceed south to the village of Stevensburg, where he could guard the left flank. It appears, however, that Hooker intended that only a portion of the 2nd Division make the move as a hedge against the remote possibility of interference via the Rapidan River. The majority of Duffié's troops were then to join their colleagues at Brandy Station, completing a three-pronged pincer movement. An entire division was not needed at Stevensburg but Gregg sent it there in full strength, again without informing Pleasonton.

Gregg also mishandled Duffié by not immediately recalling him once Buford became heavily and loudly engaged. Instead of concentrating all the manpower at his disposal, Gregg permitted his subordinate to remain well to the south, pinned down by tiny detachments of Hampton's and Lee's brigades, for most of the day. Late in the afternoon the colonel was called to the battlefield by a roundabout, time-consuming route. By then the day was spent and the battle effectively over.

Finally, Gregg erred by not taking the 2,400 officers and men of his own division on the most direct route to Brandy Station as soon as he learned of Buford's involvement. Finding that road occupied by the small brigade (two North Carolina regiments) of Brig. Gen. Beverly H. Robertson, Gregg, who had left his infantry supports behind to secure Kelly's Ford, chose to shift five miles to the west in order to take the Fredericksburg plank road. The controversial decision would attract the scrutiny of generations of historians and military analysts. Spurred onward by messages from Pleasonton informing him "of the severity of the fight on the right and of the largely superior force of the enemy," Gregg followed the plank road past Paoli Mill and across sluggish Mountain Run before veering onto the Carrico's Mill road. Despite being slowed by Duffié's rear guard less than mile from his objective, around 10:30 a.m. Gregg reached a point southeast of Brandy Station. There he found himself, as he had hoped, in a position to smite Stuart from the rear while the latter was deeply engaged in front.[30]

Gregg would describe the countryside around the depot as abounding in open fields "particularly suitable for a cavalry engagement." As soon as he arrived he decided: "I either had to decline the fight in the face of the enemy or throw upon him at once the entire division." Assured that Kilpatrick's brigade was near enough to provide ready reinforcement, he ordered Colonel Wyndham to advance at a rapid gait across the railroad to Fleetwood Heights, where Stuart had pitched his headquarters the day before and which Gregg considered the key to the enemy's position. Wyndham moved forward, the 1st New Jersey in the van, but just shy of the tracks he halted under the shelling of a single 6-pounder howitzer on the high ground. The hesitant Englishman dismounted some of his men, unlimbered a two-gun section of Lt. James W. Martin's 6th New York Battery, and, unwilling to proceed farther until certain of what he was up against, scanned the hill with his binoculars.[31]

Properly concerned that Wyndham's delay might prove fatal, Gregg instructed him to seize the western spur of the heights, which, previously unoccupied, had begun to teem with the Virginians of Jones's brigade, recalled from Buford's front. Gregg, riding with his staff, including his brother Tom, hit the incline in the midst of the New Jerseymen. Pvt. Henry C. Meyer, a clerk on the division headquarters staff, recalled that "General Gregg showed an enthusiasm that I had never noticed before. He started his horse on a gallop . . . swinging his gauntlets over his head and hurrahing." At the head of a full-throttle mounted attack, even a soldier known for his self-control could throw composure to the winds.[32]

Slashing with their sabers and spitting pistol balls, Wyndham's horsemen sliced through the first opponents they encountered, members of the 12th Virginia, then penetrated a second line of Rebels before a third column, just reaching the hill, slammed into them and drained their momentum. As more and more Confederates flooded the area, they pushed back, successively, Wyndham's 1st Pennsylvania and the 1st Maryland, while wounding the brigade leader and menacing Lt. J. Wade Wilson's artillery section. Eventually forced off the crest despite Gregg's efforts to rally and re-form it, Wyndham's command suffered 150 casualties, more than half of them missing and presumed captured.[33]

At this point "the fight," Gregg declared, "was everywhere most fierce." Next into the fray was Judson Kilpatrick's brigade, its commander having rejoined the army from Yorktown only four days earlier. Ignoring the pleas of Gregg's staff to attack Wilson's assailants and save his guns, the uber-aggressive officer known to many of his men as "Kill-Cavalry" charged up the south slope of Fleetwood Hill, the 10th New York in the lead. Before the attackers reached the summit Wade Hampton's men, now on hand in heavy numbers along with at least two batteries, collided with them, broke their formation, and sent them reeling. Kilpatrick, "wild with excitement," committed the 2nd New York, followed by the 1st Maine, but despite making some headway neither regiment secured the heights.[34]

And yet the fight went on. "For an hour and a half was the contest continued," Gregg reported, "not in skirmishing, but in determined charges. The contest was too unequal to be longer continued. The 2nd Division had not come up; there was no support at hand, and the enemy's numbers were three times my own." This last observation was an exaggeration, although from Gregg's point of view it appeared accurate. He was also incorrect in reporting that during the fighting Stuart had been reinforced by infantry brought up by rail from Culpeper. He was correct, however, as to his lack of immediate support.

The furious pace of attack and counterattack finally slackened, ending the fighting on the 3rd Division's front. Carefully disengaging, its leader withdrew, at Pleasonton's order, to the river at Rappahannock Bridge where he connected with Buford's exhausted command. Gregg crossed there under the cover of Duffié's division, finally returned from Stevensburg "without being molested by the enemy."[35]

Though forced off the heights around Brandy Station, Gregg's men had accomplished much, including killing or disabling scores of opponents and capturing eight officers, 107 men, and two battle flags. But because of the wayward path he had taken to the battlefield, compounded by Wyndham's hesitation to attack, Gregg had been unable to break Stuart's flank. Farther north, where Buford's division had been fought to a standstill and Grimes Davis killed, the Federals had gained no greater success. By 5 p.m. Pleasonton's reunited force was recrossing the river, covered by Meade's infantry. As soon as he could Gregg telegraphed Ellen in Reading: "Tom and myself all right."[36]

The fighting had been severe indeed. The casualty count was heavily tilted in Stuart's favor—fewer than six hundred killed, wounded, or missing, in contrast to nine hundred for Pleasonton, suggesting a decisive victory. The Federals had been forced to withdraw and three of their guns had been captured, a loss that left Gregg (as a subordinate given to understatement put it) "very much annoyed that such a thing could happen, and so unnecessarily." Even so, objective observers would view the fight as a draw. Especially considering they had been outnumbered throughout the day, the outcome redounded to the credit of the star-crossed horsemen of the Army of the Potomac.[37]

1. Gen. William W. Averell. Courtesy of the Library of Congress, LC-DIG-cwpb-05434.

2. Gen. George B. McClellan. Public domain.

3. Gen. George
Stoneman. Courtesy of
the Library of Congress,
LC-DIG-cwpb-05212.

4. Col. David McMurtrie Gregg and
officers of the 8th Pennsylvania Cavalry.
Courtesy of the Library of Congress.

5. Gen. Alfred Pleasonton. Courtesy of the Library of Congress, LC-DIG-cwpbh-03158.

6. Gen. Joseph Hooker. Courtesy of the Library of Congress.

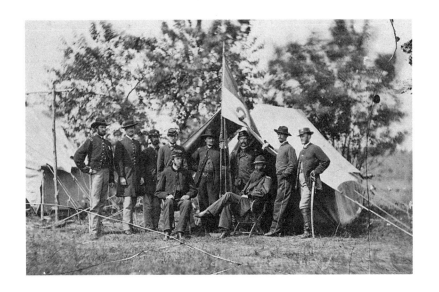

7. (*opposite top*) Gen. H. Judson Kilpatrick.
Courtesy of the Library of Congress,
LC-DIG-cwpb-00983.

8. (*opposite bottom*) Gen. George Gordon
Meade. Courtesy of the Library of Congress,
LC-USZ-62-68321.

9. (*above*) General Gregg (*seated, right*) and
his staff, ca. 1863. Courtesy of the Library of
Congress, LC-BH 841 3.

10. Gen. George Armstrong Custer. Courtesy of the Library of Congress.

11. Gen. James E. B. Stuart, CSA. Courtesy of the Library of Congress.

12. Gen. Ulysses S. Grant. Courtesy of
the Library of Congress, LC-USZ-903.

13. (*From left*) Generals Wesley Merritt, Gregg,
Philip H. Sheridan, Henry E. Davies, James H.
Wilson, and Alfred T. A. Torbert, 1864. Courtesy
of the Library of Congress, LC-DIG-ppmsca-34134.

14. Gen. Wade Hampton, CSA. Courtesy of the Library of Congress.

15. David McMurtrie Gregg, ca. 1903. Courtesy of the Library of Congress, LC-ppmsdca-49599.

16. Gregg statue, Pennsylvania State
Monument, Gettysburg Battlefield.
Gettysburg Daily.

17. (*opposite*) Gregg statue, Reading,
Pennsylvania. Photograph by Fred Paul.

18. Col. (later Gen.) John Irvin Gregg. Courtesy of the U.S. Army Heritage and Education Center, Carlisle Barracks, Pennsylvania.

7

Days of Strife and Glory

T he battle of June 9, 1863, had a lasting effect on both cavalries. Although Alfred Pleasonton had failed to deal Jeb Stuart the crippling blow that his army commander desired, he had weakened and disorganized his opponent to the point that Stuart would not start north at full strength for a week after the fight. Until a major refit was completed, other, smaller bodies of cavalry and mounted infantry would guide Robert E. Lee to, across, and above the Potomac.

The pleased, even jubilant, Federals also reorganized, but mainly on paper. On June 11 Pleasonton reduced the structure of his command by eliminating Colonel Duffié's division. The Frenchman had performed poorly enough at Brandy Station, even given Gregg's misuse of him, that Pleasonton dropped him all the way to regimental command (a contributing factor was Pleasonton's intense distrust of foreign-born officers). Gregg profited from the man's downfall; seven of Duffié's regiments were absorbed into the new 2nd Cavalry Division, including the familiar faces of the 8th and 16th Pennsylvania. Gregg organized the expanded force—which he would command for the rest of his war service—into three brigades headed by Cols. John McIntosh, Judson Kilpatrick, and John Irvin Gregg. Meanwhile, John Buford was formally given command of the 1st Division, which included not only the Reserve Brigade but also two squadrons of the 12th Illinois, formerly under David Gregg.[1]

The latter was gratified to be assigned such a mighty command, which Pleasonton reviewed along with Buford's division on the afternoon of June 11. One proud participant recalled that "the day was beautiful, and the troopers made a splendid appearance." In turn, Gregg was proud of the way the 3rd Division had comported itself two days earlier. As he wrote in an address distributed to every trooper, "Your repeated bold and resolute charges upon the enemy's brigades at Brandy Station merit the highest commendation and fully establish the superiority of the sabre as a cavalry weapon when wielded by the strong hands of brave men."[2]

Immediately after the battle the 2nd Division was assigned to patrol the river between Beverly and Kelly's Fords, connecting on the right with Buford's pickets and on the left with various infantry units. On June 13 one of Gregg's brigades was dispatched to Warrenton, from there to scout toward the Blue Ridge gaps where, according to persistent rumors, Lee was heading. By then, however, it was too late to preempt the invasion of the North. Richard S. Ewell's corps, leading the way, had left Culpeper Court House on June 10 and was now in the Shenandoah Valley; one day later it would attack and carry the major communications hub at Winchester. On June 15 Longstreet had also departed for the same valley by way of Ashby's and Snicker's Gaps. The previous day A. P. Hill had begun to pull up stakes at Fredericksburg to join the exodus.[3]

Hooker, belatedly aware of the enemy's movements, ordered an army-wide pullback in the direction of the supply depot at Manassas Junction. In that area the army would be in position to protect Washington, wherever Lee was heading. By June 14 Pleasonton's horsemen were marching up the Orange and Alexandria Railroad toward the depot; soon afterward Gregg, having drawn in his widely scattered detachments, was at Manassas, where his command enjoyed a long-overdue refit.[4]

By June 17 Jeb Stuart was finally in motion, having crossed the Rappahannock, heading for the Loudoun Valley. That morning Pleasonton, at Hooker's behest, started northwest from Manassas Junction. The previous day General-in-Chief Henry Halleck had reminded Fighting Joe of his main priority: "I do not think there is reliable information that the enemy has crossed the Potomac in any force. Where his main corps are, is still uncertain, and I know of no way to ascertain, excepting through your cavalry, which should be kept near enough to the enemy to at least be able to tell where he is."[5]

In a message sent to Lincoln that same day, Hooker promised to hunt for Lee with "vigor and power." The next morning he directed Pleasonton: "Put the main body of your command in the vicinity of Aldie, and push out reconnaissances toward Winchester, Berryville, and Harper's Ferry." Hooker vowed to hit the road by 3 a.m. but Pleasonton did not move for at least two more hours, suggesting that vigor was not one of his watchwords. Leading the column was Gregg's division minus one regiment (the 1st Rhode Island under the unfortunate Colonel Duffié, which had been dispatched by Pleasonton on an unsupported reconnaissance to Middleburg that would end disastrously). Also missing was McIntosh's brigade, having been detached for rear guard and wagon-escort duty as well as to picket the lower reaches of the Bull Run Mountains.[6]

Hooker had ordered Pleasonton to halt his first day's march at least five miles from Aldie in the vicinity of Gum Spring, but the cavalry leader, who realized that either that day or the next he would have to pass through the town and the neighboring gap, pressed ahead. Nine miles from the village he ordered Gregg to send a brigade through the defile and from there to Front Royal on the Shenandoah River. Gregg placed Kilpatrick's command, the 2nd New York, in advance. Although not at full strength—three hundred of its men remained in Yorktown, still awaiting transport north—the 2nd moved forward at a rapid clip just as Rebel horsemen neared the pass from the other side. The result was a meeting engagement, an encounter that surprised and rocked both forces.

With Kilpatrick at least temporarily checked, a reconnaissance party sized up the situation and Gregg hastened to the front, placing his field headquarters on a hill just north of the town. Informed that a heavy force blocked the road—Fitz Lee's brigade, led by Col. Thomas T. Munford—he ordered Kilpatrick to attack, supported by the just-arrived brigade of Irvin Gregg. Kilpatrick at first sought to secure two enemy-held byways, more than a mile apart at their widest divergence, that forked just west of Aldie: the Little River (or Ashby's Gap) Turnpike and, to the north, the Snickersville Pike. Because high ground rose at the junction of the roads Kilpatrick found he could not observe and thus control the fighting that broke out on both. As at Brandy Station, he elected to attack piecemeal on the lower pike, the 6th Ohio following the 2nd New York. His decision, however, may have been a product of the narrowness of the road, which left no room for a heavier attack.[7]

The opposing forces clashed violently. Following profligate use of saber and pistol and the downing of men and horses, the Federals were driven to the rear by Munford's carbineers, bolstered by a section of artillery. A lull ensued, lasting until early afternoon. By then David Gregg, influenced by Kilpatrick's inability to make progress, shifted his attention to the enemy's left flank. At his order the 1st Massachusetts, followed briefly by the soon-to-retreat 4th New York, charged up the Snickersville Pike into another collision with Munford's men. The shooting and hacking contest ended with a portion of the Massachusetts regiment cut off from its main body. Eventually both segments were forced into a bloody retreat.

As of late afternoon Gregg had exercised minimal control of the action—perhaps because Pleasonton was at his shoulder throughout the day—content to leave the tactical decisions to Kilpatrick. But around 5:30, with daylight waning, he reinforced the 2nd Brigade with one of his cousin's outfits, the 1st Maine of Col. Calvin S. Douty. A new series of attacks commenced, in one of which a member of Pleasonton's staff took part. Capt. George Custer, ever the daredevil, rode all the way through the gray ranks while downing two opponents with his Toledo-steel sword before cutting his way back to the starting point. He returned with nary a scratch thanks to a nondescript hat and a dust-covered uniform of indecipherable hue.[8]

Although three separate attacks were required, the Mainers finally pried Munford from his defenses, which included a long stone wall on a farm along the north side of the turnpike. Gregg wrote that the 1st "charged the enemy at the critical moment, and in connection with the regiments of the Second Brigade . . . drove the enemy from the field, inflicting on him severe loss in killed, wounded, and prisoners." Success came with a price: 305 casualties including 5 officers killed or mortally wounded, one being the "brave and generous" Douty, felled by rifle balls.[9]

The day after the set-to on the rim of the Bull Run Mountains, Pleasonton, hoping to get a fix on Stuart's latest position, had Irvin Gregg's brigade scout toward Middleburg and Upperville, respectively five and twelve miles to the west. Instructed to take possession of the former place if possible, the colonel did so in mid-afternoon following five hours of skirmishing with portions of two Rebel brigades. At this point the fighting degenerated into an artillery exchange. Stuart, not wishing to subject the town to cannon fire, withdrew to a westward ridge, later christened Mount Defiance. Gregg held Middleburg till early evening when Pleasonton, fearing that the 3rd Brigade was fighting mounted infantry and thus was overmatched, ordered it back to Aldie. When he realized his mistake Pleasonton countermanded the order and David's cousin bivouacked a mile and a half from the town.[10]

On June 19 Pleasonton sent the 3rd Brigade back to Middleburg, which Stuart had reoccupied, supported at a distance by Union infantry. By 6 a.m., with the temperature climbing toward a high of ninety-eight degrees, Irvin Gregg's men—supported by Kilpatrick and, at a distance, elements of Buford's division—moved out the Ashby's Gap Turnpike against heavy small-arms and artillery fire. At first progress was satisfactory. Overcoming stout resistance, the 4th Pennsylvania, supported by the 16th Pennsylvania and 10th New York, cleared Middleburg of Stuart's men, who took up positions west of the town. Stuart placed a battery just below the turnpike, at least one of its pieces in the road itself. The guns supported the dismounted North Carolinians of Beverly Robertson below the pike, and, north of the road, the Virginians of Gregg's West Point friend John Randolph Chambliss, Jr., commanding Rooney Lee's brigade following the latter's disabling at Brandy Station. Thanks largely to their artillery strength the Rebels brought their enemy's advance to a halt. By 8 a.m., half of Gregg's men, mounted and afoot, had been committed to a static skirmish line almost a mile wide.

During the two hours of indecisive skirmishing that ensued, Colonel Gregg (known to his devoted officers and men as "Long John") did his best to conceal them from plunging cannon fire. Finally General Gregg—determined to be more proactive than he had been at Aldie—resolved to break the stalemate. He desired Long John to "disregard the menaces on his flanks and to direct all his available force upon the center." Perhaps because the rest of his staff was otherwise occupied, he called on Private Meyer to "ride up to Colonel Gregg, present my compliments, and ask him why he does not drive those people out of there." The reference was to a position north of the pike where Chambliss occupied a wheat field and another stone wall.

Braving rifle and carbine fire, the headquarters clerk located Irvin Gregg and relayed the message. The colonel patiently explained: "If I order a charge across there it will be subjected to an enfilading fire from those men behind the stone wall and it will be very expensive of men." He asked Meyer to petition David to circle behind the wheat field with a dismounted force and attack the rear of the position, "whereupon the charge would be made." Meyer dutifully ran another gauntlet of fire to deliver the request, which was granted. At the division commander's order Judson Kilpatrick sent forward large detachments of two of his outfits while Irvin Gregg's 1st Maine, supported by Lt. William Fuller's Battery C, 3rd United States Artillery, bolstered the left and center of the skirmish line.[11]

Despite determined resistance the combined forces of Gregg and Kilpatrick achieved success. The 10th New York and a portion of the 1st Maine charged up the pike supported by skirmishers of the 2nd New York and 6th Ohio. After a succession of charges and countercharges the attackers forced Chambliss's men off a strategic ridge. Meanwhile, the Union left flank—the 4th and 16th Pennsylvania, augmented by additional elements of the 10th New York and 1st Maine—drove Robertson's men from the grounds of a walled cemetery and into a woods; dozens did not make it to the trees and were forced to surrender. The fighting continued until Stuart, late in the day, ordered his forces to withdraw two miles west of Middleburg. From there they could continue to deny the Yankees access to the Shenandoah Valley.[12]

Pleasonton did not contest the move, content to allow his supports to spell him. These included two regiments of the Reserve Brigade— the only portion of Buford's division to see action this day—which had crossed Goose Creek near Millville, two and a half miles northwest of Middleburg, in an ultimately unsuccessful attempt to turn Stuart's upper flank. Around 5 p.m. another supporting force, a division of Meade's V Corps, had moved to Aldie to secure the cavalry's rear. Despite having been held short of the Blue Ridge, Gregg believed that his men had outfought Stuart's vaunted cavaliers—that in fact, "all acquitted themselves well."[13]

The combatants rested and regrouped on Saturday, June 20, before going at it again the next morning. Pleasonton, now desperate to gain entrance to the Shenandoah, was authorized to call on Col. Strong Vincent's infantry brigade for close assistance. This day Gregg and Buford were supposed to work in tandem, joining forces near Upperville. But Buford experienced rough going, failing to locate Stuart's left flank and rear thanks to unexpectedly difficult terrain and the potent opposition of Grumble Jones and Chambliss even as they retired beyond Upperville at Stuart's order. In the end Buford roamed too far from the principal fighting to influence it in any significant way. At Pleasonton's order, however, late in the day he detached the Reserve Brigade, now led by Maj. Samuel H. Starr, to help Gregg battle what Buford believed to be a superior force.[14]

Gregg had received his orders for the day at his headquarters in a Middleburg hotel. They gave him to understand that he was to feint toward the enemy on the Ashby's Gap Turnpike while the 1st Division attacked to the north. About 8 a.m. he advanced skirmishers from several of Kilpatrick's regiments toward Upperville, Vincent's foot soldiers covering their left flank. The opposition this day was supplied by the dismounted troopers of Hampton and Robertson, crouching behind a series of stone walls at right angles to the Ashby's Gap Pike and along a shallow stream, Kirk's Branch. To dislodge them Colonel Vincent, moving in conjunction with the cavalry, advanced against the center of the enemy position with one of his four regiments, followed closely by two others while the fourth menaced the Rebel right.

Stuart claimed that his brigades held their ground "decidedly for a long time" despite steadily increasing pressure and the disabling of one of Hampton's cannons by a shell from Fuller's battery. At some point, however, he withdrew most of his men to high ground behind Crummey's (or Cromwell's) Run. Pressed again on the flanks by infantry and cavalry, Stuart then retired nearly four miles to the banks of Goose Creek, which crossed the turnpike four miles west of Middleburg. One of Vincent's outfits resumed its flanking efforts while another, assisted by the 2nd and 4th New York Cavalry, was poised to cross the Goose Creek bridge into the midst of Stuart's latest position. The 2nd, which Kilpatrick sent flying down the pike, was first across; on the far bank it drove the graybacks from the shelter of yet another stone wall. Closely observing his more mobile comrades, Vincent decided that "the charges of the cavalry, a sight [he] had never before witnessed, were truly inspiring." For his part, Stuart, who had not wished to defile the sabbath by engaging in a pitched battle, was inspired to withdraw about two miles to the outskirts of Upperville.[15]

"From Goose Creek to Upperville," Gregg would write, "the retreat of the enemy was rapid." Stuart halted in front of the town and deployed Hampton's brigade to defend the place. Kilpatrick responded by leading another hell-bent-for-leather charge, only to be charged in turn in front and flank and forced to withdraw. The Federals rallied and brought on another series of attacks and counterattacks during which Kilpatrick was briefly taken prisoner. Eventually the 6th Ohio fought its way into Upperville, though at heavy cost, before falling back along with the rest of its brigade.[16]

With the 2nd Brigade reeling, Gregg, accompanied by brother Tom and other members of his staff, dashed forward, perhaps to help Kilpatrick's men re-form. The gesture nearly proved fatal when a piece of shell struck the general's horse in the stomach beyond the saddle girth, grazing the rider's leg. As the animal sank to the ground Gregg dismounted and remounted on a horse provided by an orderly. Though fatally wounded, when the charge resumed the horse struggled to its feet and ran beside Gregg, "his entrails dragging on the ground," his nose pressing against the general's injured leg. At Gregg's command, "For God's sake, somebody shoot him," Private Meyer did so, pressing his pistol against the horse's ear.[17]

Upon Kilpatrick's fallback, Alfred Pleasonton ordered Major Starr's just-arrived Regulars to launch an attack of their own, aimed at Hampton's position below the turnpike. Once a bastion of military professionalism, the Reserve Brigade had become skeletonized with recruits as well as top-heavy with inexperienced officers. Two of its regiments, the 1st and 6th U.S., attempted to charge but started off before fully formed and properly aligned. Both became strung out even as they were raked by Hampton's men from behind good cover. Three of his regiments then countercharged and sent the Regulars to the rear, broken and bleeding.

Kilpatrick's brigade had also been thrown into confusion and retreat, but its commander, rescued from captivity, rallied his ranks for another assault, this one southeast of Upperville, supported by the redoubtable 1st Maine and other elements of Irvin Gregg's brigade. Plowing into Robertson's troopers north of the pike, the Federals forced many to withdraw until counterattacked by other Rebels less willing to call it a day. In turn, the Rebels were quickly taken in front and flank and brought to a halt. Re-forming, they charged again but were forced to the rear by the mounted 4th Pennsylvania and the now dismounted 1st Maine.[18]

Upon Robertson's late afternoon withdrawal, Stuart hauled his forces through Ashby's Gap. So ended a day of frenetic combat that had inflicted almost two hundred casualties on the Federals, seventy-three in Gregg's division. With the Loudoun Valley free of Rebel cavalry, Gregg could look with pride on his division's accomplishments despite a week of mixed results. In his official report he declared that "in these engagements—at Aldie, Middleburg, and Upperville—the brigades of this division demonstrated the very greatest gallantry." Further opportunities for gallantry awaited.[19]

The day following Stuart's departure from Upperville, Pleasonton fell back to rejoin Hooker, who was finally on the move. Stuart was willing to let his opponent go, for by June 22 he had completed his screening operation and was heading for the Blue Ridge Mountains to connect with Lee. The Confederate invasion was nearing high tide. As early as June 15 horsemen from the western Virginia brigade of Brig. Gen. Albert G. Jenkins had entered the Keystone State, occupying Greencastle and Chambersburg and gathering spoils from the countryside. Ewell would follow on June 22, and within five days the entire Army of Northern Virginia would be on Pennsylvania soil, pointing in the general direction of Harrisburg, the state capital.[20]

The Confederates' approach generated a combination of panic and resolve in Pennsylvania. Aware that the Army of the Potomac lay too far to the south to protect the commonwealth, Governor Curtin had mobilized militia and short-term volunteers, initially to combat an anticipated raid by Stuart. Those called out included Robert Allison McMurtrie of Hollidaysburg. David Gregg's favorite uncle would help organize troops to defend iron furnaces, railroads, and other likely targets of the invaders.[21]

Pleasonton may not have gotten the advantage of his adversary in every recent instance but his cavalry had gathered intelligence that had a bearing on the unfolding campaign. After Stuart retired late on June 21 Buford had sent scouts through Ashby's Gap; peering west, they confirmed Lee's presence in force in the Shenandoah Valley. Prodded into action, Hooker had moved his army from Fairfax Station into lower Maryland while throwing out advance forces including Buford's division, which would cross the Mason-Dixon Line before month's end.[22]

Hooker's belated efforts to curtail Lee, added to the lingering stigma of his drubbing at Chancellorsville, had made him a lame duck in the eyes of his political and military superiors. His shaky tenure ended on June 27 at the army's new headquarters at Frederick, ostensibly the result of strategic differences with Halleck and Stanton and Hooker's demands to be reinforced. George Meade, a Pennsylvanian who could be counted on to defend his state, was assigned to replace him.

By the hour of Meade's appointment most of the army's cavalry had crossed the Potomac, along with the bulk of the army, on a pontoon bridge at Edwards Ferry. Gregg and Buford, prior to the latter's plunge into Pennsylvania, had covered the crossing—except for a single brigade of infantry, theirs were the last troops to leave the south bank. At Frederick Meade called on some of his newly acquired subordinates, including Pleasonton, to whom he admitted his unfamiliarity with the strength, condition, and needs of the mounted arm. On the brigadier's advice Meade approved a new round of organizational and personnel changes quickly sanctioned by the War Department. A third division was added to the Cavalry Corps, made up of regiments previously part of the defense forces of Washington. Pleasonton was gratified by his enlarged authority, although Meade made clear that he considered his cavalry chief an administrator rather than an operational commander.[23]

The expansion produced a command consisting of some 12,700 officers and troopers. Kilpatrick, recently appointed a brigadier general, was tabbed to lead the new division, comprising two brigades to be headed by "officers with the proper dash to command cavalry," as Pleasonton put it. Those officers were Elon Farnsworth and George Custer, each of whom made an unprecedented transition from captain to star rank. A third company-level commander, Wesley Merritt, made the same jump to lead the Reserve Brigade of the 1st Division. A few days after the appointments were sanctioned, Pleasonton received his second star.[24]

Once Meade took over, the Army of the Potomac made its final push to Pennsylvania. To pave the way, the cavalry was split up, Buford guarding the army's left flank, Kilpatrick its front, and Gregg the far right. The immediate task was to relocate Stuart's cavalry—the brigades of Hampton, Fitz Lee, and Chambliss—who were traveling well east of the invasion route, having received Lee's grudging permission to go their own way northward. On June 30 Kilpatrick was the first to make contact with the Rebel raiders at Hanover, Pennsylvania, where mounted and dismounted warriors clashed for hours in the heart of the town as well as on outlying roads.[25]

Gregg got to see the effects at first hand one day after the drawn battle, by which time the adversaries had departed the area. Around midnight on July 2, following an excessively fatiguing march during which detachments had visited such disparate venues as New Market, Liberty, Ridgeville, and Westminster in response to a flurry of sometimes contradictory orders, the 2nd Division limped into Hanover. Its four thousand riders, including the men of two batteries and a separate section of artillery, cast "moving shadows" on the buildings along Centre Square. Looking about, they found every street and alley littered with the debris of combat: makeshift barricades, scattered arms and equipment, and dead horses.[26]

By this time, according to Capt. William Miller of the 3rd Pennsylvania, the 2nd Division "had become a sorry-looking body of men, having been in the saddle day and night almost continuously for three weeks, without a change of clothing or an opportunity for a general wash; moreover [it] had been much reduced by short rations and exhaustion, and mounted on horses whose bones were plainly visible to the naked eye." In addition to being worn out, Gregg's command was at two-thirds strength. The previous day Pennock Huey's brigade and Fuller's battery had been sent to Manchester, Maryland, to guard the approaches to the army's rear supply base. In coming days almost half of McIntosh's brigade would be lost to Gregg, its 1st Massachusetts and 1st Pennsylvania also assigned to detached duty.[27]

The remainder of the command spent three hours in Hanover. While dead-tired riders stretched out on the sidewalks, Gregg conferred with local residents who praised the heroics of Kilpatrick, Farnsworth, and Custer and tried to describe Stuart's departure route. Afterward Gregg caught an hour or so of sleep on a wooden horse block in the square before rising and rousing his men, who were soon trotting along the road to Littlestown, Adams County.

They rode toward the steady thump of artillery emanating from the road hub of Gettysburg, where Lee was concentrating his scattered forces. At about 10 a.m., having veered off Littlestown Road onto the more direct Hanover Road, the column halted five miles east of the battlefield. There messengers from the front found Gregg and escorted him to cavalry headquarters in the village (because Meade regarded Pleasonton as a glorified staff officer, he had tethered him to his own headquarters). Meeting his superior near the town's Evergreen Cemetery, Gregg received orders and a situation report. He learned that the battle, which had been raging at white heat since the previous morning, remained undecided. It might well have ended prematurely but for the efforts of stalwarts including John Buford, who at the head of the brigades of Cols. William Gamble and Thomas C. Devin and a battery had held back thousands of Rebels coming in from the west and north until Meade's infantry advance arrived to relieve him. Because Lee put greater weight into the fight, day one had ended with full-scale Union retreat, but the beaten men rallied and held on. With both armies now on the field in force, July 2 had become another day of extreme carnage in sweltering heat, the fate of the Union hanging in the balance.[28]

In Gregg's absence emissaries from Pleasonton led his troops, under Colonel McIntosh, a mile and a half closer to the battlefield, halting them near the intersection of the Hanover and Low Dutch (or Salem

Church) Roads. At that dusty crossroads three and a half miles east of Gettysburg Gregg's truncated command, perhaps 2,400 strong, could protect the army's right flank and rear, a mission Pleasonton had specifically assigned it. McIntosh bivouacked his own brigade, to which were attached the four guns of Capt. Alanson M. Randol's Battery E/G, 1st U.S. Artillery, north of the Hanover Road opposite Irvin Gregg's position. To seek out an enemy force known to be in the area, McIntosh placed skirmishers of the 10th New York on heavily wooded Brinkerhoff's Ridge, which intersected the Hanover Road nearly at a right angle about two miles from Gettysburg.[29]

By the time Gregg returned to the crossroads, around 6 p.m., he found the New Yorkers trading shots with foot soldiers massing among the trees. The opposition came from the 2nd Virginia Infantry of the famed Stonewall Brigade. The Virginians constituted the left flank of a column that their corps commander, Dick Ewell, was about to hurl at the Union occupants of Culp's Hill, a mile and a half to the southwest. Though doubtful that he understood what the 2nd Virginia had in mind, Gregg felt compelled to engage the regiment and keep it immobile.

The exchange of carbine fire and musketry soon escalated into a major skirmish, which Gregg hoped to end by committing a phalanx of fifty dismounted skirmishers. Advancing in some force, the 2nd Virginia compelled the dismounted skirmishers to fall back. The Rebels were forced back in turn by a detachment of the 3rd Pennsylvania, which had formed on the right of the 10th New York. Two squadrons of the 3rd dismounted, crossed a shallow stream just east of the ridge, and headed toward a stone wall that they sized up as the key to the entire position. As they ran, equally perceptive Virginians made for the wall from the other side.

The Pennsylvanians won the footrace, but just barely. From behind the wall they unleashed a "withering fire" from their repeating carbines into the faces of the enemy no more than twenty yards away. Under the fusillade and the pounding of the horse batteries on the Hanover Road, the foot soldiers conceded defeat, melting away into a wheat field and the woods beyond. They reemerged after dark, attacked again, and unhinged the cavalry's right flank, but after what the historian of the 3rd called "a considerable amount of trouble" the line was reestablished and secured.[30]

Thanks to the opposition of Gregg's men and the threat they continued to pose well into the evening, the 2nd Virginia failed to join the assault on strategic Culp's Hill, which fell short of success. In its first spate of combat during what would prove to be the war's pivotal battle, Gregg's division had made a substantial contribution to its army's security.

The fighting just ended had cost the 2nd Division more than a dozen casualties, but Gregg's men held the ground around the Hanover–Low Dutch crossroads stretching west to Brinkerhoff's Ridge. The relatively flat and open terrain, which was intersected by two watercourses, Cress and Little's Runs as well as by a second, smaller stretch of high ground, Cress Ridge, appeared a logical route of any Confederates intending to gain the rear of the Army of the Potomac. For this reason Gregg was reluctant to relinquish the position his skirmishers had hammered out in the fading light of day. And thus he was concerned when around 10 p.m. he received an order from Pleasonton to withdraw to a position along the Baltimore Pike where his brigades would share space with the guns, caissons, and limbers of the army's artillery reserve. Pleasonton described the position as an important one but Gregg doubted that it was as strategically significant as the one he had been told to vacate. Acting on that belief, he had left a small force on the recent field of fighting just in case Ewell—or Stuart, or anyone else seeking to make trouble in the Union rear—showed up there.[31]

Around 6 a.m. on the soon-to-be-scorching third of July, a courier from Pleasonton reached Gregg's bivouac with orders for him to "place a force of cavalry and battery" on a ridge along the Baltimore Pike near its crossing of Rock Creek. This force could shield the right flank of Maj. Gen. Henry W. Slocum's XII Corps against renewed attempts by Ewell to take Culp's Hill. Reportedly General Meade considered the position "so important that it must be held at all hazards," but, again, Gregg was doubtful. According to Gregg, he requested the courier to return to Pleasonton "and to state to him that I regarded the situation on the right of our army as exceedingly perilous, that I was familiar with the character of the country east of Brinkerhoff's Ridge," and that if this ground "was not covered by a sufficient force of cavalry it would be to invite an attack upon our rear with possibly disastrous results." Only Gregg seemed in position to hold the vulnerable area. Buford's fought-out troopers had been allowed to go to the rear to refit, and the whereabouts of Kilpatrick's division was not definitely known.[32]

Sometime after full daybreak, with the guns at Gettysburg again in full throat, Pleasonton's courier returned to Gregg's bivouac to confirm the order to move toward Culp's Hill. The corps commander addressed Gregg's alarm only to the extent of authorizing him to assign a replacement force to occupy the Hanover–Low Dutch Road vicinity. The nearest source of manpower was Kilpatrick, now known to be at Two Taverns on the Baltimore Pike almost three miles south of the Rock Creek crossing, He had reached that place with the men of Farnsworth and Custer and the battery of A. C. M. Pennington following an encounter with Stuart's wayward raiders at Hunterstown, twenty-nine miles above Gettysburg. The fighting featured a spirited clash between Custer's Michigan Cavalry Brigade and the troopers of Wade Hampton, guarding Stuart's rear and the Yankee supply train, 125 wagons long, that Stuart had captured five days earlier outside Rockville, Maryland. The clash ended indecisively, although Custer burnished his already secured reputation for aggressive (or reckless) leadership, having been shot out of the saddle while leading a charge on a well-defended position south of the town.[33]

Gregg sent a galloper to Two Taverns with the help-wanted summons. The courier arrived there about 9 a.m. to find that Kilpatrick and Farnsworth had ridden off to defend the army's extreme left flank near the rocky knoll known as Little Round Top. The advance element of Custer's brigade had followed but its main body was still on hand and its leader readily heeded Gregg's call for assistance (when or whether he informed Kilpatrick of his decision is not known). Sometime before 10 a.m. Custer, accompanied by Pennington's battery, was on hand where Gregg wanted him. Upon arriving he deployed units of his 5th and 6th Michigan to cover the crossroads and seek out any enemy troops in the area. He also dispatched parties of approximately

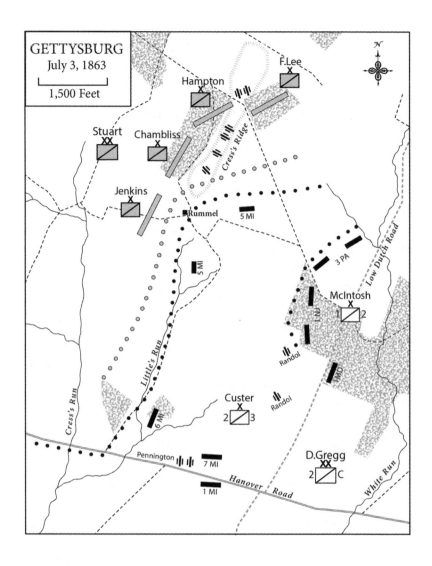

Map 5. Gettysburg, July 3, 1863. Created by Paul Dangel.

fifty men to bolster both of his flanks, one moving well up the Low Dutch Road, the other along the turnpike to York.[34]

At some point Custer reported to his superior, whereupon Gregg saw that the so-called "Boy General with the Golden Locks" had a fashion sense in keeping with his unorthodox tactics. The twenty-three-year-old brigadier was clad in a uniform of his own design: pants and coat of black velvet awash in gold lace, under the latter a navy blue shirt and a crimson-colored necktie, and on his cinnamon-colored head a wide-brimmed black hat adorned with gilt cord and a silver star. But there was more to the man than an ensemble one observer would describe as that of "a circus rider gone mad." Gregg would have been familiar with the qualities that had placed a star on a lieutenant's shoulder.[35]

Gregg learned that upon arrival Custer had unlimbered Lieutenant Pennington's four 3-inch ordnance rifles in the southwestern corner of the road junction, facing west. At that hour he did not know that a threat was emerging from the north, via Cress Ridge. Stuart was heading toward that point with Hampton, Fitz Lee, Chambliss, the recently added brigade of Albert Jenkins (led by Col. Milton Ferguson following Jenkins's wounding on July 2) and three light batteries, an aggregate of more than four thousand officers and men.

Stuart had descended from Gettysburg after reporting at Lee's headquarters the previous afternoon, seven days after cutting loose from the army that in his absence had wandered almost blindly though enemy territory. Lee was more than a bit upset with his cavalry leader, and he let Stuart know it. Today the Beau Sabreur was determined to make amends by detouring south and east of the firing lines. From a well-chosen position below the turnpike to York he could cover Ewell's lower flank, as Lee intended, and perhaps also strike the rear of the Army of the Potomac while its attention was turned in the other direction. Though not specifically coordinated with the infantry assault Lee planned to launch against the Union center, Stuart might create chaos and panic in the enemy's ranks at a propitious time, perhaps producing a breakthrough.[36]

As of 10 a.m. Gregg had no idea that Stuart was so near, but he remained concerned that the Hanover–Low Dutch intersection would provide an enterprising enemy with access to the Union rear. He was likewise concerned that Custer's 1,800 "Wolverines" were insufficient to repulse a threat such as that which the Stonewall Brigade, if still in the area, might have posed. Acting on his own judgment and fully realizing that in doing so he could be charged with refusing to obey given orders, he directed McIntosh to return his brigade to a point midway between the Baltimore Pike and the Hanover Road within supporting distance of Custer. McIntosh did so, and he remained in that position for three hours, a move seemingly validated by a message Gregg received shortly after noon from Maj. Gen. Oliver Otis Howard, commanding the XI Corps. Howard's pickets south of Gettysburg had observed a long column of Confederate horsemen, accompanied by guns and vehicles, moving out the York Pike toward Gregg's position.[37]

It would appear that Pleasonton, who had relayed Howard's communiqué, now agreed with Gregg's determination to stay and fight, for he formally ordered the return of both Irvin Gregg and McIntosh to the crossroads. Even so, the corps leader revealed his ignorance of the gravity of the situation by directing Gregg to relieve Custer and return him to Kilpatrick. Initially Gregg acquiesced; sometime after 1 p.m. McIntosh began to take over Custer's positions and the latter moved to vacate the field. Custer did so, however, only after suggesting to one of Gregg's subordinates that the trees on Cress Ridge were full of Rebels. This was alarming news. As Captain Miller of the 3rd Pennsylvania would observe, while the Confederates were well covered, "Gregg's troops were not so favorably situated. Occupying a line about three miles long . . . through an open country, they were in full view of the enemy." The relative strength of the positions bothered Gregg but there seemed no help for it.[38]

In any case, McIntosh moved his leading regiment, the 1st New Jersey, up the Low Dutch Road and onto the fields of a farmer named Lott some six hundred yards north of the crossroads. The Jerseymen deployed in woods on either side of the road, most of them in the role of mounted skirmishers. The colonel massed the rest of his men in columns of squadrons south of the timber. Initially Irvin Gregg's brigade was placed well up the Baltimore Pike, near Wolf's Hill. His 1,800 men connected with the foot soldiers of the XII Corps, its line stretching from Brinkerhoff's Ridge to the eastern flank of Cress Ridge. In this

reserve position part of the 3rd Brigade nearly came under the fire
of Confederate batteries south of Gettysburg paving the way for the
attack on Meade's center. The thunderous cannonade would endure for
almost two hours. One of Gregg's men recalled that "the very ground
shook and trembled," while the smoke from the guns made it appear
that "thousands of acres of timber [were] on fire." For all its heart-
stopping effects, the barrage would prove ineffective. Pickett's Charge
would end as it had begun—a gallant but doomed attempt to salvage
Lee's final foray in the North.[39]

Stuart opened the fighting on the cavalry's front by directing elements
of Ferguson's brigade to descend Cress Ridge and take cover behind the
outbuildings of Pennsylvania Dutchman John Rummel, some three-
fourths of a mile northwest of the Lott farm. With Gregg still at the
previous evening's bivouac conferring by courier with Custer and receiving reports from his scouts, around 2 p.m. Colonel McIntosh reacted
to the threat by dismounting much of the 1st New Jersey and sending
it through the fields toward the enemy's position. Ferguson's sharpshooters occupied the Rummel barn and a fence along the south edge
of the farm, and a quickly escalating skirmish broke out. Stuart supported Ferguson with artillery, which was promptly answered by Pennington's battery below the Hanover Road and the two sections under
Randol on the Low Dutch Road. When McIntosh saw what he was up
against he extended his line by moving two squadrons of the 3rd Pennsylvania across Little's Run onto the New Jersey regiment's left flank.
At about the same time the remainder of the 3rd, including two companies under Captain Miller, moved up the Low Dutch Road. There,
just beyond Lott's Woods, they took station as mounted skirmishers,
protecting the far right flank.

Stuart fed more men into the fight than McIntosh's understrength
command could cope with. Of necessity the colonel petitioned Gregg
to move the 3rd Brigade to his assistance, but it was too far to the rear
to be immediately available. Gregg did, however, respond by making
the most fateful tactical decision of his military career. Leaving his bivouac, he rode to the front and took command of the entire field. He
met first with Custer, some of whose men had begun to leave the area in

search of Kilpatrick. Learning of Custer's belief that Cress Ridge sheltered hundreds of Rebels, Gregg, as he later recalled, told the younger man: "If such was his opinion, I would like to have the assistance of his brigade." Gregg quoted Custer as replying, "If you will give me an order to remain I will only be too happy to do it."[40]

Leaving Custer, Gregg began making dispositions. He moved Irvin Gregg's brigade—just returned from a misguided and then countermanded order to report on Rebel dispositions inside Gettysburg—down the Hanover Road onto high ground west of the crossroads. From there his cousin could protect the division's left flank while also blocking Stuart's most direct route to the Union rear, the Baltimore Pike. At the same time, undoubtedly at Gregg's suggestion, Custer extended the left of the dismounted line along Little's Run while ordering Col. Russell A. Alger's 5th Michigan to spell the New Jersey and Pennsylvania troopers. Having worked their seven-shot repeaters for more than an hour, both outfits were low on ammunition.

As the Wolverines moved to the front, Stuart from his high ground advanced dismounted members of Chambliss's brigade. They pressed McIntosh's retiring troopers so closely that the latter were forced to turn about and confront them. With the help of Alger, whom Custer had instructed to hold his ground at all hazards, the Rebels were eventually driven back, but not far enough to prevent them from continuing to take a toll on their adversaries. At the same time they were applying a steady pressure on the far Union flanks, where both of Custer's parties were driven in.

At this point, the 5th Michigan's supply of cartridges began to dwindle. The flanks of the regiment were imperiled, and it began to look as if Alger, despite Custer's injunction, would have to relinquish his critical position. Then the highly regarded leader of Alger's skirmish line, Maj. Noah H. Ferry, was killed. Minus his guiding hand and again pressed by Ferguson and Chambliss, the entire Union line was driven back. The advantage appeared to have swung decisively toward the Confederates, but then came a lull in the fighting. Ferguson's men, too, had exhausted their ammunition, forcing them to abandon the Rummel farm and take shelter on Cress Ridge.[41]

Stuart, though hard pressed all along the line, saw an opportunity to restart and control the fighting via a maneuver that would sweep the enemy off the board. Around 2:30 p.m., units of Fitz Lee's newly arrived brigade were sent forward with the 1st Virginia, the most celebrated mounted regiment in Confederate service, in the vanguard. The men of the 1st paused briefly as their ranks were carefully aligned. Then, at a signal, they spurred toward the suddenly tenuous positions of McIntosh and Custer.

With his division depleted by more than a third and the remainder strewn in small groups across the field of battle, Gregg realized that only Custer was in a position to counter Stuart's offensive. He rode up to Col. William D. Mann of the 7th Michigan, whose regiment had begun to leave the area in response to Pleasonton's orders and had now just returned to the crossroads, and instructed him to charge the 1st Virginia, a command repeated immediately afterward by Custer. The boy general fell in with the head of the regiment as it started out. Within minutes the least experienced component of the Wolverine brigade, only 420 strong, was thundering toward the Rummel farm and the oncoming Rebels. As the opponents neared a collision parties from both armies, caught in the middle of the field, scrambled to let them pass. Other combatants, including two dismounted regiments of Chambliss's brigade ensconced behind farm fences, prepared to rake the flanks of the charging Wolverines.

The rookies sliced through the first rank of the enemy but Chambliss's sharpshooters inflicted casualties well before Custer and Mann reached their target. The flank fire caused the column to veer off course and slam into the fence from which Alger's men and their supports had fled. A huge pile-up followed, which the 1st Virginia took advantage of by firing into the mass of men and horses. About two hundred yards short of the Rummel farm Custer broke off the attack and led the survivors homeward, Lee's remounted men at his heels. "On came the rebel cavalry," wrote Capt. James H. Kidd of the 6th Michigan, "right toward the battery [Pennington's] we were supporting apparently sweeping everything before them." But when Battery M's guns started in, showering the enemy with shell and canister, the pursuers turned back, allowing the better part of the 7th Michigan to reach safety.[42]

Gregg and Custer saw that the fighting was far from over. About 3 p.m., with Pickett's Charge underway, Stuart committed his reserves to a final effort to reach the Baltimore Pike. Up came a strong, seasoned, and savvy brigade of three regiments from North and South Carolina and two regimental-size legions from Alabama, Georgia, and Mississippi. As they descended the high ground, Wade Hampton at their head, they drew expressions of awe from observers. Capt. Hampton S. Thomas of McIntosh's staff recalled that the Rebels "came on in magnificent style . . . yelling and looking like demons."[43]

Custer, covered now with as much grime as he had worn at Aldie, again rushed into the breach. He galloped to the head of the veteran 1st Michigan, which had been stationed, mounted, just west of the crossroads. To Col. Charles H. Town he calmly said, "I shall have to ask you to charge, and I want to go in with you." And he did, crying out, as the column changed from trot to gallop, "Come on, you Wolverines!"[44]

This time Custer directed the attack at the center of the oncoming Rebels, sweeping wide to avoid the fences that had waylaid the 7th Michigan. About a third of the way between the opposing lines the columns merged with a resounding crunch, horses and riders tumbling head over heels while those still in the saddle shot and swiped away at each other with abandon. Though outnumbered, the 1st Michigan made headway, assisted as it was by attacks against both of Hampton's flanks by detachments of the 1st New Jersey, 3rd Pennsylvania, and 5th and 7th Michigan as well as by division staff officers collected by Captain Thomas.

For perhaps half an hour the indecisive melee continued. A turning point occurred when Hampton was wounded by saber slashes and a gunshot, forcing him to the rear. Within minutes his men began to follow him to Cress Ridge, salvos from Pennington and Randol making "dreadful havoc in their ranks."

The Confederate withdrawal confirmed, Custer regrouped his scattered ranks and their supports and pulled back to the crossroads. The Federals retired in high spirits. With daylight waning, Stuart's grand effort to turn the Union flank and strike from the rear had failed and David McMurtrie Gregg, more than any other man on the field including George Custer, had seen to it.[45]

8

Six Months of Travail

David Gregg's role in the aftermath of Gettysburg was both anticlimactic and passing strange. Immediately on the heels of his greatest triumph, he virtually disappeared from the ranks of the army that was driving its enemy back to Virginia—as he did from the pages of history. On the rainy evening of July 4, as the Army of Northern Virginia, bloodied but unbowed, began its long trek homeward, George Meade's cavalry set out to harass and halt it short of the Mason-Dixon Line. Two-thirds of the corps did so either at full strength or greater. The divisions of John Buford and Judson Kilpatrick—the latter enlarged by absorbing Pennock Huey's brigade at Manchester—headed for Maryland, determined to overtake Robert E. Lee before he could cross the mountains en route to the Potomac. Over the next ten days, as Meade's infantry advanced ponderously in the general direction of its namesake river, Buford's and Kilpatrick's riders clashed time and again with the horsemen covering the enemy's principal retreat route, in the process destroying hundreds of supply wagons before able to clear Monterey Pass in the Blue Ridge extension known as South Mountain.

Only a portion of Gregg's division—which was fragmented on July 4, not to return to full strength until July 16—played an active role in the pursuit and it did so slowly and erratically. For the better part of that Independence Day McIntosh's brigade remained on the scene of the previous day's fighting, resting and refitting. In the evening it moved to the far left of the army near Round Top "to picket the different roads and to observe the movements of the enemy in that direction." Hampton Thomas of McIntosh's staff never forgot the conditions under which the march was made: "It was raining hard and so dark that we were compelled to use lanterns to remove the dead and dying out of our way, fearing our horses would crush them under their feet. The moans of the dying were horrible."[1]

In his new position McIntosh occupied the area recently held by Kilpatrick (to whom Gregg had returned George Custer after thanking him warmly for his assistance on July 3). The 1st Brigade remained south of Gettysburg for only a few hours; early on July 5 Alfred Pleasonton ordered it to move at once to Fairfield Gap in pursuit of Jeb Stuart's widely dispersed command. En route McIntosh clashed with enemy pickets, which, as he described it, he "drove in, while capturing a dispatch showing the position of both Generals Longstreet's and Ewell's corps"—copies of which he forwarded to both Meade and Pleasonton but apparently not to Gregg. On July 7 McIntosh fell in with a brigade of the VI Corps, which he accompanied in sparring with various enemy forces without halting their retreat. Five days later, having spent much of that period marking time near the entrance to the Cumberland Valley at Waynesboro, the brigade headed south and reported to David Gregg at Boonsboro, Maryland.[2]

While McIntosh wandered about, on July 4 John Irvin Gregg's brigade crossed the field of the previous day's struggle to inspect the position Stuart had vacated. From there it headed north, retracing the route Stuart had taken from Hunterstown to Gettysburg on July 2. Early on July 5, the 3rd Brigade crossed over to the northwestward-leading Chambersburg Pike, where it picked up the trail of a column of supply wagons and ambulances crammed with wounded and ill Confederates. The train was under escort by Brig. Gen. John D. Imboden's brigade of western Virginia cavalry, mounted infantry, and partisan rangers, accompanied by a battery and supported at a distance by elements of Fitz Lee's and Wade Hampton's commands.

Irvin Gregg overtook the Rebels late on the July 5 near Greenwood, Pennsylvania, the point at which the caravan of misery turned south, and brought on a brief, inconsequential skirmish. The next day, near Marion on the road between Chambersburg and Greencastle, a detachment of the brigade tangled with Fitz Lee's outriders without impeding

Imboden's progress. Following this, Gregg lagged behind his supposed quarry as if obliged to maintain a respectful distance until it was beyond his reach. On July 11 he broke off his languid pursuit and headed for Boonsboro, at the foot of South Mountain, where division headquarters had been established two days earlier.[3]

The official record fails to establish David Gregg's whereabouts during the critical week following the Confederates' departure from Gettysburg except for a communiqué from cavalry headquarters placing him near Frederick on July 8, where he had been ordered to round up far-flung detachments of his division. Pleasonton informed Gregg that "the remainder of [his] command will be ordered to join [him]" in a few days. The instructions confirm that Gregg accompanied none of his brigades (including Huey's) on their meandering trek through south-central Pennsylvania. Moreover, had the 2nd Division been kept intact and he at its head it seems unlikely that McIntosh and Irvin Gregg would have behaved as fecklessly as they did from July 4 to 10. Their timid, ineffective pursuit was not something the energetic and proactive brigadier would have tolerated.[4]

Gregg's report of the campaign fails to address his status during this period. He noted (perhaps with a measure of embarrassment) that "the peculiar service of the cavalry in the operations of the army subsequent to July 4, necessitated the constant detaching of brigades for special service. This was particularly the case in the Second Division." He might have added that neither Buford nor Kilpatrick marched and fought piecemeal. By avoiding fragmentation they became the only elements of Meade's army to overtake Lee before he could cross the rain-swollen river to his home state. The fact that Lee accomplished this once the water receded on July 14 was not the fault of either division commander.

Because evidence is lacking, one can only speculate as to what happened to David Gregg between July 4, when he was still at Gettysburg, and July 9, when he set up headquarters in the mountains of western Maryland. Given his performance on July 3—on which he was complimented by Meade's chief of staff, Maj. Gen. Daniel Butterfield, within hours of Stuart's repulse—it seems unlikely that he was suddenly relegated to the sidelines because of questions about his leadership. It is more likely that his absence had a physical basis, perhaps a recurrence of his tendency to fainting spells or his susceptibility to debilitating fevers. Whatever the cause, he went missing in action for a period during which his tactical acumen was sorely needed by his army.[5]

If some observers may have regarded Gregg's extended absence as suggestive of a reprimand, others close to him who had heard of his heroics at Gettysburg made certain the government knew otherwise. Over a several-week period commencing on July 7, dozens of family members, friends, and political officials petitioned the War Department not only for recognition of Gregg's recent deeds but for his immediate promotion. Congressman Samuel Calvin, who had procured the youngster's appointment to the Military Academy, requested Secretary of War Edwin M. Stanton to advance "the claims of Brig Genl David McM. Gregg for promotion to the rank of Major General—his recent achievements have won for him high position among the people of his native state." The congressman stressed: "In addition to his success as an officer . . . he is a high-toned temperate reliable gentleman." Calvin's sentiments were endorsed by the entire Pennsylvania congressional delegation, whose members wrote directly to President Lincoln on Gregg's behalf. Supporters of lower station chimed in, one telling the war secretary: "Put another star on his shoulder Mr. Stanton. He has earned it." Through the summer family members headed by David McMurtrie of Huntingdon kept up the pressure on various government officials.[6]

The campaign to promote Gregg would fall short. The unrelievedly slow process of advancement through the ranks ensured that he would not receive that second star—and then only by brevet—for sixteen months. Nevertheless, his many avid supporters helped keep his record on a par with that of other heroes of Gettysburg. In so doing they echoed the sentiments of superiors such as Pleasonton, who in his report of the campaign cited the commander of the 2nd Division for "handsomely" deflecting Stuart's thrust at the Union rear. The corps leader added his "warmest thanks for the intelligence and harmony" with which Gregg "invariably and skillfully executed every design transmitted from [Pleasonton's] headquarters."[7]

Soon after he regained command of the 1st and 3rd Brigades (Huey's 2nd Brigade would not rejoin him for a few more days) Gregg returned to the business of fighting, and in a dramatic way. On July 14, "agreeably to instructions from the major-general commanding Cavalry Corps," he led his abbreviated command to Harpers Ferry. The following day it crossed the Potomac on a pontoon bridge, thus becoming the only Union force south of the Potomac—the main army would not complete its crossing until July 19. The next day Gregg was informed by Pleasonton that the Army of Northern Virginia had returned to its home region and that he should keep within range of its left flank and rear. Told that Huey, finally freed up by Kilpatrick, was on his way to him, Gregg believed that he would soon have the strength to tackle Stuart's rear guard. Till then, however, he must be wary of being lured into a fight against unequal odds. He avoided Stuart's larger force that day and the next morning when occupying Halltown and Shepherdstown. But, as he wrote, "Having ascertained [by the morning of July 16] that with the force with me I could not successfully advance, I determined to withdraw toward Harper's Ferry, and from thence operate on another route."[8]

He was denied that opportunity. Around noon, a battalion of Irvin Gregg's 10th New York found itself assailed by a heavy force under Fitz Lee before it could depart Shepherdstown. Soon both McIntosh and Gregg were heavily involved, the former guarding the division's left flank between the roads to Harpers Ferry and Charles Town, the latter on the other flank, defending the roads to Martinsburg and Winchester. The men of both brigades, most of them dismounted and utilizing whatever cover the country afforded, including stumps and rocks, were soon fighting for their lives and hoping for Huey's immediate arrival. The 2nd Brigade did not reach the field, however, until almost too late. By then, wrote Sgt. Samuel Cormany of the 16th Pennsylvania, "we were under the hottest cross-fire we ever were in, and had to fall back on line with an old house and stone fence and stone piles."[9]

Realizing that his opponent lacked timely support, Stuart threw at him the rest of Lee's brigade as well as large helpings of John R. Chambliss's and Albert Jenkins's, supported by as many as six guns. Meanwhile, Grumble Jones's brigade took position on the Harpers

Ferry road, blocking what appeared to be the 2nd Division's only line of retreat. Hunkering down behind their meager defenses and working their repeaters as fast as they could fire and reload, Gregg's men repulsed a succession of attacks while mortally wounding Col. James H. Drake of the 1st Virginia.

As if never doubting that his line would hold, Gregg kept a firm grip on his composure. According to an officer who observed him closely, when an excited courier galloped up he found Gregg "riding leisurely along smoking his familiar meerschaum pipe." Apprised of an attack on a certain part of his line, "with that deliberation and coolness so characteristic of him, the General removed the pipe from his mouth and as he tapped the ashes from the bowl and placed the pipe in his side pocket asked, 'On which road?' On being informed the General at once proceeded to make such disposition of his troops as he deemed necessary."[10]

Not until sometime after 9 p.m. did Stuart—frustrated by the tenacity of McIntosh and Irvin Gregg and now facing Huey as well—begin to disengage. Aware of Jones's continued presence in his rear, David Gregg realigned his ranks, then retired by an old river road apparently unfamiliar to the enemy. By eight o'clock the next morning he and his men were safely in camp on Bolivar Heights, overlooking Harpers Ferry. The fighting had been severe; the division had suffered 104 casualties, almost twice as many as it had absorbed on July 2 and 3 combined. But it had survived a burgeoning crisis—that is what mattered.[11]

Within days of the clash at Shepherdstown, Meade's army crossed the Potomac before moving through the Loudoun Valley in the direction of Centreville and Manassas. Meade had failed to cut off Lee's escape; the Army of Northern Virginia had crossed into the Shenandoah Valley before passing relatively unmolested through the Blue Ridge to the Culpeper Court House vicinity.

Even so, the Army of the Potomac—in contrast to its frame of mind following Fredericksburg and Chancellorsville—was in uniformly high spirits. Only days after winning a critical struggle on Northern ground, shooing Lee back home, Meade's soldiers heard the heartening news from Mississippi, where on July 4 Maj. Gen. Ulysses S. Grant, the most consistently successful commander in the western theater, had forced the surrender of strategic Vicksburg. The capture of the stronghold gave the Union virtually unfettered access to the all-important Mississippi River while cutting the Confederacy in two. Though gained hundreds of miles away, Grant's success—following on the heels of his much-celebrated captures of garrisons on the Tennessee and Cumberland Rivers and his come-from-behind victory at Shiloh—was a potent stimulant to the morale of the Federals once again waging war in the Old Dominion.[12]

Worn down by excessive marching and some of the hardest fighting it had ever seen, the 2nd Cavalry Division desperately needed rest and refurbishment. Gregg attended to that matter as soon as he reached Harpers Ferry, where he procured enough supplies to retake the field and permitted his men a welcome respite. On July 19 he started south; two days later he was at Manassas Junction, where he secured additional rations, forage, and equipment.

By July 22, per orders from corps headquarters, he had placed McIntosh's brigade at Cedar Run, northwest of Culpeper, where it could keep tabs on Lee while guarding the railroad spur to Warrenton Junction. Huey's troopers took station at and near Gainesville on the Warrenton Turnpike, where they guarded the Manassas Gap Railroad and picketed through Thoroughfare Gap in the Bull Run Mountains. Along Broad Run Gregg positioned Irvin Gregg to guard the tracks and trestles of the Orange and Alexandria (O & A) Railroad and confront the partisan rangers of the "Gray Ghost," Maj. John Singleton Mosby, highly active in that area.[13]

From his new headquarters at Warrenton Junction Gregg on July 26 informed Pleasonton that despite the rigors of recent service at least two of his brigades—Huey's and Irvin Gregg's   were "in good and serviceable condition." Some regiments, however, had been whittled down to dangerous levels. The 2nd New York, for one, had fewer than two hundred officers and men equipped and available for duty. On the other hand there had been an infusion of new blood—in Irvin Gregg's case, the 13th Pennsylvania and (briefly) the 11th New York, formerly members of the VIII Corps and the Washington defense forces, respectively.[14]

Gregg was more concerned with the condition of McIntosh's brigade; for this reason he asked Pleasonton to expedite the return of the "large numbers of officers and enlisted men" who, lacking horses, had been sent to the remount depot on the Anacostia River near Washington that had been commanded by Percy Wyndham since his disabling at Brandy Station. The troopers' absence from the field was unavoidable, but many had remained up north long after Lee's retreat erased any threat to the capital. Pleasonton vowed to help as much as possible. On July 29 he directed Gregg to send the dozens of dismounted men still with the division to Anacostia via Warrenton Junction. He insisted: "[Wyndham] has horses to remount the men as soon as they arrive and will send them immediately back to their commands."[15]

With the force he retained, Gregg kept busy. Late in July he sent three hundred-man parties to observe Rebels picketing the Rappahannock at several points, including Beverly and Kelly's Fords. Three days later he reconnoitered enemy outposts along the south side of the Hazel (or Aestham) River, one of the Rappahannock's many tributaries. And in the first week in August—soon after reports were received that Lee had moved his army below the Rapidan—Gregg sent McIntosh toward suddenly deserted Culpeper to confirm the news. The colonel reported that the Rebels had left behind a fairly large force, primarily Stuart's troopers, to hinder access to their new position. Over the next week Gregg sent detachments to stir up other bodies of gray cavalry—most of them of manageable size—near Gaines's Cross Roads and Muddy Run.[16]

As of August 8 McIntosh's and Gregg's brigades were camped near Sulphur Springs, north of Hedgeman's River, where they maintained a twenty-mile-long picket line extending across the stream from Waterloo to Amissville and from there to Jeffersonton and Rixeyville on the south bank of the Hazel River. The next day Pleasonton had Gregg place 250 men below the Hazel, connecting with the right flank of Buford's division and patrolling west toward Sperryville. The link was broken, however, when a party sent to establish the new position encountered a force of 150 cavalry that drove it back across the river.[17]

Picket duty was always a disagreeable business but not usually a controversial one. Early in August, however, it caused a stir that embarrassed the commander of the 2nd Cavalry Division. In its edition of August 7 the *New York Herald* published a group of letters from Virginia soldiers and civilians that had been seized by Gregg's men near Sperryville. Immediately afterward Pleasonton conveyed to their commander a mild reproof from General Meade. Always sensitive about military documents ending up in the newspapers, the army leader "direct[ed] that everything of that kind which can give any information of the enemy be immediately forwarded to [his] Headquarters for his information."

In his review of his father's life and career David Gregg, Jr., strongly doubts that the general sent the correspondence to the *Herald* or caused it to be circulated. He cites as proof the "well known fact" that the general distrusted and shunned reporters. In apparent support of the "fact," Captain Thomas of the 1st Brigade staff would claim that "Gregg would never permit a newspaper correspondent about his command, and hence our division was not appreciated, outside of army circles, as it should have been." This is incorrect, for at least one reporter— the *Herald*'s Solomon T. Bulkley—accompanied the 2nd Division in the field several times during the campaigning of 1864. Even so, Gregg was troubled by newspaper reporters' access to military information. His natural inclination was to confine enemy intelligence to the operatives of the army's Bureau of Military Information, who knew not only how to use it to maximum advantage but how to safeguard it.[18]

After August 12 the force that patrolled from Sulphur Springs to Rixeyville had been noticeably diminished. On that day Gregg's command was reduced to two brigades. The move was made to conform to the structure of the divisions of Buford (whose Reserve Brigade had been detached to Washington for an extended refit) and Kilpatrick (which had never included more than two brigades). Huey's brigade was broken up, two of its outfits being reassigned to Buford and Kilpatrick and the others split between Gregg's remaining brigades. Gregg was left with thirteen regiments plus an independent company of District of Columbia cavalry. The 1st Brigade was commanded, as before, by Colonel McIntosh (and in McIntosh's occasional absence by Col. John P. Taylor of the 1st Pennsylvania, an officer with whom Gregg had forged an especially close relationship), while the new 2nd Brigade was led by Irvin Gregg.

A few weeks later their common superior formally recommended his brigade leaders for promotion, both having displayed "great ability in their respective positions" while proving themselves "familiar with their professional duties, strict disciplinarians and of irreproachable moral character." His efforts produced no quick result; McIntosh would not gain a star until the following July, and Irvin Gregg, who had already been passed over for promotion more than once, would finish the war as a brigadier only by brevet.[19]

On August 21 Gregg applied for a ten-day leave "in consequence of ill health, which almost entirely [incapacitated him] for duty, and which increasing daily" would "produce a total disability." Recent campaigning had taken a toll of those at the top—Buford had only recently returned from sick leave—but no details are available as to the nature and degree of Gregg's condition. Even so, it was deemed serious enough that Pleasonton approved the application one day later, and the leave would be extended until mid-September. Because it was spent at Philadelphia's Continental Hotel "with the bride he had seen so little of since their marriage," Gregg's son mistakenly describes the visit as "a very happy one for him." It appears, however, that he spent most of his homecoming ministered to by Ellen and her sister—assuming that Kate was strong enough to do so, she having given birth to a son six weeks earlier.

By September 3 Gregg had recovered sufficiently to receive visitors and well-wishers, including Governor Curtin and a small party of city officials. His recent heroics, which a reporter for the *Inquirer* described as "so familiar to our readers that they need not be alluded to here," were such that a crowd that included veterans of the 8th Pennsylvania gathered on the street below his room, accompanied by a brass band playing the "Star Spangled Banner" and "John Brown's Body." When the music ceased the reluctant orator was prevailed upon to step onto the balcony and offer a few remarks. Acknowledging the compliment paid him, Gregg declared that he accepted it on behalf of "the brave men under [his] command" whose claim to the credit for the cavalry's recent success he felt deeply. When he ceased speaking the governor delivered a brief address after which "the assemblage quietly dispersed."[20]

By September 6 Gregg was back in central Virginia, where his troopers continued to picket the south side of Hedgeman's River while also patrolling the Manassas Gap Railroad toward the mountains. The picket lines, as always, were exposed to the roving enemy. On the day of his return the outpost at Carter's Run, west of Warrenton, was attacked with the loss of seven men. Investigating the incident, Gregg learned that in his absence several members of the division had been captured, mostly the result of "improper dispositions, and from want of care and vigilance on the part of those responsible for the safety of the parties." He would make changes in the way the pickets were positioned and supported, and to make an example of those guilty he arrested and confined a sentinel who when attacked had abandoned his post and failed to sound the alarm.[21]

Operations on a larger scale soon claimed Gregg's attention. On September 13, at Meade's order, Pleasonton's cavalry, supported by a portion of Maj. Gen. Gouverneur K. Warren's II Corps, launched a reconnaissance-in-force against Culpeper Court House and Lee's old headquarters. Only cavalry and artillery still held the town; the brief skirmish that followed cost Gregg few casualties while nabbing dozens of prisoners and three artillery pieces. The day's most dramatic event was a "dashing" charge that drove the Rebels fifteen miles, at which point the pursuit came to an abrupt halt and the 6th Ohio came dashing back, "demoralized" by a swarm of angry insects. Its abashed colonel explained to Gregg that his men "could stand all the shot and shell the damned rebels could give them, but not a hornet's nest."[22]

Gregg's reduced command was soon engaged in its heaviest round of campaigning since Gettysburg, the result of a great battle in the western theater whose tremors spread far from its epicenter. Late in July Maj. Gen. William S. Rosecrans, a one-time subordinate of Grant's, led his Army of the Cumberland in a masterful campaign of threat and maneuver that drove Gen. Braxton Bragg's Army of Tennessee from its longtime base at Chattanooga and into northern Georgia. Fearing the strategic implications of the city's loss and Rosecrans's pursuit of the evacuees, Jefferson Davis, with Lee's reluctant assent, detached James Longstreet with two of his divisions from the Army of Northern Virginia and sent them by rail to augment Bragg for the showdown to come.

The strategy bore fruit; on September 19–20, along Chickamauga Creek near Rossville, Georgia, Bragg and Longstreet throttled the overconfident and overextended Rosecrans and sent his troops flying back to Chattanooga, to which the triumphant Confederates lay siege. The sudden crisis prompted a round of high-level deliberations in Washington, one result being the transfer of Meade's XI and XII Corps to Tennessee, along with reinforcements from Grant at Vicksburg. In October Grant himself would be sent to Chattanooga to raise Bragg's siege in the role of commander of the newly created Military Division of the Mississippi.[23]

The loss of almost 20 percent of his manpower forced Meade to abort a wide turning movement against his enemy, the first step of which had been the occupation of Culpeper. In addition to relieving Lee of this threat, the Union transfer to Tennessee gave him an opportunity to assume the offensive by threatening to outflank his foe and interpose between him and Washington. On October 9 Lee began to cross the Rapidan; the following day he moved his headquarters to Madison Court House, endangering Meade's right. By October 12 he was at Sulphur Springs within reach of the Army of the Potomac's rear.[24]

The bold maneuver forced Meade to retire north of the Rappahannock and hasten toward more defensible positions less than thirty miles from the capital whose security he was sworn to ensure. As always, Lee's advance was covered by Stuart. Over the next ten days Pleasonton's horsemen were kept furiously busy protecting the rear and flanks of their infantry comrades while striving to avoid being overtaken and cut off by the swift-moving enemy.

On the day Lee's offensive got underway Gregg, whose headquarters were then at Bealton on the O & A, was ordered to concentrate his division at Culpeper, "marching by night & day" to get there before Stuart arrived—which he did. He was likewise directed to patrol the banks of the Rappahannock from Kelly's Ford to Hartwood Church and United States Ford while keeping four regiments of the 1st Brigade, under Colonel Taylor, farther north at Morrisville.[25]

On October 10 a portion of the division, along with members of the III Corps, was sent to the aid of Kilpatrick, who while reconnoitering Lee's movements had been struck by the Confederate advance and driven back to James City, south of Culpeper. Gregg's assistance was not needed, however, and on October 11 he crossed Hedgeman's River to Sulphur Springs to guard the rear of the withdrawing infantry. About dark on the same day Taylor's and Irvin Gregg's brigades reached, respectively, Sulphur Springs and Jeffersonton. Their march had been made out of sight of the enemy but Gregg knew that Stuart was not far off and could be counted on to oppose Meade's continuing withdrawal.[26]

Around midnight Meade's chief of staff, Maj. Gen. Andrew A. Humphreys, ordered Gregg to move one or more of his outfits to Sperryville and Little Washington "to obtain certain and early information of the enemy's movements." Gregg selected the 1st Maine while directing the rest of the 2nd Brigade, minus one regiment, to picket the east side of Hedgeman's. The outfit left on the west bank, the 13th Pennsylvania, was attacked at Jeffersonton sometime after 9 a.m. and driven in. At once Gregg's cousin sent his 4th Pennsylvania across the stream to help out. "After some skirmishing," the general reported, "all became quiet, and I was informed that the enemy had disappeared from the front and was moving off to the left." But as soon as Irvin Gregg hunkered down to hold his position he was so hard pressed that both regiments were ordered back to the east side, their crossing covered by a third. After they recrossed General Gregg lined the river above and below the nearest bridge with dismounted sharpshooters. As he wrote, "the enemy advanced with a long and strong line of skirmishers, but were checked by the fire of our carbines" supported by an artillery piece that "gave them rapid discharges of spherical case."

Gregg claimed that the Rebels replied with no fewer than twenty guns, under cover of which Stuart's men forced a crossing at the bridge. He directed Irvin Gregg to retire slowly while ordering Taylor, whose brigade occupied the road to Warrenton, to resist Stuart's advance as long as possible. Taylor met Stuart with what Gregg called a "daring charge" by the 1st New Jersey. The attack, however, was only temporarily successful, being repulsed with heavy loss.[27]

Not only Stuart was delivering the blows Gregg's division was absorbing. At three p.m. the 4th Pennsylvania (led that day by a company-grade officer, Capt. Samuel S. B. Young, who four decades later would become the first chief of staff of the U.S. Army) had reported that large numbers of infantry were joining Stuart in attacking at Jeffersonton. The pressure was so intense that Young doubted he could hold his position much longer. Irvin Gregg sent a courier to notify his cousin of the presence of Dick Ewell's corps at Jeffersonton, but the man never completed the errand, supposedly wounded and captured.

Pressed in front by Ewell and on both flanks by Stuart, Irvin Gregg withdrew "in some confusion" to the bridge at Sulphur Springs. During the frantic movement twenty-three-year-old Capt. William Henry Harrison Gregg of the 13th Pennsylvania had his horse shot under him and fell into enemy hands. "Harry" Gregg would spend several months in Richmond's notorious Libby Prison, a period of severe trial not only for him but for his older brother and every member of his family. When Irvin Gregg pulled back to the other side of the stream Stuart's troopers forded it and captured the bridge, enabling elements of Ewell's corps to occupy the east bank before darkness fell.[28]

His attention absorbed by the worsening situation, David Gregg did not report to cavalry headquarters until shortly before 5 p.m., eight hours after skirmishing began on his front. Until then, Meade and Pleasonton were ignorant of the enemy's movements and the frightening prospect that the army's right flank was being turned. Absent any information that Lee was attempting a full-scale envelopment, Meade at about ten a.m. had dispatched a sizable expeditionary force—the II, V, and VI Corps, preceded by Buford's troopers—to Culpeper and Brandy Station, where Lee had been observed the previous afternoon. But Lee was no longer there, and even when informed of the fact Meade remained unaware of his adversary's position and intentions. He did not receive Gregg's report of his all-day fight until around 9 p.m., at which hour Ewell was close to uniting with A. P. Hill at Warrenton.[29]

Finally apprised of his perilous situation, Meade recalled the forces sent below the Rappahannock, positioned the III Corps to counter a

possible attack from Sulphur Springs, and moved the I Corps to Warrenton Junction, less than five miles from Lee's imminent concentra-
tion point. By one a.m. on October 13 the army was moving on the
road to the defensible heights of Centreville. The march, much of it
made along the roadbed of the O & A, continued through the night and
well into the morning. By this movement Meade slipped the trap Lee
had so masterfully set for him, but it had been a near thing indeed.[30]

Questions would persist about Gregg's role in the potential disaster. Why had he taken so long to report Ewell's presence north of the
Rappahannock and, when he did, why had the dispatch taken four
hours to reach army headquarters, only ten miles from the position
Gregg had occupied for much of the day? The general's son excused
his father's conduct—which at least one nineteenth-century historian
described as "culpable negligence" and "inexcusable error"—by noting how distracted the general had been after being attacked at Sulphur Springs, the severity of the fighting that ensued—costing the 2nd
Division upwards of five hundred casualties—and the fact that he had
his hands full conducting an orderly retreat, late in the day, to Fayette-
ville on the road to Bealton. Gregg, Jr., also points to Irvin Gregg's
inability to inform David of his early afternoon troubles on the river.
He also faults Pleasonton, whom he implicitly criticizes for failing to
relay David's report to Meade as soon as he received it (though that
hour is unknown).[31]

Still, Gregg seems vulnerable to censure on at least three counts.
The orders he received from General Humphreys at midnight on
October 12 emphasized that he should monitor and report the enemy's movements, not engage him in sustained combat. Although
fighting of some extent had been unavoidable, Gregg could have disengaged sooner and have devoted himself for the remainder of the
day to accomplishing his primary mission. Then, too, since he had
received his instructions from Meade's headquarters, why had he not
reported to the same source, thus shortening the time it took Meade
to receive it? Finally, given that the information Gregg reported was
absolutely critical why did he not relay it by multiple couriers, expecting that one would have covered those ten miles more quickly than
all or some of the others?

Certainly army headquarters did not consider Gregg blameless in the matter. Though not identifying him by name, General Humphreys excoriated the cavalry leader in a letter to his family four days later. Humphreys related: "I had sent an officer who was gone all night to take certain measures to ascertain where the enemy was; to report instantly when he ascertained the fact. It was 9 o'clock Monday before any report was received from him, although he engaged the enemy at 11 o'clock in the morning and was not many miles from us. . . . Lee was within a hair's breath [*sic*] of getting between us and Washington. We beat him, however, in the game. You may be assured that it was well for the cavalry officer that I am not in command of the Army. He would have got no mercy from me. I was furious." Humphreys's son, writing almost forty years later, claimed his father strongly believed that for "placing our army in a dangerous position," Gregg should have been "arrested, brought before a Drum Head Court Martial, tried and shot."[32]

As it had done so often over the past year and a half, the cavalry covered the retreat of the Army of the Potomac—Gregg's division protecting its rear component, Warren's II Corps—on the road to Auburn and Greenwich. Temporarily outdistancing Stuart, Gregg found time on the march to forage for his horses and distribute rations to their riders. On reaching Auburn at about 9 p.m. on October 13 he placed his brigades in bivouac in front of the infantry, picketing the roads to the south and west. At daylight the next morning the troops of Ewell and Stuart overtook the 2nd Division and struck it head-on. As Gregg wrote, "I at once formed my whole division, and made every disposition to receive and repel the attack. The ambulances and a portion of the troops of the Second Corps were still on the west side of Cedar Run and in my rear; the advance of the Second Corps had been fired upon in the vicinity of Saint Stephen's," a church southeast of Auburn near the line of the O & A. Warren's strung-out posture meant "the situation was difficult." But when he asked Gregg to keep back the enemy till his men could cross the run, the latter realized: "There was one but one thing to do, to hold my position at any cost."

And he did. His troopers and their artillery supports—James W. Martin's 6th New York and Lt. Horatio B. Reed's Battery A, 4th Artillery—

repulsed repeated attacks. Their steadfastness kept the Rebels away from Warren's left and rear until his corps could strike the railroad and follow the tracks toward Bristoe Station in rear of Maj. Gen. George Sykes's V Corps. Thanks to Gregg's delaying action Ewell failed to cut off Warren's withdrawal short of Bristoe. Hill's corps, however, by harder marching on a more roundabout route came within striking distance of the depot ahead of most of Warren's troops. A last-minute hesitation doomed Hill's plans, for by the time he attacked more of the II Corps had come up and had dug in on the east side of the railroad embankment. From this advantageous position the Federals shredded two Rebel brigades, inflicting almost 1,400 casualties and snuffing out any hope Lee might have entertained of intercepting Meade short of Centreville.[33]

But the Confederates did not give up easily. While the uneven contest raged at Bristoe, Gregg continued to cover Warren's left and rear as the II Corps crossed Kettle and Broad Runs. After Gregg's 1st Brigade had waded Broad Run, Rebels concealed in a thicket so dense no horseman could have penetrated it fired into its exposed flank. Colonel Taylor coolly dismounted the 1st Pennsylvania and 6th Ohio, whose men also went to ground, firing volley after volley into the enemy's sanctuary. Under the fusillade no Rebel dared show his head and few returned fire, although the Federals' rapid firing left the brigade ammunition-poor.

While the 1st Brigade pinned down its enemy, Irvin Gregg found his men cut off from the rest of the division by a column of Rebel infantry that had seized the railroad bridge on Kettle Run. Maintaining his aplomb, he shifted farther to the right, crossed the stream near Brentsville, and resumed covering the II Corps, including its 125 ambulances and several field hospitals. Describing these adroit dispositions in his official report, Gregg proudly declared: "To my command, Major-General Warren assigned the duty of holding the left of his position. Without ammunition, and having only their drawn sabers to rely upon, the position was held until darkness made the position safe, and I moved to Brentsville to assist General Buford with the [army's] wagon train."[34]

Gregg was justified in reporting that his officers and men had performed capably and on occasion superbly in guarding the army's rear

in its race to Centreville. Statistics would testify to their heavy involvement in the campaign. From October 9 to 16, the day that Lee, failing
to maneuver Meade out of his impregnable positions, broke contact
and started back to the Rappahannock, the 2nd Division had accumulated just shy of six hundred casualties, almost twice as many as
Buford and Kilpatrick combined. Gregg expected that his command's
achievements, though not necessarily deserving of celebration, would
not be overlooked. Therefore he was terribly upset when on October
15 Meade published a general order announcing Lee's repulse at Bristoe and praising the "skill and promptitude" of Warren's men. The
army leader made no mention of the cavalry's role in protecting the II
Corps by foiling Lee's attempts to cut it off from the rest of its army.[35]

In the mind of an old veteran like Gregg, failure to praise suggested
censure. He aired his grievance in an unusually emotional letter to his
wife, noting that on three occasions during October 14 General Warren had "acknowledged that he owed his safety" to Gregg. "My officers
and men are astonished," Gregg wrote. "My forbearance has ceased. I
have applied for a Court of Inquiry, with the view of bringing to light
all the facts and having justice done myself and [my] Division. . . . I
have asked, if a Court is not granted me, that I may be relieved from
duty with the Army of the Potomac."[36]

On October 17 General Williams at army headquarters replied to
Gregg, refusing his request for an inquiry and explaining that the omis-
sion of a reference to the services of his command was "purely acciden-
tal and not intentional." The following day an amended order admitted
the oversight and commended the "activity, zeal, and gallantry, not only
of the 2nd Division, but of the whole cavalry corps, and to the effi-
cient and arduous service rendered in all the recent operations from
the Rapidan to this place." The apology had the desired effect. Considering himself exonerated, a mollified Gregg made no further comments about leaving the army, a threat that if carried out would have
scarred him emotionally for the rest of his life.[37]

On October 18 Meade's cavalry reported the enemy's withdrawal
from the Centreville area. As he retired, Lee destroyed track, bridges,
and telegraph poles on the O & A, thereby preventing Meade from
launching a quick pursuit for want of easily accessible supplies. With

the infantry immobilized, only the army's horsemen followed closely upon the heels of the Army of Northern Virginia. The job fell mainly to Kilpatrick's division, Buford and Gregg being assigned to guard Meade's flanks and rear. On October 19 Kilpatrick again displayed ill-considered aggressiveness when his command, the brigades of Custer and Brig. Gen. Henry E. Davies, was cut off and nearly surrounded by Stuart and Fitz Lee at Buckland Mills, south of Broad Run. Fortunate timing and the tenacity of Custer's Wolverines allowed Kilpatrick to escape the trap but only after a five-mile retreat at high speed that the exultant enemy would refer to as the "Buckland Races."[38]

The following day Stuart's people, at the tag end of Lee's army, passed over the Rappahannock, putting an end to a campaign that had produced 2,292 Federal and 1,381 Confederate casualties without significant strategic gain to either army. For the next three weeks the decisive theater of the war shifted to Tennessee, where Grant and Maj. Gen. George H. Thomas, Rosecrans's successor, were preparing to lift the siege of Chattanooga and thrash the besiegers. In late November the campaign would culminate in Bragg's successive defeats at Orchard Knob, Lookout Mountain, and Missionary Ridge, followed by his headlong return to north Georgia.[39]

In the temporarily quiet sector along the Rappahannock Gregg's cavalry continued to patrol the north bank of the river while also seeking to refit and rebuild. Irvin Gregg's brigade had been whittled down by the recent fighting to 1,200 men fit for duty; Taylor's brigade had suffered comparably; and since mid-September the division had lost the services of 950 horses to brutal campaigning and 458 others to diseases such as "rotten hoof"—almost 1,500 had been condemned and turned in. But no longer would dismounted men go to Washington and remain there indefinitely. As Gregg announced in a division-wide circular on October 28, "horses and equipments required" would be "received in the field."[40]

The grueling pace of the war was having a command-wide effect. On November 4 an exhausted Capt. Charles Adams of the 1st Massachusetts wrote that "marches, scouts, reconnaissances and battles have done their honest work and not much more can be gotten out of the Cavalry Corps this year." And yet a spell of combat, limited though it was, remained to be endured. On November 7 Meade, his railroad supply line restored, bulled his way across the Rappahannock, spawning heavy fighting—almost all of it by the infantry—at Rappahannock Station and Kelly's Ford, where the Federals laid pontoon bridges. Caught off-guard by his opponent's sudden aggressiveness, Lee once again withdrew south of the Rapidan, pitching headquarters at Orange Court House. And there, in the positions in which they had so long faced each other, the armies remained until the last week in the month when Meade, prodded by Washington to strike a blow before the weather shut down operations, crossed the lower fords of the Rapidan in an attempt to envelop Lee's supposedly lightly held right flank west of Mine Run. Before Meade could strike, however, Lee shifted his forces eastward to meet the threat and perhaps launch a preemptive attack.[41]

As had been the case with previous offensives, the Mine Run Campaign—with a single glitch—got underway promisingly, only to founder on delay, missed opportunity, and Lee's exasperating ability to outsmart, outmaneuver, and outfight his enemy. An undaunted Meade headed south from the Rapidan in three columns, Gregg's division covering the left flank and Buford's the right, while Kilpatrick's guarded the crossing sites. Gregg, however, got off to a false start. On November 24 he crossed the river at Ely's Ford only to be ordered back across the stream. That morning, facing a hard rain and a rising river, Meade ordered a two-day postponement of the movement. Early on November 26 Gregg recrossed and took position in advance and to the left of Sykes's V Corps.

On the south bank Gregg plunged into the Wilderness, where seven months earlier Joe Hooker had lost his nerve, a battle, and, in the end, his army. Early on November 27 Gregg left his evening's bivouac at Parker's Store on the Orange Plank Road, heading southwest toward New Hope Church. Sometime after 11 a.m., according to Sykes, Gregg's advance ground to a halt when it encountered Stuart's pickets and skirmishers in a thicket of pine trees and along the bed of an unfinished railroad. The 1st Brigade being in front, Colonel Taylor dismounted three squadrons of the 3rd Pennsylvania and 1st Massachusetts. The squadrons drove in their opponents thanks largely to the support they received from the 6th New York Battery, which put an opposing artillery unit out of action.[42]

"At this point," Gregg would report, "the enemy's cavalry disappeared behind a line of infantry" from Maj. Gen. Henry Heth's division of Hill's corps. Portions of Taylor's brigade—dismounted detachments of four regiments—made short work of these Rebels, too, who sought shelter inside a woodlot from which they did not reemerge. Taylor reported capturing thirty-four foot soldiers, "besides killing and wounding a large number." More than eighty of his own men having become casualties, Gregg fell back as soon as Sykes came up to spell him on the firing lines.

Throughout the following day, as Meade moved slowly but confidently to the attack, Gregg posted his men both at New Hope Church and Parker's Store, the latter force covering the former's rear. He believed he had secured the area in between; thus he was surprised around noon of November 29 when attacked by Stuart, riding at the head of Brig. Gen. Thomas L. Rosser's Virginia brigade. Caught flat-footed while distributing rations, portions of two of Taylor's regiments ran for their lives; dozens were captured, and the rest of the force was "attacked on all sides." Gregg reacted immediately, hastening three regiments of the 2nd Brigade and a section of Reed's battery to the scene of chaos. He soon had Stuart and Rosser on the ropes, but then Wade Hampton, recently recovered from his injuries at Gettysburg and now in command of Stuart's 1st Division, galloped to Parker's Store and joined the fight, tilting the odds in the Rebels' favor.

Now it was Gregg's men who were in a tight corner, from which they escaped only when reports of advancing infantry persuaded Stuart to withdraw. Before departing the cavalry leader had been repeatedly attacked by the 4th and 16th Pennsylvania, who freed many of their comrades from captivity. Even so, Gregg's casualties had been heavy: more than a hundred all told, half of them missing. He would claim that "the loss of the enemy in killed and wounded was as great as our own."[43]

Neither Stuart nor Hill gave Gregg further trouble, permitting him to concentrate on supporting the infantry's attempts to attack below Mine Run. In preparation for the assault Gregg accompanied General Warren on a reconnaissance of the enemy's position along the railroad bed. The mission helped alter the strategic situation. By late on November 29 Meade's original plan had been changed to simultaneous assaults against both of Lee's flanks beginning at eight o'clock the next morning. But at the assigned hour Warren, whose 28,000-man column was to strike the first blow, unilaterally suspended operations in the face of visibly strengthened defenses in his front. A frustrated Meade elected to abort the entire offensive. On the evening of December 1 he turned back to the Rappahannock, north of which he would go into winter quarters. Thus ended—with a whimper, not a bang—the final spasm of a year characterized by incessant maneuvering, desperate fighting, and dreadful carnage.[44]

9

The Winds of Change

Following the aborted campaign on Mine Run the 2nd Cavalry Division returned to the prosaic work of patrolling and reconnoitering the north side of the Rappahannock, its brigades grouped at familiar places, Bealton Station and Warrenton. There and elsewhere they were not disturbed by the appearance of regular Confederate forces in any strength. As unrelievedly cold weather descended on the river Gregg's men settled down—if not to a long winter's nap then to a reduced schedule of operations. Flurries of activity included some highly destructive attacks on the picket lines and wagon parks around Warrenton. One such affair took place in early January 1864 when a fifty-man party of John Mosby's battalion launched a pre-dawn attack on the picket reserve of the 3rd Pennsylvania, resulting in the capture of eighteen men and forty-some horses "with equipments." Gregg sent a hundred troopers in pursuit but they failed to overhaul the partisans. The loss was substantial enough that George Meade ordered an investigation. At least one head rolled, that of an officer whom Gregg faulted for "inattention and gross neglect of duty."[1]

Outpost security was tightened and stringent methods were adopted to enforce it. One involved the closure of Warrenton, one of Mosby's most notorious enclaves, to ingress and egress. Gregg regretted having to resort to such an extreme tactic, which had been approved by army headquarters, but he considered it necessary to protect the units stationed in and around the town. Appreciating the human impact, he reported to his superiors: "Cut off from all markets . . . these families are suffering for the necessities of life." At his urging, Meade agreed to supply the townspeople with rations from the army until the quarantine could be lifted.[2]

Such humane efforts did not stop Mosby from bedeviling Gregg's pickets. Early in February his partisans attacked another stretch of the line, seizing seven members of the 1st New Jersey. A pursuit was effective but only to the extent of freeing five of the captives. Wishing to make a bigger impact, a few days later Gregg sent four hundred men to sweep a wide sector of Mosby's Confederacy. Near Manassas Gap they captured almost thirty rangers, some of them caught in farm houses and barns, others dragged from closets in the bedrooms of women who protested "the intrusion on their maidenly modesty." Subsequent expeditions through the Luray and Loudoun Valleys not only depleted Mosby's band but also that of another noted partisan leader, Maj. Harry Gilmor.[3]

Activity unrelated to combat was a constant burden, most of it generated by the necessity of refitting, remounting, and reorganizing the corps for active service and infusing it with new blood in the form of a steady stream of recruits, conscripts, and substitutes. With this exception, however, the general level of activity was low enough that Gregg, Pleasonton, and other leading lights of the cavalry were permitted short leaves in the North. On two occasions while Pleasonton was gone, Gregg commanded the corps to the entire satisfaction of all concerned, including Meade.[4]

In December, with Gregg visiting his family over Christmas, Pleasonton heard a rumor that some of his relatives, apparently including Ellen and her sister, were attempting to persuade him to seek a desk job in Washington. "Should such be the case," he telegraphed Gregg, "do not accept it. . . . Your career has been so brilliant with this army, that I would not permit myself to be separated from it at this time, not even for 'the amiable young ladies' at Reading."

Pleasonton need not have worried for Gregg had no intention of absenting himself longer than ten days. However, perhaps to ensure that his senior subordinate did not grow restless at his estrangement from loved ones, Pleasonton ensured that on at least one occasion Mrs. Gregg availed herself of an opportunity granted to many officers' wives, a visit to the army on the Rappahannock. When not in attendance in her husband's camp at Warrenton, Ellen and the family members who accompanied her roomed at the Warren Green Hotel. The Warrenton hostelry, where Ambrose Burnside had resided prior to the battle at Fredericksburg, was notable for its glamorous clientele. Gregg, Jr., recalled that his mother "always spoke with enthusiasm of the charming people she met there."[5]

Ellen enjoyed the few social engagements that winter quarters afforded, the premier event being the Washington's Birthday Ball, attended by a star-studded collection of the army's officers and held in a building specially constructed for the occasion. In mid-March the 2nd Cavalry Division held a grand soiree of its own. General Gregg, a member of the organizing and invitation committee, danced the evening away with his wife—as well as, perhaps, with some of the numerous other ladies in attendance.[6]

As soon as the weather turned cold the army's rumor mill heated up. Many of its gleanings were wholly unfounded, such as the curious report, bruited about in December, that one of Gregg's brigades was to be transferred to Texas. A surprising number of other rumors proved accurate; more than a few had lasting effects on cavalry organization and personnel. Within days of the army's return from the Rapidan, New York newspapers published a report that Pleasonton was soon to replace Meade in army command. The story was without basis but it created "a great stew" among officers who feared the result if it came to pass. One of these, a captain in the 6th Pennsylvania, called the idea "absurd. . . . He [Pleasonton] is not fit to command a reg[imen]t in active service."[7]

A diametrically opposite rumor that began to circulate almost three months later proved all too true for Pleasonton. Having performed less than brilliantly in Meade's eyes while habitually dispensing the same unsolicited advice he had given the man's predecessors, by March 1864 Pleasonton was already on shaky ground. That month, during an appearance before the congressional watchdog panel known as the Joint Committee on the Conduct of the War, the cavalryman offered some harshly worded criticism of Meade's generalship during and after Gettysburg. The army leader, who claimed to have defended Pleasonton more than once against the criticisms of Halleck and Stanton, con-

sidered his testimony an act of betrayal and thereafter sought to jetti-
son him. On March 24 Pleasonton was relieved of his command and
exiled to duty in the Trans-Mississippi theater. Gregg succeeded him
in command of the corps but only on a provisional basis.[8]

Thanks to the early arrival of the first of several high-ranking officers
to join the Army of the Potomac that winter, Gregg's tenure lasted less
than two weeks. The newcomer was Ulysses S. Grant, whose smashing
victory over Braxton Bragg had solidified his standing as the Union's
preeminent soldier. Called east by Lincoln, on March 9 Grant was elevated to the post of lieutenant general in command of the field armies
of the United States. In his role as general-in-chief (Halleck would
maintain his desk job as the army's chief of staff), Grant could have
exercised his sweeping authority from Washington or from any theater of operations. Early on he decided that the war would be won or
lost in Virginia and thus he would accompany the Army of the Potomac in the field, formulating broad strategy. Meade, who from their
first meeting had impressed Grant as a capable and unselfish soldier,
would continue to make the tactical decisions governing the army.
With Grant in the East, his ranking subordinate in Tennessee, Maj.
Gen. William T. Sherman, assumed command of the three armies
that composed the Military Division of the Mississippi. Sherman was
charged with furthering Grant's overall design with specific reference
to seizing Atlanta, the logistical and manufacturing center of the lower
Confederacy.

Upon reaching Washington Grant was given *carte blanche* to make
top-level personnel decisions in accordance with the views of Stanton and Halleck. One of his first moves was to send to Tennessee for
the services of Maj. Gen. Philip Henry Sheridan, the feisty, bandy-
legged commander of one of the infantry divisions that had helped
Grant overwhelm Bragg. Sheridan (West Point, 1853) had spent five
months in 1862 as colonel of a Michigan cavalry regiment, and Grant
considered him the perfect man to lead to glory a service arm that in
many ways, even in victory, had underperformed. Lincoln approved of
Grant's choice (though Meade was not keen on acquiring such a free-
thinking subordinate), and on April 4 Sheridan replaced Pleasonton
on a permanent basis.[9]

The cavalry greeted the unimpressive-looking newcomers warily, uncertain if the success they had gained against inferior opponents such as Bragg would continue in a theater ruled by Robert E. Lee. Charles Adams of the 1st Massachusetts, whose finger was ever on the pulse of the army, described the corporate feeling toward Grant as "peculiar—a little jealousy, a little dislike, a little envy, a little want of confidence . . . and only brilliant success will dissipate the elements."[10]

The army's attitude toward Sheridan appeared somewhat more charitable. Although his hard-driving style would antagonize more than a few of his newly acquired officers, within days of his coming a 3rd Pennsylvania trooper wrote that the man "seem[ed] to be growing popular rapidly." One reason was that upon assuming command "Little Phil" persuaded Meade to shorten the cavalry's circuitous picket lines—for instance, by assigning infantry units to patrol their own grounds. This played well with Sheridan's new charges, one of whom had recently complained of the "shameful . . . way the cavalry" were "kept at work while the infantry [did] nothing at all in their camps." Meade, who continued to underestimate cavalry's value, agreed to the change reluctantly, but he wished to make a good impression on Grant's protégé. The gesture went for naught; the Meade-Sheridan relationship was doomed to deteriorate to the point of mutual enmity.[11]

The relations Sheridan forged with David Gregg also had the potential to create friction, principally because of the men's widely differing and sometimes conflicting personalities. Whereas Gregg was modest, gentlemanly, and unflappable (although he could become exercised when his reputation or that of his command was besmirched), Sheridan was boisterous, supremely self-confident, sometimes crude in manner and speech, and unforgiving of errors even when committed by old comrades. Still, Sheridan respected Gregg's war record and came to regard him as trustworthy and dependable. For his part, Gregg was aware of the success Sheridan had achieved in two arms of the service and was willing to give the man time to prove himself in his new arena. No doubt he suspected, as others did, that Sheridan brought to the army qualities lacking under his predecessors. As Lt. Col. Theodore Lyman of Meade's staff put it, "[If Sheridan] is an able officer, he will find no difficulty in pushing along this arm, several degrees."[12]

On the other hand, Gregg would not have been human had he not, at least to a degree, resented the assignment of Sheridan, for it appeared to reflect negatively on him. Years later another mounted leader who had come to know Gregg well pondered the failure of the army's senior cavalryman to attain overall command: "Seen as lacking in enthusiasm and possibly in aggressive temper, he was a man of modesty but of far more unusual capacity . . . [but] for some reason not easy to define, he had not impressed himself sufficiently upon his immediate commanders to secure the position which was given to Sheridan." The commentator might have added that this was not the first time Gregg had been outranked and overshadowed by officers demonstrably less capable than he but more skillful at ingratiating themselves with the people who advanced soldiers' careers. Gregg's aversion to self-promotion was almost legendary. To those who wondered why newsmen were rarely seen at his headquarters, he explained: "I do not propose to have a picture reputation."[13]

If the upper echelons of the army did not seem to fully appreciate Gregg's worth, his men certainly did. More than a few fairly idolized him; Private Henry Meyer wrote: "I was more or less in awe of him, when in his presence." To Surgeon Alphonso Rockwell, Gregg was "modesty itself, and his reputation for calm and steady bravery was of the best," to the point of gaining the moniker "Old Stand-by Gregg." The historian of the 10th New York agreed that "no one could handle a mounted body of men better than Gregg, and none enjoyed the confidence of his men more than he."[14]

Other observers commented on his hard horse sense and dependence on facts, not rumors. Whenever a subordinate brought word of events whose significance was unclear to him, the general replied: "You should not think, sir, you should know. Go and find out." Still others reflected on the human side of the soldier. One of his orderlies recalled: "I never heard Gregg utter a profane word and never saw any drinking with him or in his tent. He was always the same kind hearted and true friend of all the men that served under him." Such testimonials suggest that whatever qualities or circumstances may have hindered Gregg's advancement the army could have used more men like him.[15]

Grant and Sheridan were not the only newcomers to the winter quarters that stretched from Brandy Station through Stevensburg and Warrenton. Two additions to the cavalry followed closely on the heels of Sheridan's appearance. Their assignment must have surprised and may have troubled Gregg, for neither had previously commanded mounted forces. The situation would make Sheridan ever mindful that Gregg "was the only division commander I had whose experience had been almost exclusively derived from the cavalry arm."[16]

On April 10 Brig. Gen. Alfred T. A. Torbert, Gregg's West Point classmate, who for the past two and a half years had led a brigade and for brief periods a division in the VI Corps, reported for duty as commander of the 1st Cavalry Division. Torbert may not have come highly recommended but he had connections, one being his long friendship with Phil Sheridan. Gregg would have forgiven (had he even remembered) the drunken slur Torbert directed at him during the West Point Christmas 1853 festivities, but he may well have looked askance at the man's inexperience and been troubled by the on-the-job training he must undergo short weeks before the resumption of active campaigning. Certainly Gregg would have been saddened by the vacancy that Torbert had been selected to fill. It had opened following the death of the estimable John Buford, who in mid-December had succumbed to a virulent strain of typhoid aggravated by overwork and overexposure to the elements.[17]

One week after Torbert arrived at Brandy Station he was joined by James Harrison Wilson, a young (twenty-five-year-old) brigadier who had received his star less than six months before without ever commanding in the field. Wilson was, like Sheridan, a protégé of the general-in-chief. A West Point–trained engineer, he had served on Grant's staff in the role of all-purpose troubleshooter. Brash and headstrong, a stranger to doubt despite his callowness and inexperience, the Illinois native had impressed Grant as possessing multiple talents. In January he had recommended Wilson for the post of chief of the Cavalry Bureau, a War Department agency that oversaw the mounting, equipping, and staffing of horse soldiers across the war zone. Wilson had justified Grant's faith in him; despite lacking high-level administrative experience, in less than four months he had turned a poorly functioning office susceptible to corruption into a model of efficiency and honesty. Division command in his preferred branch had been his reward.[18]

Wilson's promotion came at the expense of Judson Kilpatrick, who, in the words of Colonel Lyman, had "dished himself" when planning and leading a winter assault on lightly defended Richmond. Kilpatrick envisioned the feat as eclipsing his raid on the city under George Stoneman. The assault's objectives were to destroy the capital's military infrastructure, distribute copies of an amnesty proclamation for Virginians approved by Lincoln, and liberate Harry Gregg and the hundreds of other inmates of Libby and Belle Island Prisons.

With the blessing of the president and Secretary Stanton but against the better judgment of Meade, on February 28 two columns of horsemen had descended on Richmond, planning to unite for a climactic assault on the "hateful city." The larger column, some 3,500 men under "Kill-Cavalry" (Kilpatrick), approached from the north while a satellite force of 500 under Col. Ulric Dahlgren—a former member of Hooker's and Pleasonton's staffs who rivaled Kilpatrick for derring-do and self-confidence bordering on arrogance—approached the city from below the James River.

The raiders had the advantage of surprise, but bad weather, unfamiliarity with the countryside, and the quick response of defenders, including elements of Hampton's division fresh from winter quarters, prevented the forces from joining and entering Richmond. Turned back at the city's defenses, Kilpatrick retreated, as he had ten months earlier, down the Peninsula, while Dahlgren's band was surrounded and shot up by local troops and their leader killed. The repercussions of the fiasco expanded when documents found on the colonel's body revealed plans to capture and assassinate Confederate officials, including Jefferson Davis. Though Kilpatrick disavowed such an intent, the ensuing controversy cost him his command. In mid-April he was relieved from duty with the Army of the Potomac and shunted west to serve under William T. Sherman.[19]

The Kilpatrick-Dahlgren Raid and its aftermath came as a shock to the Cavalry Corps as a body, but since less than half of it had taken part the effect on morale was minimal and would be erased by the influx of fresh blood at the upper levels. David Gregg, for one, regretted the folly that had cost the career of one injudicious officer and the life of another, but he could take comfort in the knowledge that fewer than 400 members of his 2nd Brigade had been attached to Kilpatrick's column. Five hundred others, culled from the 1st Brigade, had taken part in a diversionary expedition under George Custer that involved burning bridges near Charlottesville and downing telegraph wire between Gordonsville and Lynchburg. Because he encountered few enemy forces other than Stuart's horse artillery in winter camp outside Charlottesville, Custer failed to draw many opponents from Kilpatrick's and Dahlgren's paths. A series of minor actions cost him only 6 men wounded, for which Gregg was grateful. No casualties occurred among the 469 men of the 2nd Division sent to Stevensburg to occupy the picket lines vacated by Kilpatrick.[20]

All in all, it had been an eventful winter for the horsemen of the Army of the Potomac especially given that the local weather tended to shut down operations for weeks at a time. With warmer days on the way and roads beginning to dry, officers and troopers could expect their workload to increase geometrically in the not-distant future.

By the last week of April Grant had honed his plans for the Virginia campaign as well as his vision of simultaneous operations by Sherman's armies and Union forces in the Shenandoah Valley, West Virginia, and Louisiana. Yet another force, to be governed by Grant at long range, was the newly formed Army of the James, 35,000 strong, led by the war's preeminent politician-soldier, Maj. Gen. Benjamin F. Butler of Massachusetts. Butler's command was instructed to imperil Richmond from the south by moving up the James while Meade attacked from the north, driving Lee inside the capital's defenses. The armies were then to join in attacking Richmond or besieging the city with the aim of starving out its defenders. Though he had served in the field since 1861, Butler remained a novice warrior, but as a prominent Democrat who supported the military policies of a Republican administration, his influence and support might secure Lincoln's reelection in the fall. Thus the general-in-chief was committed to working with the man as smoothly as possible during the campaigning to come.

Grant's strategy for the Virginia front began with a gamble, one that both Hooker and Meade had taken to their regret: a crossing of the Rapidan and a march through the twelve-mile-wide, six-mile-long Wilderness. Grant's object was to threaten Lee's right flank and drive him from Orange Court House. The operation—the first steps of an offensive destined to consume the next two and a half months and in a sense continue until war's end—got underway in the pre-dawn darkness of May 4. As the army filed out of its camps around Brandy Station, it displayed a streamlined look. Sadly reduced by the losses of 1863, especially those at Chancellorsville and Gettysburg, Meade's I and III Corps were gone, their manpower merged into the remaining components, the II, V, and VI Corps, commanded by, respectively, Generals Hancock, Warren, and Sedgwick. A fourth corps, the IX, under Ambrose Burnside, who after his failure at Fredericksburg had achieved some success in East Tennessee, had only recently joined the army.[21]

The combined forces gave Grant and Meade almost 120,000 troops and 274 pieces of artillery with which to oppose Lee's army of 62,000. The disparity in numbers had long existed but once battle was joined it had not given the Army of the Potomac anything close to a lasting advantage. Still, Meade's strength was one reason Lee did not contest his opponent's crossing of the Rapidan. He would wait to oppose the Federals amid the second-growth pine and tangled thicket that barred their path.

Meade's army marched in two parallel columns five miles apart, crossing the Rapidan at Germanna and Ely's Fords. The right-hand column, the V and VI Corps, was covered in front and on its flanks by Wilson's 3rd Cavalry Division, a daunting mission for a first-time leader of cavalry. Gregg's command (whose 1st Brigade was now commanded by General Davies, a recent transferee from Torbert's division) cleared the way of the Ely's Ford column, the II Corps. Burnside's corps, which had farther to march to reach the river, would not cross at Germanna Ford until early on May 5.

Originally the 2nd Division had been assigned to cover the crossing of the army's vast train of supply and baggage wagons and its artillery reserve via the pontoon bridge laid at Ely's Ford and to march with them, guarding Meade's left. Before Gregg started for the river, however, his superior countermanded his orders. Concerned by reports that Rebel cavalry under Fitz Lee (now in command of a full division of horse) had congregated at Hamilton's Crossing, ten miles east of Gregg's position at Alrich's farmstead, Meade instructed Torbert's 1st Division to ford at Ely's, move to Alrich's, and accompany Gregg to Hamilton's Crossing.

This proved to be the first mistake of the campaign. Fitz Lee was no longer in his assumed location, having moved out to rejoin Stuart on the less-than-commodious Orange Plank Road (only one side of whose roadbed was actually covered with planking), which met the Orange Turnpike (made of crushed stone) west of Chancellorsville. Gregg and Torbert had been assigned to what one historian calls a "wild goose chase," the result being that Gregg would linger inactively near Alrich's and Torbert would find himself hemmed in by 1,400 supply wagons and ambulances on the trails between Ely's Ford and Chancellorsville. Neither division would be in a position to support the inexperienced Wilson on the far right.[22]

The first day's march ended with Wilson's two brigades and twelve horse-artillery pieces far in advance of the entire army. He made stops at a couple of venues on the plank road well known to Gregg from the Mine Run Campaign: New Hope Church, where he skirmished with some outpost members, and Parker's Store, where he spent the night. At 5 a.m. on May 5 Wilson resumed the march south along a narrow trail toward Craig's Meeting House on the Catharpin Road. He had been ordered to place large detachments on the plank road and the Orange Pike, but being reluctant to deplete his force in the face of a lurking enemy he had failed to do so, leaving Meade's right flank unsecured. Furthermore, unknown to Wilson, two corps of Rebel infantry and attached cavalry were bearing down on him via both of those roads.

Shortly after daybreak on May 5 the 3rd Division reached Craig's Meeting House, where it was suddenly attacked by the Virginians of Thomas Rosser. Wilson's vanguard reeled from the shock of the collision, but troops toward the rear stood firm. By early afternoon, following hours of heavy skirmishing, Wilson's recently reinforced opponents charged him on foot, scattering the brigade of Col. George H. Chapman. The division's two batteries finally contained the attack, but then

Wilson discovered cavalry under Rosser in his rear on the road from Parker's Store, cutting him off from his army. Refusing to panic, the engineer turned cavalryman located a country road that led to what he hoped was a safe haven: Todd's Tavern, three miles to the southeast near the reported location of Hancock's infantry. To reach there Wilson had to cross the Po River, which would take time; compounding his problem was his discovery that the enemy was heading in the same direction on the Catharpin Road. Through speed born of desperation Wilson's brigades and batteries crossed the river at Corbin's Bridge minutes before Rosser could overtake him.

Even beyond the stream the 3rd Division was in trouble, from which, at a most opportune time, it was extricated by Gregg, who had been sent cross country to Todd's Tavern in support of his colleague. While most of the couriers Wilson had sent to inform army headquarters of his predicament had been captured, at least one got through. Meade had notified Sheridan that Wilson needed help and Sheridan had dispatched the 2nd Division as soon as he got the word.[23]

Gregg, his men drawn up in dismounted lines of battle, cradling their seven-shot Spencers, had been waiting at the tavern for Rosser to appear. At about 3 p.m. Wilson's men took station in rear of their deliverers, whereupon the 2nd Division went into action. Davies's advance echelon, the 1st New Jersey and 1st Massachusetts, mixed with Rosser's troopers and despite absorbing heavy blows drove them, as Gregg reported, "a distance of 3 miles, and beyond Corbin's Bridge." The severity of the fight—made necessary by Wilson's inexperience and disobedience of orders—is indicated by Gregg's losses, nearly a hundred men killed or wounded.[24]

The numbers paled in contrast to those suffered by the main armies on May 5, which saw some of the fiercest combat of the war. Around noon Meade had moved to attack an enemy force assumed to be of division size and found himself engaging Richard S. Ewell's corps. When the fight began Grant ordered Meade's lieutenants to attack on the Orange Plank Road "without taking time for dispositions," but the assaults were so sluggish as to raise the hackles of the lieutenant general. Eventually the battle expanded to involve the greater part of both armies—the II, V, and VI Corps versus Ewell and A. P.

Hill (Longstreet's corps, delayed en route, failed to reach the battle-field in time to take part). The fighting petered out at 8 p.m. with the Confederates barely holding their ground, waiting for Longstreet to arrive and secure it.

Meade's three-corps attack resumed at 5 a.m. on May 6 in such strength that Hill's corps almost went under before Longstreet finally reached the field two hours later. At 11 a.m. the newcomers emerged from the cover of an unfinished railroad cut south of the plank road, counterattacked, and began to roll up the left flank of the II Corps. Before they could be overrun Hancock's men withdrew eastward, occupying earthworks along the Brock Road. Longstreet, pivoting to attack the new position, was severely wounded by friendly fire and the Confederate drive stalled. Late in the day, the chronically slow Burnside (Grant had ordered him to attack soon after dawn) advanced against the center of Lee's line but suffered a sharp repulse. Later still, Ewell smashed into the VI Corps on the Union right but the day ended before a limited breakthrough could be exploited. Stalemate resulted, to the tune of 18,000 Union and 11,000 Confederate casualties. Grant's opening offensive of his tenure in the East had been thwarted, yet he refused to retreat to salve his wounds in the manner of McClellan, Burnside, and Hooker. As he told his erstwhile staff officer on May 7, "It's all right, Wilson; the army is moving toward Richmond!"[25]

While the infantries grappled on May 6, Gregg's division at Todd's Tavern spent the day skirmishing with Fitz Lee's horsemen. Unsurprisingly, given the lack of maneuvering room, the Rebels fought dismounted and, as Gregg wrote, "studiously kept under the cover of the dense woods surrounding the tavern." The 2nd Division operated within supporting distance of Torbert's command, the brigades of Custer (recently transferred from Wilson's division, whose leader he personally detested) and Thomas C. Devin, but the heated fighting was all Gregg's to handle. As one officer put it, "from the start Lee's cavalry was aggressive, and by its ceaseless activity in that densely wooded region reminded one of a swarm of bees suddenly disturbed by strange footsteps." Even so, Gregg would note that the day "closed without any decisive result."[26]

Surveying the results of his command's operations, Phil Sheridan proposed to hold the positions it had gained, including Todd's Tavern. The tavern he viewed as an anchor for Meade's left flank as well as a jumping-off point for a southeastward advance on the road to Spotsylvania Court House, which he supposed to be Grant's next objective. At his order Gregg and Wilson constructed breastworks and set up picket lines in the clearing around Todd's. Early that afternoon, however, Meade began to fear for the safety of his left flank. Acting on erroneous reports, he informed Sheridan that Hancock's position had been turned; he ordered the cavalry to be withdrawn to Chancellorsville to better protect the army's invaluable supply train. Sheridan, with great reluctance, withdrew Custer's men from the Brock Road—the most direct route to Todd's Tavern and Spotsylvania—to the Union rear.[27]

Sheridan's misgivings were validated on May 7 when Grant ordered the Army of the Potomac to move to Spotsylvania, where it could threaten Lee's communications and cut his route of retreat. Meade was to march there on the road his ill-advised order had uncovered. Advancing once again toward Todd's Tavern—now firmly in the hands of Fitz Lee—Sheridan planned to recapture the place with the divisions of Gregg and Torbert, the latter commanded by Wesley Merritt, his superior having gone north for surgical removal of a spinal abscess. Wilson's battered troopers would rest and refit at Chancellorsville.

Gregg would advance by two routes. Davies's brigade was to move out the Catharpin Road to Piney Branch Church, then veer south to the Brock Road in order to gain the rear of Lee's division, the brigades of Brig. Gens. Williams C. Wickham and Lunsford L. Lomax. Meanwhile, John Irvin Gregg would also move down the Catharpin Road to the tavern, there to strike Lee's right flank in conjunction with Davies's maneuver. The plan had merit but it fell apart when Lee slipped the trap by vacating Todd's Tavern and moving closer to Spotsylvania, where he erected breastworks to contest the Yankees' further progress. Around the same time two more Rebel brigades—those of Brig. Gens. James B. Gordon and Pierce Young—had taken position across Irvin Gregg's path between Todd's Tavern and Corbin's Bridge.[28]

Merritt, not Davies, now drew the primary assignment of taking on Fitz Lee. Just after 7 a.m. the 1st Division, Custer's Wolverines in the lead, advanced on Todd's Tavern and encountered Wickham and Lomax. The struggle for the lower stretch of the Brock Road was heated— literally so, for balls and shells set the dry brush around the breastworks ablaze although the fire failed to halt the fighting. Eventually Merritt's men captured the defenses only to see them reoccupied late in the day following the Federals' withdrawal.

While Merritt—eventually with help from Davies—slugged it out with Lee, Irvin Gregg prepared to attack Gordon and Young, as per Sheridan's revised plan for the day. He found the enemy holding high ground on the near bank of the Po River, a position so strong that the colonel quickly withdrew to Todd's Tavern. There he went on the defensive, throwing up field works and sending back for Battery A, 4th Artillery. Gordon and Young promptly attacked, filling the fields west of Todd's with fierce but inconclusive fighting that consumed the balance of the day and personally involved the cousins Gregg. According to Sergeant Samuel Cormany, soon after the shooting started "along came General D. Mc. M. Gregg and Genl [*sic*] J. I. Gregg noting our lines and positions and adding to our courage."[29]

Though the Confederates gave at least as well as they got, they had been forced to vacate the Catharpin Road–Brock Road intersection. By early evening Gregg and Merritt had linked at Todd's Tavern and Sheridan's primary mission—opening the road to Spotsylvania—had been accomplished. The achievement, however, had come at heavy cost, including nearly a hundred casualties in one of Merritt's regiments, supposedly the most ever absorbed by a cavalry outfit in a single engagement. Moreover, Sheridan's success was of short duration. By failing to cross the Po and hold Corbin's Bridge Irvin Gregg had opened it as well as several lower bridges to the Rebels as they raced Meade to Spotsylvania. The failure to drive away Gordon and Young would enable Lee's vanguard—Longstreet's corps, now under Maj. Gen. Richard H. Anderson—to cut a woods road, four miles long, from the Wilderness toward the Catharpin and Shady Grove Church Roads. This was a major error. Another would follow.[30]

Within ninety minutes of Sheridan's success Meade, with Grant peering over his shoulder, was on his way to Spotsylvania, Warren's V Corps in advance along the upper reaches of the Brock Road. To ensure that the enemy did not bar Warren's path Sheridan, some time before 1 a.m. on May 8, penned the orders he would give to his division commanders this day. At five a.m. he expected to send Gregg and Merritt back down the Catharpin Road and across the Po at separate bridges before advancing to Spotsylvania. Meanwhile, Wilson's now-restored command would move to the courthouse village on a roundabout route from the northeast, securing the place and a strategic Po River bridge south of it. Wilson was to hold his new-won position until Warren's foot soldiers relieved him.

Sheridan's dispositions appeared to be logical ones but were based on erroneous suppositions, including his belief that Lee's army would remain immobile for some time to come. In any case they would not be put into effect, at least partly due to General Meade's interference in the cavalry's affairs. Wilson duly got his orders and started for Spotsylvania before dawn. Before Gregg and Merritt received their instructions, however, Meade, his headquarters on the move, found them at Todd's Tavern. The army leader was surprised and perturbed to learn that neither subordinate had heard from Sheridan, who was then at Alrich's, several miles off. In their leader's absence he gave Gregg and Merritt orders of his own based on a misunderstanding of the strategic picture. Believing that Stuart's men had been driven beyond Spotsylvania, he instructed Merritt to head there immediately; Gregg he sent west on the Catharpin Road to Corbin's Bridge to guard against an enemy advance from that direction. Meade shot Sheridan a hasty note explaining that he had acted because Gregg and Merritt "are in the way of the infantry and there is no time to refer to you." Sheridan would claim that he never received notice of Meade's action. When he learned of the revised dispositions, the hot-tempered Irishman blew up and damned Meade for his meddling.[31]

Morning confirmed Sheridan's worst suspicions. By 8 a.m. Wilson was in Spotsylvania but with no support at hand. Soon after dawn Anderson's command, which had stolen a night march on its enemy, had reached the town. Anderson had crossed the Po unhindered thanks to Irvin Gregg's inability to secure Corbin's Bridge and Meade's meddling in cavalry affairs; the exhausted but enthusiastic foot soldiers had been directed into position by Stuart's scouts. A one-sided fight ensued; by ten-thirty Wilson had been evicted from the village and the second phase of Ulysses S. Grant's grand strategy was a dead letter.

The proximate cause of Grant's inability to beat Lee to Spotsylvania was a traffic jam. In the early morning darkness of May 8 Warren's men had found their path clogged with Merritt's troopers, who were in turn stymied by barriers laid across the road by the Confederates. Warren and Merritt exchanged sharp words over the foul-up and later in the day Sheridan and Meade did so as well. Each blamed the other for a precious opportunity lost, Sheridan adding the charge that Meade had deliberately undermined his authority. The cavalryman ended the confrontation with a parting shot: if Meade would stop interfering in its affairs and permit it to act independently, the Cavalry Corps would seek out Stuart, engage him on open ground, and give him a sound drubbing.

Meade wasted no time complaining to Grant about what he considered Sheridan's insubordination. He expected a sympathetic hearing because the cavalryman had not been blameless in the matter at hand, if only because of the untoward delay in delivering Gregg and Merritt their orders for May 8. Instead, Grant was receptive to the boast Meade told him Sheridan had made. Aware that the Wilderness was no place for cavalry to fight in, the lieutenant general decided that before the army made its next move Sheridan should cut loose with his entire force, head for Richmond, and draw Stuart into a finish fight. The major drawback to this strategy was that by ranging far afield of the main army for an unknown length of time, Sheridan would deprive Meade of mounted support at a critical point in the campaign. Lacking an important source of intelligence collection, the Army of the Potomac would stumble through the coming weeks much as Lee had when invading Pennsylvania the previous summer.[32]

On the morning of May 9, some ten thousand horsemen, accompanied by six batteries and dozens of ammunition wagons and ambulances, headed south around the right flank of the army on the old Telegraph Road. The presumed destination of the thirteen-mile-long column, Richmond, conjured up memories of another expedition. Though Sheridan's primary objective—a climactic confrontation with the enemy, not simply the destruction of materiel—had not been George Stoneman's mission, enough parallels existed to give those who had participated in the earlier raid an uncomfortable sense of déjà vu. Sheridan was adamant that this operation had an attainable goal. As he informed Gregg and the other division leaders before starting out, "I know we can beat him [Stuart], and in view of my recent representations to General Meade I shall expect nothing but success."[33]

From the first hours on the march, Stuart tracked the raiders more or less closely, a chore made easier by Sheridan's decision to stretch out his column on a single road. Stuart, as though to downplay the threat his enemy posed, pursued at the head of a much smaller force, the two brigades of Fitz's Lee's division under Lomax and Wickham and James B. Gordon's brigade of Hampton's division, an aggregate of fewer than five thousand men. Thus far unimpressed by Sheridan's tactics, the Beau Sabreur doubted he needed more than half his opponent's manpower to deter him from his objectives, whatever they turned out to be.

Stuart confined his early blows to the rear of the Yankee column, the position of Gregg's division. The first of these was landed by Wickham's Virginians near Jerrell's Mill, where Davies's brigade, in the extreme rear, was driven back a short distance before the 6th Ohio and 1st Pennsylvania rallied, fending off this and later attempts to limit the raiders' progress. While Davies fought, the main body kept marching. Sheridan did not intend to engage Stuart at this point, preferring to place two bodies of water, the North and South Anna Rivers, between him and his pursuers. South of the streams he could halt long enough to supply his men and mounts—who had drawn only three days' rations and half a day's forage—from local farms and fields.[34]

Late in the afternoon the raiders turned off the Telegraph Road and made for Beaver Dam Station on the Virginia Central Railroad, Lee's forward supply base. The regiments at the head of the column fell upon the depot, destroying two locomotives, three trains of cars, eight to ten miles of track, local telegraph lines, and more than a million rations of flour and meat. They also liberated four hundred Union soldiers, captured in the Wilderness, who had been on their way to the prisons of Richmond.[35]

The following morning Stuart caught up to his quarry, his artillery providing a wake-up call for Gregg's men on the upper bank of the North Anna. Their leader reported that "the enemy was again repulsed, and the crossing easily effected." Hours later Wickham's men again nipped at the division's rear but were dispersed by one of Irvin Gregg's regiments. Stuart then crossed the North Anna downriver from the Yankees. But instead of directly following Sheridan he turned southeastward, intending to outpace his opponent and interpose between him and the capital. The effort was a success; by 9 p.m. Stuart's brigades had reached Hanover Junction on the road to Richmond. From there they would move to a point six miles north of the city near an abandoned public house, Yellow Tavern.[36]

That night Sheridan, eagerly anticipating his confrontation with the great Confederate leader, encamped along the South Anna near Ground Squirrel Bridge, the span that Gregg had destroyed under Stoneman and that had been rebuilt—only to be burned again by the raiders. Before dawn on May 11 Sheridan had Gregg dispatch Davies's brigade to cut the Richmond, Fredericksburg and Potomac Railroad at well-defended Ashland, another of Stoneman's ports of call almost exactly one year earlier. Davies had to fight his way into the station, suffering nineteen casualties, but once there he did a thorough job of tearing up "quite a section of railroad," putting the torch to Confederate government stores, and destroying another engine and a train of cars.[37]

Sheridan decided that when the main body moved out Irvin Gregg's brigade would remain on the South Anna as a rear guard. With Ground Squirrel Bridge in ruins and the river around it believed to be unfordable, the colonel felt secure in what might seem a precarious position. He was proven wrong when, not long after the rest of Sheridan's force rode off, three North Carolina regiments under James B. Gordon successfully negotiated the river's fifteen-foot-high banks and, screaming the Rebel yell, launched multiple assaults. Hard pressed throughout the day, Gregg managed to retain his hold on the river, although, as one of his men put it, "for a few moments it was every man for himself and the rebels take the hindmost." In his report of the campaign David Gregg would claim that his cousin's brigade "without difficulty, in every attack, was more than able to drive the enemy at all points, inflicting upon him severe loss." Historians beg to disagree.[38]

Meanwhile, the main body, Merritt's division in front, advanced along Mountain Road to the tavern where, Sheridan had learned, Stuart was waiting. Upon reaching the vicinity at about 11 a.m. Little Phil sent one of Merritt's brigades around his opponent's left to take position on the Brook Turnpike between the tavern and Richmond, while deploying Wilson's and Irvin Gregg's troopers north of the 1st Division on Mountain Road. Over the next five hours the cavalries sparred, each lashing the other with small arms and artillery.

At about 4 p.m. Sheridan, his dispositions complete, ordered Custer's brigade of Merritt's division to attack Stuart's left while one of Wilson's brigades pressed the other flank. The result gladdened Sheridan's heart. Thanks to aggressive leadership and weight of numbers Custer and his comrades broke Stuart's flank, capturing hundreds of prisoners and two cannons. Lomax's men were forced back so far that they became entangled with Wickham's regiments; a counterattack by the vaunted 1st Virginia finally stemmed the blue tide, at least temporarily. At the height of the action Stuart exposed himself to enemy fire and was shot at close range by a Wolverine fleeing on foot from the 1st Virginia. The pistol ball struck Stuart in the abdomen, perforating an intestine. Borne from the field to a home in Richmond, he would succumb to the wound the next evening.[39]

After Jeb's fall his forces steadily melted away. Pressed on all sides by mounted and dismounted Yankees, they made their way, in groups large and small, toward Richmond. As they withdrew, Gordon's North Carolinians, still lodged in the rear of Sheridan's column, launched a series of attacks on Irvin Gregg's new position three miles northwest of Yellow Tavern. Sheridan, anticipating the blows, had ordered Gregg to place his 2nd Brigade behind a line of breastworks. From these hastily erected but effective defenses Gregg repelled the assault and then counterattacked under a rainstorm, pushing Gordon away and opening a path to Richmond via the Brook Pike.

This action ended the day's combat on a high note for Sheridan's rough riders, for it appeared to place Richmond at their mercy. Little Phil may not have annihilated his enemy but he had backed up his boast that in a fight on open ground he would get the better of it. Not only had he beaten Stuart, he had removed him bodily from the war.[40]

Having already gained much of importance (though he would not learn of Stuart's death for three days), Sheridan considered his expedition effectively at an end. Richmond, however, lay in front of him and even if he had no intention of entering the city he would have to be careful in detouring around its layers of defense. Having found a country road that ran between Richmond's outer and inner works, he planned to reach the suburb of Mechanicsville via a crossing of the Chickahominy. Then he intended to lead his weary, rain- and mud-spattered force south via Fair Oaks Station to Ben Butler's supply base at Haxall's Landing on the James, where he might rest and refurbish beyond enemy range.[41]

Sheridan left Yellow Tavern on the still-sodden morning of May 12, heading for a campsite between Walnut Grove and the old Peninsula Campaign battlefield of Gaines's Mill. He did so as stealthily as such a large force would permit, but Richmond's defenders, expecting an assault on their works for the third time in a year, roused up, as did the cavalry under General Gordon, still dogging Sheridan's rear guard under David Gregg. The result was chaotic and almost disastrous to the raiders' fortunes. Wilson, at the head of the column, lost his way in pre-dawn darkness, blundered into the first line of works, and took a beating.[42]

The opposition was stout enough to persuade Sheridan to detour east of the city. He would do so by a roundabout course: crossing to the north side of the Chickahominy at Meadow Bridge and recrossing downriver. His plan was almost upset when Merritt, in the vanguard of the column, discovered that Meadow Bridge had been partially unplanked and its approaches covered by dismounted troopers and artillery under Fitz Lee, who had assumed command of Stuart's corps. At the same time troops from the city's defenses launched an offensive against Wilson and Gregg.

At Merritt's direction, members of Custer's brigade dismounted and stripped timber from abandoned dwellings along the riverbank. Under a covering fire engineer units laid a new floor on the structure upon which Custer would cross, chasing off Lee's men. The repair project, however, took time, and with Merritt immobilized Gregg's men bunched up behind him on the Brook Pike, their flank exposed to the occupants of Richmond's second line of defense as well as to Gordon's hard-hitting troopers.[43]

His options limited, Gregg battened down to resist assault, his artillery poised to sweep the approaches to the pike. "Not doubting the success of their attack," he wrote, "the enemy moved boldly against our lines despite the fire of two of our batteries." Sheltered by log-and-rock breastworks, the defenders not only repulsed three attacks but mortally wounded Gordon. "So complete was their defeat," Gregg added, "that they offered no further opposition to the passage of the division over the Chickahominy."[44]

Once on the north side Sheridan rested for nine hours before leading the way to Bottom's Bridge. After recrossing, he headed for the James, which he reached on May 14. Three days later the corps started on a week-long return to the Army of the Potomac, putting a final touch to an expedition that highlighted Phil Sheridan's aggressive leadership and nimble thinking, his men's combat prowess, and Jeb Stuart's mortality.

10

Hot Work under Sheridan

While the cavalry was away, Grant and Lee had spent a hellish fortnight grappling north and west of Spotsylvania Court House in a series of engagements that piled corpses high without materially affecting the strategic situation. Meade's army had launched major attacks on May 9, 10, 12, and 18 while every day in between saw smaller-scale but no less desperate fighting. Though revolted by the carnage—no fewer than thirty-three thousand Union casualties since the start of the Wilderness Campaign—Grant never relinquished his determination to pass his opponent's flank in the direction of Richmond. On May 11 he wired General Halleck in Washington that he proposed "to fight it out on this line if it takes all summer."[1]

Finally admitting that his path had again been blocked, late on May 20 Grant had the Army of the Potomac swing south and east toward its next geographical landmark, the North Anna River in the vicinity of Hanover Junction. As ever, Lee correctly interpreted his strategy and through the invaluable advantage of interior lines (the shorter, more direct routes at the disposal of a defender as opposed to the circuitous exterior lines an attacker is saddled with) beat him to his latest objective. The result was four more days of inconclusive combat ending late on May 26 with another side-step to the southeast by Meade's army, this time in the direction of Hanovertown on the Pamunkey River.

Phil Sheridan and his raiders rejoined Meade's main body on May 24 near Chesterfield Station on the Richmond, Fredericksburg and Potomac Railroad. The cavalry's march from the Chickahominy to the North Anna had been action-packed although the level of the opposition must have seemed tame compared to that encountered at Yellow Tavern and inside the Richmond defenses. Gregg's operations had been confined to cooperating with James Harrison Wilson to cover George Custer's Wolverines as they destroyed bridges on the South Anna. To accomplish the mission the 2nd and 3rd Divisions were sent as far southeast as Cold Harbor on the Pamunkey River, a future battlefield of the Army of the Potomac whose name would become synonymous with mass murder.[2]

To properly support Grant and Meade on the North Anna, Sheridan was compelled to disperse his command. Wilson's division he sent on May 25 to Little River on the army's far right where it probed the western end of Lee's line. The following day the rest of the cavalry corps moved out to facilitate the army's departure. The 1st and 2nd Divisions (the former again under Alfred Torbert, recently returned from medical leave), subsequently supported by a division from Maj. Gen. Horatio G. Wright's VI Corps (John Sedgwick having been killed at Spotsylvania), took the advance with an eye to securing the Pamunkey fords while making efforts to deceive Lee as to which one Meade would use. As Sheridan would write, "To attain this end in the presence of an ever-watchful foe . . . required the most vigorous and zealous work on the part of those to whom had been allotted the task of carrying out the initial maneuvers."

Torbert demonstrated at one crossing, Taylor's Ford, while Gregg marched farther north to Littlepage's Bridge, ten miles upriver from where Grant intended to cross the Pamunkey. At both places the horsemen made ostentatious movements as if heralding Meade's imminent arrival. On May 27 Torbert, Custer's brigade in advance, crossed at Taylor's Ford and drove away a hundred members of the Cavalry Corps, Army of Northern Virginia, now led by Wade Hampton, Stuart's de facto successor by virtue of seniority. From the crossing site Torbert continued south to Hanovertown Ferry, where he was confronted by the brigade formerly led by James Gordon. He maneuvered the Rebels into retreating by sending Custer's men by a right-hand road to Haw's Shop, an abandoned farm equipment factory three miles from the river. As Sheridan noted in his memoirs, "This completed our task of gaining a foothold south of the Pamunkey, and on the 28th the main army crossed un-harassed and took up a position behind my line, extending south from the river."[3]

Because Grant remained uncertain of Lee's whereabouts, he ordered the cavalry to demonstrate in the direction of Mechanicsville, ten miles south of the Pamunkey crossings. On May 28 Sheridan sent Gregg in that direction via Haw's Shop. The 2nd Division progressed unhindered for about three-quarters of a mile beyond the shop but at that point ran into Hampton's main body. The Confederates, who had been expecting their opponents, were dug in behind fieldworks braced with artillery. Having recently been augmented by two thousand mounted riflemen from South Carolina, Hampton outweighed Gregg, and the preponderance of long-range rifles gave him an added advantage.[4]

Sheridan described the ensuing engagement as "of the severest character," and he did not exaggerate. Gregg detailed the conditions under which it was fought: "The enemy[,] dismounted, were strongly posted in a dense woods, and, in addition to defensive works, were still further protected in their position by swamps [tributaries of Crump's and Mill Creeks]. Having chosen their ground advantageous positions had been selected for batteries." Ignoring the odds against him, the brigadier dismounted four regiments of Henry Davies's brigade and sent them to feel out the enemy, ascertaining their strength and position. The 1st New Jersey and 1st Pennsylvania formed the center of this line astride the road to Mechanicsville with the 10th New York on their right and the 6th Ohio to the left. The 6th New York Battery, which had ably supported Gregg's command since before Second Brandy Station almost a year ago, moved its six 3-inch rifles into position in the 10th New York's rear.[5]

Appropriating whatever cover the area offered—mostly fence rails and fallen logs—the 1st Brigade directed the fire of its seven-shot carbines at Hampton's right flank, which was ensconced in the trees behind Enon Church, one mile west of Haw's Shop. The Rebels—members of Williams C. Wickham's and Thomas Rosser's brigades, covered by Hampton's horse artillery—replied with a fire of their own that Gregg described as "exceedingly stubborn." Under the fusillade General Davies barely escaped injury when a rifle ball split his scabbard in two and clipped off the tail of his horse.[6]

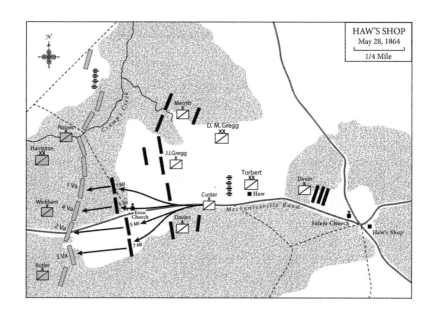

Map 6. Haw's Shop, May 28, 1864. Created by Paul Dangel.

The standoff was relatively brief, however, for Davies's men, finding it impossible to turn either of Hampton's swamp-protected flanks, were steadily forced to the rear. To stabilize the position and extend his right flank, Gregg had his cousin send in the 13th and 16th Pennsylvania, which had just reached the field. Hampton took Irvin Gregg's arrival as a cue to attack mounted, one of the few such charges early in the fight. The 1st Pennsylvania managed to disrupt and turn back the effort, only to see both of its flanks threatened. The dismounted men of the 1st New Jersey then rushed into the breach and a fragile stalemate set in, the opposing artilleries carrying on the fight for a time.

At this point Hampton played his ace in the hole, committing the pea-green but highly motivated 4th South Carolina of Brig. Gen. M. Calbraith Butler's brigade, its men toting long-range, English-made Enfield rifles. A sudden blizzard of balls took a savage toll of Davies's outfits, particularly the 1st New Jersey which absorbed 64 of the 256 losses the 2nd Division would count at day's end. In minutes the center as well as the left of the 1st Brigade began to waver. Looking on from the rear, Custer's position, Captain James Harvey Kidd of the 6th Michigan wondered if "the hitherto invincible Gregg might have the worst of it. . . . The attack was such that only the bravest men could have withstood it."[7]

Reluctantly, one imagines, but of necessity Gregg messaged Sheridan that if reinforcements were not promptly sent his division might go under. His superior complied by releasing two-thirds of Torbert's division. The Reserve Brigade, again under Wesley Merritt, hurried forward to bolster and lengthen the right flank, thwarting an attempt to envelop the position by John R. Chambliss' brigade. Then, around 4:00 p.m., Custer's Michiganders reached the field and deployed in the center of Gregg's line, the 1st and 6th Michigan on the north side of the Mechanicsville road, the 5th and 7th below it. Preparations complete, the flamboyant Custer led his men forward, their morale stimulated by patriotic airs provided by the brigade band.

As it happened, Custer struck just as the enemy was disengaging. From captured Federals Hampton had learned what he had been sent to Haw's Shop to find out: Meade's infantry—Hancock's II Corps—was already on the south side of the Pamunkey within supporting reach of Sheridan and presumably at his call (conversely, Sheridan had gained no definitive information on Lee's dispositions). Now Hampton's plan was to retire southeast to Cold Harbor, placing a water barrier (Totopotomoy Creek) between him and any pursuers.

When the Wolverines attacked, they stampeded Wickham's withdrawing troopers, creating a gap between Rosser's brigade and the raw but ready South Carolinians. Rosser's veterans cleared out, avoiding heavy loss, but the new recruits refused to run and suffered accordingly, especially after Gregg threw in a large portion of his command to enlarge Custer's gains. Finally forced to retreat or suffer annihilation, Butler's men nevertheless gave Gregg and Custer a shellacking they would not quickly forget. The seven-hour struggle at Haw's Shop would find its niche in history as the largest and most fiercely contested dismounted cavalry engagement of the war.[8]

If Grant was to drive the Confederates inside their capital, he was running out of maneuvering room. Now well to the northeast of Richmond, after crossing the Pamunkey he directed the Army of the Potomac toward the crossroads village of Old Cold Harbor, about ten miles from his ultimate objective. If he could beat his enemy to that nondescript but strategic venue he might turn Lee's right and threaten his rear, a futile effort since May 5. As always, however, effective intelligence-gathering, combined with interior lines and adroit maneuvering, thwarted Grant. Fitz Lee's horsemen reached Cold Harbor first on the morning of May 31 and were soon augmented by a brigade of infantry.[9]

Sheridan, who after the fighting at Haw's Shop had moved the divisions of Gregg and Torbert to Old Church, north of Cold Harbor, appreciated the strategic importance of the crossroads with the curious name. "Indeed," he would recall, "it was absolutely necessary that we should possess it, to secure our communications with the White House [a supply base on the Pamunkey River], as well as to cover the extension of our line to the left toward the James River. Roads from Bethesda Church, Old Church, and the White House centered at Cold Harbor, and from there many roads diverged also toward different crossings of the Chickahominy which were indispensable to us." For this reason on May 30 he hustled Torbert's division from Old

Church to Cold Harbor via a crossing of Matadequin Creek. North of the stream fighting less extensive than at Haw's Shop but of a similarly violent nature broke out. Thanks to his superior numbers Torbert drove to within a mile and a half of Cold Harbor, where Lee was trying to nail down a defensive position.[10]

Gregg's division played no part in the action on May 30 other than guarding Torbert's flanks and keeping open the road from White House. The latter mission was especially important, for that landing on the Pamunkey was the debarkation point of a ten-thousand-man column detached from Ben Butler's Army of the James under Maj. Gen. William Farrar Smith and sent by water to reinforce Meade for his next confrontation with Lee. Irvin Gregg's brigade was assigned to meet and guide Smith to Cold Harbor, but it failed to find him; mistakes by the army headquarters staff had sent Smith to the wrong destination, forcing him to countermarch.[11]

Early on May 31 Sheridan moved on Cold Harbor with Torbert, who after a severe struggle and with support from Davies's brigade wrested the town from Fitz Lee and his infantry comrades. Learning that large numbers of Rebels were heading his way and aware that he was too far afield to receive adequate support, Sheridan was compelled to withdraw during the night. But as he later wrote, "The last of my troops had scarcely pulled out . . . when I received a dispatch from Meade directing me to hold Cold Harbor at every hazard" until the infantry's advance echelon, the VI Corps, could relieve him. Sheridan—undoubtedly with sharp memories of the same foul-up at Todd's Tavern—began at once to return his troopers to the place where Grant and Meade expected to fight their next battle. Torbert, now augmented by Davies's brigade, occupied and reversed the temporary breastworks that the Confederates had constructed at the crossroads. Sheridan used them to repulse an attack just after daylight on June 1 by Maj. Gen. Joseph B. Kershaw's infantry division. Later in the morning Kershaw's men came on a second time; again Torbert and Davies beat them back with their repeating carbines. "After this second failure we were left undisturbed," Sheridan recalled, and by 10:00 a.m. Wright's foot soldiers began filing into the cavalry's works and building new ones.

Allowed to go to the rear, Sheridan marched Gregg and Torbert to the north side of the Chickahominy, placed them in camp near a familiar landmark, Bottom's Bridge, and picketed the riverbank. Rebel cavalry and artillery confronted them on the south side, but because "it was not intended that we should cross," Sheridan remained virtually stationary until June 6, thus sparing his men from the ordeal suffered by their infantry comrades. On June 1–3, while the cavalry rested, Grant had Meade assault various sectors of Lee's entrenched lines northwest of Old Cold Harbor. Each attack failed in spectacular fashion with an aggregate loss of almost thirteen thousand. Grant would never cease to regret the misguided tactics that had produced such a slaughter.[12]

On June 6, having gained no advantage in the direction he was moving, the general-in-chief made a major revision of strategy. Having nearly reached the banks of the Chickahominy, too far from Richmond to threaten the city effectively, he decided to cross Meade's troops over that river and the James as well. Bypassing the Confederate capital, he would push twenty-two miles south to Petersburg, Richmond's primary supply and transportation center. Should Meade seize and occupy the "Cockade City," Lee would have to evacuate his trenches and rifle pits in search of foodstuffs, forage, ammunition, and equipment. Once on open ground his army would be vulnerable to defeat piece by piece.

Grant realized that even as lightly defended as it then was, Petersburg was not ripe for the taking. On June 9 that portion of the Army of the James not sent to Cold Harbor had attempted to fight its way into the city from the northeast and south but had blundered and been checked. Grant would attack with a much larger force, under abler generals than Ben Butler.

In mapping his plans, he saw a major role for Sheridan's cavalry in keeping Lee ignorant of his intentions for as long as possible. While Wilson remained with Meade, guarding the army's front and flanks as it moved to and across the James, Gregg and Torbert would march well to the west, drawing Hampton's horsemen, Lee's primary intelligence-gathering force, from Meade's path. Grant saw additional objectives for Sheridan, including destroying the railroad bridge over the Rivanna River near Charlottesville and ripping up track on the Lynchburg branch of the Virginia Central Railroad at Gordonsville "and, if practicable, from Gordonsville back toward Hanover Junction." An ancillary mission would be making contact with an army under Maj. Gen. David Hunter that had been operating in the new state of West Virginia and which Grant had ordered to move to Charlottesville. If able to join forces, Sheridan and Hunter were to destroy further the Virginia Central and also the James River Canal, which George Stoneman's raiders had struck but failed to put out of operation.[13]

On June 6 Sheridan, in response to orders, concentrated his strike force—which had been whittled down by the recent campaigning to around six thousand officers and men—at New Castle Ferry on the Pamunkey. Next day the raiders started northeast via Aylett's Mills on the lower bank of the Mattapony, then turned west toward Chilesburg via a crossing of the Richmond, Fredericksburg and Potomac Railroad. For most of the journey Torbert's men took the lead while Gregg's division—perhaps because of its effective performance on the road to Yellow Tavern—guarded the rear.

Over the next three days the raiders kept moving at a moderate, even a leisurely, pace, their principal opposition being irregular forces who hit and ran, discomfiting but not seriously harming the column. The only truly uncomfortable features of the journey were the steadily climbing heat of each day on the march and the almost impenetrable clouds of dust stirred up by horses' hooves and wagon wheels. By late on June 10 Sheridan had crossed the North Anna at Carpenter's Ford and gone into bivouac on a road leading to Trevilian Station on the Virginia Central, seven miles away. At this point the free-and-easy gait of the expedition was at an end. "During the evening and night," Sheridan wrote, "the boldness of the enemy's scouting parties, with which we had been coming into collision more or less every day, perceptibly increased, indicating the presence of a large force." That force, Hampton's, had been keeping pace with the raiders on parallel loads; having sped up, it was now stationed about three miles north of Trevilian, while an equally sizable contingent under Fitz Lee had reached Louisa Court House, six miles east of the station.[14]

Hampton, who expected to link with Lee at a critical point in the fight to come, was determined that Sheridan would progress no farther. When the Federals descended on the railroad soon after day-

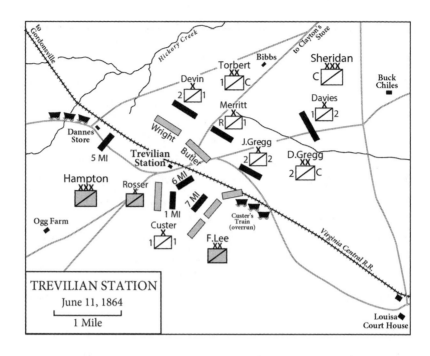

Map 7. Trevilian Station, June 11, 1864. Created by Paul Dangel.

light on June 11, he met them head on. Intent on breaking through the roadblock, Sheridan advanced on the Fredericksburg Road, the most direct route to the depot, with two-thirds of Torbert's division, while Custer's brigade, on the far left flank, came in from the east to seize Trevilian. The fighting began with Merritt's brigade attacked by some of the same South Carolinians who had given Gregg a rough time at Haw's Shop. Charges, countercharges, and dismounted combat would consume the balance of the intensely hot day.

While Torbert and Hampton clashed, the Wolverine Brigade passed to the rear of the preoccupied enemy. Custer's intervention appeared fortuitous, but the young brigadier had not reconnoitered the area thoroughly enough. Reaching the depot, he plowed into a mass of led horses, wagons, and artillery caissons that Hampton had left there. His conspicuous presence alerted Rosser's brigade, which fell upon Custer from the west. At approximately the same time Fitz Lee's late-arriving troopers stormed in from the east, catching Custer in a pincer movement. Through hard fighting and good fortune he made his escape, but he was forced to relinquish the horses and other spoils he had captured while his own baggage wagon, four caissons (and, briefly, one cannon) fell into Rebel hands. Custer's near-encirclement, the result of faulty planning, has struck many historians as a presentiment of his fatal struggle on the Little Bighorn a dozen years later. The difference was that at Trevilian Station his route to the battlefield had been assigned to him by his superiors.[15]

Up to this point half of Gregg's command had been reduced to the role of spectator, only the 2nd Brigade having been sent in support of Torbert's main body early in the fight. But when Sheridan learned of Custer's predicament he not only ordered Torbert to cut his way through to the depot but instructed Irvin Gregg, on the 1st Division's left, to exploit a gap that had opened between Hampton and Lee. According to his cousin, it took only twenty minutes for Colonel Gregg—supported by Alanson Randol's battery and three regiments of Davies's brigade, which had been guarding Sheridan's own wagons—to clear the enemy from a position it was clinging to along the railroad bed.

Much of the credit for the success in this sector went to the 10th New York of Davies's brigade (temporarily assigned to Irvin Gregg).

Attacking dismounted, the New Yorkers imperiled one of Lee's batteries, which from the grounds of a tavern east of the depot had been harassing Custer. It took two attacks, but the 10th forced the battery to limber up and speed to the rear. The charging men then dismounted, jumped into a nearby railroad cut, and scooped up numerous Rebels whose chosen position had effectively trapped them. Meanwhile, Davies's 1st New Jersey, which had been picketing near the route Custer had taken to Trevilian, swept around Hampton's left flank toward Louisa Court House. En route it encountered the pickets of a large force of Rebels strung out along the railroad. The Jerseymen charged, causing the main body of Col. Gilbert J. Wright's Georgia brigade to flee. The 1st's commander would describe the attack as "managed so cleverly that it excited the admiration of all who saw it."[16]

Irvin Gregg's regiments were also more or less heavily engaged, and their leader narrowly escaped being struck in the face by a rifle ball. In his diary Sam Cormany of the 16th Pennsylvania, now a lieutenant, described his brigade's "wild and dashing mounted charge upon the enemy's right, getting almost in rear of their artillery—we caused them [Lee's men] to concentrate on the center—and put up a hot resistance. . . . But we gained the day and held the Field." By early evening Sheridan had driven his opponent "so far that many miles now intervened between the two Confederate divisions, precluding their union until about noon the next day." Although not engaged as long or as desperately as Torbert, Gregg had sustained a considerable loss: seventy-seven officers and enlisted men killed or wounded.[17]

With the exception of a spell of manual labor on June 12, this was the extent of the 2nd Division's involvement in the two-day battle of Trevilian Station, the war's largest all-cavalry engagement. Perhaps the physical condition of its commander had something to do with its absence from combat. According to a newspaper correspondent traveling with Sheridan, although Gregg remained on duty he was "under severe indisposition all day." The nature of his ailment remains unknown but the rigors of the expedition may well have aggravated one of his several recurrent health issues.[18]

Early on June 12 Sheridan relinquished hope of linking with the capricious General Hunter, who according to captured Confederates had moved not to Charlottesville but well to the southwest near Lexington. At the same time, said Sheridan's informants, a considerable force of the enemy had occupied both Charlottesville and Gordonsville, negating any profit the raiders might gain from heading there. "In view of this," Sheridan wrote, "[I] made up my mind to abandon that part of the scheme" and to return to the army at or near Petersburg "by leisurely marches."

That morning, at per their orders from Sheridan, Gregg's troopers gave their attention to the railroad in the direction of Louisa Court House, "breaking it pretty effectually." Using fence rails and other makeshift tools as levers, they pried up at least a mile of track—probably much more—which they piled and set on fire. When heated to the point of malleability the rails were bent around tree trunks and telegraph poles until utterly useless.[19]

While the 2nd Division labored, Torbert was sent on a reconnaissance on the road to Gordonsville with the object of securing a byway to a ford at which Sheridan wished to cross the North Anna. The expeditionary leader intended to follow the river as far as Spotsylvania and then, via Bowling Green and Dunkirk, to the Pamunkey at White House, Meade's primary supply base. He soon discovered, however, that the path to his chosen destination was neither open nor free. Hampton had placed his men behind freshly dug entrenchments about two miles west of Trevilian. Hoping to clear the road, Torbert attacked, but when Fitz Lee appeared on Hampton's right flank the opposition was strong enough to prevent further progress and produce casualties "very heavy on both sides." Torbert got the worst of it but apparently did not receive adequate assistance. Sheridan claimed to have sent Davies to his support but in his official report Gregg insisted that his 1st Brigade was "not engaged" that day.[20]

Stymied, no longer hopeful of gaining his several objectives, Sheridan pocketed the thought of passing the North Anna at Mallory's Ford. To do so would have precipitated a third day of carnage; already his ammunition supply was running low and he was burdened by four hundred wounded, five hundred prisoners, and some two thousand fugitive slaves who had fallen in with the raiders in hopes of being led out of bondage. As a result, at midnight he withdrew, recrossed the river at Carpenter's Ford, and on the other side gave his weary, grimy troopers a breather while turning their mounts out to graze.[21]

The journey home resumed on June 14 and continued for the next ten days, the whole time under careful observation from a respectful distance. As James Kidd of Custer's brigade would write, "during the entire march from Trevilian to the James, Hampton hovered on the flank of Sheridan's column, watching for a favorable opportunity to inflict a blow, but avoiding a general engagement." As when en route to the Virginia Central, the march was "hot—sultry—dusty" but proceeded at a comfortable pace, the column stopping frequently to enable the men to "lay around resting" and forage for themselves and their horses. The trek covered familiar ground: Todd's Tavern on June 14, the gory, still-littered battlefields of Spotsylvania the next day.[22]

On June 16 the raiders crossed the Mattapony and continued south toward the Pamunkey. Three days later they added destruction of enemy property to their itinerary as one of Gregg's detachments burned a mill at Walkerton. Also on June 19 Sheridan, who had been out of touch with Meade's headquarters since the raid began, learned that Grant, in preparation for his move to Petersburg, had begun to break up Meade's logistical base at White House prior to transferring it to Petersburg. Because the Army of the Potomac's nine-hundred-wagon supply train reportedly remained at the base, Sheridan turned in that direction.[23]

The train would become the bane of the cavalry's existence. When Sheridan neared White House on June 20 he discovered that Fitz Lee had attacked its small garrison with artillery from the surrounding bluffs. Lee withdrew on his approach, and Sheridan lay over for two days, taking on rations, forage, ammunition, and equipment. While there he finally got in touch with army headquarters and learned that he must escort the ponderous caravan to the James, a distance of twenty miles. The assignment rankled him, "knowing full well the dangers which would attend" the rest of the march.[24]

Lee had withdrawn from White House but Hampton, apparently ready to fight, had reached the Pamunkey. To meet any opposition from him Sheridan at dawn on June 21 sent both divisions across the river bridge, Gregg's on foot, Torbert's mounted. On the south bank Gregg, supported by Merritt's brigade, took the road to Tunstall's Station on the Richmond and York River Railroad. Upon arriving the Federals offered battle to their foe, now posted on the west side of Black Creek. According to Sheridan, Hampton, perhaps resolved to defer a strike until the train was in motion, demurred. Gregg, however, reported that Hampton's command advanced threateningly "with the view of retaking the position held by it on the preceding day, but in this it failed, and during the night retired to the Chickahominy." Gregg's claim of a somewhat busier day than Sheridan recalled was upheld by Lieutenant Cormany, who wrote that Irvin Gregg's brigade attacked and drove "a few of the enemy" for a mile and a half toward Tunstall's.[25]

The wagons began trundling south next day, escorted by Torbert in front and Gregg on the exposed right flank. The divisions became widely separated, however, as result of a change in Sheridan's instructions for the train. Originally the wagons were to be transported to a pontoon bridge at Deep Bottom, a horseshoe-shaped bend in the James at the top of Butler's enclave at Bermuda Hundred. But on June 24, the vehicles having passed the Chickahominy at Jones Bridge, Sheridan learned that a lengthy stretch of his westward route by way of Harrison's Landing and Malvern Hill was in enemy hands. Unwilling to court danger, he directed the train south via Charles City Court House to Wilcox's Wharf. The new plan placed Torbert in charge of the train while Gregg was instructed to "hold fast," securing the rear until the wagons were safely parked on the James. Torbert did his job well, escorting the train to the river without loss of a single vehicle, but his separation from Gregg left the latter on his own to face the combined might of Hampton and Lee.[26]

Despite the vexing problems he had encountered on the march from White House—teamsters losing their way on unfamiliar roads, their wagons assailed by pursuers who hit and ran—the 2nd Division made relatively smooth progress until around 10:00 a.m. on June 24. At that hour Gregg's column neared a place of worship six miles northwest of Charles City Court House variously known as Samaria Church or St. Mary's Church. Within a mile of the church grounds Irvin Gregg, leading the advance, encountered a small mounted force in gray. Though it was quickly driven off, larger forces were reported to be advancing on the roads to the west, suggesting that Gregg and his men were in a certain amount of trouble.

Seeing no alternative to standing and fighting if the supply train were to clear Charles City Court House, Gregg dismounted his leading ranks, deployed them on both sides of the church, placed his batteries in "commanding positions," and made "every disposition . . . to resist an attack of the enemy." His constant activity attracted notice. A member of the 4th Pennsylvania found the general "looking anxious and riding to and fro in different directions; then I knew there was something interesting on hand." The trooper was later told that Gregg sent couriers to report his situation but that none got through to Sheridan.[27]

Hampton, whose men had been on starvation rations or something close to them, had been tailing the supply column in hopes of capturing it whole or at least in part. Now the South Carolinian was committed to an all-out attack on the train's escort, using his entire force on hand—six brigades. Because he handily outnumbered Gregg, he must have envisioned crushing him or at least driving him off, then falling on the tag end of the train. But Hampton's opponent did not shrink from the challenge. As the 4th Pennsylvania trooper noted, "Gen. Gregg stood by us nobly." He quoted the division leader as saying: "Here was the end of the line. We must hold this point till after dark."[28]

Facing westward, Gregg built a defense line with Irvin Gregg's brigade on the right, Davies's men on the left, and the cavalry's own wagons in between, parked in the fields behind the church. The division's batteries were unlimbered in the rear of both brigades, and pickets were thrown out several hundred yards in front of the main line. The dismounted troopers on the left threw up breastworks that Hampton later described as quite strong, but the works on Irvin Gregg's part of the field, built on more open ground and thus more exposed, were susceptible to being turned.

The morning and half of the afternoon was consumed in skirmishing, but by 3:00 p.m. the Rebels were prepared to strike. Within minutes all sectors of Gregg's position came under heavy pressure as Hampton

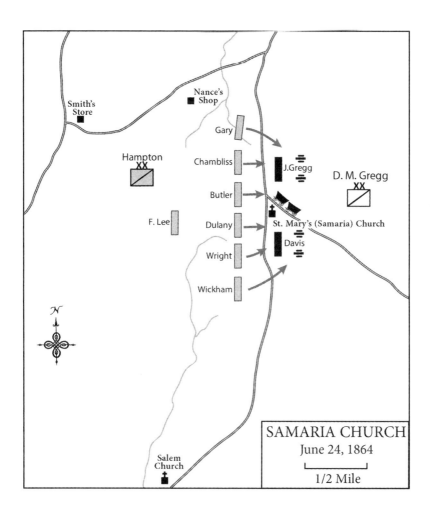

Map 8. Samaria Church, June 24, 1864. Created by Paul Dangel.

attacked both frontally with his main force and against the upper Union flank with two brigades, every man dismounted. As they crossed the field of approach, some two hundred yards long, his men were met with a sheet of carbine fire that staggered them but, quickly rallying, they pressed ahead. The preponderance of attackers eventually drove some of Irvin Gregg's troopers from their works. Reacting swiftly, General Gregg called up mounted supports; their timely arrival helped steady the flank and dashed Hampton's first wave. The Rebels came on again, confident they had their opponents in an inescapable corner. Whenever sectors of his line wavered, Gregg threw in more reinforcements, as did Hampton. As Hampton Thomas of the staff described it, the antagonists "came together like two battering rams, then backed off for vantage-ground, and went at each other again and again."[29]

The seesaw fighting raged for more than two hours, Hampton driving in sectors of Gregg's line through a series of dismounted attacks but achieving limited success. Gregg responded with counterstrikes, including a rare mounted charge by his old 8th Pennsylvania, which drove off a force that came close to capturing the guns of Randol's battery but in so doing lost Col. Pennock Huey to capture. Eventually, inevitably, the tide of battle began to engulf the outnumbered Federals, especially once they ran low on cartridges and shells. By late afternoon Gregg faced the necessity of making a run for it to the James and the prospect of hundreds of his men cut off and captured. But he knew that by now the supply train was beyond the possibility of being overtaken and pillaged by Hampton.

At his reluctant order one unit after another disengaged, fell back, regained its led horses, and galloped to the rear. Enemy pressure was unrelenting; numerous times Gregg's men were forced to turn about and make a stand before being compelled to resume their retreat. Their fight-and-fall-back tactics bought time, as did their passage through wooded areas behind the church almost inaccessible to pursuers. But when the Federals gained the road to Charles City Court House they found themselves in a mammoth snarl, enmeshed with wagons, ambulances, guns, caissons, limbers, and pack animals. When Hampton rallied his men and attacked the congealed mass of humanity and horseflesh, the retreat became complete. For up to six miles cheering, screaming

Rebels lashed the rear and flanks of the 2nd Division before calling off the chase under evening darkness. By then Gregg had suffered 357 casualties to his enemy's fewer than 200.[30]

The heavy losses were bad enough, but for want of adequate transportation Gregg had been forced to leave behind dozens of his wounded. The highest ranking of these unfortunates was Lt. Col. George H. Covode of the 4th Pennsylvania, son of U.S. Congressman "Honest John" Covode and one of Gregg's most trusted subordinates. Shot through the arm and body, the portly officer could not be moved from the stretcher his men had improvised for him. When the retreat began Gregg, realizing that Covode was mortally wounded, took the time to dismount, shake his hand, and bid him goodbye. The gesture nearly resulted in his being snatched up by the swarming Rebels. He escaped only because his adjutant general, Capt. Henry C. Weir, "forced him upon his horse" and galloped off at his side.[31]

Putting the best face on the beating he had taken, Gregg reported that "the movement" to Charles City Court House was made "in the best possible order, without confusion or disorder. The enemy pressed hard upon the rear of the command, but without advantage." By 8:00 p.m. he and the other runaways had reached the courthouse, where they joined Torbert, ensuring that no further molestation would occur. The next day the rear section of the supply train was ferried over the James, followed by the 1st and 2nd Divisions. On the south bank officers and men went into camp at Jordan's (or Light House) Point, six and a half miles upriver from the parked wagons. There they would spent the next three weeks recovering from fifty-six consecutive days of marching and fighting.[32]

Thus ended a dark day for the 2nd Cavalry Division. Objective critics would not minimize the scope of the defeat but neither would they declare it an unmitigated disaster. An enlisted man of the 10th New York described Samaria Church as "the first and only time the colors of the 2nd Division were lowered." A correspondent of the *Philadelphia Inquirer* agreed that Gregg's command "was for the first time in the history of the organization compelled to retire, but in a masterful manner." In his memoirs Sheridan cast the battle in a different light: "Gregg's losses were heavy, and he was forced to abandon his dead and most seriously wounded, but the creditable stand made ensured the safety of the train. . . . His steady, unflinching determination to gain time for the wagons to get beyond the point of danger was characteristic of the man."[33]

While two-thirds of its cavalry had been away, the Army of the Potomac had blundered again, in spectacular fashion. It had failed to evade Lee in the Wilderness or beat him to Spotsylvania and Cold Harbor, but this time it managed to steal a march on its opponent, gaining an opportunity to decisively alter the course of the war—only to throw it all away through sloppy staff work, miscommunication, and an inability to coordinate relatively simple maneuvers. Beginning on June 12, following several days of ill-considered, indecisive, and extremely costly attacks at Cold Harbor, Grant, in a feat that approached miracle status, had slipped away from his adversary, sending Meade's troops, including Wilson's horsemen, across the Chickahominy and James on pontoon bridges that would stand as marvels of engineering. Then the army moved on unsuspecting Petersburg. The advance was taken by Smith's contingent of Butler's army, which was shipped in transports down the Pamunkey, York, and James Rivers to Petersburg's northern doorstep. An overland march by Hancock's II Corps would give Smith the support he needed to attack and seize Grant's new objective.

By rights, Petersburg should have fallen almost at first contact. Commanded by Gen. Gustave Toutant Beauregard of Bull Run fame, its garrison consisted of barely 5,500 troops, including those stationed north of the Appomattox River inside a line of works opposite Bermuda Hundred. Further, neither the "Great Creole" nor his men knew that the Yankees were heading their way. Smith, however, moved ponderously and reluctantly to the attack. Finally in position to strike by early evening, for reasons never fully explained he handed overall command to Hancock upon the latter's belated appearance and went to the rear. The result was that no attack was made that night. The next day, with the IX Corps now at Petersburg, Beauregard's outer works were attacked and some captured, but the defenders withdrew to their interior line and battened down. Their leader stripped the Bermuda Hundred defenses to augment the garrison while sending distress calls to Cold Harbor. Lee, still not convinced that Grant had left his front, did not reinforce the city until around noon on June 18, following two more days of disjointed Union assaults that produced no breakthrough. The failed offensive cost Meade more than eleven thousand casualties to no strategic gain.

A supremely frustrated Grant appeared to be left with no alternative to besieging Petersburg. Before making a final decision he decided to attempt to starve out the city by breaking some of the five railroads that serviced it, especially the one that led to Wilmington, North Carolina, the last open Southern seaport. His first effort, while Sheridan was on his return from Trevilian Station, was to send Hancock's corps, supported by Wright's, down the Jerusalem Plank Road southeast of Petersburg, then west toward the railroad. The plan miscarried when two divisions of A. P. Hill's corps attacked and shoved the uncoordinated Federals back to the plank road.[34]

Though the movement had extended his siege lines across the railroad, Grant was not satisfied. This time he targeted the line with more mobile forces. On June 22 Wilson's horsemen were sent to destroy it as well as the westward-leading South Side (or Petersburg and Lynchburg) Railroad and, via Burkeville Junction, the Virginia Central. Prior to starting out, the 3rd Division was joined by the small (four-regiment) division of cavalry attached to Butler's army under Brig. Gen. August V. Kautz, Wilson's former chief subordinate, then his successor, as head of the Cavalry Bureau. This effort, too, fell short of Grant's hopes. The raiders tore up sixty miles of track on all three roads, but on June 29 they were intercepted and almost surrounded by Hampton (now freed from pursuing Sheridan) with his and Fitz Lee's divisions as well as two brigades of Hill's infantry. In the lopsided clash near Reams Station, ten miles from Petersburg, Wilson lost all his artillery and wagons and more than a thousand men; the survivors were stampeded and forced to cut their way back to their starting point. Upon returning to the army Sheridan, along with the VI Corps, was ordered to rescue the raiders, but by the time he reached Reams Station the antagonists were long gone.[35]

A few days later Gregg's division was sent back to the depot, which was again in enemy hands, to estimate the number of its defenders.

North of Reams Davies's brigade clashed with Williams Wickham's brigade, drove its men to a line of freshly dug entrenchments, and held them there while two of Irvin Gregg's regiments probed southward along the Jerusalem Plank Road and across Warwick Swamp to Lee's Mills. There Long John encountered a much larger mounted force under Tom Rosser and Lunsford L. Lomax and was forced to fall back. With his main body David Gregg returned the favor, shooing his cousin's assailants back to Reams Station. The reconnaissance, which cost more than forty casualties, now complete, he returned his men to their camp on the James. A few days later Gregg was forced to deny to army headquarters that at Lee's Mills Davies had lost almost a hundred men captured, as reported in a Richmond newspaper.[36]

Grant seethed over another opportunity squandered, but an unlikely prospect for redemption appeared in late July. The day after Samaria Church a Pennsylvania regiment in the IX Corps composed largely of coal miners began tunneling under a Confederate salient east of Petersburg. Initially regarded as a means of keeping Burnside's men busy, within a month, to the astonishment of Grant and Meade, the coal-crackers had dug a shaft 511 feet long and more than 20 feet below the enemy position. They stocked it with 320 kegs (8,000 pounds) of gunpowder, to be detonated by a multi-spliced fuse that ran the length of the shaft. At last attuned to the possibility of gaining entrance to Petersburg via explosives, Grant authorized Burnside to select and train troops to attack in the wake of the blast, set for the predawn hours of July 30.[37]

Meade belatedly set in motion supporting operations mainly intended to draw enemy troops from the mine area. On July 26 Sheridan pulled Gregg's and Torbert's divisions out of their camps at Jordan's Point and led them to the James, which they crossed at the Deep Bottom bridge before dawn next day. At that point they were joined by Kautz's brigade-sized command, now recovered from its drubbing at Reams Station. En route to the Northside (as the area above the James was known) Sheridan also met up with General Hancock, whose corps would supply the bulk of the manpower for the mission. While the infantry pinned down the nearest Rebels, occupants of the fortificd camp at Chaffin's Bluff, Sheridan was to swing north and west to make yet another attempt to put the Virginia Central out of commission as well as to wreck some bridges on the North and South Anna and Little Rivers.

The combined-arms operation, later known as First Deep Bottom, would fall short of fruition on both ends of the twelve-mile front. The first day out the II Corps attacked a line of Rebel works on the east side of Bailey's Creek and, supported on the right by Sheridan, took 250 prisoners and three guns. As Little Phil wrote, "this opened the way for Hancock to push out his whole corps" on the New Market and Charles City Roads toward the capital, an advance in which the cavalry joined. The Rebels were pushed back to a stronger line of entrenchments on the west bank.

A stretch of high ground on the Union right was soon occupied by Gregg and Torbert, supported by Kautz, most of their men mounted. Confederate infantry advanced on the position, shoving back the horsemen, who soon regrouped, dismounted, and, at Sheridan's order, lay down in line of battle about fifteen yards from the crest. He described the result: "Such a severe fire" was opened on the Rebels "and at such close quarters, that they could not withstand it, and gave way in disorder."[38]

Initially Gregg's division had a hard time of it. While supporting Torbert's embattled pickets on the road between Malvern Hill and Richmond, Davies's brigade was attacked by Kershaw's infantry and threatened with heavy loss. Covered by a section of Battery A, 2nd United States Artillery, Davies's men resisted fiercely but were forced to give ground until the 2nd Brigade came up in their rear, whereupon the enemy beat a hasty retreat through impenetrable woods. Gregg reported inflicting at least thirty casualties but also losing one of Battery A's guns, whose horses had been shot down, preventing its escape when attacked.[39]

The cavalry's stand reestablished Hancock's line but the weight of the opposition told Sheridan that Lee had sent up more troops from Petersburg, under Gen. Richard H. Anderson, than Grant had anticipated: "This development rendered useless any further effort on Hancock's part or mine to carry out the plan of the expedition" for "there was no longer any chance for the cavalry to turn the enemy's left."

The Federals, however, held their ground. July 28 was spent in diverting Anderson's attention from the goings-on at Petersburg. Sheridan helped achieve this by marching Torbert's division and one of Gregg's brigades after dark to the south side of the river, their crossing muffled with moss and grass spread on the bridge, and returning them to the north bank, on foot, the next morning "to create the impression of a continuous movement of large bodies of infantry." That night, in preparation for the detonation of the Petersburg mine, Hancock, followed by the cavalry, withdrew to the Southside.[40]

The infantry and cavalry's maneuvering went for naught. The absence of the troops Lee had transferred from Petersburg achieved nothing once the mine was detonated at 4:44 on the morning of July 30. The explosion itself was a spectacular success, creating a smoking crater 170 feet in length, more than 100 feet wide, and 30 feet deep. Almost 300 Confederates were killed by the blast and supporting forces were so stunned by the unearthly effects they failed to respond quickly enough to block access to the city.

Burnside had been ready to attack with a specially trained division of United States Colored Troops (USCT) but at the last minute—for reasons military, or political, or both—the black soldiers were replaced with a white division that lacked training in the type of assault tactics called for here. Commanded by an incompetent drunkard who refused to go in with his troops, the division not only failed to exploit the breakthrough but allowed the enemy to cobble together a new line which proved impossible to surmount. Too late to salvage the situation, the USCT were thrown into to the cauldron, to be shot down in droves by maddened Rebels. By 2:00 p.m. the criminally bungled assault had run its course and Grant was left to ponder the demise of another golden chance to end the war in a single stroke.[41]

11

Commander of Cavalry, Army of the Potomac

For Gregg and his horse soldiers the last five months of 1864 were filled with frequent, intense, and sometimes hectic activity, the fruit of Grant's decision to lay siege to Petersburg. In a sense it was a time of career progression, for at the outset Gregg attained perhaps his loftiest personal ambition, command of the cavalry of Meade's army. The elevation came about upon the opening of a major theater of operations 150 miles to the west, to which Grant dispatched Phil Sheridan, along with the VI Corps and a mounted force of undetermined size.

In another sense this period was a time of disappointment, dissatisfaction, and professional decline for the general who was left at Petersburg. As the eminent military historian Russell F. Weigley has observed, David McMurtrie Gregg attained a long-deferred goal "when it had lost much of its former meaning, and when circumstances deprived the cavalry of the spectacular qualities it often displayed in other periods and areas of the war." During this stage of the conflict the opposing leaders, "having exhausted their armies in pursuit of smashing victories they could not win, had reconciled themselves to the more measured triumphs of inducing in the enemy a greater exhaustion than they themselves suffered." Weigley describes the altered landscape, in which horse soldiers were regularly reduced to fighting on the defensive and on foot, as "the twilight of mounted cavalry." The metaphor was applicable to Gregg himself, whose presence on war's stage was drawing to a close.[1]

Gregg's ascendency effectively dated from June 12, 1864, when Lee ordered ten thousand troops under Lt. Gen. Jubal Anderson Early, the senior division commander in Richard S. Ewell's corps, to Staunton to help the local forces deal with David Hunter's Federals. After Hunter's defeat eight days later at Lynchburg, Early remained in the Shenandoah Valley at the head of two infantry divisions and a division of cavalry and began an invasion of the North. Lee authorized the move as a means of drawing besiegers from Petersburg; other objectives included freeing the inmates of prisons in and around Washington. Early carried out his orders so well that he threw the Union capital into a panic by assaulting its outer works on July 11–12. Forced to withdraw when Meade dispatched the VI Corps to the city's defense, Early returned to the lower Shenandoah, where his presence threatened Grant's operations while safeguarding the "Breadbasket of the Confederacy," which succored the defenders of Petersburg and Richmond.[2]

Grant's response, after consultation with Lincoln, Stanton, and Halleck, was to send Sheridan to the Valley with orders to clear it of Early's feisty and fast-moving army. Little Phil was assigned command of a vast domain known as the Middle Military Division, consisting initially of some 43,000 troops, including the VI Corps, two other infantry corps (the VIII and XIX), and a substantial force of cavalry. A portion of the latter would be led by William Averell, who since his ouster from middle Virginia had operated, more or less capably, in the western regions of the state. At least one mounted division would be sent to Sheridan from Petersburg, leaving the others, with the assistance of August V. Kautz's small command, to support Meade.[3]

Briefly there was some question as to who would lead the Valley horsemen, though it appears that Alfred Torbert, at the head of the 1st Division, was selected at an early date. On August 3, one day after Sheridan was relieved "temporarily from duty" in the Army of the Potomac, General Halleck telegraphed the newly established headquarters of the combined armies of George Meade and Benjamin F. Butler at City Point (at the confluence of the James and Appomattox Rivers), noting that Sheridan had requested that a second division be sent to him via Washington. Grant left the choice of which one up to Meade. When Gregg learned of the situation he applied for the position: "I have the honor to designate the Second Division (that commanded by myself) as the division to proceed to Washington." He noted that his brigades, both of which were posted east of Petersburg, could "most conveniently be moved to City Point for shipment."

On the afternoon of August 4 Meade made his choice: James Harrison Wilson would serve under Sheridan. No explanation was given for declining Gregg's request. It was probably a combination of factors including Meade's preference for a seasoned commander of horse—one he could depend on based on past experience—to continue under him. Sheridan's preference for Torbert, who led the largest of the army's mounted divisions, may have rested on his belief that the man was somewhat more aggressive and assertive than the quietly competent Gregg. He may well have felt the same about the less experienced but self-confident Wilson, who exuded potential. By naming Torbert as his chief of cavalry, Little Phil permitted the multi-talented Wesley Merritt to succeed to permanent command of the 1st Division. In late September Wilson would be sent west to command Sherman's cavalry; he would be replaced by Sheridan's favorite subordinate, Custer.[4]

One of Gregg's men would recall less than fondly the period following Torbert's and Wilson's departure: "The division that remained with the Army of the Potomac . . . moved from right to left and from left to right of the line in front of Petersburg without any regard for rest or comfort." The command's peripatetic existence began on the day of the mine explosion, when to better cover the army's lower (left) flank it was moved to the area around Prince George Court House, east of the city and along and above the railroad to Norfolk. John Irvin Gregg's brigade went into camp in that area, picketing toward Lee's Mill on the other side of the railroad. There it connected with the pickets of Davies's brigade, who patrolled northeastward to Mount Sinai Church.

On August 5 both brigades were abruptly recalled to Jordan's Point where they had camped upon returning from the Trevilian expedition. From his new headquarters Gregg ordered Kautz, over whom he had been given authority, to post his sentinels at various points farther east near Sycamore Church and, toward the south, at Mount Zion Church. Kautz's picket line was to connect with Gregg's and all roads leading to Prince George Court House were to be well covered.[5]

The 2nd Division's rest period at "Light House Point" lasted only four days before it was ordered back to Prince George, where it remained until August 13. At 4 p.m. on that day Gregg broke camp and headed for the James to take part in a second expedition on the Northside via Deep Bottom. The operation, conducted in cooperation with Hancock's command and one of Butler's corps, had a trio of objectives. Grant believed, erroneously, that Lee had depleted his lines around Richmond to reinforce the Valley army (it was later learned that he had detached Joseph B. Kershaw's infantry and Fitz Lee's cavalry from Petersburg). Grant hoped the offensive would prompt Lee to recall the reinforcements; if able to break through the supposedly reduced defenses, Butler and Hancock might take another crack at the enemy capital. Finally—as part of a plan indicating that Grant remained fixated on waylaying Petersburg's communications—the operation would support a simultaneous advance against the Petersburg and Weldon Railroad by the V Corps in the vicinity of Globe Tavern, three and a half miles below the Cockade City. When Gregg vacated the Southside, Kautz would take over the job of guarding the army's left and rear.[6]

After dark on the August 13 Gregg's people crossed the pontoon bridges on the flanks of Bermuda Hundred and connected with the X Corps of Maj. Gen. David Bell Birney, an erstwhile division commander under Hancock. To mask the move, the soldiers of the II Corps were shipped to the target area by transports from City Point as if bound for Washington and from there to the Shenandoah.[7]

The next day, August 14, the combined forces moved to the attack. While Birney, to the south, struck toward Chaffin's Farm, Hancock advanced against the capital's defenses via the New Market Road and, farther north, Fussell's Mill. While the opposing infantries clashed Gregg was to move around the north flank and make for the supposedly distracted capital. Because of the faulty intelligence at the heart of the operation, however, Birney's and Hancock's advances were halted on August 14 and 16 by the local defenders, augmented by troops hustled up from below the James.

Gregg's troopers were demonstrably more successful. On August 14 they made good progress on the Charles City Road, driving enemy cavalry from and then seizing a line of rifle pits whose construction dated

from the Peninsula Campaign. Gregg reported that his position astride
the road and on either side of it extended for five miles, connecting
with Hancock's right flank. The next day mounted and dismounted
troopers under Wade Hampton launched "a spirited advance" that
drove Gregg from the captured trenches, although the 2nd Division
fell back slowly and grudgingly. Despite the setback, by early afternoon
Gregg had secured the strategic intersection of the Charles City, New
Market, and Quaker Roads, about ten miles southeast of Richmond.[8]

On August 16 Gregg, supported part of the time by the II Corps
brigade of Brig. Gen. Nelson A. Miles, fought his way across Deep
Bottom Creek. He drove Hampton toward White's Tavern, within
seven miles of the city. Hancock wished Gregg to reconnoiter farther
up the road but his path was blocked by Rooney Lee's division, including the brigade of Gregg's West Point comrade John Chambliss. Eventually Gregg was forced back across the creek, effectively ending his
participation in the operation, though not before he bore witness to
a personal tragedy. In the fighting that day a dismounted member of
the 16th Pennsylvania pointed his pistol at a fleeing horseman, a "fine
looking man in grey," and knocked Chambliss from his saddle, killing
him instantly. Lieutenant Cormany, whose men had brought down
the brigadier, removed Chambliss's sword, belt, and pipe, which he
intended to keep as souvenirs. After Cormany departed Gregg arrived,
inspected Chambliss' body, and collected a few personal items. At his
direction the Virginian was buried near the point where the Charles
City Road crossed Bailey's Creek.[9]

Two days later a Rebel truce party exhumed the remains and placed
them in a coffin, to which Gregg added the items he had taken from
the corpse, a pair of gold sleeve buttons and Chambliss's West Point
ring. Apparently he later sent the general's widow a pocket Bible with
the deceased man's name in it (Lieutenant Cormany also returned to
the Chambliss family the pipe he had appropriated). Gregg did not
return another item found on Chambliss's body, a detailed map of the
Richmond defenses, which he had copied for distribution throughout the army. Another casualty of the fight was Gregg's cousin; Irvin
Gregg had received a disabling wound in the right arm, forcing him to
relinquish brigade command to Col. Michael Kerwin. Subsequently

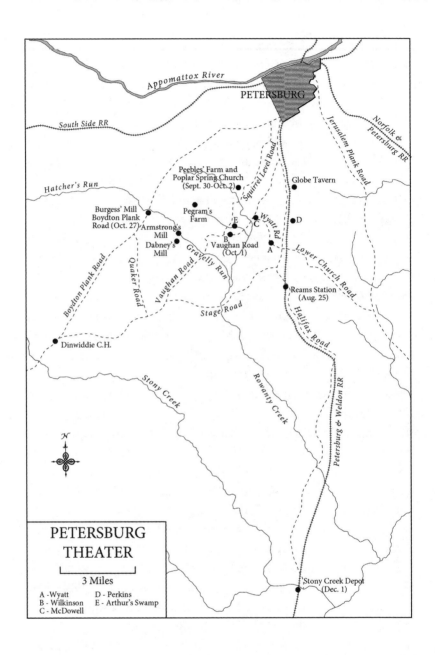

Map 9. Petersburg theater. Created by Paul Dangel.

Kerwin was supplanted by Col. Charles H. Smith of the 1st Maine, a more tried and trusted subordinate of the division commander.[10]

On August 17 Grant, having learned of the troop transfer from Petersburg, doubted that the II Corps, even with support from Gregg and Birney, could survive on that front. He held the troops north of the river for three more days but changed their operation to a reconnaissance in force. By then Birney's efforts to strike the southern flank of the works above the James had foundered on questionable tactics—not his, but Hancock's. On August 16 the X Corps had made a promising advance against the main line west of Bailey's Creek only to be ordered to relinquish its gains by Hancock, who had failed to make similar progress and desired closer cooperation from Birney. At his order the X Corps made a roundabout march to a point opposite the upper end of the enemy line near Fussell's Mill. Birney assaulted and overran the position, only to be halted, counterattacked, and held at bay for the balance of the operation.[11]

After dark on August 20 the entire expedition crossed to Bermuda Hundred and then back to Petersburg. By now Grant had set in motion the offensive against the Weldon line near Globe Tavern. This operation would garner only slightly more success than the one at the opposite end of the Union lines. Although the V Corps advanced only a few hundred yards west of the tracks before being thrust back, it held the ground left to it, denying a key section of the railroad to the enemy. Now Lee would have to bring up supplies by wagon via a thirty-mile detour from Stony Creek Depot to and then up the Boydton Plank Road.[12]

On the morning of the August 21 Hancock and Gregg, although fatigued and frustrated after a week of fighting and maneuvering to no discernable purpose, were unexpectedly committed to the operations on Gouverneur K. Warren's front. The aborted offensive had taken its toll: 2,900 casualties, including 231 in the ranks of the 2nd Cavalry Division. Now Grant wished the railroad to be torn up as far south as Rowanty Creek, nine miles from Globe Tavern. That much damage should permanently deny Lee access to the railroad, forcing him to rely even more heavily on the poorly maintained plank road from Boydton.

As always, the cavalry led the march. Upon recrossing the river Gregg had returned to Prince George Court House, but his men got minimal rest there. Within a few hours of arriving they were heading down the Jerusalem Plank Road toward Reams Station. The march was not hindered by impedimenta; as Gregg's chief surgeon noted, "The condition of the roads was so very bad, owing to the late rains, that it was almost impossible to bring any wheeled vehicles along" including the divisional artillery, a significant deprivation.[13]

When it reached the railroad on the morning of August 22 the division began to picket the Jerusalem Plank Road and the left flank of Warren's corps. "Just before dark," Gregg reported, "a reconnaissance was made to Reams' Station and no enemy found." The next day, in response to Meade's orders, Gregg moved the entire command to Reams. There he established a picket line between Warren's troops and two divisions of the II Corps, which had occupied previously constructed breastworks south of the depot.

Gregg soon learned that one of August Kautz's brigades under Col. Samuel P. Spear, which had been attached to Hancock, had encountered Rebel troopers coming in from the west along the stage road to Dinwiddie Court House. To ascertain the strength and position of the enemy Gregg directed two regiments of Smith's brigade down the road. About a mile and a half from Reams they discovered what appeared to be a full division or more of dismounted cavalry, which soon advanced against them. Before the Rebels could strike Gregg called up seven more regiments, all but one of which he dismounted, the seventh being kept in the saddle to guard the flanks and held in reserve should the enemy attack mounted. By 5 p.m. the fight was on; it continued "without abatement until about 8:30 when the enemy withdrew, having failed to reach Reams' Station, his evident purpose."[14]

The enemy did reach the station on August 25, following a fairly quiet day during which the main activity was the of destruction of tracks and ties by Hancock's working parties. That morning—only hours after Gregg informed Hancock that the enemy had not been reinforced, relieving the latter's mind about his vulnerable position—Rebel horsemen attacked through a swamp west of the depot, where Gregg had assembled the bulk of his division. They scattered the pickets of the 13th Pennsylvania, but the 4th Pennsylvania, with the assistance of foot soldiers from the division commanded that day by General Miles, struck back and chased them away. "Scarcely had the enemy retired," Gregg reported, than his patrols on the Dinwiddie Road and in front of Hancock's picket line were again attacked by mounted cavalry. These too, however, were forced to withdraw fairly quickly.

Then around 2 p.m. disaster befell the expeditionary force when suddenly attacked by more than 8,000 Confederates—four brigades of infantry under Maj. Gen. Cadmus M. Wilcox and the cavalry of Wade Hampton. They struck in waves against Miles's command, manning the northern section of the 700-yard-long main face. For upward of four hours Miles held firm under mounting pressure even after reinforcements pitted 13,000 Rebels against 8,000 Federals. Finally, inevitably, the attackers penetrated Miles's line while others, including two divisions of Hampton's horsemen, wrested the southern sector of the works from the division of Maj. Gen. John Gibbon. Physically and psychologically stunned, hundreds of Gibbon's men broke and fled to the rear. His entire line on the verge of collapse, Hancock engineered a last-ditch stand that gave most of the infantry time to clear the field. His loss would approach 2,000 (more than 1,700 of them missing and presumed captured) and eight cannons.[15]

The scale of the defeat was an eye-opener for all involved. Since the Peninsula Campaign Hancock's command had been the bulwark of the army, its leader the most aggressive, acute, and dependable of the corps commanders. But the II Corps, which had performed sluggishly at Deep Bottom, had been gutted by battle loses, and Hancock, still suffering from a wound received on the third day at Gettysburg, was no longer the soldier he had been for so many years.

Gregg's men were equally tired and stressed from their recent exertions, but they gave a strong account of themselves throughout August 25. Early in the afternoon, after repulsing the mounted assaults on his lines west of the depot, Gregg transferred the 4th and 8th Pennsylvania to the east side of Hancock's works to prevent the Confederates from gaining possession of the road linking Reams with the Jerusalem Plank Road. Once Wilcox advanced Gregg shifted the rest of his force, including the dismounted 1st Maine and mounted 16th Pennsylvania, to shore up Hancock's left. With the additional support of portions of two of Colonel Spear's regiments, he easily turned back a "feeble demonstration" against the front of his new line. When, minutes later, the Rebels turned their attention to Hancock's corps, the cavalry poured a "galling fire" into the assailants' exposed flank.[16]

Gregg's men remained on the field long after Hancock's troops vacated it in haste and panic. The 2nd Cavalry Brigade covered the infantry's flight, not being withdrawn until hours after the shooting ceased. The 1st Brigade, led by Col. William Stedman of the 6th Ohio (General Davies was on sick leave), maintained its position on the Dinwiddie Road until ten o'clock the next morning. As one of Hancock's men lamented, August 25, 1864, had been the "blackest of all days" for the once-proud II Corps; but Gregg's troopers, in the words of its leader, "acquitted themselves handsomely." Hancock avidly concurred. In dispatches sent during the battle he noted that the cavalry "did particularly well." Five days later he recommended Gregg for promotion "for highly meritorious and distinguished conduct throughout the campaign" and especially at Reams Station.[17]

Because Wilcox, Hampton, and their supports ultimately vacated the battlefield, Lee's army failed to recover another lost stretch of railroad. Compounding his army's onerous supply problems, the Weldon Railroad was now open only as far north as Stony Creek Depot, sixteen miles from Petersburg. Grant and Meade took note; there would be subsequent attempts to bridge the gap between the rail line and the Boydton Road. These would continue for the remainder of Gregg's war service.

The day after Hancock's disaster the 2nd Cavalry Division went into camp on the Jerusalem Plank Road north of the Blackwater River. There its 3,900 troopers established their ubiquitous picket lines, covering the left flank of the V Corps at and near Globe Tavern and circling around the rear of the army. To the east they connected with Kautz's horsemen, now only 1,500 strong, who were picketing between the plank road and the James River. In these areas Gregg's men, as one of their officers wrote, "remained quiet [for] some time." During this period the only item worthy of note was the soul-inspiring news, received on September 3, that on the previous day Sherman had forced Lt. Gen. John Bell Hood to evacuate Atlanta, which the combined Union armies had then occupied.[18]

The prolonged spell of inactivity gave Gregg the opportunity to apply for a ten-day leave, which was granted on September 13. The leave enabled him to visit home for the first time in nine months. Upon his departure General Davies, his own leave now over, assumed command. While its leader was gone the division officially went into reserve, Kautz's men replacing it on the picket lines. With some exceptions, it would remain off-duty until Gregg came back.[19]

For Davies his return was a case of unfortunate timing. Three days after Gregg started north Wade Hampton made one of the most audacious and spectacular raids of the war, capturing the beef cattle herd of the combined Union armies that had been grazing at Coggins Point on the James northeast of Petersburg. The operation's success—the Rebels rustled almost 2,500 cattle and got away scot free—was quite remarkable considering the daunting logistics and the lengthy riding involved. Because Coggins Point was within Kautz's patrol area the Army of the James received most of the blame for the theft and for failing to overtake the herders on their way back to their army. But Davies, who was sent in pursuit at the head of 2,100 men, neither recovered any cattle nor seriously harassed the thieves. Moreover, a 150-man force of his 13th Pennsylvania that had been guarding the herd put up a feeble defense when attacked and lost twenty-some men to capture. These included the detachment's commander, Capt. Harry Gregg—his second stint as a prisoner of war. Thus both Davies and his superior came in for their share of embarrassment at the hands of Wade Hampton.[20]

Upon David Gregg's return from leave he received a warm welcome, a contrast to Davies's contretemps. On the evening of September 22, perhaps in response to word of the efforts being made to grant him a second star, several subordinates and staff officers greeted him at his headquarters. The egalitarian-minded Lieutenant Cormany called it "a truly pleasant hour to be thus associated with the men away above us in rank and yet in many ways simply our equals! Our Comrades! And to find we had so many things in common, while all the while we were ever ready to lift our hats and recieve [*sic*] orders from them and obey."[21]

Conviviality was probably enhanced by the recent receipt of more glad tidings from other theaters. After a month of maneuvering on the defensive, on September 19 Sheridan had smashed Early's Confederates outside Winchester, driving them south to Strasburg and Fisher's Hill. At the latter place, on the day of Gregg's return, Little Phil resumed the beating he had given Early three days earlier, capturing more than a thousand Rebels and twelve guns.

Less than a week after Gregg returned from leave he and his division, no longer in reserve, were back in action, heavily so. Having failed to attain critical objectives above and below the James with consecutive offensives, Grant now planned simultaneous movements that would constitute his fifth offensive against Petersburg. On September 29 he sent both of Butler's corps and Kautz's horsemen across the river from Bermuda Hundred to threaten Richmond and prevent Lee from reinforcing Early. One column attacked the entrenched camp at Chaffin's Bluff, seizing its largest work, Fort Harrison, after desperate fighting. Farther east, a second column assailed the heavy defenses on New Market Heights but failed to take Fort Gilmer, commanding Richmond's intermediate line of defense. Concerned for the safety of his upper flank and his capital, Lee came up from Petersburg to direct in person a series of counterattacks. These failed to recover lost ground, but by sealing off the captured works they preserved the capital's security. Butler's somewhat disjointed offensive had cost him 3,300 casualties but had prevented Lee from detaching troops to the Valley. Of equal importance, the Army of the James had clamped a grip on the Northside that it would never relinquish.[22]

Soon after Butler crossed the James, Grant set in motion on the other side a strike force under Meade's supervision composed of two divisions of Maj. Gen. John G. Parke's IX Corps (Ambrose Burnside had quit the army following the powder mine fiasco) plus two divisions of Warren's corps and Gregg's cavalry. Unsurprisingly, Meade did not consider adding Hancock's used-up command to the effort. Potentially, the expeditionary force had a two-fold purpose: a show-of-force to make Lee concentrate his attention on the Southside and refrain from reinforcing Butler's opponents, and a full-head-of-steam push toward Lee's communications should Meade find few Rebels barring his path.

Early on September 30, after a day of maneuvering and with the battle to the north at white heat, Warren, followed by Parke, marched via

Poplar Spring Church toward the outer line of works south of Petersburg on the Squirrel Level Road. One of the V Corps divisions attacked and overran the position, but a cautious follow-up by Parke toward Oscar Pegram's farm was defeated by the weight of four brigades from the main defensive line along the Boydton Plank Road under Henry Heth, Wilcox, and Hampton. Parke, losing heavily, fell back to William Peebles's farm, where his men erected works that connected with those at Globe Tavern. The following day, October 1, Heth advanced again but tactical mistakes and miscommunication resulted in his repulse and the securing of the extension of Meade's line. On October 2 Meade reconnoitered the plank road position. Finding it too strong to attack with assured success, he withdrew to the permanent works at Pegram's and Peebles's farms.[23]

Gregg's role in the operation was both offensive and defensive in nature: to locate and engage the enemy, preventing it from interfering with the infantry's operations, and to secure the left flank and rear of the expeditionary force. The general had concentrated his far-flung division on the evening of September 28 and before daylight the next morning sallied forth, accompanied by two batteries—I of the 1st and A of the 2nd U.S. Artillery—but few supply wagons. From the Halifax Road, which ran roughly parallel to the Weldon line, he moved his two brigades onto the northwestward-leading Lower Church Road. At Wyatt's Crossing, named for the owner of a nearby plantation, he sent Smith's brigade to the right to locate the Vaughan Road, which led to Dinwiddie Court House and gave access to the Confederate defenses below Petersburg. Davies's troopers he dispatched to a point one mile north of Reams Station to guard the division's left and rear.

Sometime after 7 a.m. Gregg, riding with Smith, found the crossover he was seeking and gained the Vaughan Road at its intersection with another strategic thoroughfare, the Wyatt Road, near McDowell's (sometimes called "Snyder's" or "Mrs. Davis's") farmstead. Leaving the 1st Maine at the farm, he continued west with Smith's four other regiments, nearing Rebel-infested territory (he had informed army headquarters that he intended to fight "wherever [he found] the enemy"). About three-quarters of a mile past the crossroads he found what he was searching for, outpost troops from one of Hampton's brigades.

No match for the invaders, the Rebels quickly yielded their position and Gregg pushed on toward Hatcher's Run, which crossed the Boydton Plank Road at Burgess's Mill, five miles southwest of Petersburg.

Along Hatcher's Run more resolute defenders from Hampton's main body—M. Calbraith Butler's division—protested the Yankees' coming, and a sharp fight broke out. Meade had intended that Gregg not engage in a pitched battle but demonstrate before the enemy, getting a fix on their position and numbers, especially along the Boydton Plank Road. To comply Gregg tried to outflank his opponent, but he was so thoroughly checked that shortly after noon he warned headquarters: "[Although] a strong effort is being made [to gain the plank road,] I do not think we will reach it."[24]

He was right. Blocked in front and disturbed by reports of entrenched infantry not far ahead, he recalled his flanking force. Around 1 p.m. he had Smith fall back almost two miles to the area around McDowell's and assume a defensive position along the branch of a morass known as Arthur's Swamp. The 2nd Brigade maintained its foothold there despite being attacked around 5 p.m. by Hampton under cover of his horse artillery. The Federals replied with carbines and shells from Battery I. A newspaper correspondent on the scene wrote that the Confederates "poured the solid shot and shell" into Gregg's position "at a lively rate," but his gunners "returned shot for shot" until an errant shell struck one of their caissons, exploding it and inflicting casualties. The reporter highlighted one of the verities of the campaign when he added that "the country was entirely unsuited to mounted charges," which compelled Gregg's troopers "to rely solely upon their carbines, at short range. The fight continued until it became too dark to distinguish the enemy, when, by mutual consent, the firing ceased, and each side withdrew to count the[ir] losses."

Thus ended the first day of the great offensive south of the James. Despite having met "considerable opposition to [his] advance," Gregg that morning had dealt some blows to enemy communications, such as by chopping down telegraph poles "from Petersburg to Stony Creek," including near Armstrong's Mill along Hatcher's Run. Yet he had been prevented from gaining the Boydton Plank Road; in fact, he had been halted short of the outer line of Confederate defenses along the Squirrel Level Road. After the antagonists disengaged he brought up Davies's brigade from the railroad to hold the day's hard-won position while placing Smith's now-exhausted command near the Perkins house on the Halifax Road to recruit its strength.[25]

The 2nd Cavalry Division was back in action at 9 a.m. on September 30. That day Gregg intended to reach, seize, and secure the lower flank of the Squirrel Level Road while Meade's infantry stormed the defenses on and near Peebles's farm. While the 2nd Brigade continued to rest Davies's men resumed moving west on the Vaughan Road. North of Hatcher's Run they encountered the heavy outposts manned by Butler's division, but the latter withdrew in unexpected haste. Davies pursued but Gregg elected not to force his way across the run. His job, as army headquarters saw it, was to continue to protect the left rear of the infantry and keep tabs on the enemy's horse. Thus, at Meade's mid-evening order he withdrew his scouting parties and retired to a position from which to block any enemy incursion toward the infantry's flank.[26]

Meade determined that on October 1 the troops below the James, spearheaded by Parke's IX Corps, would make a supreme effort to reach the Boydton Plank Road, the cavalry keeping pace with the infantry. Neither Parke nor Gouverneur Warren, however, was enthusiastic about the plan in light of the heavy losses they had suffered near Peebles's farm on September 30. Thus Meade assigned Gregg a defensive role when the forward movement began. Late on the thirtieth the cavalry leader was directed to move out at daylight and ascertain the enemy's positions opposite the Federal left. Although the instructions were not received until after five a.m. on October 1 Gregg got moving as expeditiously as possible. The errand turned out to be unnecessary—when reporting to Parke after 8 a.m. Gregg learned that "the object of the intended reconnaissances has been fully accomplished—the enemy found."[27]

The day did, however, bring on the heaviest cavalry fighting of the offensive. It began with a late morning attack by Calbraith Butler, supported by artillery, on Gregg's advance position at E. Wilkinson's house between the Squirrel Level and Vaughan Roads. The attack was strong enough to force the rear guard, the 1st Maine, to fall back on

Davies's main body east of the Vaughan and Wyatt Roads intersection. Gregg resolved to regain the position, however, and by late on that rainy afternoon his dismounted troopers were driving the Rebels back to Wilkinson's.

He did not expect the enemy, although forced back, to stay put. As Maj. Myron H. Beaumont of the 1st New Jersey later reported, "Disposition was immediately made . . . to meet any emergency." Under Gregg's supervision, the 6th Ohio was moved forward, dismounted, north of the Vaughan Road, while the 1st Massachusetts and 10th New York dug in along the road itself. Three guns of Battery A had unlimbered behind Gregg's right flank with the fourth piece on the road just behind the division's newly erected breastworks. The balance of the 1st Brigade was positioned in the rear, on both sides of the road and west of Arthur's Swamp. Meanwhile, with the exception of the 1st Maine on Davies's far right, Smith's brigade guarded the division's other flank and rear in a discontinuous line stretching as far east as the Weldon Railroad.

The wisdom of these dispositions, Beaumont wrote, "soon became apparent," for around 3 p.m. Hampton attacked from the west with the brigades of Brig. Gens. John Dunovant and Pierce Young and Col. J. Lucius Davis. Handily outnumbered, the New York and Massachusetts outfits were driven in. "An ominous silence ensued for a moment," the overly dramatic major noted, "when suddenly the dense woods in our front became alive with rebels, who came on at a double-quick, shouting and yelling like so many fiends, firing as they advanced." Beaumont claimed that his steadfast regiment blunted the assault; in fact, the Confederates had been done in by the untimely convergence of two assault columns that nearly triggered a friendly-fire incident.[28]

Hampton recovered from the error to gain a foothold on the eastern side of Arthur's Swamp. From there, influenced by his fire-eating subordinate Dunovant, he authorized a frontal assault. The attack, in which the brigadier was killed, was spirited but Davies withstood it with admirable aplomb. Two hours later Hampton attempted to turn Davies's left—his intention all along. Before he could be enveloped, however, Gregg's senior subordinate withdrew to the division's critical reserve position near McDowell's.

Hampton followed and launched additional assaults, each of which was repulsed by Davies, greatly assisted by Battery A. Then the 1st New Jersey and 10th New York counterattacked on foot, driving the Rebels back two hundred yards. Just before nightfall Hampton attacked yet again, this time sending Young's brigade against the Union right. The effort went awry when a company of the 1st New Jersey, cut off by the attackers, fought its way back to Davies's position by striking Young from the rear, nearly capturing him. In the gathering darkness, believing that he faced a much larger force, Young withdrew. By the time he saw his mistake and came on again, Gregg had shored up the embattled flank; this attack also failed, effectively ending the fighting. As the preeminent historian of Grant's fifth offensive summed up the contest, at a lesser cost "Gregg had inflicted approximately 130 casualties. More importantly, he had repulsed repeated Confederate efforts to capture the key road junction at McDowell's. In his hands the Federal left rear was secure."[29]

Although one day remained before Grant called off his westward push, October 2 was anticlimactic. This was so even though Meade, probably without any great expectations, reinforced Parke and Warren with a division of the II Corps. The heavier effort fared no better than its predecessors, being arrested well short of the plank road. Meanwhile, Gregg and Hampton, each blocking the other's path, had reached a standoff. Both cavalries, utterly spent, went over to the defensive, then slowly disengaged.[30]

The following day the 2nd Division fell back to its old camp on the Jerusalem road. It remained in that area, picketing and maintaining a "thorough system of scouting," until October 26. In the interim Gregg received permission to mount three cavalry regiments that had been serving for the past several months as infantry attached to the V and IX Corps. The addition of the first two of these outfits to receive horses would give him almost six thousand officers and men available for duty. This provided a basis to seek permission to form a third brigade, something he had lacked for more than a year. Headquarters duly approved the request and Gregg selected Colonel Smith to lead the new organization, which consisted of his own 1st Maine, the 6th

Ohio, and the newly mounted 21st Pennsylvania. General Davies continued to lead the 1st Brigade, comprising the 1st Massachusetts, 1st New Jersey, 1st Pennsylvania, 10th New York, and the erstwhile foot soldiers of the 24th New York. Colonel Kerwin, pending the return from convalescent leave of Irvin Gregg, again took charge of the 2nd Brigade: the 2nd, 4th, 8th, 13th, and 16th Pennsylvania.[31]

Outside of the normal camp duties the only activity of any note during the three weeks following Grant's latest offensive was a reconnaissance on October 12 to Stony Creek Station, which disproved reports that as many as ten thousand Confederate infantry had gathered there en route from North Carolina. The following day an equally erroneous report had Hampton's cavalry readying an attack on the left and rear of the army; the faulty intelligence nevertheless produced a strengthening of Gregg's picket lines on the lower stretches of the plank road. Yet another report, received a week later, proved gloriously true; at Cedar Creek on October 19 Sheridan had gained his third and most complete victory over Early after recovering from a surprise assault that nearly spelled disaster. The triumph, which virtually cleared the Shenandoah Valley of organized defenders, led to the subsequent return to Petersburg of the VI Corps, giving Meade his most substantial manpower advantage over Lee since mid-August.[32]

Buoyed by Sheridan's success, Grant set in motion still another simultaneous operation against Petersburg and Richmond. On the morning of October 27 both of Butler's corps again crossed to the Peninsula to attack the capital's defenses on the Darbytown Road. They did not get far; when counterattacked, the Army of the James was chased back to Bermuda Hundred in overwhelming defeat as exemplified by the disparity of casualties: 1,600 for Butler, fewer than 100 for his opponents. This, the latest in a long series of failures and disappointments, would eventually lead to the politician-general's relief from command.[33]

While Butler fought and lost, Meade, as per Grant's plan, sent Hancock's corps, reinforced by elements of Warren's and Parke's commands, toward the Boydton Plank Road and, beyond, the South Side Railroad. On October 27 the II Corps crossed Hatcher's Run and angled around the Rebel flank near Burgess's Mill. Although the infantry of A. P. Hill and the horse soldiers of Hampton resisted fiercely, Hancock's momentum carried him up the plank road toward Petersburg, supported by Warren. But when a gap opened between the poorly coordinating corps and the enemy took advantage, the operation ended abruptly.[34]

Throughout the day Hancock was ably assisted by his longtime comrade in cavalry command. This was not Gregg's first venture toward the Boydton Road; on September 2, at Meade's order, he had led Smith's brigade in a rapid move in that direction, supported by a division of the V Corps. Less than a mile from the target area, the raiders were turned back by a much larger force of cavalry and artillery, while entrenched infantry was discovered guarding the road itself. Gregg, however, was able to take notes on a stretch of countryside critical to Petersburg's defense.[35]

Leaving its camps along the Weldon Railroad before dawn on October 27, the 2nd Cavalry Division fell in on the left of the II Corps. It moved west until striking the Quaker Road, where it turned north toward the Boydton Plank Road. Barring the cavalry's path were three streams under control of the enemy, Rowanty Creek, Gravelly Run, and Hatcher's Run. The first was passed easily enough; portions of Smith's 1st Maine and 6th Ohio waded across to drive away some irresolute defenders. Prisoners told Gregg that Rooney Lee's division was in camp within reach of the Boydton Road and that Calbraith Butler's was "on the Quaker Road, in [Gregg's] front."

Two miles farther on at Gravelly Run, Smith encountered a much hardier force on better ground and supported by two guns. Gregg went to his well-thumbed dragoon manual, attacking with two regiments afoot and the recently mounted 21st Pennsylvania in the saddle. The Pennsylvanians' charge—a rarity at this stage of the conflict—surprised and disarranged the graycoats and put them to flight even as the II Corps came up on the right, forcing other sectors of the Gravelly Run line to give way.[36]

Apparently under a full head of steam, the II Corps pushed on to the plank road where, at Meade's order, it halted to await Warren's arrival. At around 1 p.m. Gregg halted there as well so as not to get ahead of the infantry he was shielding. To provide maximum support he deployed his three brigades in as many positions: Kerwin's west of the road, close upon Hancock's flank; Smith's on the road itself, facing south; and Davies's to the rear on the Quaker Road. This was as far as infantry and cavalry would progress. Separated by a considerable distance from the V Corps, with reports of heavy enemy forces coming his way, Hancock in mid-afternoon received verbal orders from Grant and Meade, who had taken the field to oversee the operation, to hold his position till morning and then retire by the road he had taken to the front.[37]

Until then Hancock and Gregg faced a dicey situation. A. P. Hill's infantry under Heth and Maj. Gen. William Mahone plus five brigades of Hampton's cavalry were quick to exploit it. Around 4 p.m. the Rebels struck the II Corps in front and flank with almost overwhelming force, seizing the Dabney's Mill Road. Hancock was so endangered that at his urgent request Gregg dismounted Smith's and Kerwin's regiments and sent them to his assistance. This left Davies's brigade in a predicament similar to Hancock's, especially when Rooney Lee's division circled around and struck from the rear with dismounted riflemen supported by four guns. The inexperienced horsemen of the 21st Pennsylvania bore the brunt of the surprise assault but held firm until the 1st Maine and 6th Ohio "came at a run" to their aid.

Even now the advantage of numbers and ordnance remained with Hampton. Under his pounding the Federals were steadily forced back, imperiling the II Corps's flank that Gregg had sought to shore up. At his plea Hancock returned to his colleague three of Kerwin's outfits, which arrived "successively as fast as their legs could carry them." This was all the corps commander could spare—Gregg would have to hold his ground with his seven regiments and single section of Battery I, 1st Artillery.

Swiftly but precisely the general and his subordinates deployed their forces to cover all sides of their precarious position. Fighting in every direction from behind whatever cover the countryside provided, they held the line for at least six hours till able to fall back in tandem with Hancock. With ammunition running low and the retreat route via the Dabney's Mill Road threatened, Hancock had decided not to wait till morning to clear out. According to Gregg, Hampton retired before he or Hancock did, "without having accomplished other than his own punishment, which was severe." Hancock regretted his inability to return more of his comrade's men in that hour of need, but as he noted, "[I] trusted General Gregg to hold his own, and I was not disappointed." Emphasizing his appreciation, on November 4 (only three weeks before his accumulated wounds compelled him to surrender corps command) Hancock issued a general order lauding not only the conduct of his troops but that of the "gallant cavalry under General Gregg" who by warding off Hampton's attack had secured the II Corps's rear and route of withdrawal.[38]

Gregg and his troopers got a couple of weeks of comparative rest, during which they completed construction of their winter habitations, before being ordered out again on expedition, this time to no purpose. On November 7 Gregg led 2,400 men in three columns down the Weldon Railroad and the Jerusalem Plank Road to scout the trails to Rowanty Creek. Rebel infantry and cavalry were thought to be in some force along the route but few were found north of the creek. The wild goose chase, conducted in bitter weather, pleased few of the participants, but warmth of a sort returned the following day when Abraham Lincoln won a second term in the White House. To everyone but the densest observer the president's victory effectively doomed Confederate fortunes if military attrition and civilian-sector privation had not already done so.[39]

The next two missions in which Gregg took part, both with the same objective, produced more visible results than the probe of Rowanty Creek. At 4 a.m. on December 1 he pulled his troopers and horse artillerymen out of their tents and cabins and led them back to Rowanty Creek via the plank road. This time Rebel cavalry were found north of the stream; they were driven across too quickly to burn the local bridge as intended. Leaving Smith's brigade to secure the bridge and Davies's men to cover the Halifax Road, Gregg pushed on with the 2nd Brigade, once again commanded by cousin John Irvin, just returned from convalescent leave. The target was Stony Creek Depot, fifteen miles below Petersburg, where an immense cache of Confederate stores awaited transportation to the embattled city.

The supply cache was too precious to lack a strong guard. On the opposite side of Stony Creek the cavalry's outriders discovered a "strong earth-work, with two pieces of artillery, with which the enemy opened as soon as we came in sight." Irvin Gregg promptly attacked with the mounted 4th Pennsylvania, which charged across the water a few hundred yards below the work while the 16th Pennsylvania advanced on foot across the local railroad bridge. Their attention distracted by the mounted charge, the defenders were forced to surrender when outflanked and taken in rear by the 4th Pennsylvania. Almost two hundred Rebels were captured along with two cannon. The guns were spiked, their carriages destroyed, and the depot and storehouses burned. Some three thousand sacks of corn, five hundred bales of hay, and a large quantity of bacon, along with an untold amount of equipment and ammunition, went up in flames. By late afternoon the regrouped division was back in camp, Gregg reporting his loss as "very small."[40]

A few days after his return from Stony Creek, Gregg acknowledged receipt of his just-received appointment as brevet major general of volunteers. The long-overdue promotion, backdated to August 1, was awarded "for highly meritorious and distinguished conduct throughout the campaign," with special reference to his efforts to protect the army's vital supply train at Samaria Church.[41]

Although gratefully received, the award was in a sense a hollow honor, as the general's role in the war was approaching a finale. On December 7 a second Stony Creek raid, much larger than the first, got underway. Gregg's troopers took the advance and also protected the flanks of the main strike column, composed of the V Corps and a II Corps division. Warren's men were ordered to tear up the tracks to a point beyond the Nottoway River, thus increasing the distance Lee had to cover to haul supplies to Richmond and Petersburg, many of whose defenders were already on starvation rations. The raiders would suffer too; throughout the six-day operation they were assailed by biting winds, icy rain, and sleet. Few would forget the experience, especially when conditions other than the weather turned ugly.

In advance of the infantry, Gregg's 4,200-man column moved confidently down the Jerusalem Plank Road, then across the Nottoway on a pontoon bridge. Early on the second day out it turned west to strike the tracks of the Weldon where they crossed the river. After members of Smith's brigade destroyed the railroad bridge the column continued to Jarratt's Station, where Irvin Gregg was attacked by one of

Rooney Lee's regiments, speedily repulsed by the 4th Pennsylvania. When other Confederates sought to interpose between Gregg and Warren, the 8th Pennsylvania cleared the road and reestablished contact with the infantry.

The next day, December 9, Gregg reached Three Creek, where he found two hundred cavalry opposing him, the hundred-foot-long railroad bridge on fire, and all fords obstructed. Patiently and carefully the fords were cleared and the march continued to Belfield and Hicksford on the Meherrin River, long stretches of track being destroyed on the way. At Hicksford defenders were driven into a line of fieldworks and rifle pits on the north bank. As if the mounted offensive was not an antiquated tactic after all, those works were carried by an old-fashioned cavalry charge by Davies's 1st Massachusetts, whose commander was mortally wounded by a shell fragment. Scrambling across the stream, the Rebels rallied inside three redoubts sheltering a total of nine artillery pieces. Before Gregg could order another attack General Warren made contact with him. Having destroyed the railroad for several miles below Stony Creek, he told Gregg to cease his advance, assist the V Corps in doing still more damage to the line, and then head for home.[42]

The return march, which began on December 10, was a study in torment. All the way home Gregg's and Warren's forces were assailed by the weather (several men suffered frozen feet) as well as by pursuers who hit and ran, inflicting casualties and waging war at its most hideous. During the retreat reports circulated of stragglers found by the roadside, their bodies stripped and mutilated, the victims of bushwhackers. Their cold, angry comrades took revenge by looting and burning farmhouses and barns. Reportedly, some residents suspected of perpetrating the atrocities were seized and hanged before officers could intervene. Some of these acts were blamed on the wholesale confiscation of locally brewed whiskey, which gave the expedition the enduring nickname "Applejack Raid."[43]

Gregg and his men returned to camp shortly before midnight on December 11. With active operations at last at an end, the division settled into winter quarters and numerous officers and men took leave. Three days before Christmas Gregg, worn down by months of stress and overexertion, packed his personal items, bade farewell to his subordinates, and went home to Ellen.[44]

12

A Man of Unimpeachable Character

On January 25, 1865, three weeks after returning from his holiday leave, General Gregg sat at a portable desk inside his headquarters tent and wrote a letter to Adjutant General of the Army Lorenzo Thomas. "Having for more than 3 years been on uninterrupted service in the field commanding Cavalry in the Army of the Potomac," he wrote, "I at this time find such an imperative demand for my command presence at home, that my personal attention may be given to pressing private duties and business, that I can no longer defer action to secure my discharge from the Service." The next day Gregg's application was endorsed by Gen. John G. Parke, commanding the Army of the Potomac in the absence of General Meade, who had been called to Washington. In so doing Parke noted: "The eminent services rendered by [Brevet] Major General Gregg are well known to this Army and Country. His resignation will be a serious loss to the Service, but under the circumstances it is approved and respectfully forwarded for the decision of the [War] Dept."[1]

Until his departure from the army received War Department approval, the war went on and Gregg went with it. On February 5 he embarked upon the final operation of his military career, the result of Grant's determination to extend the Union lines ever farther to the south and west of Petersburg. The lieutenant general's ultimate objective was the seizure of Lee's last line of supply, the South Side Railroad. Grant also wished to choke off other routes by which the Cockade City might be supplied including the Boydton Plank Road, which ran northeast from Dinwiddie Court House. Reports had wagon trains, carrying all manner of provisions, ammunition, and forage, operating with some regularity on the road. According to rumors, a supply depot at Belfield, on the railroad thirty miles south of Reams Station, was still operating for benefit of Lee's army. Grant feared that unless these resources were cut off Petersburg might hold out indefinitely.

Although obviously a job for cavalry, the interdiction mission expanded exponentially when Grant decreed that large elements of the II and V Corps should accompany the horsemen. While G. K. Warren's men closely supported Gregg on the stage road east of Dinwiddie Court House, the II Corps, now under Meade's former chief of staff, Andrew Humphreys, would advance on Warren's north flank, interposing between his colleague and the permanent line of enemy earthworks and trenches that extended outward from Petersburg's lower environs. Humphreys was to take position on Hatcher's Run near its crossing of the Vaughan Road, some two miles north of Warren's position. Against his better judgment but in accord with Grant's wishes, Meade eventually assigned seven infantry divisions and a portion of an eighth to an operation that appeared to promise limited gains.[2]

Answering his last call to duty, at 3 a.m. on February 5 Gregg led his division—every trooper who had a serviceable horse, toting three days' rations and half a day's forage—down the Jerusalem Plank Road, then to Reams Station. Around 8 a.m. the column turned west toward Dinwiddie Court House over what one Pennsylvanian called "the muddiest roads I ever saw." The artillery-free column, John Irvin Gregg's brigade in the lead, passed deserted Rebel camps where, as one New Yorker put it, "the fires, like the Confederacy, were still burning, but very low."[3]

Reaching the courthouse settlement late in the morning, Gregg fulfilled his orders by probing "up and down" the Boydton Road. Grant's expectations notwithstanding, pickings were slim, the result of the recent destruction of bridges on the Weldon Railroad and the plank road that had offered access to Petersburg. That evening Grant informed General Halleck that "but few stores were remaining at Belfield and but few wagons were on the road. He [Gregg] captured 18 wagons and 50 prisoners." Presumably most were escort troops, although the haul may have included civilian teamsters. By 4:30 p.m. Gregg was withdrawing toward Malone's Bridge on Rowanty Creek, where he expected to spend the night.[4]

At least one of his infantry colleagues had a busier day. Humphreys, moving on Warren's right flank, had reached his assigned position on the Vaughan Road about a thousand yards from a newly erected line of Confederate defenses; meanwhile, the V Corps took position at Monks Neck Bridge on Rowanty Creek. The city defenders responded vigorously to these movements. Late in the afternoon Humphreys came under attack from the north by elements of two Rebel corps. The II Corps fought off the attackers; Warren, however, saw little action. Even so, Meade was alarmed enough to dispatch supports to the scene of the confrontation, a division each from the VI and IX Corps.

As the scope of the offensive widened, the army leader became concerned that enemy forces might slip between Gregg and Warren and cut off the cavalry. At 10:30 p.m. he ordered Gregg to detach a force to convey the V Corps's wagon train to the rear and report with the rest of his command to Warren. Only a half-hour earlier the 2nd Division had gone into bivouac; now its men were rooted out of their blankets and escorted by Warren's aides to V Corps headquarters at the Gravelly Run crossing of the Vaughan Road. By 7 a.m., after a grueling march in frigid weather, the sleep-deprived horsemen were covering Warren's renewed push toward Hatcher's Run.[5]

En route to Warren, the rear of Gregg's command was attacked by enemy cavalry "in some force." The initial effort was repulsed by Davies's brigade, but they kept coming, and Gregg finally halted to deal with them properly. He dismounted Irvin Gregg's 2nd Brigade and the 3rd Brigade, led that day by Col. Oliver B. Knowles of the 21st Pennsylvania, Charles Smith being on leave. Their men snaked to within carbine range of the enemy and for an hour or more a vicious little skirmish gyrated across the fields and woods on both sides of the Vaughan Road. A 16th Pennsylvania trooper reported that his regiment "made a dismounted charge, killing, wounding and capturing quite a number of rebels. We also repulsed a charge with heavy loss to the rebels."[6]

David Gregg could be found, as usual, at the head of the storm, dispelling any notion that he had tendered his resignation because his nerves had gotten the better of him. At some point, in fact, he proposed to do some reading under fire. Petersburg and Richmond newspapers often contained information about Confederate military movements unobtainable elsewhere, and Gregg, through a most improbable source, gained access to a couple of recent editions. During a lull in the fighting he heard the call of a resourceful—and fearless—newsboy who had accompanied the Federals into action. Whether or not Gregg knew it, there was a precedent for such daring behavior on the part of sales representatives of the fourth estate. During the fighting at Meadow Bridge on the Chickahominy during the previous year's Richmond Raid, Phil Sheridan had been amazed to discover that "two young newsboys with commendable enterprise had come inside [the Union] lines from the Confederate capital to sell their papers. They were sharp youngsters, and having come well supplied, they did a thrifty business."

The general sent one of his orderlies to the rear; the man obtained two newspapers, which he folded and stuffed inside his jacket. Returning to the front, he was shot off his horse, a minie ball striking him over the heart. A comrade rushed to the orderly, thinking him dead, but found him merely stunned by the blow. When his jacket was opened a spent bullet, cushioned by the newspapers, fell to the ground.[7]

Throughout February 6 the horsemen continued to provide close support to Warren's corps as it moved to join Humphreys. Around 1 p.m. Warren ordered Gregg to drive the Rebels across Gravelly Run while continuing to cover the infantry's lower flank. The general assigned his cousin's brigade to the job, but as Irvin Gregg reported, the Confederates were "too strongly and advantageously posted in the woods and behind rifle-pits to be dislodged." Subsequently Gregg's entire command was attacked by infantry, part of Brig. Gen. John Pegram's division of Lee's Second Corps. Supported by one of Warren's divisions, the cavalry, most of its men fighting afoot, held its ground, then advanced, its Spencer repeaters blazing. In the end, as Irvin Gregg reported, the enemy was "driven from his position and a mounted force sent to Gravelly Run bridge."[8]

The infantry again saw heavy fighting on February 6. Early that afternoon the V Corps reconnoitered toward Dabney's Mill, two miles short of the Boydton Road. The move was met by Pegram's division but the latter was repulsed and its leader killed. Warren then discengaged, ending Meade's attempt to gain a lodgment on the plank road, although on the evening of February 6–7 both Federal corps fortified the ground they had seized along Hatcher's Run.[9]

While the infantry dug in, Gregg moved Davies's and Knowles's troopers across the run and into position on the Halifax Road, where they could cover the approaches to Reams Station and Monk's Neck Bridge. Late on February 7, following a day filled with "rain falling and freezing as it fell," the division was withdrawn to Reams Station. On February 9 the men returned to what one called "our comfortable winter quarters—which we appreciate more highly now, than we did before we set out" on such a body- and soul-trying mission. The three-day operation had cost Meade more than 1,500 casualties, 117 in the ranks of the 2nd Cavalry Division including the slight wounding of both General Davies and Colonel Gregg on February 6. Whether or not the cost was worth the slight extension of Meade's lines, it would be the last westward push the army would make until the opening of the Appomattox Campaign almost two months hence.[10]

Following his return from the interdiction mission Gregg received official notice (issued on February 4) of the acceptance of his resignation from both the regular service and the volunteer army. On February 9 he was relieved of command of the 2nd Cavalry Division. That day he released a farewell address to his troops in which he expressed "profound regret" at parting with them after two years of shared successes and hardships: "The officers and enlisted men of the 2nd Division will always be remembered in friendship by him, and with them he will ever cherish recollections of the virtues of the brave men of his command who had fallen on its battle fields."[11]

On February 10 he left again for home, this time never to return to the army. Upon his departure command of the division passed to General Davies, although in less than two months he would be superseded by Maj. Gen. George Crook, a veteran of campaigning in the West and a future Indian fighter of renown. Crook would lead the 2nd Cavalry Division through the campaign that lay ahead, culminating with Lee's forced evacuation of Richmond and Petersburg on April 2–3 and his surrender to Grant one week later at Appomattox Court House.[12]

Because Gregg never provided an explanation for his sudden exit from the war other than the vague reference to "private duties and business," historians have speculated ever since about his motives. Most have doubted that the cited reason was a legitimate one, although Gregg had used it as the basis for earlier leave requests, such as in December when he stated a need to visit relatives in Centre and Blair Counties with whom, as he wrote, he had "business[,] the settlement of which has been postponed during the last three years." It does not strain credulity that in so writing he was looking ahead to his postwar civilian career with a view to securing his family's financial future.[13]

Another possible basis was the issue of his health, which had suffered relatively frequently and for weeks at a time while he was on active duty and more than once had failed, effectively disabling him. There is also the possibility that his decision was influenced by the view of his wife and family friends that he had served his country long and faithfully enough and should leave the field before either his constitution or the enemy did him in. There is an unverified anecdote to the effect that upon his return home at Christmas Ellen was horrified to find a bullet hole in her husband's slouch hat.

Other potential reasons are not difficult to accept. One encompasses the professional disappointments Gregg experienced from the earliest days of his war career to the very end, during which younger, less experienced, and arguably less talented officers achieved ascendency over him in matters of rank and position. Although he had rendered capable and distinguished service throughout the conflict, his low-key, self-effacing persona seemed out of synch with the personalities of Sheridan, George Custer, Judson Kilpatrick, and other colleagues who fit the mold of the aggressive, flamboyant centaur and profited thereby.

Certainly, too, there is the prospect that the gentlemanly, old-school Gregg—especially in the wake of the Applejack Raid, during which he personally witnessed the effects of military atrocities—no longer believed he could function creditably in such an environment. Although never a chivalric exercise in the manly arts, the war had once respected certain boundaries and observed certain niceties. Now, however, the border between semi-civilized warfare and killing for its own sake seemed not only to have blurred but to have disappeared. Gregg may well have wondered if such a war was worth waging even given the monumental issues at stake.

Two suggested motives that have received much scrutiny over the years can be dismissed fairly readily. Supposedly, during a Thanksgiving Day dinner at his headquarters Gregg had informed Colonel Smith, in the hearing of Surgeon Alphonso Rockwell of the 6th Ohio Cavalry, that he was soon to resign his commission because he had lost his nerve. The surgeon quoted him as telling his subordinate, "I am a good deal of a coward. Every engagement tells upon my nervous system to the last degree, and it is only by the exercise of all my will power than I can appear natural and unafraid." Although a credible witness, Rockwell did not publish his account for almost sixty years; moreover, he believed Gregg was exaggerating what he saw as a flaw in himself that no one else did—a self-deprecatory exercise in sarcasm. Rockwell had seen Gregg under fire too many times to credit his self-evaluation; more than once he had thought of the general: "You certainly are a very cool and courageous man."[14]

Another oft-repeated but unsupported stimulus for Gregg's resignation—his unwillingness to serve again under Sheridan once the latter, having disposed of Early, vacated the Shenandoah Valley—is unsupportable. For one thing, there was no guarantee that Sheridan would return to Petersburg for the closing months of the war. Little Phil's itinerary following his fourth and final defeat of Early at Waynesboro in March 1865 was cloaked in uncertainty, for Grant had not yet determined whether his long-time cavalry chief would rejoin the Army of the Potomac for the Appomattox Campaign. The general-in-chief's original plan was to have Sheridan, after disposing of Early, cross the James at Columbia, damage the nearby railroads, then head for North Carolina to join forces with Sherman, who had begun his March to the Sea in mid-November and had turned north from Savannah in late January.[15]

The case for bad blood between Gregg and Sheridan is a weak one if only because their relationship fostered no observable friction during the war and because in postwar years they interacted and corresponded with apparent cordiality. Gregg's son would emphatically declare that he never heard his father demean Sheridan's character and that the elder

Gregg always spoke highly of his services in command of Meade's cavalry, "loyalty being almost as strongly developed a trait of his character as was modesty."[16]

Perhaps the most telling indication that Gregg would not have feared reestablishing a relationship with Sheridan was his appeal to go to the Valley instead of James Harrison Wilson. By early August he had been subordinated to the fiery Irishman for three and a half months; by then he would have known whether he could serve under Sheridan with peace of mind and self-respect. Given that he had not been in contact with Little Phil in the months since, it seems unlikely that his opinion of the man would have changed materially by the outset of 1865.

Gregg may have had early cause to regret leaving the conflict before its conclusion. The following January—by which time he and Ellen were likely residing somewhere in Reading—he learned that the regular army was about to be reorganized and expanded. A new regiment, the 8th U.S. Cavalry, was being formed, and he applied for reinstatement to the ranks as its colonel. The application may have been born of financial need (he had not secured a paying job since returning home and none appeared to be on the horizon) or ennui and disappointment over his current situation. His son suspected the latter, believing that the change from the intense activity of military life to the slow pace of affairs in a city the size and location of Reading must have been unsettling.

To promote his qualifications for the position he coveted, Gregg sought and received endorsements from such stalwarts as George Meade, Winfield Hancock, and Phil Sheridan as well as civilian officials including Governor Andrew Gregg Curtin and former Secretary of War Simon Cameron. Their recommendations were duly forwarded to Commanding General Grant, Secretary of War Edwin Stanton and, eventually, President Andrew Johnson, Lincoln's successor.[17]

The efforts of these patrons, although they must have carried much weight, were unavailing. When in July 1866 President Johnson signed the legislation that increased the army threefold, command of the 8th Cavalry went to another Gregg—cousin John Irvin. Long John had remained in the army after Appomattox, having won several brevets for gallantry and meritorious service including major general of volunteers and brigadier general of regulars. Some of David's relatives and friends professed to believe the appointment came about through a clerical error at the War Department, but he himself did not doubt the correctness of the selection and considered the promotion well-earned. Still, his son would wonder if "the same influences that had operated against his advancement in the Regular Service, in which he had remained a Captain throughout the entire war, had again asserted themselves and prevented his appointment."[18]

There is no record of where the Greggs lived for the first two years after the war, though it is supposed they spent considerable time among Ellen's relatives in and near Reading; over time the seat of Berks County assumed the role of the general's adopted city. Their son suggests that they renewed old friendships and family ties in Centre, Blair, and Huntingdon Counties, sometimes staying with Ellen's sister, at other times checking into hotels, including the Continental in Philadelphia, where David had roomed in the fall of 1861 prior to rejoining the 6th Cavalry. By the spring of 1867 the couple enjoyed a more settled existence, residing with her aunt, Mrs. John Pringle Jones, in the old John S. Hiester home at 404 Penn Street, Reading, where Ellen's parents had been wed in 1829.

Strangely enough, except for a brief period, through the rest of their life together the couple did not own a home of their own, and the general was employed only intermittently. Apparently the "private duties and business" affairs he mentioned in his resignation request had more to do with securing the family's existing finances than seeking business opportunities. Despite the almost rootless nature of their existence, however, the Greggs appear to have enjoyed a contented family life. They became parents for the first time on March 9, 1867, upon the birth of George Sheaff Gregg. Their second son, David, was born on October 3 of the following year while the family was living at Slott's Hotel in Reading, Ellen's aunt being "unable to entertain her niece at this time."

Between the birth of their sons, David and Ellen purchased property in Milford, Delaware, where they bought a small farm in hopes of making a living as peach growers. The southern part of the state was then developing a fruit growing culture; other factors that made the relocation attractive were neighbors including Gen. Alfred T. A. Torbert (a native of nearby Georgetown) and Ellen's uncle Frederick A. Hiester, who had moved to Milford after selling his farmstead in Reading. The enterprise began promisingly but when nine-month-old George developed a severe case of malaria and the local climate was implicated in it, the Greggs sold out at a small profit and returned to Reading to seek a more permanent home.

That search initially took them to the Midwest. Early in 1870, anticipating a business boom in what had formerly been the Confederate heartland, the family established themselves in Carthage, Missouri, close to the homestead of David's brother Harry, who had settled there soon after his release from the army and was about to marry. The happy event was followed by a sad one; soon after Harry's wedding came news of the death of Ellen's sister Kate, prompting a long journey back to Reading. It is not known how long the family spent in Pennsylvania, but in the summer of 1871 they were back in Missouri, where the general was asked to become a director of a local bank, an invitation that he declined or was later withdrawn. This did not prevent him from winning "recognition as a public spirited citizen" in a bustling community that boasted an iron foundry (an industry that would have appealed to a member of the Gregg family), lead mines, and limestone quarries.[19]

Eventually the spirited citizen outlived his simple life on the prairie and by late 1872 or early 1873 he and Ellen returned once again to Pennsylvania, settling this time in Norristown, fifteen miles northwest of Philadelphia, close to the home of Ellen's cousin J. P. Hiester Jones and his wife and son. At first they rented rooms at a local hotel, the Montgomery House, before moving seven miles east to Flourtown, not far from the church in White Marsh where David and Ellen had wed.

The family remained in Flourtown until early in 1874, by which time their financial situation seems to have become acute. To salvage it Gregg applied to President Ulysses S. Grant for a State Department post, preferably in the consular service. In February Grant appointed him consul at Prague in the Kingdom of Bohemia, then part of the Austro-Hungarian Empire, and the family sailed from Philadelphia for Europe on February 20, 1874.

The portents were grave even before Gregg reached his posting. The voyage aboard the liner *Indiana* was a nightmare of cramped accommodations and severe weather. As he wrote a friend after reaching Europe, "We have had about as stormy and disagreeable [a] passage as you can well conceive—to be tossed in a gale for five days, losing life boats, and knowing that the seas that are thundering over the decks, will, unless all things are exactly right, book you for Davy Jones' locker." There were compensations, too, once land was reached, including weeks of sightseeing in Queenstown, Liverpool, London, Dover, Ostend, and Hanover, much of the time accompanied by Ellen's aunt and uncle, Judge and Mrs. Jones, whose trip to West Point in 1854 had introduced their niece to her future husband and who had been living abroad for the past year and a half.[20]

Upon reaching Prague, Gregg found the affairs of his office in the capable hands of the chief clerk. To this civil servant, he quickly decided, he owed whatever success he made of his appointment, which turned out to be short-lived. The brevity of his tenure owed principally to the unhappiness of Ellen, who did not speak German and felt isolated and alone in an European setting. Her failure to enjoy the local life contrasted with the experience of their sons, who, it was said, "wandered about the ancient city to their heart's content." The loneliness Ellen felt and her longing to return home were exacerbated by the sudden death of Judge Jones in London only three days after the Greggs reached Prague. David sympathized with Ellen's desire to live again in the house in Reading to which her widowed aunt would return. Moreover, he found his position something of a sinecure and he considered his salary—twenty-five hundred dollars a year—inadequate to the demands of maintaining even a small home in the city. Thus, less than five months after accepting the consulship, he resigned the position and in mid-July the family sailed for the United States aboard the *Pennsylvania*.[21]

Reaching home in early August, the Greggs moved into a hotel near Reading, which they occupied until the fall, when they began residing as "paying guests" in Mrs. Jones's home in the city. They would remain in her household for the next twelve years. When the venerable family home was sold in 1886, the Greggs again relocated to a local hotel for the winter while spending most of their summers at the New Jersey seashore. Not until November 1896 would they acquire a permanent residence, moving into a home on North Fourth Street that they rented from Col. Edward P. Pearson, a regular army veteran and a close friend of the family. David and Ellen would live out their lives in this comfortable but unostentatious edifice.[22]

Perhaps because the Greggs never owned a home of their own, they traveled extensively, often in pursuit of the general's personal interests and in furtherance of his professional associations. At other times Ellen and he spent extended periods visiting their many relations in various states. Almost every summer they vacationed at resorts and tourist locations including Atlantic City and Asbury Park, New Jersey, Rehoboth Beach, Delaware, and Ephrata in the Pennsylvania Dutch country. On several occasions in the summer of 1876 they took the train to Philadelphia to view the Centennial International Exhibition. They also traveled to cities to attend gatherings of two Union veterans' associations, the Grand Army of the Republic (GAR) and the Military Order of the Loyal Legion of the United States. In April 1877 Gregg joined such wartime luminaries as McClellan, Hancock, and Burnside in Philadelphia to mark the eleventh anniversary of the founding of the GAR. Two years later, when the Gen. William H. Keim Post no. 76 was organized in Reading, Gregg became a charter member as well as its first commander. And in May 1886 he was elected commander of the Pennsylvania Commandery of the Loyal Legion. He headed the state chapter of that Union officers organization for the next eighteen years.[23]

Although not heavily active politically, Gregg maintained a consistent affiliation with the Republican Party, mainly at the county level, which undoubtedly furthered his involvement in the semi-political organizations he belonged to such as the GAR. Occasionally he deviated from party adherence, such as during the presidential campaign of 1880, when from a sense of loyalty he voted for his old comrade Winfield Hancock, the Democratic candidate. When Hancock was defeated by James A. Garfield, however, Gregg expressed himself in private as pleased by the result.[24]

The general visited the battlefield of Gettysburg, where he had reached the apogee of his career, on numerous occasions, the last being on the eve of the First World War. Although described as a "graceful and forcible speaker," he did not seek speaking engagements and declined many invitations to orate on various military and civic occasions. In October 1884 he was prevailed upon to deliver a few remarks during the dedication of a thirty-foot-high granite shaft honoring those in both blue and gray who fought on what had become known as Gettysburg's East Cavalry Field. Twelve years later he spoke at the unveiling of statues of Generals Meade and Hancock. In later years, however, he would vocally object to a proposal to erect an equestrian statue of Lee on the battlefield, arguing that "a memorial in honor of any soldier who there bore arms against the Union" would foster sectional discord: "Let every personal monument on that field teach its lesson of loyalty and patriotism."[25]

In July 1889, Pennsylvania Day at Gettysburg, Gregg served as chief marshal of the elaborate and well-attended ceremonies. And on September 27, 1910, age seventy-seven, he made a brief address upon the dedication of the Pennsylvania Memorial in the role of the only surviving general officer from the state to have taken part in the battle. The sixty-foot structure bore the name of every member of a Pennsylvania regiment or battery who fought on that field. Two and a half years later eight portrait statues were added to the monument to honor President Lincoln, Governor Curtin, and six general officers. Next to his old comrade Hancock on the east face of the monument is Gregg, standing erect, his gloved hands resting on the hilt of his saber.[26]

On more than one occasion he was chosen to take a prominent role in ceremonies commemorating an important site in another great war, Valley Forge. On June 19, 1878, during the centennial observances held on the grounds of the Continental Army's winter encampment, Gregg served as grand marshal of the day's parade as well as a member of the reviewing party that also included Governor John F. Hartranft. Over time he became involved in a campaign to preserve as a national shrine Washington's headquarters. The effort failed, but in 1893 the site attained the status of a state park.[27]

Most of the general's travels were remunerative only in that they brought him pleasure, gratification, and a sense of participation in the affairs of respected organizations in pursuit of worthy causes. Even when he was at home, demands on his time prevented him from seeking steady employment. In January 1880, for instance, the Greggs withdrew their sons from the private school they had been attending in Reading after both boys contracted diphtheria-like conditions. For the next two years Gregg spent much of his time home-schooling them. His tutoring was successful enough that by the time they were of high-school age George and David were "both thoroughly grounded in the ordinary studies of boys of their ages."

Outside the home he gave a great deal of his time to state and local commissions of one kind or another, none of which provided a salary. His son notes that he was "much in demand on all public occasions in Reading, and elsewhere" where he "presided at public meetings, sat on Boards and Committees," and promoted municipal improvement projects. When asked, he helped coordinate local relief efforts, such as in the wake of a cyclone that leveled a portion of Reading in January 1889 and killed several of its residents.[28]

Gregg continued to lack a full-time job well into his mid-fifties. By 1889 the family's finances had become so strapped that he felt constrained to seek the position of head of the Soldiers' and Sailors' Home at Erie, Pennsylvania. Because he lacked the necessary political connections, the post eluded him, a "serious disappointment to him," according to his son. That same year supporters, including the editors of some of the state's more influential newspapers, promoted him for state commissioner of pensions. This opportunity he declined, ostensibly because he had no wish to enter public life but probably because his selection appeared a long shot and he lacked the energy to pursue a lost cause.

Although he had long rejected the idea of public and political office, he finally gained a paying position in the summer of 1891 when elected to a four-year term as auditor general of Pennsylvania. His candidacy owed to a scandal that threatened to have dire consequences for the state's Republican machine. The city treasurer of Philadelphia, John Bardsley, had been caught embezzling almost $300,000 in state personal tax receipts and board of education funds, precipitating a bank failure and prompting the commonwealth to sue the city for the lost revenues plus interest and penalties. In order to secure the election of the party ticket that fall, G O P leaders turned to candidates with unblemished reputations and little if any political experience. It was thought that a military hero would fill the bill nicely and a "Gregg Republican Club" soon sprang to life in various parts of the state.[29]

Gregg's son reports that the general "said nothing, and did nothing, to further his own nomination, but his interests were in the hands of his friends." Strangely, this did not include the officers of the Republican organization of Berks County, who refused to support him, claiming that he had voted for the Democratic ticket during more than one election. David, Jr., notes that "the fight went on until Convention time came around," by which time his father had publicly declared that "the only vote cast by me for a Democratic candidate for President, was that for my lifelong friend and fellow soldier, Gen. Hancock." The statement had the desired effect, as did the public appearances he made throughout the state to promote himself and his views. This necessity he attended to reluctantly but effectively, assisted by the presence in the audience of numerous old soldiers who "took charge of the meetings" and displayed "so much enthusiasm" on his behalf that victory appeared assured. And so it was; on election night in November he defeated his Democratic opponent by more than 58,000 votes.

Before his term began in January 1892 the family secured rented quarters in Harrisburg, the state capital. From the first Gregg's personal habits were defined by military-like precision, "his custom being to breakfast at 8, reach his office by 9, remain at his desk until 12, dine, return to the office at 1:30, and leave for the day at 4 or 4:30." The schedule extended to Saturdays, on which he worked a half day. His administrative methods were similarly inflexible, based as they were on a strict interpretation of state law even when it conflicted with long-established practices and customs. His most controversial reform involved compelling every institution that received state aid to file accounts clearly showing receipts and expenditures and when appropriations exceeded demonstrated needs to return the balance to the treasury. "Very naturally," his son relates, "a grand wail was set up all over the State," but his course was sustained by the state's Democratic governor, Robert E. Pattison, and opposition eventually subsided.

With this notable exception, Gregg's tenure proceeded smoothly, so much so that when it ended in December 1895 he was prominently mentioned in the state's newspapers as a suitable candidate for governor. At one point a petition signed by almost three hundred "prominent Republicans of Reading" was sent to the county party committee asking that delegates to the next state convention advance his candidacy should a groundswell of support develop. In the end, having helped restore the party's good name, his influence was no longer needed and he failed to receive serious consideration for a post he probably never coveted in the first place.

Three years later he was again being touted in some circles as gubernatorial material and even won the conditional support of Matthew S. Quay. The powerful United States senator declared that should William A. Stone, the choice of a large segment of the state party, decide not to seek the nomination he would back Gregg for the office. Although the potential candidate was always quick to give the impression that he had no desire to reenter public life—reportedly, he had recently declined an offer to become deputy treasurer of Philadelphia—his sons always believed that if his party had come calling, this time their father would have paid heed. In the end, however, Stone threw his hat in the ring, received the support of Quay and many another official, and succeeded Pattison.[30]

Senator Quay was not Gregg's only influential patron. On April 20, 1897, Pennsylvania's other Republican senator, Boies Penrose, introduced a bill authorizing President William McKinley to appoint and retire Gregg as a regular army captain, immediately qualified to receive a pension based on his prewar and wartime service at that rank. Penrose noted in sponsoring the legislation: "[The bill] seeks to give some slight measure of justice to one of the most brilliant, daring and intelligent soldiers of the Union Army, and I am sure that it will awaken a responsive chord in the breasts of every Pennsylvanian." The senator added a personal touch, recalling that some years earlier, while touring the battlefields of Virginia, he had made the acquaintance of several former Confederates whom he found "unanimous in their opinion that General Gregg was one of the greatest soldiers on the Union side." The recipient of Penrose's support being "old and far from prosperous," he deserved the gratitude his government would display by granting him the small but needful pension he sought.

The adjutant general of the army agreed with Senator Penrose. When invited to express an opinion "adverse or otherwise" on the appointment, Gen. George D. Ruggles ("Tub" Ruggles, Gregg's West Point classmate) on May 10 wrote Secretary of War Russell A. Alger (who as colonel of the 5th Michigan Cavalry had served under Gregg and Custer at Gettysburg) describing Gregg as "a very gallant and distinguished officer in the volunteer service and the regular establishment." Several notable personages, military and civilian, added their support, some writing directly to McKinley to express it.[31]

Senate Bill no. 1747's journey through Congress' slow and antiquated committee system was a study in promise, hope, and, in the end, rejection. At first, passage appeared assured, Penrose's effort being endorsed at both the state and federal level. The Pennsylvania legislature passed a joint resolution (in the peculiar jargon of the time) "praying Congress for the passage of the bill." Subsequently it was cosponsored by U.S. Congressman Marlin Olmsted, a close friend of Gregg dating from his Harrisburg years. "Subjected to the usual delays," the bill was finally reported out of the Senate Military Committee with the notation: "While the reappointment and retirement of officers should not be the rule, yet an examination of General Gregg's record and case notes a peculiarly justifiable exception." Subsequently the measure was passed by unanimous consent of the full Senate.[32]

According to David Gregg, Jr., despite a wealth of favorable opinion and solid support, the bill failed on the House floor when Democratic Congressman Nicholas N. Cox of Tennessee, former Confederate colonel and subordinate of the famed cavalry commander Nathan Bedford Forrest, objected to the motion of unanimous consent on procedural grounds—whereupon the solon promptly fell asleep at his desk. The circumstances surrounding the bill's demise may have been more complicated than this almost humorous anecdote would suggest. On April 18, 1898, Cox's Democratic colleague James M. Robinson of Indiana specifically inquired of the War Department's Record and Pension Office as to the circumstances surrounding Gregg's resignation from the service. No evidence links the request for information to a coordinated effort to block the bill's passage, but one wonders if legislators who strongly believed that the reappointment of officers should not be the rule might have used Gregg's unwillingness to finish out the war as ammunition to scuttle his retirement application.[33]

Retreating forever from the public spotlight, General Gregg devoted increasing attention to personal interests and hobbies, including a local whist club in which for over two decades he indulged his fondness for that four-player card game. As the new century dawned he was elected to the board of the Historical Society of Pennsylvania, became an honorary life member of the Union League of Philadelphia, and was active in the Associates of Graduates of the United States Military Academy. In 1903 he gained one of his most cherished positions when named commander-in-chief of the Loyal Legion. He tenure lasted two years before health issues began to limit his active participation.

Even in advancing years, military affairs continued to claim his attention and involvement. He corresponded regularly with many of his old colleagues and subordinates, reliving shared experiences and refreshing his memory as to the service of his various commands on and off the battlefield . In June 1895 he happily attend the fortieth annual reunion of his West Point class though saddened to find that only a dozen other survivors could attend. And in April 1898, when years of diplomatic and political wrangling over the island of Cuba provoked the United States to declare war against the Spanish Empire, he wrote to Secretary of War Alger offering his active support: "I will be happy to render any military service in the field, for which I may be deemed fitted by my education and experience and which it may be your pleasure to request."[34]

Unsurprisingly, Alger turned down the offer with an expression of warm regard for Gregg's long and distinguished service. The family's contribution to the conflict thereafter rested with twenty-nine-year-old David, Jr., who, according to one biographer, "marched off with the Governor's Troop, Pennsylvania Volunteers, and served in [training camp in] Virginia and [in the field in] Puerto Rico." Years earlier David Sr., hoping to extend the family's military tradition, had sought for his younger son a commission in the regular service. Although numerous "prominent gentlemen with whom [he had] been associated in the Army" endorsed his efforts, the campaign failed for reasons unknown, as had his own attempt to reenter the army a quarter century before.[35]

Curiously, given his lifelong involvement in things military, Gregg wrote and spoke little about his Civil War experiences. In his relatively few public remarks he publicized the careers of Meade, Hancock, and other leading lights of the war. Yet published reflections on his own service were limited to a summary of the cavalry's operations at Gettysburg, first published in March 1877 in the *Philadelphia Weekly Times* as part of a series of recollections by prominent veterans. Two years later Gregg's piece was included in a book-length compilation, *Annals of the War: Written by Leading Participants North and South*, edited by Alexander K. McClure of the *Times*, an avid promoter of Gregg, whom he considered a paragon of military virtue. The only other notable work of the general's to see print—originating as an address delivered before the Pennsylvania Commandery of the Loyal Legion on May 1, 1907—was a slightly longer account of mounted operations at Gettysburg with specific reference to the 2nd Cavalry Division. Brief as it is (fourteen pages), the piece remains not only a well-crafted account of the command's activities throughout the campaign but also a thoughtful analysis of cavalry's evolution from war's outset to its critical mid-war period.[36]

Death began to stalk the Gregg family long before the eighty-year-old general made a sad pilgrimage, along with his older son, to his father's grave in the cemetery of New Valley Church near Point of Rocks, Virginia, in September 1913. By this time only one of the general's siblings, Harry, seventy-three, was still alive; their longest-living sister, Mary, wife of the proprietor of Barree Forge, Pennsylvania, had passed away the previous year.

Most of the members of Ellen's family were also gone, and her own health was failing. It had been fragile for almost a decade though she had enjoyed sustained periods of renewed vigor and spirit. At least since 1912, however, she had been unwell on a continuing basis and her death on October 27, 1915, from a paralytic stroke came as a terrible blow to her husband and sons, though not an unexpected one. In the aftermath of her passing, the general's health experienced a sharp decline. His son would recall that although he survived the subsequent winter, "he appeared to have lost all interest in life, and seemed to be willing for his own call to come."

The last bugle sounded the following summer. On July 1, 1916, he suffered a "violent trembling attack" from which he appeared briefly to recover, but within days the condition, which initially affected his digestive system, worsened and he lapsed into semi-consciousness. Toward the end—as seemed true of so many aged soldiers—"his mind wandered back to his old army days," of which he would speak fondly when awakening from a fitful sleep. Death came at 7:48 p.m. on August 7. He had lived eighty-three years and four months.

The funeral service was held at his rented home on North Fourth Street just after noon on August 11. Presided over by the rector of Saint Barnabas, the Episcopal church the family regularly attended, it attracted a large group of mourners. These included, in a "most touching" show of respect, a few members of Gregg's wartime circle, including one of his long-time orderlies, who must have related fond memories of their service together. Interment, attended by family members only, was in the local cemetery of which he had long served as director.[37]

His passing attracted eulogistic commentary from political figures, editors, and the common folk of Reading, to whom he had long been a favorite son, seen and spoken to respectfully during his daily walks through its streets. Accordingly, the city council offered a deeply felt tribute:

> As an army officer he commanded the respect and laudation of his country. As a citizen of Pennsylvania and of Reading he labored industriously for the cause of good government. During the closing years of his life he showed his love for man, regardless of creed, caste or condition by a multitude of charitable works.

A similarly heartfelt expression came from West Point's Association of Graduates:

A man of unimpeachable personal character, in private life affable and genial but not demonstrative, he fulfilled with modesty and honor all the duties of the citizen and [as the] head of an interesting and devoted family.[38]

Eventually his adopted city would put its recognition of his contributions and achievements in bronze. In the summer of 1922 it dedicated, with appropriate ceremonies including a gala parade, a life-size equestrian statue of the general, erected in Centre Parke at the triangular intersection of Centre Avenue, Fourth Street, and Olney Street. Restored and rededicated seven decades later, it continues to stand as a fitting tribute to an officer who achieved a measure of greatness and renown despite seeking neither, committed as he was to serving his army and his country to the utmost of his ability and with unfailing dignity and unpretentiousness.[39]

In many respects, David McMurtrie Gregg embodied the mid-nineteenth century American cavalry officer. By early 1861 he had attained a high degree of proficiency in his service branch based on a finished education, a thorough training regimen, and six years of garrison duty in the Southwest and on the Pacific Coast. Hard experience had taught him both the basics and the nuances of mounted service while involving him in hand-to-hand combat with Native American warriors. When the Civil War broke out his professional education continued at a steady pace as he assumed the responsibilities incumbent on leaders of larger bodies of troops. He quickly won the respect of his men and the trust of his superiors, although it took longer to gain the rank of brigadier general of volunteers and, by February 1863, command of a division of cavalry.

Promotion might have come sooner had Gregg not rejected the image of the typical cavalry commander of the time—a flamboyant publicity hound dedicated to advancing his career and reputation by any and all means. Such was not Gregg's style; to the end of the conflict he remained content to allow his performances in camp, on the march, and in battle to define his worthiness for rank and position. Unlike many of his colleagues, if those performances sometimes fell short, Gregg owned up to it. In later years his corps commander, Alfred Pleasonton, recalled that whereas other brigade and division leaders "would never tell enough in their reports," forcing him to "read between the lines . . . Gregg would ka-plunkity, plunk write down the truth. If he got licked, he would say so."[40]

Gregg was no military innovator—he pioneered no body of tactics, created no new formations—but he absorbed and exploited to the full the lessons he and other mounted leaders learned in action. Like many prewar officers bred on European doctrines of warfare, he was a strong advocate of the tactical offensive, carried out principally via fighting in the saddle. As late as the Bristoe Campaign of October 1863, when seeking to prevent Lee's army from outflanking Meade's near Rixeyville, Virginia, Gregg noted that it was "to be regretted" that several of his regiments "had to fight almost entirely on foot."[41]

For Gregg as for many of his fellow commanders, the offensive featured heavy use of the saber. He did not view cold steel (as many Confederates professed to) as a terror weapon of antiquity, but as an easy-to-wield tool highly effective at close quarters against mounted opponents. Under his influence his troopers employed the arm with success in many actions, including Second Brandy Station, Aldie, Gettysburg, and the early battles of the 1864 Overland Campaign when he alone, among Sheridan's division commanders, had prior experience in cavalry operations. In his report on Brandy Station Gregg enthusiastically described the attack delivered by one of his subordinates: "The whole brigade charged with drawn sabers, fell upon the masses of the enemy, and, after a brief but severe contest, drove them back, killing and wounding many and taking a large number of prisoners."[42]

By May 1864 he had learned to fight his troopers with greater frequency on foot, relying on shoulder arms—principally the state-of-the-art seven-shot Spencer carbine—not only to defend territory but to advance and take ground even when opposed by long-range rifles in the hands of foot soldiers and mounted infantry. Gregg adopted this versatile approach months before it gained widespread application in the ranks of Robert E. Lee's cavalry following the mortal wounding of Jeb Stuart, a devotee of the offensive as exemplified by the mounted attack.

Skilled in fighting independent of infantry assistance, Gregg was also adept at providing close support to the other arms. He did so especially well during the multiple offensives that Grant and Meade launched throughout the Petersburg Campaign. During this period Gregg was frequently teamed with Hancock's II Corps. The latter praised the "gallant cavalry under General Gregg" for shielding his corps against attack by Confederate infantry and horsemen. On those occasions when the 2nd Cavalry Division found itself isolated, Hancock trusted Gregg to hold his own and, he noted, "I was not disappointed."[43]

Gregg was equally adept in his use of horse artillery. Although he usually permitted the commanders of the batteries attached to his division to select their own positions, he was not reluctant to provide input based on a keen eye for suitable terrain. He enjoyed a cordial relationship with those officers and, unlike some of his colleagues, was quick to record his appreciation of their services. In his report of his division's operations on the third day at Gettysburg, where his horsemen were supported by the batteries of Alanson Randol and Alexander Pennington, he described the fire their guns delivered as "the most accurate that I have ever seen." Other occasions on which he teamed especially well with his attached artillery included at Auburn during the Bristoe Campaign, on Sheridan's 1864 raids, at Reams Station, and in several of the engagements during the Petersburg siege.[44]

As the war wore on, Gregg increasingly relied on mixed formations, forming a dismounted line in front with a mounted phalanx in the rear ready to charge if its comrades dislodged the enemy. In their seminal study of Civil War tactics Grady McWhiney and Perry D. Jamieson cite Gregg's handling of "a typical dismounted and mounted action" near Hatcher's Run on February 5–6, 1865, the general's last spell of field service before he resigned his commission and departed the army. On February 5 Gregg attacked with one regiment dismounted "and drove a Confederate force in its front." A mounted regiment held in the rear then charged, "scattering the retreating Confederates." The following day Gregg repeated the process, sending two regiments forward on foot against entrenched Rebels and, in the words of a subordinate, "driving the enemy out of his works, capturing 66 men and 1 stand of colors." At the same time, two regiments launched a mounted attack farther to the right, shoved infantrymen inside their works, and held them there.[45]

At times Gregg seemed indefatigable, willing to take on any and all missions. His finest hour may have come on July 3, 1863, when he not only fought Jeb Stuart to a standstill but defied given orders that might have compromised his ability to hold his position. And yet he shouldered his heaviest workload during the Petersburg Campaign, seemingly without breathing hard and certainly without complaining. With Torbert's and Wilson's divisions fighting under Sheridan in the Shenandoah Valley, Gregg's command was assigned a never-ending series of responsibilities as Grant steadily extended his lines around Petersburg and Richmond. In addition to a daily schedule of picketing, reconnoitering, and escorting supply wagons, in the space of six months the 2nd Cavalry Division played a prominent part in such major actions as Second Deep Bottom, Reams Station, Poplar Spring Church and Oscar Pegram's and William Peebles's farms, Stony Creek Station (on two occasions), Hatcher's Run and the Boydton Plank Road, two raids on the Petersburg and Weldon Railroad, and Dabney's Mills. On each of these operations he accorded himself with distinction and to the complete satisfaction of those in overall command.

Such satisfaction was not sufficient, however, to grant him the position his services entitled him to: commander, Cavalry Corps, Army of the Potomac. He achieved a measure of distinction only in the fall of 1864 when left in charge of mounted operations on the Petersburg front. Why he had been passed over for corps command upon Alfred Pleasonton's relief the previous March remains a matter of speculation, although the proximate cause was the trust General-in-Chief Grant reposed in his long-time subordinate Sheridan and his unfamiliarity with Gregg beyond the latter's sterling record at the division level.

Although it cannot be confirmed, it is possible that Gregg's political orientation as well as his publicity-averse personality factored into his inability to win higher rank. Although his cousin, Pennsylvania governor David Gregg Curtin, was a powerful supporter, Gregg lacked political patrons on the national level. Though seemingly apolitical, he was of a conservative bent, owing perhaps to his family's long affiliation with the Democratic Party and its precursors. He was not a favorite of the Republican congressmen and the Lincoln administration officials who conferred military appointments. His perceived political views caused him to be branded a "traitor" by one fellow officer, a staunch Republican and avid supporter of the wartime president.[46]

Also impossible to evaluate is the effect of the impression Gregg gave to some observers as lacking enthusiasm and an aggressive temperament. These critics may have concluded that because he did not seem to care about career enhancement he did not care about prosecuting the war with sufficient vigor. His low-key personality, avoidance of flamboyance, and refusal to seek a "picture reputation" may also have influenced generations of historians. To be sure, he continues to lack the attention regularly accorded to more colorful but perhaps less worthy comrades and superiors.

Whatever the men in power may have thought of him, Gregg's officers and men knew him for the stalwart he was. They fully appreciated his value to their division, to the army as a whole, and to the cause of saving the Union. After the war one of those troopers paid his old commander perhaps the highest tribute any officer could aspire to, declaring that

> in action he was brave to a fault, as he was always in the thickest of the fight, and his very appearance on any part of the field, no matter how discouraging the situation, was enough to inspire the men with renewed energy and courage, for they always felt that wherever he took them he would certainly bring them out with the least loss possible. Whilst he was noted as being the most tenacious cavalry fighter of the war, they felt that he was watching over them and that not a life would be sacrificed needlessly.[47]

NOTES

Abbreviations

ACPF	Appointment, Commission, and Personal Branch Files
BHC	Berks [County PA] History Center
E	Entry
HQ	Headquarters
HSP	Historical Society of Pennsylvania, Philadelphia
JCCW	Report of the Joint Committee on the Conduct of the War
LC	Library of Congress, Washington DC
M	Microcopy
MRRRP	Muster Rolls, Returns, and Regimental Papers
MSS	Correspondence, Papers
NA	National Archives, Washington DC
OR	*War of the Rebellion: A Compilation of the Official Records of the Union and Confederate Armies* (all references are to volumes in series 1)
RCCAP	Records of the Cavalry Corps, Army of the Potomac, 1861–65
RG	Record Group
TCOSW	Records of the Secretary of War, Telegrams Collected
USAHEC	U.S. Army Heritage and Education Center, Carlisle Barracks PA
USMA	U.S. Military Academy, West Point NY

1. Man in the Invisible Circle

1. Gregg Jr., "David McMurtrie Gregg," Gregg MSS, LC, 1–5; Burgess, *David Gregg*, 4; *National Cyclopaedia of American Biography*, 4:330; *Philadelphia Inquirer*, August 8, 1916; *Forty-Eighth Annual Report of the Association of the Graduates of the USMA*, 51.

2. Gregg Jr., "David McMurtrie Gregg," Gregg MSS, LC, 2–4.

3. Gregg Jr., "David McMurtrie Gregg," Gregg MSS, LC, 8, 16–18, 21–26; Burgess, *David Gregg*, 3–4, 6–7.

4. David McMurtrie to Edwin M. Stanton, July 10, 1863, ACPF, RG-94, E-297, part 2, NA.

5. Gregg Jr., "David McMurtrie Gregg," Gregg MSS, LC, 27–28; *Forty-Eighth Annual Report of the Association of the Graduates of the USMA*, 53.

6. Gregg Jr., "David McMurtrie Gregg," Gregg MSS, LC, 29, 37–38; Mitchell, *Within an Invisible Circle*, 1–5.

7. Gregg Jr., "David McMurtrie Gregg," Gregg MSS, LC, 28–29; *Reading News-Times*, June 19, 1922.

8. Gregg Jr., "David McMurtrie Gregg," Gregg MSS, LC, 29–31; Burgess, *David Gregg*, 11–12.

9. Gregg Jr., "David McMurtrie Gregg," Gregg MSS, LC, 31; Averell, *Ten Years in the Saddle*, 15.

10. Gregg Jr., "David McMurtrie Gregg," Gregg MSS, LC, 31–32; Comstock, *Diary of Cyrus B. Comstock*, 11–12; Heitman, *Historical Register and Dictionary*, 1:401.

11. *Official Register of the Officers and Cadets of the U.S. Military Academy* (1852), 17; (1855), 7.

12. Averell, *Ten Years in the Saddle*, 47. Averell mistakenly includes in his list of future general officers one "J. H. Hill," apparently misidentifying Robert Clinton Hill of the Class of '55, who never rose above the rank of colonel in the Confederate service. See Krick, *Lee's Colonels*, 193.

13. Gregg Jr., "David McMurtrie Gregg," Gregg MSS, LC, 39; Comstock, *Diary of Cyrus B. Comstock*, v–vii, 389–90; Heitman, *Historical Register and Dictionary*, 1:319.

14. Gregg Jr., "David McMurtrie Gregg," Gregg MSS, LC, 38.

15. Gregg Jr., "David McMurtrie Gregg," Gregg MSS, LC, 37–38, 392; Longacre, *General William Dorsey Pender*, 27; Comstock, *Diary of Cyrus B. Comstock*, 162. Gregg's curious nickname may bear some relation to the fact that his name was misspelled "Daniel Gregg" on the published register of the academy's officers and cadets for the first three years of his studies.

16. Averell, *Ten Years in the Saddle*, 17; Morrison, *"Best School in the World"*, 71–72; Crackel, *Illustrated History of West Point*, 133–36.

17. Gregg Jr., "David McMurtrie Gregg," Gregg MSS, LC, 32–33.

18. Averell, *Ten Years in the Saddle*, 25.

19. Morrison, *"Best School in the World"*, 87, 91–96.

20. *Official Register of the Officers and Cadets of the U.S. Military Academy* (1852), 13; (1853), 11.

21. Averell, *Ten Years in the Saddle*, 35; Crackel, *Illustrated History of West Point*, 140; Robbins, *Last in Their Class*, 129.

22. *Official Register of the Officers and Cadets of the U.S. Military Academy* (1854), 9; (1855), 7.

23. *Official Register of the Officers and Cadets of the U.S. Military Academy* (1852), 17; (1853), 11; (1854), 9; (1855), 7; Morrison, *"Best School in the World"*, 73–74, 121; Comstock, *Diary of Cyrus B. Comstock*, 186–87; Averell, *Ten Years in the Saddle*, 43–44.

24. Gregg Jr., "David McMurtrie Gregg," Gregg MSS, LC, 37; Burgess, *David Gregg*, 16; Comstock, *Diary of Cyrus B. Comstock*, 103.

25. Comstock, *Diary of Cyrus B. Comstock*, 50, 172–73; Averell, *Ten Years in the Saddle*, 36.

26. Comstock, *Diary of Cyrus B. Comstock*, 109–10, 138, 168; Averell, *Ten Years in the Saddle*, 38.

27. Comstock, *Diary of Cyrus B. Comstock*, 148; Crackel, *Illustrated History of West Point*, 110–11, 143–44; Morrison, *"Best School in the World"*, 75–76.

28. Averell, *Ten Years in the Saddle*, 41–42.

29. Comstock, *Diary of Cyrus B. Comstock*, 153.

30. Averell, *Ten Years in the Saddle*, 36–37; Johnson, *Winfield Scott*, 278n14.

31. Gregg Jr., "David McMurtrie Gregg," Gregg MSS, LC, 38–39, 163–64, 166–68; Burgess, *David Gregg*, 17.

2. Lieutenant Gregg's Frontier

1. Comstock, *Diary of Cyrus B. Comstock*, 206; Averell, *Ten Years in the Saddle*, 50.

2. Crackel, *Illustrated History of West Point*, 143–44, 149.

3. Gregg Jr., "David McMurtrie Gregg," Gregg MSS, LC, 43, 45; Burgess, *David Gregg*, 19.

4. Rodenbough and Haskin, *Army of the United States*, 174; Rodenbough, *From Everglade to Cañon*, 17–39.

5. Arnold, *Jeff Davis's Own*, 12–14.

6. Scott, *Military Dictionary*, 110–11

7. Rodenbough and Haskin, *Army of the United States*, 153.

8. Edwards, *Civil War Guns*, 135–37; Steffen, *Horse Soldier, 1776–1943*, 1:128–36; Huntington, *Hall's Breechloaders*, 89–90, 207, 217.

9. Rosebush, *Frontier Steel*, 158.

10. Averell, *Ten Years in the Saddle*, 54–55.

11. Averell, *Ten Years in the Saddle*, 55–56; Gregg Jr., "David McMurtrie Gregg," Gregg MSS, LC, 45–46.

12. Comstock, *Diary of Cyrus B. Comstock*, 162.

13. Averell, *Ten Years in the Saddle*, 55–59; Bauer, *Mexican War*, 60–62; McWhiney and Jamieson, *Attack and Die*, 39.

14. Gregg Jr., "David McMurtrie Gregg," Gregg MSS, LC, 46; Burgess, *David Gregg*, 20.

15. Gregg Jr., "David McMurtrie Gregg," Gregg MSS, LC, 46; Frazer, *Forts of the West*, 143–44.

16. Gregg Jr., "David McMurtrie Gregg," Gregg MSS, LC, 47–49.

17. Gregg Jr., "David McMurtrie Gregg," Gregg MSS, LC, 49; Longacre, *General William Dorsey Pender*, 27.

18. Gregg Jr., "David McMurtrie Gregg," Gregg MSS, LC, 64. Pages 74–99 include excerpts from a journal kept by Lieutenant Gregg on the march from Fort Thorn to Fort Tejon. For the Cooke expedition, see Bauer, *Mexican War*, 138–39. For details on Forts Thorn and Tejon, see Frazer, *Forts of the West*, 32, 104–5.

19. Gregg Jr., "David McMurtrie Gregg," Gregg MSS, LC, 64, 78–79; Rosebush, *Frontier Steel*, 152.

20. Gregg Jr., "David McMurtrie Gregg," Gregg MSS, LC, 76.

21. Gregg Jr., "David McMurtrie Gregg," Gregg MSS, LC, 64–68, 78; Utley, *Frontiersmen in Blue*, 105.

22. Rodenbough and Haskin, *Army of the United States*, 159; Gregg Jr., "David McMurtrie Gregg," Gregg MSS, LC, 68.

23. Gregg Jr., "David McMurtrie Gregg," Gregg MSS, LC, 68–73; Frazer, *Forts of the West*, 177.

24. Gregg Jr., "David McMurtrie Gregg," Gregg MSS, LC, 69, 104–7; Manring, *Conquest of the Coeur D'Alenes, Spokanes and Palouses*, 28–48; Utley, *Frontiersmen in Blue*, 187–201; Johanson and Gates, *Empire of the Columbia*, 254–55.

25. Rosebush, *Frontier Steel*, 132–33; Utley, *Frontiersmen in Blue*, 202.

26. Gregg Jr., "David McMurtrie Gregg," Gregg MSS, LC, 108–15; Utley, *Frontiersmen in Blue*, 202; Manring, *Conquest of the Coeur D'Alenes, Spokanes and Palouses*, 89–95, 127–29.

27. Gregg Jr., "David McMurtrie Gregg," Gregg MSS, LC, 115–18; Manring, *Conquest of the Coeur D'Alenes, Spokanes and Palouses*, 110–13, 124, 129–30; Utley, *Frontiersmen in Blue*, 203.

28. Utley, *Frontiersmen in Blue*, 203; Manring, *Conquest of the Coeur D'Alenes, Spokanes and Palouses*, 114–24; Gregg Jr., "David McMurtrie Gregg," Gregg MSS, LC, 119–20.

29. Utley, *Frontiersmen in Blue*, 203–6; Manring, *Conquest of the Coeur D'Alenes, Spokanes and Palouses*, 158–59, 186–201.

30. Gregg Jr., "David McMurtrie Gregg," Gregg MSS, LC, 124–27.

31. Utley, *Frontiersmen in Blue*, 207; Longacre, *General William Dorsey Pender*, 33; Manring, *Conquest of the Coeur D'Alenes, Spokanes and Palouses*, 205.

32. Utley, *Frontiersmen in Blue*, 207–8; Gregg Jr., "David McMurtrie Gregg," Gregg MSS, LC, 131, 135–36; Burgess, *David Gregg*, 28.

33. Utley, *Frontiersmen in Blue*, 208.

34. Gregg Jr., "David McMurtrie Gregg," Gregg MSS, LC, 137–42.

35. Gregg Jr., "David McMurtrie Gregg," Gregg MSS, LC, 146; Burgess, *David Gregg*, 29; Heitman, *Historical Register and Dictionary*, 2:405; Frazer, *Forts of the West*, 127–28; *Reading News-Times*, June 19, 1922.

36. Gregg Jr., "David McMurtrie Gregg," Gregg MSS, LC, 143–49; Burgess, *David Gregg*, 29; *OR*, vol. 50, part 1, 442–43.

37. *OR*, vol. 50, part 1, 450, 483–84; Heitman, *Historical Register and Dictionary*, 1:476.

3. From the Pacific to the Potomac

1. Gregg Jr., "David McMurtrie Gregg," Gregg MSS, LC, 150; Heitman, *Historical Register and Dictionary*, 1:476; Rodenbough and Haskin, *Army of the United States*, 232; Carter, *From Yorktown to Santiago*, 13.

2. Heitman, *Historical Register and Dictionary* 1:477.

3. Brackett, *History of the United States Cavalry*, 219.

4. *OR*, vol. 50, part 1, 561.

5. *OR*, vol. 50, part 1, 561–62; Gregg Jr., "David McMurtrie Gregg," Gregg MSS, LC, 152; Burgess, *David Gregg*, 31.

6. Gregg Jr., "David McMurtrie Gregg," Gregg MSS, LC, 153, 157.

7. Gregg Jr., "David McMurtrie Gregg," Gregg MSS, LC, 153; Heitman, *Historical Register and Dictionary* 1:176; Regimental History Committee, *Third Pennsylvania Cavalry*, 17.

8. Averell, *Ten Years in the Saddle*, 289–302.

9. Davis, *Common Soldier, Uncommon War*, 65.

10. Benjamin Hutchins to "Dear Bob," December 31, 1861, courtesy of Mrs. Tillie Clement, Haddonfield NJ.

11. William W. Averell to "My dear Sister," September 25, 1861, Averell MSS, New York State Library, Albany; Scott, *Military Dictionary*, 62–63.

12. George Stoneman to Seth Williams, September 3, 1861, Stoneman MSS, Simon Gratz Coll., HSP; George Stoneman to Randolph B. Marcy, September 17, October 18, 1861, RCCAP, RG-393, part 2, E-1469, NA.

13. Gregg Jr., "David McMurtrie Gregg," Gregg MSS, LC, 154–57.

14. Averell, *Ten Years in the Saddle*, 340–41; Bates, *History of Pennsylvania Volunteers*, 3:111; Fitz John Porter to Seth Williams, December 16, 1861, George B. McClellan MSS, LC.

15. *Philadelphia Inquirer*, January 23, 1862.

16. Robert Cummings to "Dear Sister," December 23, 1861, Cummings MSS, Alexander Library, Rutgers University, New Brunswick NJ; Edward McLaughlin to "Dear Sallie," December 23, 1861, McLaughlin MSS, HSP.

17. Robert Cummings to "Dear Sister," December 23, 1861, Cummings MSS, Alexander Library, Rutgers University, New Brunswick NJ.

18. Robert Cummings to "Dear Nephew," January 30, 1862, Cummings MSS, Alexander Library, Rutgers University, New Brunswick NJ.

19. Bates, *History of Pennsylvania Volunteers*, 3:111.

20. Longacre, *Lincoln's Cavalrymen*, 47; Gregg Jr., "David McMurtrie Gregg," Gregg MSS, LC, 159; Crowninshield and Gleason, *First Massachusetts Cavalry*, 111.

21. *Philadelphia Inquirer*, February 14, 1862; Collins, "A Prisoner's March from Gettysburg to Staunton," 430; Crowninshield and Gleason, *First Massachusetts Cavalry*, 291.

22. The list of officers who either resigned or were discharged from the service during Gregg's first months in command in 1862 include: Chief Quartermaster William Frederick (disch., March 18); Asst. Surg. J. Ralston Wells (resig., March 23); Capt. William Murray, Co. E (resig., March 5); 1st Lt. George Bertram, Co. E (resig., February 26); 1st Lt. Jackson McFadden, Co. G (disch., February 28); 2nd Lt. Christian Kneass, Co. G (resig., March 17); Capt. Bennet Fulmer, Co. K (disch., February 11); 1st Lt. Thomas B. Whitney, Co. K (resig., March 18); 2nd Lt. George O. McMullin, Co. K (disch., February 26); Capt. T. James Hardy, Co. L (resig., February 26); and 1st Lt. Thomas Furness, Co. L (disch., March 17). Several other officers left the regiment the following summer (Bates, *History of Pennsylvania Volunteers*, 3:118, 131, 135, 144, 147–48). Gregg Jr., "David McMurtrie Gregg," Gregg MSS, LC, 158–59, claims that Gregg also rid the regiment of its first major (presumably Albert G. Enos), but Bates, *History of Pennsylvania Volunteers*, 3:118, says Enos did not resign until mid-October 1862.

23. Averell, *Ten Years in the Saddle*, 341.

24. Sears, *To the Gates of Richmond*, 3–5.

25. Gregg Jr., "David McMurtrie Gregg," Gregg MSS, LC, 160–63.

26. Gregg Jr., "David McMurtrie Gregg," Gregg MSS, LC, 168–70; *Philadelphia Inquirer*, February 20, 1862; Long and Long, *Civil War Day by Day*, 174.

27. Gregg Jr., "David McMurtrie Gregg," Gregg MSS, LC, 171; *OR*, vol. 5, 19; vol. 11, part 3, 36–37; vol. 51, part 1, 558.

28. Longacre, *Lincoln's Cavalrymen*, 68–72; Davis, *Common Soldier, Uncommon War*, 98–101; William W. Averell to "My dear Father," March 13, 1862, Averell MSS, New York State Library, Albany.

29. *OR*, vol. 5, 548–49, 740–42.

30. William W. Averell to "My dear Father," March 13, 1862, Averell MSS, New York State Library, Albany; William W. Averell to "My dear Sister," March 28, 1862, Averell MSS, New York State Library, Albany.

31. Sears, *To the Gates of Richmond*, 9–20.

32. *OR*, vol. 5, 1; vol. 11, part 1, 283, part 3, 36; Regimental History Committee, *Third Pennsylvania Cavalry*, 45; Rufus Ingalls to James A. Van Alen, March 31, 1862, Smith MSS, USAHEC; William W. Averell to "My dear Brother," April 27, 1862, Averell MSS, New York State Library, Albany.

33. Sears, *To the Gates of Richmond*, 35–36; *OR*, vol. 11, part 1, 9, 285, 298, 358, part 3, 141; Burgess, *David Gregg*, 34.

34. Sears, *To the Gates of Richmond*, 36–39; *OR*, 11, part 1, 9–11, 403–11.

4. Averell and Pleasonton

1. Sears, *To the Gates of Richmond*, 61–62, 65–67; Longacre, *Lincoln's Cavalrymen*, 75–76.

2. Thomas W. Smith to "Dear Joe," August 7, 1862, Smith MSS, HSP; Gregg Jr., "David McMurtrie Gregg," Gregg MSS, LC, 111–12, 180–82, 229–30. A third Gregg brother to serve in the conflict, though not in the army—George, in prewar years a mechanic, fireman, and engineer on the Pennsylvania Central Railroad—was transferred to service on a military railroad in Virginia in June 1861. His duties frequently took him into enemy territory; twice captured by guerrillas, on one occasion he was imprisoned for several weeks until exchanged and released.

3. William W. Averell to "My dear Brother," April 27, 1862, Averell MSS, New York State Library, Albany.

4. *OR*, vol. 11, part 1, 424–28, 430–32, 436–46; *New York Times*, May 6, 1862; Averell, "With the Cavalry on the Peninsula," 429; O'Neill, "What Men We Have Got Are Good Soldiers and Brave Ones Too," 101–4. Army headquarters specifically ordered the 6th and 8th Pennsylvania to remain at Yorktown during the fighting on May 5. See *OR*, vol. 11, part 3, 141.

5. William H. Emory in Generals' Reports of Service, RG-94, E-160, NA, 6:301–2, 319–20; O'Neill, "What Men We Have Got Are Good Soldiers and Brave Ones Too," 105.

6. *OR*, vol. 11, part 3, 168, 173; *New York Tribune*, May 15, 1862; Adams, *Story of a Trooper*, 452.

7. *OR*, vol. 11, part 3, 171, 212.

8. *OR*, vol. 11, part 3, 642, 644–45; George W. Flack, diary, May 20, 1862, Alexander Library, Rutgers University, New Brunswick NJ.

9. *OR*, vol. 11, part 3, 191–92; Sears, *To the Gates of Richmond*, 110–13.

10. *OR*, vol. 11, part 3, 649.

11. *OR*, vol. 11, part 3, 648–49, 670–73; Bates, *History of Pennsylvania Volunteers*, 3:111–12; *Philadelphia Inquirer*, May 31, 1862.

12. Sears, *To the Gates of Richmond*, 117–45.

13. William H. Medill to "Dear Sister Kate," March 15, 1862, Medill MSS, LC.

14. Bates, *History of Pennsylvania Volunteers*, 3:112.

15. Robert Cummings to "Dear Sister," June 17, 1862, Cummings MSS, Alexander Library, Rutgers University, New Brunswick NJ.

16. *OR*, vol. 11, part 2, 192, part 3, 820, 825.

17. *OR*, vol. 11, part 3, 281; vol. 51, part 1, 671; David M. Gregg to HQ IV Army Corps, June 18, 1862, MRRRP, 8th PA Cav., RG-94, box 4142, NA; Robert Cummings to "Dear Sister," June 17, 1862, Cummings MSS, Alexander Library, Rutgers University, New Brunswick NJ; Robert Cummings to "Dear Nephew," June 17, 1862, Cummings MSS, Alexander Library, Rutgers University, New Brunswick NJ.

18. *OR*, vol. 11, part 3, 238; Robert Cummings to "Dear Nephew," June 17, 1862, Cummings MSS, Alexander Library, Rutgers University, New Brunswick NJ; Kelsey, *To the Knife*, 13.

19. David M. Gregg to HQ IV Army Corps, June 18, 1862, MRRRP, 8th PA Cav., RG-94, box 4142, NA; *OR*, vol. 11, part 1, 233.

20. *OR*, vol. 11, part 2, 30; vol. 51, part 1, 715; Longacre, *Lincoln's Cavalrymen*, 87–89, 92.

21. Sears, *To the Gates of Richmond*, 183–335.

22. Burgess, *David Gregg*, 35; Bates, *History of Pennsylvania Volunteers*, 3:112; *OR*, vol. 11, part 2, 192.

23. Averell, "With the Cavalry on the Peninsula," 432; Miller, *War History*, 11.

24. *OR*, vol. 11, part 2, 192–95.

25. *OR*, vol. 11, part 2, 193, 195; Averell, "With the Cavalry on the Peninsula," 432.

26. *OR*, vol. 11, part 2, 194–95, 206, 220–21, part 3, 288–89.

27. Sears, *To the Gates of Richmond*, 339, 355.

28. *OR*, vol. 11, part 3, 281.

29. David M. Gregg to George Stoneman, July 6, 1862, MRRRP, 8th PA Cav., RG-94, box 4142, NA.

30. *OR*, vol. 11, part 3, 307–8; vol. 51, part 1, 716–17; O'Neill, "What Men We Have Got Are Good Soldiers and Brave Ones Too," 135.

31. Gregg Jr., "David McMurtrie Gregg," Gregg MSS, LC, 172; O'Neill, "What Men We Have Got Are Good Soldiers and Brave Ones Too," 134, 217n132; *OR*, vol. 19, part 1, 180; Longacre, *Lincoln's Cavalrymen*, 101.

32. *OR*, vol. 11, part 3, 369; Longacre, "Alfred Pleasonton," 11–14.

33. *OR*, vol. 11, part 2, 951–52; *JCCW* 2 (1868), 5; O'Neill, "What Men We Have Got Are Good Soldiers and Brave Ones Too," 136–37; Sears, *To the Gates of Richmond*, 343, 354–55.

34. *OR*, vol. 51, part 1, 118–19.

35. Hewett, Trudeau, and Suderow, *Supplement to the OR*, vol. 2, 481–83.

36. Sears, *To the Gates of Richmond*, 353; *OR*, vol. 11, part 2, 964–66; William W. Averell to "My dear Father," August 22, 1862, Averell MSS, New York State Library, Albany; William W. Averell to "My dear Brother," September 15, 1862, Averell MSS, New York State Library, Albany; Averell, *Ten Years in the Saddle*, 385.

37. Hennessy, *Return to Bull Run*, 5–6, 22–25.

38. Hennessy, *Return to Bull Run*, 90–91; *OR*, vol. 11, part 1, 85–89, part 3, 376–77.

39. Hennessy, *Return to Bull Run*, 27–29, 200–451.

40. Sears, *Landscape Turned Red*, 180–297.

41. *OR*, vol. 12, part 3, 789; Bates, *History of Pennsylvania Volunteers*, 3:112; Seth Williams to Jacob D. Cox, August 31, 1862, MRRRP, 8th PA Cav., RG-94, box 4142, NA.

42. *OR*, vol. 19, part 1, 180, part 2, 242, 337; vol. 51, part 1, 754; Sears, *Landscape Turned Red*, 103; Alfred Pleasonton to Seth Williams, September 10, 1862, McClellan MSS, LC.

43. HQ Defenses of Washington to Seth Williams, September 27, 1862, McClellan MSS, LC; Welsh, *Medical Histories of the Union Generals*, 141. Gregg Jr., "David McMurtrie Gregg," Gregg MSS, LC, 177, states that Gregg "was in the battles of South Mountain on the 14th [of September] and Antietam on the 17th." This does not seem likely; the illnesses that struck him down must have predated these battles. It would have taken weeks for him to recover, a process only nearing its end by September 27.

44. Gregg Jr., "David McMurtrie Gregg," Gregg MSS, LC, 172–75.

5. Brigadier General of Volunteers

1. William W. Averell to "My dear Brother," October 2, 1862, Averell MSS, New York State Library, Albany; Alfred Pleasonton to Randolph B. Marcy, October 11–12 (several dispatches), Pleasonton Dispatch Book, 1862, Alderman Library, University of Virginia, Charlottesville; Longacre, *Lincoln's Cavalrymen*, 109–12.

2. John B. McIntosh to "My dear Wife," October 15, 1862, McIntosh MSS, John Hay Library, Brown University, Providence RI.

3. *OR*, vol. 19, part 2, 39; Alfred Pleasonton to Randolph B. Marcy, October 11, 1862, Pleasonton Dispatch Book, 1862, Alderman Library, University of Virginia, Charlottesville; Gregg Jr., "David McMurtrie Gregg," Gregg MSS, LC, 174.

4. Marvel, *Burnside*, 99–100, 111, 159–61; O'Reilly, *Fredericksburg Campaign*, 1–3.

5. *OR*, vol. 19, part 2, 460.

6. *OR*, vol. 19, part 1, 377, part 2, 109–12, 494, 518–19, 526; Alfred Pleasonton to George D. Bayard, October 30–31, 1862, Pleasonton Dispatch Book, 1862, Alderman Library, University of Virginia, Charlottesville; Alfred Pleasonton to Randolph B. Marcy, October 31 (two dispatches), November 1, 1862 (three dispatches), Pleasonton Dispatch Book, 1862, Alderman Library, University of Virginia, Charlottesville; Bayard, *Life of George Dashiell Bayard*, 259–62.

7. *OR*, vol. 19, part 1, 152, part 2, 112–13, 125, 129, 141–42.

8. Alfred Pleasonton to Randolph B. Marcy, November 1, 1862 (three dispatches), Pleasonton Dispatch Book, 1862, Alderman Library, University of Virginia, Charlottesville.

9. Alfred Pleasonton to Randolph B. Marcy, November 2, 1862 (five dispatches), November 3 (two dispatches), Pleasonton Dispatch Book, 1862, Alderman Library, University of Virginia, Charlottesville; *OR*, vol. 19, part 2, 113–14, 129, 143; McClellan, *Life and Campaigns of Stuart*, 176–80.

10. *OR*, vol. 19, part 2, 125–26, 130, 143–44, 148, 693–94.

11. *OR*, vol. 19, part 2, 117, 126, 130, 144; vol. 51, part 1, 927, 929–30; Alfred Pleasonton to George D. Ruggles, November 5, 1862 (two dispatches), Pleasonton Dispatch Book, 1862, Alderman Library, University of Virginia, Charlottesville; Moore, *Rebellion Record*, 6:177–679; *New York Herald*, November 11, 1863; Davis, *Common Soldier, Uncommon War*, 268–70; O'Neill, "Col. Benjamin 'Grimes' Davis at Barbee's Cross Roads."

12. *OR*, vol. 19, part 2, 695, 701, 709.

13. *OR*, vol. 19, part 2, 127, 130, 144–45, 701, 704; Alfred Pleasonton to Albert V. Colburn, November 7, 1862 (four dispatches), Pleasonton Dispatch Book, 1862, Alderman Library, University of Virginia, Charlottesville; Alfred Pleasonton to William W. Averell, November 7, 1862, Pleasonton Dispatch Book, 1862, Alderman Library, University of Virginia, Charlottesville; Alfred Pleasonton to Ambrose E. Burnside, November 7, 1862, Pleasonton Dispatch Book, 1862, Alderman Library, University of Virginia, Charlottesville.

14. *OR*, vol. 19, part 1, 89, part 2, 127, 130–31, 707; Alfred Pleasonton to John G. Parke, November 10, 1862, Pleasonton Dispatch Book, 1862, Alderman Library, University of Virginia, Charlottesville.

15. Marvel, *Burnside*, 163–65; O'Reilly, *Fredericksburg Campaign*, 20–25; *OR*, vol. 19, part 2, 583–84; vol. 21, 962, 986.

16. *OR*, vol. 21, 785–86, 987.

17. *OR*, vol. 19, part 2, 129; vol. 21, 23–28, 1021.

18. *Official Records of the Union and Confederate Navies*, 5:186; *OR*, vol. 21, 841.

19. *OR*, vol. 19, part 2, 572, 580–81; vol. 21, 790, 793–95, 798–800, 802.

20. *OR*, vol. 19, part 2, 715–16; vol. 21, 84–87, 1017–20, 1026, 1031–32, 1035, 1037; O'Reilly, *Fredericksburg Campaign*, 44–47.

21. *OR*, vol. 21, 85, 786; *JCCW* 1 (1863), 747.

22. *OR*, vol. 21, 90–95, 546–47, 553–55; O'Reilly, *Fredericksburg Campaign*, 127–429.

23. Adams *Cycle of Adams Letters*, 1:211; *OR*, vol. 21, 220–21; Alfred Pleasonton's Generals' Reports of Service, RG-94, E-160, NA, 1:120.

24. Bayard, *Life of George Dashiell Bayard*, 272–74; *New York Times*, December 15, 1862; Thomas, *Some Personal Reminiscences*, 8.

25. *OR*, vol. 21, 61, 935; "Gen. Gregg Succeeds Gen. Bayard," article copied in *Camden* [NJ] *Democrat*, January 3, 1863.

26. Gregg Jr., "David McMurtrie Gregg," Gregg MSS, LC, 179; Heitman, *Historical Register and Dictionary*, 1:476; David M. Gregg to Lorenzo Thomas, January 17, 1863, ACPF, RG-94, E-297, part 2, NA; Oath of office as brigadier general of volunteers, January 17, 1863, ACPF, RG-94, E-297, part 2, NA; Chief of the Record and Pensions Office, War Dept., "Statement of Volunteer Military Service of David McM. Gregg," May 18, 1897, ACPF, RG-94, E-297, part 2, NA.

27. David G. Curtin to Abraham Lincoln, October 21, 1862, ACPF, RG-94, E-297, part 2, NA.

28. O'Reilly, *Fredericksburg Campaign*, 467–75; Marvel, *Burnside*, 208–11.

29. O'Reilly, *Fredericksburg Campaign* 476–89; *OR*, vol. 21, 752, 755; Myron H. Beaumont to David M. Gregg, January 26, 1863, RCCAP, RG-393, part 2, E-1449, NA.

30. Glazier, *Three Years in the Federal Cavalry*, 123; Marvel, *Burnside*, 215–17; *OR*, vol. 21, 1004–5.

31. Sears, *Chancellorsville*, 62–75, 80–82; Sears, *Controversies and Commanders*, 184–85; *JCCW* 4 (1865), 73–74.

32. *OR*, vol. 25, part 2, 59, 71–72, 82–83.

33. "Skirmishes of the [1st Pennsylvania Cav.] Regiment," n.d., Taylor MSS, HSP.

34. Gregg to Martin T. McMahon, January 3, 1863, RCCAP, RG-393, part 2, E-1532–33, NA; Kelsey, *To the Knife*, 22; Nathan B. Webb, diary, January 23, 1863, William L. Clements Library, University of Michigan, Ann Arbor.

35. David M. Gregg to Edward A. Fobes, January 8, 1863, RCCAP, RG-393, part 2, E-1532–33, NA.

36. *OR*, vol. 25, part 2, 91, 111.

37. *OR*, vol. 25, part 2, 116–17.

6. Failed Raid, Drawn Battle

1. David M. Gregg to Seth Williams, February 18, March 5, 1863; Endorsements by George Stoneman, February 18, 22, 1863, David M. Gregg's Generals' Papers, RG-94, E-159, NA.

2. *OR*, vol. 25, part 1, 21–26; Adams, *Cycle of Adams Letters*, 1:256–57.

3. *OR*, vol. 25, part 1, 47–64; Longacre, *Lincoln's Cavalrymen*, 134–38.

4. Gregg Jr., "David McMurtrie Gregg," Gregg MSS, LC, 84–87; Burgess, *David Gregg*, 44–45.

5. *OR*, vol. 25, part 1, 1066–67, part 2, 199–200, 204–5; Davis, "Stoneman Raid," 536.

6. David M. Gregg to Officers and Soldiers of the 3rd Division, June 11, 1863, David M. Gregg's Generals' Papers, RG-94, E-159, NA.

7. *OR*, vol. 25, part 1, 1068, 1081, part 2, 213–14, 223; A. J. Alexander to David M. Gregg, April 27, 1863, RCCAP, RG-393, part 2, E-1449, NA; Longacre, *Mounted Raids of the Civil War*, 154–55.

8. *OR*, vol. 25, part 1, 1057–58, 1065.

9. *OR*, vol. 25, part 1, 1058–59, 1072–80; Doster, *Lincoln and Episodes of the Civil War*, 190; Longacre, *Mounted Raids of the Civil War*, 157–61.

10. *OR*, vol. 25, part 1, 1060, 1082–83, 1085–86; Gracey, *Annals of the Sixth Pennsylvania Cavalry*, 139–45.

11. *OR*, vol. 25, part 1, 1085–87; Longacre, *Mounted Raids of the Civil War*, 165–71; Brackett, *History of the United States Cavalry*, 308–10; Moore, *Rebellion Record*, 6:607–8; *New York Times*, May 10, 1863; "Stoneman's Raid in the Chancellorsville Campaign," 152–53.

12. *OR*, vol. 25, part 1, 1083–84, part 2, 441, 452–53; Glazier, *Three Years in the Federal Cavalry*, 181; Moore, *Kilpatrick and Our Cavalry*, 49–50.

13. *OR*, vol. 25, part 1, 1062–63, 1082–83.

14. George A. Custer to Isaac P. Christiancy, May 31, 1863, Custer MSS, USMA Library; George G. Meade to "Dear Margaret," June 12, 1863, Meade MSS, HSP; Gregg, "Union Cavalry at Gettysburg," 374.

15. *OR*, vol. 25, part 1, 1069, part 2, 463.

16. *OR*, vol. 25, part 1, 1081; Sears, *Chancellorsville*, 161, 191, 266; Robbins, *War Record and Personal Experiences*, 55–56; Johnston, *Virginia Railroads in the Civil War*, 149; Longacre, *Lincoln's Cavalrymen*, 139–40.

17. Sears, *Chancellorsville*, 172–424.

18. *OR*, vol. 25, part 1, 1080.

19. *OR*, vol. 25, part 2, 513.

20. *JCCW* 2 (1868), 7–9; *OR*, vol. 25, part 1, 772–76, 786–88; vol. 27, part 1, 51; Pleasonton, "Successes and Failures of Chancellorsville," 179–82; Kelsey, *To the Knife*, 43–47; Huey, Carpenter, and Wells, "Charge of the Eighth Pennsylvania," 186–88.

21. John B. McIntosh to "My own dear Wife," May 13, 1863, McIntosh MSS, John Hay Library, Brown University, Providence RI; Walter S. Newhall to his father, May 14, 1863, Newhall MSS, HSP; Beck, "Letters of a Civil War Surgeon," 152; Adams, *Cycle of Adams Letters*, 2:8.

22. Alfred Pleasonton to John F. Farnsworth, June 23, 1861, Pleasonton MSS, LC; Elon J. Farnsworth to John F. Farnsworth, June 23, 1863, Pleasonton MSS, LC.

23. *OR*, vol. 25, part 1, 905–6, part 2, 516–17, 584–85; Alfred Pleasonton to Seth Williams, May 22, 1863, RCCAP, RG-393, part 2, E-1449, NA.

24. David M. Gregg to Charles G. Sawtelle, May 22, 1863, RCCAP, RG-393, part 2, E-1534, NA; David M. Gregg to A. J. Cohen, May 28, 1863, RCCAP, RG-393, part 2, E-1534, NA; General Orders No. 1, HQ 3rd Cavalry Div., May 27, 1863, RCCAP, RG-393, part 2, E-1534, NA; *OR*, vol. 25, part 2, 524–25; vol. 27, part 3, 23.

25. *OR*, vol. 25, part 2, 518, 543.

26. *OR*, vol. 25, part 2, 528, 531, 536, 593; vol. 27, part 3, 5–8, 12–14; *New York Times*, June 10, 1863; Coddington, *Gettysburg Campaign*, 536, 623n; Nye, *Here Come the Rebels!*, 32–36.

27. *OR*, vol. 27, part 2, 293, part 3, 859, 863–64, 876; McClellan, *Life and Campaigns of Stuart*, 261–63; Wert, *Cavalryman of the Lost Cause*, 235–40.

28. Alfred Pleasonton to David M. Gregg, June 8, 1863, Smith MSS, USAHEC; Circular, HQ 3rd Cavalry Div., June 8, 1863, RCCAP, E-393, part 2, E-1532–33, NA; *OR*, vol. 27, part 1, 170, 1043, part 3, 15–17, 27–30; vol. 51, part 1, 1047.

29. *OR*, vol. 27, part 2, 679–80; Pleasonton, "Campaign of Gettysburg," 448–49; McClellan, *Life and Campaigns of Stuart*, 264–68; Longacre, *Cavalry at Gettysburg*, 66–73.

30. *OR*, vol. 27, part 1, 949–50, 961. I am indebted for much of the analysis of Gregg's operations at Second Brandy Station to the acknowledged expert on this battle, Clark B. Hall. Hall to the author, June 18, 26–27, 2018.

31. *OR*, vol. 27, part 1, 950–51, 965–66, 1053, part 2, 681, 684, 755, 769; Hewett, Trudeau, and Suderow, *Supplement to the OR*, vol. 5, 249; Meyer, *Civil War Experiences*, 28; Downey, *Clash of Cavalry*, 118–19. Gregg partially blamed his slow, roundabout advance to the depot on the roads being blocked by "felled trees and other obstructions" (Gregg, *Second Cavalry Division in the Gettysburg Campaign*, 6–7; Gregg, "Union Cavalry at Gettysburg," 376), but no accounts by other members of the 3rd Division bear this out.

32. Meyer, *Civil War Experiences*, 28.

33. *OR*, vol. 27, part 1, 169, 951, 965–66; Thomas, *Some Personal Reminiscences*, 10–11.

34. *OR*, vol. 27, part 1, 951, 966–67, 985–86, 1023–28, part 2, 755, 763; Thomas, *Some Personal Reminiscences*, 11; Glazier, *Three Years in the Federal Cavalry*, 218–19; Moore, *Kilpatrick and Our Cavalry*, 59; McClellan, *Life and Campaigns of Stuart*, 270–79; Downey, *Clash of Cavalry*, 134–35, 140.

35. *OR*, vol. 27, part 1, 903, 951, part 3, 49; Gregg, *Second Cavalry Division in the Gettysburg Campaign*, 6–7; Pleasonton, "Campaign of Gettysburg," 450.

36. *OR*, vol. 27, part 1, 1045–48, part 2, 681–83; *New York Times*, June 11, 1863; David M. Gregg to Ellen S. Gregg, June 11, 1863, TCOSW, RG-107, M-504, NA. Stuart's adjutant general would write that "General Gregg retired from the field defeated, but defiant and unwilling to acknowledge a defeat." See McClellan, *Life and Campaigns of Stuart*, 279.

37. *OR*, vol. 27, part 1, 906, 1025; Gregg, *Second Cavalry Division in the Gettysburg Campaign*, 7; Gregg, "Union Cavalry at Gettysburg," 376; Thomas, *Some Personal Reminiscences*, 11. According to Pleasonton, writing immediately after the battle (*OR*, vol. 27, part 1, 903–4), "Stuart was to have started on a raid into Maryland, so captured papers state." He repeated and embellished this claim in postwar years: Pleasonton, "Campaign of Gettysburg," 450. Meyer, *Civil War Experiences*, 31, claims that Kilpatrick's men fought through to Stuart's headquarters, "capturing Stuart's adjutant-general and his papers," but he does not describe their contents. An authoritative refutation of these claims can be found in Coddington, *Gettysburg Campaign*, 61–62.

7. Days of Strife and Glory

1. *OR*, vol. 27, part 3, 64; Gregg, *Second Cavalry Division in the Gettysburg Campaign*, 8.

2. *OR*, vol. 27, part 3, 58; Glazier, *Three Years in the Federal Cavalry*, 223–24; Circular to Officers & Soldiers of the 3rd Division, June 11, 1863, RCCAP, RG-393, part 2, E-1532–33, NA; copy in David M. Gregg's Generals' Papers, RG-94, E-159, NA.

3. *OR*, vol. 27, part 2, 295–96, 305–6, 313–15, part 3, 57; A. J. Alexander to David M. Gregg, June 13, 1863, RCCAP, RG-393, part 2, E-1449, NA.

4. *OR*, vol. 27, part 1, 952, part 3, 87–89, 104–5, 116–17; vol. 51, part 1, 1054–55; Norman Ball, diary, June 14, 1863, Connecticut Historical Society, Hartford; Charles Adams, Jr., diary, June 15, 1863, Adams MSS, Massachusetts Historical Society, Boston; Gracey, *Annals of the Sixth Pennsylvania Cavalry*, 253; A. J. Alexander to David M. Gregg, June 15, 1863, Smith MSS, USAHEC.

5. *OR*, vol. 27, part 1, 45.

6. *OR*, vol. 27, part 1, 47, 66–76, 955, 962–64, part 3, 171–73; Regimental History Committee, *Third Pennsylvania Cavalry*, 252; Nye, *Here Come the Rebels!*, 181–85.

7. *OR*, vol. 27, part 1, 171, 906, 952–53, 962, 972–73, part 3, 105; *JCCW* 4 (1865), 32–33; Ulric Dahlgren to Daniel Butterfield, June 17, TCOSW, RG-107, M-504, NA; Gregg, *Second Cavalry Division in the Gettysburg Campaign*, 8; Adams, *Cycle of Adams Letters*, 2:36–37; Moore, *Kilpatrick and Our Cavalry*, 66–67; O'Neill, *Cavalry Battles of Aldie, Middleburg and Upperville*, 38–44; Robert F. O'Neill to the author, March 5, 6, 2019; Stonesifer, "Union Cavalry Comes of Age," 280; Nye, *Here Come the Rebels!*, 171–78; McClellan, *Life and Campaigns of Stuart*, 296–302.

8. *OR*, vol. 27, part 1, 171, 953, 979–80, 1052, part 2, 688–89, 739–40; Crowninshield and Gleason, *First Massachusetts Cavalry*, 144–49; O'Neill, *Cavalry Battles of Aldie, Middleburg and Upperville*, 45–60; *New York Times*, June 22, 1863; Custer and Custer, *Custer Story*, 55–56; Whittaker, *Complete Life of Gen. George A. Custer*, 159.

9. *OR*, vol. 27, part 1, 171, 907, 953, 979–80, 1052; O'Neill, *Cavalry Battles of Aldie, Middleburg and Upperville*, 61–65; Nye, *Here Come the Rebels!*, 179–80.

10. *OR*, vol. 27, part 1, 953, 975.

11. *OR*, vol. 27, part 1, 909, 953, 972, 975–76, part 2, 689–90; Meyer, *Civil War Experiences*, 37–39; Cormany and Cormany, *Cormany Diaries*, 319–20; Norman Ball, diary, June 19, 1863, Connecticut Historical Society, Hartford; McClellan, *Life and Campaigns of Stuart*, 308–12; O'Neill, *Cavalry Battles of Aldie, Middleburg and Upperville*, 102–4; Nye, *Here Come the Rebels!*, 189–93.

12. *OR*, vol. 27, part 1, 953–54; Tobie, *First Maine Cavalry*, 165–68; O'Neill, *Cavalry Battles of Aldie, Middleburg and Upperville*, 105–13; Nye, *Here Come the Rebels!*, 193–95.

13. O'Neill, *Cavalry Battles of Aldie, Middleburg and Upperville*, 109–12; *OR*, vol. 27, part 1, 954.

14. O'Neill, *Cavalry Battles of Aldie, Middleburg and Upperville*, 121, 131–44, 148; *OR*, vol. 27, part 1, 920–21, 932–33, part 2, 750–51.

15. *OR*, vol. 27, part 1, 614–15, 954, 1034–35, part 2, 690; O'Neill, *Cavalry Battles of Aldie, Middleburg and Upperville*, 126–29.

16. *OR*, vol. 27, part 1, 954, 972–73, part 2, 690–91; O'Neill, *Cavalry Battles of Aldie, Middleburg and Upperville*, 147–51.

17. Meyer, *Civil War Experiences*, 39–40. Evidently the horse killed on this field was not the one Gregg purchased immediately before the army review of April 6.

18. *OR*, vol. 27, part 1, 946–48, 954, part 2, 690–91; O'Neill, *Cavalry Battles of Aldie, Middleburg and Upperville*, 151–54.

19. *OR*, vol. 27, part 1, 172, 954.

20. *OR*, vol. 27, part 2, 306–7, 313–16.

21. *OR*, vol. 27, part 3, 347–48; Burgess, *David Gregg*, 52.

22. *OR*, vol. 27, part 1, 913, part 3, 255; Coddington, *Gettysburg Campaign*, 121–22.

23. *OR*, vol. 27, part 3, 374–76; Pleasonton, "Campaign of Gettysburg," 452; Coddington, *Gettysburg Campaign*, 220–21; Longacre, *Lincoln's Cavalrymen*, 174–75.

24. Alfred Pleasonton to John F. Farnsworth, June 23, 1863, Pleasonton MSS, LC; *OR*, vol. 27, part 1, 154; Longacre, "Alfred Pleasonton," 17–18.

25. *OR*, vol. 27, part 1, 986–87, 992, 999; Robertson, *Michigan in the War*, 578, 580–81; Wert, *Cavalryman of the Lost Cause*, 257–79; Longacre, *Lincoln's Cavalrymen*, 179 80.

26. Gregg Jr., "David McMurtrie Gregg," Gregg MSS, LC, 201–2; Gregg, *Second Cavalry Division in the Gettysburg Campaign*, 9–10; Cormany and Cormany, *Cormany Diaries*, 323; Longacre, *Lincoln's Cavalrymen*, 176.

27. Miller, "Cavalry Battle near Gettysburg," 398; *OR*, vol. 27, part 1, 166n, 958, 970, 169; Longacre, *Cavalry at Gettysburg*, 167.

28. Meyer, *Civil War Experiences*, 47; Gregg Jr., "David McMurtrie Gregg," Gregg MSS, LC, 202; *OR*, vol. 27, part 1, 927; Longacre, *Lincoln's Cavalrymen*, 178, 181–89.

29. Miller, "Cavalry Battle near Gettysburg," 400–401; Preston, *Tenth New York Cavalry*, 106–7; Rawle, *With Gregg in the Gettysburg Campaign*, 14; Regimental History Committee, *Third Pennsylvania Cavalry*, 266; Longacre, *Cavalry at Gettysburg*, 206–7, *OR*, vol. 27, part 1, 956, part 3, 489.

30. *OR*, vol. 27, part 1, 956, part 2, 518–19; Longacre, *Lincoln's Cavalrymen*, 191–92; Regimental History Committee, *Third Pennsylvania Cavalry*, 267–68; Rawle, *With Gregg in the Gettysburg Campaign*, 15; Preston, *Tenth New York Cavalry*, 110.

31. Gregg, *Second Cavalry Division in the Gettysburg Campaign*, 10; Rawle, *With Gregg in the Gettysburg Campaign*, 17; William Rawle Brooke, diary, July 2, 1863, Rawle MSS, Union League of Philadelphia. Brooke changed the order of his middle name and surname after the war; with regard to his postwar writings he is identified as William Brooke Rawle.

32. *OR*, vol. 27, part 1, 956, part 3, 502; Gregg, *Second Cavalry Division in the Gettysburg Campaign*, 10; Gregg Jr., "David McMurtrie Gregg," Gregg MSS, LC, 207; Longacre, *Cavalry at Gettysburg*, 223.

33. *OR*, vol. 27, part 1, 482, 998–1000; Gregg, *Second Cavalry Division in the Gettysburg Campaign*, 10–11; Robertson, *Michigan in the War*, 576, 580–81; Kidd, *Personal Recollections of a Cavalryman*, 134–35; Gregg Jr., "David McMurtrie Gregg," Gregg MSS, LC, 207.

34. *OR*, vol. 27, part 1, 992–93; Robertson, *Michigan in the War*, 582–83.

35. Longacre, *Cavalry at Gettysburg*, 166–67; Lyman, *Meade's Headquarters*, 17.

36. Robertson, *Michigan in the War*, 582–83; Kidd, *Personal Recollections of a Cavalryman*, 139–40; James H. Kidd to "Dear Father and Mother," July 9, 1863, Kidd MSS, Bentley Historical Library, University of Michigan, Ann Arbor; *OR*, vol. 27, part 2, 697; Wert, *Cavalryman of the Lost Cause*, 285–86. In *Protecting the Flank at Gettysburg*, 155–57, Eric J. Wittenberg advances the novel thesis (perhaps an ironic one in light of his book's title) that Stuart, rather than bent on assaulting Gregg and gaining access to the rear of Meade's army, intended to "ambush" the Union commander and provoke him into attacking so as to secure the flank of Ewell's corps. Only if successful in this would Stuart attempt to fight his way west and "make some mischief in the Union rear." Wittenberg clearly makes his point but his findings strike this author as unpersuasive.

37. *OR*, vol. 27, part 1, 956, 1050; Regimental History Committee, *Third Pennsylvania Cavalry*, 270; Miller, "Cavalry Battle near Gettysburg," 401.

38. John B. McIntosh to William Brooke Rawle, June 21, 1878, Rawle MSS, HSP; Hampton S. Thomas, "Notes as to the Cavalry Fight on the Right Flank at Gettysburg," n.p., Rawle MSS, HSP; Miller, "Cavalry Battle near Gettysburg," 402.

39. *OR*, vol. 27, part 1, 956, 977; Robertson, *Michigan in the War*, 583; Kidd, *Personal Recollections of a Cavalryman*, 146; Miller, "Cavalry Battle near Gettysburg," 401–2; Longacre, *Cavalry at Gettysburg*, 225.

40. *OR*, vol. 27, part 1, 956; Robertson, *Michigan in the War*, 583; Kidd, *Personal Recollections of a Cavalryman*, 146; McClellan, *Life and Campaigns of Stuart*, 338–39; Wert, *Cavalryman of the Lost Cause*, 286–89. Carhart, *Lost Triumph*, 187–95, 209–12, 269, lodges some serious but unwarranted and unsubstantiated criticisms of Gregg's generalship on July 3 while assigning Custer credit for singlehandedly winning the battle. He describes Gregg as "neither much of a fighter nor a skilled or even competent battlefield

commander." Moreover, according to Carhart, Gregg acted cowardly for preserving the condition of his own command at Custer's expense and lied by claiming credit for what Custer accomplished. Carhart overlooks the fact that Custer's brigade was the logical choice to do most of the fighting July 3, and was well supported throughout by the 2nd Division. Custer's command had been resting since Hanover, only one of his regiments having been heavily engaged at Hunterstown on July 2, while Gregg's division had been reduced by the loss of one brigade (Huey's) and the detaching of two of McIntosh's regiments (1st Massachusetts and 1st Pennsylvania). A third regiment of McIntosh's, the 1st Maryland, was not available for offensive operations, protecting as it was the far right flank on the Hanover Road, a sector Gregg considered vulnerable to assault. One of Irvin Gregg's regiments (4th Pennsylvania) was detached to cavalry headquarters throughout the day. Then, too, prior to the arrival of Stuart's forces Irvin Gregg's entire brigade had been detached as well, sent on a reconnaissance down the Low Dutch Road before being returned to the strategic intersection in mid-afternoon. Upon rejoining the division the 3rd Brigade was required to protect the rear, blocking Stuart's direct route via the Baltimore Turnpike to Meade's army three miles away. Finally, Custer's brigade was already on the ground to be fought over when Gregg, having talked cavalry headquarters into allowing him to remain at the strategic crossroads, returned there from his evening bivouac. Having already deployed against the approach of enemy forces from west and then north, Custer was in position to bear the brunt of the action once Stuart swept down from Cress Ridge. Gregg's appropriation of the Wolverines was critical to success; only when they were added to his one and a half brigades did he have the strength to make an even fight against Stuart's approximately 4,500 troopers and artillerymen. Under the circumstances Gregg made the right decision to absorb Custer's command and use it to spearhead the defense of the army's right and rear.

41. *OR*, vol. 27, part 1, 956, 977, part 2, 698; Regimental History Committee, *Third Pennsylvania Cavalry*, 274; Hampton S. Thomas, "Notes as to the Cavalry Fight on the Right Flank at Gettysburg," n.p., Rawle MSS, HSP; Kidd, *Personal Recollections of a Cavalryman*, 140–41, 146; Robertson, *Michigan in the War*, 578; Longacre, *Cavalry at Gettysburg*, 225–30.

42. *OR*, vol. 27, part 1, 956, part 2, 698; Gregg, *Second Cavalry Division in the Gettysburg Campaign*, 11; John B. McIntosh to William Brooke Rawle, June 21, 1878, Rawle MSS, HSP; William Brooke Rawle to J. W. Kirkley, December 21, 1883, Rawle MSS, HSP; Regimental History Committee, *Third Pennsylvania Cavalry*, 275–77; Robertson, *Michigan in the War*, 578, 582–83; Kidd, *Personal Recollections of a Cavalryman*, 148–52; Miller, "Cavalry Battle near Gettysburg," 403–4; McClellan, *Life and Campaigns of Stuart*, 340–41; Meyer, *Civil War Experiences*, 50.

43. *OR*, vol. 27, part 2, 697–98, 724–25; Thomas, *Some Personal Reminiscences*, 13; Wert, *Cavalryman of the Lost Cause*, 289–90; Regimental History Committee, *Third Pennsylvania Cavalry*, 277.

44. James H. Kidd to "Dear Father and Mother," July 9, 1863, Kidd MSS, Bentley Historical Library, University of Michigan, Ann Arbor; Hewett, Trudeau, and Suderow, *Supplement to the OR*, vol. 5, 257–58; Robertson, *Michigan in the War*, 578, 587.

45. *OR*, vol. 27, part 1, 1051; John B. McIntosh to "My dear Wife," July 17, 1863, McIntosh MSS, John Hay Library, Brown University, Providence RI; Miller, "Cavalry Battle near Gettysburg," 404–5; Thomas, *Some Personal Reminiscences*, 13; James H. Kidd to "Dear Father and Mother," July 9, 1863, Kidd MSS, Bentley Historical Library, University of Michigan, Ann Arbor; Meyer, *Civil War Experiences*, 51–52; H. S. Newhall to William Brooke Rawle, December 3, 1877, Rawle MSS, HSP; William E. Miller to William Brooke Rawle, June 5, 1878, Rawle MSS, HSP; William E. Miller to John B. McIntosh, June 8, 1878, Rawle MSS, HSP; William Brooke Rawle to William E. Miller, June 12, 1878, Rawle MSS, HSP; Gilmore, "With General Gregg at Gettysburg," 110–11; Wister, *Walter S. Newhall*, 111–13.

8. Six Months of Travail

1. Longacre, *Cavalry at Gettysburg*, 246–69; *OR*, vol. 27, part 1, 967; Regimental History Committee, *Third Pennsylvania Cavalry*, 282; Thomas, *Some Personal Reminiscences*, 14.

2. *OR*, vol. 27, part 1, 80, 959, 967–68, part 3, 560–61, 653–54; John B. McIntosh to "My dear Wife," July 6, 17, 19, 22, 1863, McIntosh MSS, John Hay Library, Brown University, Providence RI; Regimental History Committee, *Third Pennsylvania Cavalry*, 283–86; Coddington, *Gettysburg Campaign*, 550–51.

3. *OR*, vol. 27, part 1, 959, 967, 977–78, 981, part 3, 517, 559–62, 595–96; vol. 51, part 1, 196–97; Meyer, *Civil War Experiences*, 56–57; Doster, *Lincoln and Episodes of the Civil War*, 232–33; Norman Ball, diary, July 4–5, 1863, Connecticut Historical Society, Hartford; Tobie, *First Maine Cavalry*, 180.

4. *OR*, vol. 27, part 3, 602, 627. Burgess, *David Gregg*, 88, makes the dubious claim that Gregg went missing from the official record after Gettysburg due to a studied effort by his superior to neglect and downgrade his accomplishments: "Retaining Custer on the right wing [on July 3] was not Pleasonton's idea, and he never became enthusiastic about it. His report passes over rather abruptly what was done by the men under Gregg at Gettysburg." In fact, as demonstrated in the text following, Pleasonton praised Gregg, as he also did Buford and Kilpatrick, in the warmest terms.

5. *OR*, vol. 27, part 1, 958; Meyer, *Civil War Experiences*, 52–53.

6. The following letters, each addressed to Secretary of War Edwin M. Stanton recommending Gregg's promotion for his achievements at Gettysburg, can be found in ACPF, RG-94, E-297, part 2, NA: Thomas A. Scott , July 7, 1863; Samuel Calvin, July 8, 1863; David McMurtrie, July 10, 1863; Samuel S. Blair, July 28, 1863; and B. Morhead, August 4, 1863. The file also contains this letter, sent for the same purpose: W. M. Stuart, Thomas White, C. A. Baxter, John Covode, Edgar Cowan, George Potter, James Veech, Samuel S. Blair, W. Robinson, Jr., C. M. Moyer, C. I. Mailborn, P. Hager Smith, William F. Johnston, Samuel Calvin, and George D. Lawrence to Abraham Lincoln, August 4, 1863.

7. *OR*, vol. 27, part 1, 916–18.

8. *OR*, vol. 27, part 1, 959, 971–72.

9. *OR*, vol. 27, part 1, 959; Cormany and Cormany, *Cormany Diaries*, 345–46; Comte de Paris, *Civil War in America*, 3:735–36.

10. *OR*, vol. 27, part 1, 959–60, part 2, 303, 706; Gregg, *Second Cavalry Division in the Gettysburg Campaign*, 13–14; Gregg Jr., "David McMurtrie Gregg," Gregg MSS, LC, 222. Perhaps it was on this day that a surgeon of the 6th Ohio Cavalry overheard Gregg, whose field headquarters had come under fire, telling staff officers anxious to find shelter, "Be calm, gentlemen—no occasion for haste." Rockwell, *Rambling Recollections*, 164.

11. *OR*, vol. 27, part 1, 193, 960.

12. *OR*, vol. 27, part 1, 17, 83, 118, part 3, 621.

13. *OR*, vol. 27, part 1, 960, part 3, 713, 720, 756; Cormany and Cormany, *Cormany Diaries*, 347–48.

14. David M. Gregg to A. J. Cohen, July 26, 1863, RCCAP, RG-393, part 2, E-1449, NA; *OR*, vol. 27, part 1, 979.

15. Circular, HQ 2nd Cavalry Div., July 29, 1863, RCCAP, RG-393, part 2, E-1532–33, NA.

16. David M. Gregg to C. Ross Smith, July 28, 1863, RCCAP, RG-393, part 2, E-1449, NA; David M. Gregg to "Colonel," July 31, 1863, RCCAP, RG-393, part 2, E-1449, NA; David M. Gregg to A. J. Alexander, August 4, 5, 1863, TCOSW, RG-107, M-504, NA; Gregg Jr., "David McMurtrie Gregg," Gregg MSS, LC, 226; *OR*, vol. 27, part 1, 27–28, part 3, 839.

17. David M. Gregg to A. J. Alexander, August 8, 1863, RCCAP, RG-393, part 2, E-1449, NA.

18. Gregg Jr., "David McMurtrie Gregg," Gregg MSS, LC, 227–28; Thomas, *Some Personal Reminiscences*, 15.

19. *OR*, vol. 29, part 2, 35; David M. Gregg to Lorenzo Thomas, September 11, 1863, RCCAP, RG-393, part 2, E-1532–33, NA; W. L. Martin to President Abraham Lincoln, October 3, 1863, ACPF, RG-94, E-159, NA; Heitman, *Historical Register and Dictionary*, 1:477, 669; Gregg Jr., "David McMurtrie Gregg," Gregg MSS, LC, 352, 360.

20. Gregg Jr., "David McMurtrie Gregg," Gregg MSS, LC, 228–29; *Philadelphia Inquirer*, September 3, 1863; David M. Gregg to Seth Williams, August 21, 1863, and endorsement by Alfred Pleasonton, August 22, 1863, Gregg's Generals' Papers, RG-94, E-159, NA.

21. David M. Gregg to C. Ross Smith, September 6, 1863, RCCAP, RG-393, part 2, E-1533, NA; *OR*, vol. 29, part 1, 103–4.

22. Circular, HQ 2nd Cavalry Div., September 12, 1863, RCCAP, RG-393, part 2, E-1532–33, NA; Alfred Pleasonton to David M. Gregg, September 12, 1863, RCCAP, RG-393, part 2, E-1532–33, NA; John B. McIntosh to "My dear Wife," September 16, 1863, McIntosh MSS, John Hay Library, Brown University, Providence RI; Thomas, *Some Personal Reminiscences*, 14–15.

23. Cozzens, *This Terrible Sound*, 139–521.

24. *OR*, vol. 29, part 1, 405–6, part 2, 794.

25. Charles C. Suydam to David M. Gregg, October 10, 1863, TCOSW, RG-107, M-504, NA; David M. Gregg to John P. Taylor (two dispatches), October 9, 1863, RCCAP, RG-393, part 2, E-1532–33, NA.

26. C. Ross Smith to David M. Gregg, October 10, 1863 (two dispatches), Smith MSS, USAHEC.

27. *OR*, vol. 29, part 1, 356–57, 361, 444–45; McClellan, *Life and Campaigns of Stuart*, 384–86.

28. *OR*, vol. 29, part 1, 365–66; Gregg Jr., "David McMurtrie Gregg," Gregg MSS, LC, 232–37; Cormany and Cormany, *Cormany Diaries*, 360–62; Norman Ball, diary, October 12, 1863, Connecticut Historical Society, Hartford.

29. *OR*, vol. 29, part 1, 406, 410, part 2, 290, 294, 298–99.

30. *OR*, vol. 29, part 2, 290, 293, 295–97; George Gordon Meade to "Dear Margaret," October 12, 1863, Meade MSS, HSP.

31. Comte de Paris, *Civil War in America*, 3:761–64; Gregg Jr., "David McMurtrie Gregg," Gregg MSS, LC, 233, 236–37.

32. Humphreys, *Andrew Atkinson Humphreys*, 210; Humphreys, *Critical Examination of Pennypacker's Life of Meade*, 6; Cleaves, *Meade of Gettysburg*, 197.

33. *OR*, vol. 29, part 1, 238–43, 357–58, 411, 426–27.

34. *OR*, vol. 29, part 1, 358, 361, 365–66; Gregg Jr., "David McMurtrie Gregg," Gregg MSS, LC, 241–43.

35. *OR*, vol. 29, part 1, 250, 343, 359.

36. Gregg Jr., "David McMurtrie Gregg," Gregg MSS, LC, 242; Burgess, *David Gregg*, 96.

37. *OR*, vol. 29, part 1, 360.

38. *OR*, vol. 29, part 2, 345; Longacre, *Lincoln's Cavalrymen*, 230.

39. *OR*, vol. 29, part 1, 438; Cozzens, *Shipwreck of Their Hopes*, 143–342.

40. *OR*, vol. 29, part 1, 363, part 2, 382–83, 400–401; Circular, HQ 2nd Cavalry Div., October 28, 1863, RCCAP, RG-393, part 2, E-1532–33, NA.

41. Adams, *Cycle of Adams Letters*, 2:101; Gregg Jr., "David McMurtrie Gregg," Gregg MSS, LC, 248; *OR*, vol. 29, part 1, 12–14, 576, 609–11, 823–24.

42. *OR*, vol. 29, part 1, 806–10, 897–99; Walter S. Newhall to "My Dear Mother," December 5, 1863, Newhall MSS, HSP; Regimental History Committee, *Third Pennsylvania Cavalry*, 365–69; *New York Times*, November 30, 1863; Luvaas and Nye, "Campaign That History Forgot," 12–17.

43. *OR*, vol. 29, part 1, 802, 807, 899–903, 905–7; Hewett, Trudeau, and Suderow, *Supplement to the OR*, vol. 5, 631, 635–36; Cormany and Cormany, *Cormany Diaries*, 387; McClellan, *Life and Campaigns of Stuart*, 397.

44. *OR*, vol. 29, part 1, 16–18, 696–98.

9. Winds of Change

1. *OR*, vol. 33, 12–16, 361, 457–60.

2. David M. Gregg to E. B. Parsons, January 8, 1864, RCCAP, RG-39, part 2, E-1449, NA; Marsena R. Patrick to David M. Gregg, January 26, 1864, RCCAP, RG-39, part 2, E-1449, NA; *OR*, vol. 33, 398; vol. 51, part 1, 1137–38.

3. Gregg Jr., "David McMurtrie Gregg," Gregg MSS, LC, 252–53; *OR*, vol. 33, 620; Allen L. Bevan to "Dear Sister," February 19, 1864, Bevan MSS, USAHEC.

4. *OR*, vol. 33, 399, 459, 778n; Gregg Jr., "David McMurtrie Gregg," Gregg MSS, LC, 250–51, 255; David M. Gregg to Seth Williams, January 1, 1864, Gregg's Generals' Papers, RG-159, NA; C. Ross Smith to David M. Gregg, January 21, 1864, Gregg's Generals' Papers, RG-159, NA.

5. Gregg Jr., "David McMurtrie Gregg," Gregg MSS, LC, 250–52.

6. David M. Gregg to "Dear General" [Meade], March 8, 1864, John Wanamaker Coll., HSP; Allen L. Bevan to "My Dear Sister," March 5, 11, 1864, Bevan MSS, USAHEC.

7. William Rawle Brooke diary, December 6, 1863, Rawle MSS, Union League of Philadelphia; Charles B. Coxe to John Cadwalader, Jr., December 10, 1863, Cadwalader MSS, HSP.

8. George G. Meade to "Dear Margaret," March 24, 1864, Meade MSS, HSP; *OR*, vol. 33, 732–33, 741; Cleaves, *Meade of Gettysburg*, 220.

9. Catton, *Grant Takes Command*, 104–40, 166; Heitman, *Historical Register and Dictionary*, 1:881; *OR*, vol. 33, 798, 806.

10. Adams, *Cycle of Adams Letters*, 2:128.

11. Joseph D. Galloway, diary, April 7, 1864, New York Public Library, New York; William Rawle Brooke to "Dear Mother," January 17, 1864, Rawle MSS, Union League of Philadelphia; Charles B. Coxe to John Cadwalader, Jr., April 21, 1864, Cadwalader MSS, HSP.

12. Lyman, *Meade's Headquarters*, 81.

13. Wilson, *Under the Old Flag*, 1:385; Meyer, *Civil War Experiences*, 96–97.

14. Rockwell, *Rambling Recollections*, 164; Noble D. Preston to Thomas T. Munford, February 18, 1903, Munford-Ellis MSS, William R. Perkins Library, Duke University, Durham NC.

15. Meyer, *Civil War Experiences*, 96; Gregg Jr., "David McMurtrie Gregg," Gregg MSS, LC, 309.

16. Sheridan, *Personal Memoirs*, 1:352.

17. *OR*, vol. 33, 830. According to his obituary in the *Army and Navy Journal*, November 13, 1880, Torbert did not seek a command in the cavalry and attempted to turn it down, but was forced to accept it by Meade.

18. Wilson, *Under the Old Flag*, 1:321–41.

19. Lyman, *Meade's Headquarters*, 79; Venter, *Kill Jeff Davis*, 127–271.

20. Venter, *Kill Jeff Davis*, 112–26; *OR*, vol. 33, 599–600, 607, 620–21.

21. Catton, *Grant Takes Command*, 144–65.

22. Sheridan, *Personal Memoirs*, 1:359–61; *OR*, vol. 36, part 1, 787, part 2, 331–34, 342–43, 365–66; McClernand, "Cavalry Operations," 324–25; Scott, *Into the Wilderness with the Army of the Potomac*, 9–14, 32–33; Rhea, *Battle of the Wilderness*, 60–66, 91–95. A handwritten draft of Gregg's official report of operations, May 4–July 7, 1864, is in Gregg MSS, box 2, folder 9, BHC.

23. *OR*, vol. 36, part 1, 876–77; Wilson, *Under the Old Flag*, 1:379–82.

24. *OR*, vol. 36, part 1, 853, 857, 860, 877; Wilson, *Under the Old Flag*, 1:383–84; McClernand, "Cavalry Operations," 326; Moore, *Rebellion Record*, 11:452.

25. Rhea, *Battle of the Wilderness*, 94–282; Scott, *Into the Wilderness with the Army of the Potomac*, 30–108; Wilson, *Under the Old Flag*, 1:389.

26. *OR*, vol. 36, part 1, 853; Longacre, "Cavalry Clash at Todd's Tavern," 15.

27. *OR*, vol. 36, part 1, 788; Sheridan, *Personal Memoirs*, 1:362–63.

28. Sheridan, *Personal Memoirs*, 1:363–64.

29. *OR*, vol. 36, part 1, 853; Cormany and Cormany, *Cormany Diaries*, 418.

30. *OR*, vol. 36, part 1, 788–89, part 2, 514–16; Cormany and Cormany, *Cormany Diaries*, 419–21; Rhea, *Battles for Spotsylvania Court House*, 30–36; Longacre, "Cavalry Clash at Todd's Tavern," 16–19.

31. *OR*, vol. 36, part 1, 788–89, part 2, 551–53; Sheridan, *Personal Memoirs*, 1:365–67; McClernand, "Cavalry Operations," 330; Rhea, *Battles for Spotsylvania Court House*, 14–16, 40–42; Humphreys, *Virginia Campaign of '64 and '65*, 67–69.

32. *OR*, vol. 36, part 1, 878; Sheridan, *Personal Memoirs*, 1:367–69; Wilson, *Under the Old Flag*, 1:393–94; Rhea, *Battles for Spotsylvania Court House*, 49–52, 59, 65–69, 211–12.

33. Sheridan, *Personal Memoirs*, 1:372–74; Rodenbough, "Sheridan's Richmond Raid," 189; Longacre, *Mounted Raids of the Civil War*, 263–64.

34. *OR*, vol. 36, part 1, 853, 861; Sheridan, *Personal Memoirs*, 1:374; Hartley, *Stuart's Tarheels*, 339–40; McClernand, "Cavalry Operations," 331.

35. *OR*, vol. 36, part 2, 615–16; Sheridan, *Personal Memoirs*, 1:789–90.

36. *OR*, vol. 36, part 1, 853; Cormany and Cormany, *Cormany Diaries*, 422; Longacre, *Mounted Raids of the Civil War*, 268–69.

37. *OR*, vol. 36, part 1, 790, 857; Crowninshield and Gleason, *First Massachusetts Cavalry*, 206–8.

38. *OR*, vol. 36, part 1, 790, 817–19; Sheridan, *Personal Memoirs*, 1:377–79; Rodenbough, "Sheridan's Richmond Raid," 191; McClellan, *Life and Campaigns of Stuart*, 413–17; Cormany and Cormany, *Cormany Diaries*, 423; Wert, *Cavalryman of the Lost Cause*, 356–62; Rhea, *Battles for Spotsylvania Court House*, 198–99, 203–12, 212n.

39. *OR*, vol. 36, part 1, 790–91, 817–18; Rhea, *Battles for Spotsylvania Court House*, 209–11; Wert, *Cavalryman of the Lost Cause*, 356–62.

40. Sheridan, *Personal Memoirs*, 1:378–80; *OR*, vol. 36, part 1, 791, 853.

41. Sheridan, *Personal Memoirs*, 1:381; Wilson, *Under the Old Flag*, 1:410–13; *OR*, vol. 36, part 1, 791, 879–80.

42. *OR*, vol. 36, part 1, 791, 813–14; Sheridan, *Personal Memoirs*, 1:382–83; Thomas, *Some Personal Reminiscences*, 17.

43. *OR*, vol. 36, part 1, 854; Sheridan, *Personal Memoirs*, 1:385; Hartley, *Stuart's Tarheels*, 358–61. Thomas, *Some Personal Reminiscences*, 17, claims that at the height of the combat early on May 12 "General Sheridan seemed at a loss what to do, and suggested that General Gregg mount his division and try to break through the enemy's lines, so as to draw off the forces attacking our other two divisions, and thus allow Wilson's command to cross the Chickahominy, and that he (Gregg) rejoin the Army of the Potomac the best way he could, leaving his artillery with Sheridan and the rest of the corps. Gregg, however, concluded to hold fast where he was." Neither Sheridan nor Gregg made mention of such a proposition, and no evidence can be found to substantiate the staff officer's claim.

44. *OR*, vol. 36, part 1, 778–79, 791–92, 880, part 2, 765; Sheridan, *Personal Memoirs*, 1:387–90; Wilson, *Under the Old Flag*, 1:414; McClernand, "Cavalry Operations," 335; *New York Times*, May 15, 1864.

10. Hot Work under Sheridan

1. Rhea, *Battles for Spotsylvania Court House*, 45–307; *OR*, vol. 36, part 2, 627.

2. *OR*, vol. 36, part 3, 82–83, 86, 98–99, 171, 854; Rhea, *To the North Anna River*, 255–354; Sheridan, *Personal Memoirs*, 1:388–89.

3. Sheridan, *Personal Memoirs*, 1:394–98; *OR*, vol. 36, part 1, 662, 792–93, 804–5, part 3, 258–59, 363, 413–14; Wilson, *Under the Old Flag*, 1:421–22.

4. *OR*, vol. 36, part 1, 793, 854; Sheridan, *Personal Memoirs*, 1:298–99; Williams, "Haw's Shop," 12–14.

5. *OR*, vol. 36, part 1, 855, 858; Williams, "Haw's Shop," 15–16.

6. *OR*, vol. 36, part 1, 854; *Philadelphia Inquirer*, June 2, 3, 1864; Humphreys, *Virginia Campaign of '64 and '65*, 164–65.

7. *OR*, vol. 36, part 1, 854; Williams, "Haw's Shop," 15–17; Kidd, *Personal Recollections of a Cavalryman*, 323.

8. *OR*, vol. 36, part 1, 793, 820–21; James H. Kidd to "Dear Father and Mother," June 3, 1864, Kidd MSS, Bentley Historical Library, University of Michigan, Ann Arbor.

9. Rhea, *Cold Harbor*, 163, 182–90; Humphreys, *Virginia Campaign of '64 and '65*, 171.

10. Sheridan, *Personal Memoirs*, 1:402–3; *OR*, vol. 36, part 1, 794, 805.

11. *OR*, vol. 36, part 1, 854; Longacre, *Army of Amateurs*, 115–16.

12. *OR*, vol. 36, part 1, 794, 805, 822, 854, 858, part 3, 411–12, 469; Sheridan, *Personal Memoirs*, 1:405–6; Rhea, *Cold Harbor*, 224–359 *passim*.

13. Sheridan, *Personal Memoirs*, 1:413; *OR*, vol. 36, part 1, 795, part 3, 599, 603, 628–29; Longacre, *Army of Amateurs*, 128–35.

14. *OR*, vol. 36, part 1, 795–96, 854–55, part 3, 716, 735–36; Sheridan, *Personal Memoirs*, 1:417–19; Rodenbough, "Sheridan's Trevilian Raid," 233; Wittenberg, *Glory Enough for All*, 37–62.

15. *OR*, vol. 36, part 1, 796, 807, 1095; Kidd, *Personal Recollections of a Cavalryman*, 347–59; Wittenberg, *Glory Enough for All*, 69–125.

16. *OR*, vol. 36, part 1, 796, 855, 862; Sheridan, *Personal Memoirs*, 1:420–21; Wittenberg, *Glory Enough for All*, 142–43.

17. *OR*, vol. 36, part 1, 807–8; Cormany and Cormany, *Cormany Diaries*, 434.

18. *OR*, vol. 36, part 1, 858; Rodenbough, "Sheridan's Trevilian Raid," 234; *New York Herald*, June 22, 1864.

19. *OR*, vol. 36, part 1, 797; Sheridan, *Personal Memoirs*, 1:423–24; Cormany and Cormany, *Cormany Diaries*, 434–35.

20. *OR*, vol. 36, part 1, 808–9, 855; Sheridan, *Personal Memoirs*, 1:424.

21. *OR*, vol. 36, part 1, 797; Sheridan, *Personal Memoirs*, 1:425–26.

22. *OR*, vol. 36, part 1, 797, 1096; Sheridan, *Personal Memoirs*, 1:426; Kidd, *Personal Recollections of a Cavalryman*, 370; Cormany and Cormany, *Cormany Diaries*, 436.

23. *OR*, vol. 36, part 3, 779–80; Sheridan, *Personal Memoirs*, 1:427–28.

24. *OR*, vol. 36, part 1, 787, 798, part 3, 784; vol. 40, part 3, 14; William S. Keller to "Dear Sister," June 22, 1864, Keller MSS, USAHEC; *Philadelphia Inquirer*, July 4, 1864; Sheridan, *Personal Memoirs*, 1:430.

25. *OR*, vol. 36, part 1, 798, 810, 855, 1096, part 3, 787, 789; vol. 40, part 3, 14; Sheridan, *Personal Memoirs*, 1:430; Cormany and Cormany, *Cormany Diaries*, 436–37.

26. *OR*, vol. 36, part 1, 798–99, 810, 855, part 3, 792–95; Sheridan, *Personal Memoirs*, 1:432, 434.

27. *OR*, vol. 36, part 1, 799, 855, 1096; Rodenbough, "Sheridan's Trevilian Raid," 235; William S. Keller to "Dear Sister," June 26, 1864, Keller MSS, USAHEC.

28. *OR*, vol. 36, part 1, 1096–97; Wittenberg, *Glory Enough for All*, 263–64; William S. Keller to "Dear Sister," June 26, 1864, Keller MSS, USAHEC.

29. *OR*, vol. 36, part 1, 855, 1096; Thomas, *Some Personal Reminiscences*, 19.

30. *OR*, vol. 36, part 1, 855–56; Wittenberg, *Glory Enough for All*, 279–84.

31. *A Brief History of the Fourth Pennsylvania Veteran Cavalry*, 97; Gregg Jr., "David McMurtrie Gregg," Gregg MSS, LC, 278.

32. Sheridan, *Personal Memoirs*, 1:445; *OR*, vol. 36, part 1, 856; vol. 40, part 1, 612; Cormany and Cormany, *Cormany Diaries*, 455–61.

33. Preston, *Tenth New York Cavalry*, 211–12; Gregg Jr., "David McMurtrie Gregg," Gregg MSS, LC, 310–11; *OR*, vol. 36, part 1, 799; Sheridan, *Personal Memoirs*, 1:435.

34. Greene, *Civil War Petersburg*, 115; Trudeau, *Last Citadel*, 29–87.

35. Wilson, *Under the Old Flag*, 1:455–520; *OR*, vol. 36, part 1, 799; vol. 40, part 1, 620–30, 730–33; Sheridan, *Personal Memoirs*, 1:438–45.

36. *OR*, vol. 40, part 1, 613–15, part 3, 183–86, 198–99, 207; Gregg Jr., "David McMurtrie Gregg," Gregg MSS, LC, 281–83.

37. Trudeau, *Last Citadel*, 98–108; Marvel, *Burnside*, 390–92.

38. *OR*, vol. 36, part 1, 800; vol. 40, part 1, 308–11, part 3, 437–38, 443, 458, 513, 531, 551; Sheridan, *Personal Memoirs*, 1:445–48; Humphreys, *Virginia Campaign of '64 and '65*, 247–49.

39. *OR*, vol. 40, part 1, 612–13, 615–20, part 3, 569.

40. *OR*, vol. 40, part 1, 801, part 3, 504, 553, 568–69, 592–93, 596, 600, 602, 613–14, 616, 639–40, 649, 669; Sheridan, *Personal Memoirs*, 1:448–51.

41. Trudeau, *Last Citadel*, 108–27; Marvel, *Burnside*, 392–408.

11. Commander of Cavalry

1. Weigley, "Twilight of Mounted Cavalry," 81, 95.

2. Early, *Autobiographical Sketch*, 371–95; Sheridan, *Personal Memoirs*, 1:457–62.

3. Sheridan, *Personal Memoirs*, 1:452, 462–67; Wert, *From Winchester to Cedar Creek*, 12–13, 16, 21–22; *OR*, vol. 40, part 3, 669.

4. *OR*, vol. 37, part 2, 558, 582–83; vol. 42, part 2, 21, 46–47.

5. Tobie, *Service of the Cavalry in the Army of the Potomac*, 36; *OR*, vol. 40, part 1, 618–20, part 3, 671–72, 674, 709; vol. 42, part 1, 615–16, part 2, 60–61, 65–66, 132, 135–36, 143, 148–50.

6. *OR*, vol. 40, part 3, 437–38; vol. 42, part 1, 615–16, part 2, 131–32, 135–36, 164–67.

7. *OR*, vol. 42, part 1, 216–17, part 2, 61, 76, 135–36; Longacre, *Army of Amateurs*, 195–96.

8. Longacre, *Army of Amateurs*, 198–200; *OR*, vol. 42, part 1, 30, 217–19, 616, 628, 637, part 2, 174, 179, 198, 204, 229–30; Trudeau, *Last Citadel*, 152.

9. *OR*, vol. 42, part 1, 216, 219–21, 223–24, 228–30, 243, 616–17, 637, 639–40, part 2, 199–200, 215; Cormany and Cormany, *Cormany Diaries*, 464–69; Norman Ball, diary, August 16, 1864, Connecticut Historical Society, Hartford; *A Brief History of the Fourth Pennsylvania Veteran Cavalry*, 98; Patterson, "Friends More Than Enemies," 30–32.

10. *OR*, vol. 42, part 1, 637, 639, part 2, 216, 228; Patterson, "Friends More Than Enemies," 33.

11. *OR*, vol. 42, part 1, 220, part 2, 301–2; Longacre, *Army of Amateurs*, 200–203.

12. *OR*, vol. 42, part 1, 220–21, 428–30, 617, part 2, 327, 332, 334, 337.

13. *OR*, vol. 42, part 1, 222, 617, part 2, 300, 306, 321, 374–75.

14. *OR*, vol. 42, part 1, 222, 606–7, 617–18, part 2, 407–8, 426–27, 436, 441–42.

15. *OR*, vol. 42, part 1, 223–28, 293–94, 607–8, part 2, 472, 482, 486–87, 491–92, 497, 524–25; Steven R. Clark to "Dear Del," August 28, 1864, Clark MSS, USAHEC; Thomas, *Some Personal Reminiscences*, 20; Humphreys, *Virginia Campaign of '64 and '65*, 282; Trudeau, *Last Citadel*, 181–90.

16. *OR*, vol. 42, part 1, 607, part 2, 482, 486–87, 491, 497; Trudeau, *Last Citadel*, 178–89.

17. Longacre, "Battle of Reams' Station," 18–19; *OR*, vol. 42, part 1, 607–8, part 2, 524–25, 594.

18. *OR*, vol. 42, part 1, 618, 936, part 2, 560, 565.

19. Gregg Jr., "David McMurtrie Gregg," Gregg MSS, LC, 292.

20. *OR*, vol. 42, part 1, 26, 28–29, 614–15, 619, 944–47, 952, part 2, 16, 88, 852–54, 856, 859–63, 867–70, 873–79, 884–85, 891–92, 896–98, 935; Trudeau, *Last Citadel*, 195–201.

21. Cormany and Cormany, *Cormany Diaries*, 479. Upon Gregg's return from leave Grant proposed sending him to Sherman's armies, explaining to Meade that "to this time, there has not been an officer with the cavalry in the West who it was safe to trust, without infantry to guard them from danger." In reply Meade pointed out that with the exception of Davies, Gregg was the only general officer of cavalry with the Army of the Potomac whereas Sheridan's command had several. Subsequently Wilson was selected to lead Sherman's horsemen: *OR*, vol. 42, part 2, 1008–9.

22. *OR*, vol. 36, part 2, 963, 978; Longacre, *Army of Amateurs*, 211–19; Trudeau, *Last Citadel*, 208–11, 213–14, 216–17, 228–30.

23. *OR*, vol. 42, part 1, 31–33, 545–48, 852, part 2, 1090; Trudeau, *Last Citadel*, 202–15; Sommers, *Richmond Redeemed*, 178–417.

24. *OR*, vol. 42, part 1, 619, part 2, 1069, 1078–79, 1091, 1093, 1106–8; Sommers, *Richmond Redeemed*, 190–93, 197–201, 431–32.

25. *OR*, vol. 42, part 2, 1094, 1107–8; Trudeau, *Last Citadel*, 207–8; Sommers, *Richmond Redeemed*, 201–5, 220.

26. Sommers, *Richmond Redeemed*, 222, 235, 238–39, 260–61, 319–25.

27. *OR*, vol. 42, part 2, 1141–42, part 3, 7, 27–29; Sommers, *Richmond Redeemed*, 318–19.

28. *OR*, vol. 42, part 1, 634–36, 947–48, part 3, 5, 23, 27–29; Sommers, *Richmond Redeemed*, 331–33, 340–51.

29. *OR*, vol. 42, part 1, 636, 948; Sommers, *Richmond Redeemed*, 348–51.

30. *OR*, vol. 42, part 1, 32, 546–47, 948, part 3, 47, 64; Sommers, *Richmond Redeemed*, 373, 399–401, 411, 413.

31. *OR*, vol. 42, part 1, 620–21, part 3, 64, 77, 82, 88–89, 97, 241, 250, 259, 267, 463–64, 1053.

32. *OR*, vol. 42, part 3, 160–61, 182.

33. Longacre, *Army of Amateurs*, 228–31; Trudeau, *Last Citadel*, 224–25, 228–30, 237–41.

34. *OR*, vol. 42, part 1, 35–37, 231–34, 434–39, 949–50; Trudeau, *Last Citadel*, 225–28, 230–37, 243.

35. *OR*, vol. 36, part 2, 638, 644, 665, 669–71.

36. *OR*, vol. 42, part 1, 949, part 3, 359, 366, 373, 380–85; Thomas, *Some Personal Reminiscences*, 21; Trudeau, *Last Citadel*, 233–34.

37. *OR*, vol. 42, part 1, 234–35.

38. *OR*, vol. 42, part 1, 231, 234–36, 608–10, 621–22, 629, 641, 645–48, 853–54, 950, part 3, 380, 385, 387, 509; Merrill, *First Maine and First District of Columbia Cavalry*, 288–92; Cormany and Cormany, *Cormany Diaries*, 485–88; Norman Ball, diary, October 27, 1864, Connecticut Historical Society, Hartford; Weigley, "Twilight of Mounted Cavalry," 86, 89; Trudeau, *Last Citadel*, 243–47.

39. *OR*, vol. 42, part 1, 610, part 3, 537, 549–50, 566.

40. *OR*, vol. 42, part 1, 610–11, 623–24, 632, part 3, 758–60, 766–67, 770–71, 774, 776, 790–91; Norman Ball, diary, December 1–2, 1864, Connecticut Historical Society, Hartford.

41. David M. Gregg to Lorenzo Thomas, December 5, 1864; Gregg's oath of office as brevet major general of volunteers, December 5, 1864, ACPF, RG-94, E-297, part 2, NA; *OR*, vol. 42, part 3, 483.

42. *OR*, vol. 42, part 1, 350–51, 443–46, 611–13, 625–27, 630–34, 638, 649, part 3, 828–31, 833–34, 842, 856, 877–78, 881, 885–86, 891–92, 915, 919–20, 927, 934, 937–38, 951, 964–65, 968, 980, 991; Robbins, *War Record and Personal Experiences*, 100–2; Norman Ball, diary, December 7–12, 1864, Connecticut Historical Society, Hartford; Merrill, *First Maine and First District of Columbia Cavalry*, 294–98; Trudeau, *Last Citadel*, 262–79.

43. Thomas, *Some Personal Reminiscences*, 21–22; Merrill, *First Maine and First District of Columbia Cavalry*, 300; Weigley, "Twilight of Mounted Cavalry," 93, 95; Trudeau, *Last Citadel*, 280–85.

44. David M. Gregg to Seth Williams, December 15, 1864, Gregg's Generals' Papers, RG-94, E-159, NA; *OR*, vol. 42, part 1, 613, 627, part 3, 980; Gregg Jr., "David McMurtrie Gregg," Gregg MSS, LC, 302–3.

12. Man of Unimpeachable Character

1. Gregg Jr., "David McMurtrie Gregg," Gregg MSS, LC, 305–6.

2. *OR*, vol. 46, part 2, 367–69; Humphreys, *Virginia Campaign of '64 and '65*, 312; Trudeau, *Last Citadel*, 312–13.

3. *OR*, vol. 46, part 2, 370, 382; J. Wright Miller to "My dear Aunt Chattie," February 18, 1865, Miller MSS, USAHEC; Trudeau, *Last Citadel*, 312.

4. *OR*, vol. 46, part 2, 380, 388, 401, 410; Humphreys, *Virginia Campaign of '64 and '65*, 314.

5. *OR*, vol. 46, part 1, 191–93, 253–54, part 2, 389–91; Trudeau, *Last Citadel*, 314–17; Greene, *Breaking the Backbone of the Rebellion*, 143–46.

6. *OR*, vol. 46, part 2, 390–91, 410, 416–17; J. Wright Miller to "My dear Aunt Chattie," February 18, 1865, USAHEC.

7. Williams, "Letter from W. W. Williams," 55; Sheridan, *Personal Memoirs*, 1:385.

8. *OR*, vol. 46, part 1, 113–19, 366–71, part 2, 434; Humphreys, *Virginia Campaign of '64 and '65*, 314–15.

9. *OR*, vol. 46, part 1, 193, 254–56, part 2, 425, 438, 458, 474–75, 1206; Trudeau, *Last Citadel*, 317–21; Greene, *Breaking the Backbone of the Rebellion*, 146–49.

10. *OR*, vol. 46, part 1, 63–69, part 2, 450–51, 454–55, 458–59, 463, 465, 485–86.

11. Special Orders No. 57, Adjutant General's Office, February 4, 1865, Gregg's Generals' Papers, RG-94, E-159, NA; HQ 2nd Cavalry Div., February 8, 1865 (conveying Gregg's receipt of the acceptance of his resignation), Gregg's Generals' Papers, RG-94, E-159, NA; *OR*, vol. 46, part 2, 499–500. A typical statement of appreciation, issued upon Gregg's relief from command, came from the officers and men of his 1st Pennsylvania: "By the resignation of Brevet Major General D. McM. Gregg, we have lost a commander whom we were proud to follow when duty called us to danger, and in whom we placed implicit confidence for qualities possessed only by the true soldier, a commander whom we had learned to love and were proud to claim as the successor to our own gallant Bayard." In later months, Gregg's 1st New Jersey presented him with its "battle stained flag, which has so often followed you, under whose teachings we became a first class regiment. We feel that no one is more worthy to be its custodian, and that no one will prize it more highly." See Gregg Jr., "David McMurtrie Gregg," Gregg MSS, LC, 313, 326.

12. *OR*, vol. 46, part 1, 113, part 2, 788, 829–30, part 3, 198, 391; Longacre, *Cavalry at Appomattox*, 33.

13. Gregg Jr., "David McMurtrie Gregg," Gregg MSS, LC, 305, 311–12; Burgess, *David Gregg*, 106.

14. Rockwell, *Rambling Recollections*, 163–64.

15. Longacre, *Cavalry at Appomattox*, 39–43.

16. Gregg Jr., "David McMurtrie Gregg," Gregg MSS, LC, 384. An unverified account, contained in an error-marred manuscript in the Gregg MSS, BHC (Charles Schuyler Castner, "The Saga of Brigadier General David McMurtrie Gregg"), states that the general "trenchantly refused to attend the memorial dedication ceremonies at Gettysburg for his own Second Cavalry unit in 1880, ostensibly because the program chair was being shared by Generals Sheridan and [Daniel E.] Sickles. When a newspaperman asked if his demurrer had been lodged because the event called for the presence of his former adversary . . . he gave neither an affirmative nor negative response. By way of reply, he simply asked a question of his own: 'What do you mean by former?'"

17. Gregg Jr., "David McMurtrie Gregg," Gregg MSS, LC, 329–30; David M. Gregg to Edwin M. Stanton, March 29, 1866, ACPF, RG-94, E-297, part 2, NA; Andrew Johnson to Edwin M. Stanton, September 27, 1866, ACPF, RG-94, E-297, part 2, NA. In addition to the recommendation from Hancock, this file contains statements endorsing Gregg's application from Generals Meade, Sheridan, and John W. Geary, as well as from Governor Curtin, former Secretary of War Simon Cameron, Gregg's uncle David McMurtrie, and numerous other supporters.

18. Gregg Jr., "David McMurtrie Gregg," Gregg MSS, LC, 330; Heitman, *Historical Register and Dictionary*, 1:477.

19. Gregg Jr., "David McMurtrie Gregg," Gregg MSS, LC, 321, 326–32.

20. Gregg Jr., "David McMurtrie Gregg," Gregg MSS, LC, 334–39; *Forty-Eighth Annual Report of the Association of the Graduates of the USMA*, 52; David M. Gregg to "My dear Carpenter," April 23, 1874, Gregg MSS, BHC.

21. Gregg Jr., "David McMurtrie Gregg," Gregg MSS, LC, 339–42; Burgess, *David Gregg*, 108–9; David M. Gregg to "My dear Carpenter," April 23, 1874, Gregg MSS, BHC.

22. Gregg Jr., "David McMurtrie Gregg," Gregg MSS, LC, 342–43, 370.

23. Gregg Jr., "David McMurtrie Gregg," Gregg MSS, LC, 343–51; David M. Gregg to J. W. Hoffman, March 12, 1890, Ferdinand J. Dreer Coll., HSP; David M. Gregg to "My dear Colonel," July 6, 1899, Autograph Coll., HSP. GAR Post #95, in Bellefonte, Pennsylvania, was named for Gregg. Posts in Michigan and New York also bore his name.

24. Gregg Jr., "David McMurtrie Gregg," Gregg MSS, LC, 349–50; David M. Gregg to J. Edward Carpenter, November 7, 1880, Gregg MSS, BHC.

25. *Forty-Eighth Annual Report of the Association of the Graduates of the USMA*, 52; "Address Delivered October 15, 1884 by William Brooke-Rawle, Secretary of the Historical Society of Pennsylvania, When the Cavalry Monument was Dedicated at Gettysburg," Gregg MSS, BHC; Gregg Jr., "David McMurtrie Gregg," Gregg MSS, LC, 369–70, 382, 390–91; Burgess, *David Gregg*, 110.

26. David M. Gregg to "My dear Colonel," September 2, 1889, Gregg MSS, Simon Gratz Coll., HSP; Gregg Jr., "David McMurtrie Gregg," Gregg MSS, LC, 393–94.

27. Gregg Jr., "David McMurtrie Gregg," Gregg MSS, LC, 344–46; David M. Gregg to J. Edward Carpenter, July 11, 1878, Gregg MSS, BHC.

28. Gregg Jr., "David McMurtrie Gregg," Gregg MSS, LC, 346, 350, 355–56.

29. Gregg Jr., "David McMurtrie Gregg," Gregg MSS, LC, 355–61; *Third Annual Message of Charles F. Warwick, Mayor of the City of Philadelphia*, 77–79.

30. Gregg Jr., "David McMurtrie Gregg," Gregg MSS, LC, 356–68, 372–75, 378–81.

31. Gregg Jr., "David McMurtrie Gregg," Gregg MSS, LC, 371; George D. Ruggles to Chairman, Senate Military Committee, May 4, 1897, ACPF, RG-94, E-297, part 2, NA; S. 1747, U.S. Senate, April 20, 1897 ("A Bill Authorizing the President to Appoint and Retire David McMurtrie Gregg"), April 20, 1897, ACPF, RG-94, E-297, part 2, NA.

32. Gregg Jr., "David McMurtrie Gregg," Gregg MSS, LC, 372; House of Representatives, 55th Cong., 2nd Sess., Report No. 1326, "Gen. David McMurtrie Gregg," May 16, 1898, ACPF, RG-94, E-297, part 2, NA.

33. Gregg Jr., "David McMurtrie Gregg," Gregg MSS, LC, 372; James M. Robinson to Record and Pension Office, April 18, 1898, ACPF, RG-94, E-297, part 2, NA. Attempts to revive Gregg's retirement bill in February 1900 and again two years later were similarly unsuccessful, though no details of their failure are available.

34. David M. Gregg to John W. Jordan, June 7, 1878, Autograph Coll., HSP; Gregg Jr., "David McMurtrie Gregg," Gregg MSS, LC, 343–44, 349, 367, 377, 387, 390; *Forty-Eighth Annual Report of the Association of the Graduates of the USMA*, 52; David M. Gregg to Russell A. Alger, April 23, 1898, ACPF, RG-94, E-297, part 2, NA.

35. Gregg Jr., "David McMurtrie Gregg," Gregg MSS, LC, 377; Burgess, *David Gregg*, 110; David M. Gregg to J. C. Kelton, April 27, 1891, ACPF, RG-94, E-297, part 2, NA; David M. Gregg to Matthew S. Quay, April 27, 1891, ACPF, RG-94, E-297, part 2, NA; David M. Gregg to John M. Schofield, June 8, 1891, ACPF, RG-94, E-297, part 2, NA; David M. Gregg to Benjamin Harrison, June 13, 1891, ACPF, RG-94, E-297, part 2, NA. ACPF, RG-

94, E-297, part 2, NA, contains letters from several former military commanders endorsing young Gregg's application for a commission.

36. David M. Gregg to J. Edward Carpenter, December 29, 1875, January 18, 1876, Gregg MSS, Unger Coll., HSP; David M. Gregg to Alexander K. McClure, January 15, 1877, Gregg MSS, Simon Gratz Coll., HSP; Burgess, *David Gregg*, 109–10; McClure, *Old Time Notes of Pennsylvania*, 2:110.

37. Gregg Jr., "David McMurtrie Gregg," Gregg MSS, LC, 382, 388, 393, 401, 404–6, 409–13; Burgess, *David Gregg*, 110–13.

38. Gregg Jr., "David McMurtrie Gregg," Gregg MSS, LC, 417–18; *Forty-Eighth Annual Report of the Association of the Graduates of the USMA*, 52; Resolution passed by the Council of the City of Reading, August 9, 1916, Gregg MSS, BHC.

39. Gregg Jr., "David McMurtrie Gregg," Gregg MSS, LC, 419–22; *Reading News-Times*, June 19, 1922; *Reading Times*, April 25 and September 15, 1961, June 17, 1993; "The Gregg Monument," 95. A few years after Gregg's passing memorial tablets featuring his portrait, the work of two well-known sculptors, were placed in Cullum Hall at West Point by the Pennsylvania Commandery of the Loyal Legion and in the hall of the Union League of Philadelphia by the administrators of the organization. His younger son pronounced both likenesses "very good."

40. Styple, *Generals in Bronze*, 116.

41. *OR*, vol. 29, part 1, 356–57.

42. *OR*, vol. 27, part 1, 950.

43. Winfield S. Hancock to Lorenzo Thomas, January 21, 1866, ACPF, RG-94, E-297, part 2, NA.

44. *OR*, vol. 27, part 1, 951–52, 957; vol. 40, part 1, 613–16.

45. *OR*, vol. 46, part 1, 365–67; McWhiney and Jamieson, *Attack and Die*, 138. The latter source misidentifies the commander of the Second Cavalry Division in this operation as John Irvin Gregg, who led only his own brigade under his cousin's direction.

46. William H. Medill to "Dear Sister Kate," March 15, 1863, Medill MSS, LC.

47. Gregg Jr., "David McMurtrie Gregg," Gregg MSS, LC, 309.

BIBLIOGRAPHY

Archives and Manuscript Materials

Adams, Charles F., Jr. Correspondence. Library of Congress, Washington D C.

———. Diary, 1863. Massachusetts Historical Society, Boston.

Appointment, Commission, and Personal Branch Files. Record Group 94, entry 297, National Archives, Washington D C.

Averell, William W. Diaries, 1861–63. Gilder Lehrman Institute of American History, New York.

———. Papers. New York State Library, Albany.

Ball, Norman. Diaries, 1863–64. Connecticut Historical Society, Hartford.

Bayard, George D. Correspondence. U.S. Military Academy Library, West Point N Y.

Bevan, Allen L. Correspondence. U.S. Army Heritage and Education Center, Carlisle Barracks P A.

Brooke, William Rawle. Correspondence and Diaries, 1863–65. Heritage Center, Union League of Philadelphia, Philadelphia.

Cadwalader, Charles E. Correspondence. Historical Society of Pennsylvania, Philadelphia.

Clark, Steven R. Correspondence. U.S. Army Heritage and Education Center, Carlisle Barracks P A.

Cummings, Robert. Correspondence. Alexander Library, Rutgers University, New Brunswick N J.

Custer, George Armstrong. Correspondence. U.S. Military Academy Library, West Point N Y.

Flack, George W. Diaries, 1861–64. Alexander Library, Rutgers University, New Brunswick N J.

Galloway, Joseph D. Diaries, 1861–64. New York Public Library, New York.

Generals' Papers. Record Group 94, entry 159, National Archives, Washington D C.

Generals' Reports of Service, War of the Rebellion. Record Group 94, entry 160, National Archives, Washington D C.

Gregg, David McMurtrie. Cadet Application File and Delinquency Log. U.S. Military Academy Archives, West Point N Y.

———. Correspondence. Claude W. Unger Collection, Historical Society of Pennsylvania, Philadelphia.

———. Correspondence. Simon Gratz Collection, Historical Society of Pennsylvania, Philadelphia.

———. Correspondence. Society Collection, Historical Society of Pennsylvania, Philadelphia.

_____. Letter of July 6, 1899. Autograph Collection, Historical Society of Pennsylvania, Philadelphia.

———. Letter of March 8, 1864. John Wanamaker Collection, Historical Society of Pennsylvania, Philadelphia.

———. Letter of March 12, 1890. Ferdinand J. Dreer Collection, Historical Society of Pennsylvania, Philadelphia.

———. Letter of March 13, 1903. Hampton L. Carson Papers, Historical Society of Pennsylvania, Philadelphia.

———. Papers. Henry Janssen Library, Berks History Center, Reading PA.

———. Papers. Library of Congress, Washington DC.

Gregg, David McMurtrie, Jr. "Brevet Major General David McMurtrie Gregg." Gregg Papers, Library of Congress, Washington DC.

Gregg, J. Irvin. Papers. Historical Society of Pennsylvania, Philadelphia.

Hutchins, Benjamin. Letter of December 31, 1861. Courtesy of Mrs. Tillie Clement, Haddonfield NJ.

Keller, William S. Correspondence. U.S. Army Heritage and Education Center, Carlisle Barracks PA.

Kidd, James H. Correspondence. Bentley Historical Library, University of Michigan, Ann Arbor.

McClellan, George B. Papers. Library of Congress, Washington DC.

McIntosh, John B. Correspondence. John Hay Library, Brown University, Providence RI.

McLaughlin, Edward. Correspondence and Diaries, 1861–64. Historical Society of Pennsylvania, Philadelphia.

Meade, George Gordon. Papers. Historical Society of Pennsylvania, Philadelphia.

Medill, William H. Correspondence. Library of Congress, Washington DC.

Miller, J. Wright. Correspondence. U.S. Army Heritage and Education Center, Carlisle Barracks PA.

Muster Rolls, Returns, and Regimental Papers, 8th Pennsylvania Cavalry, 1861–65. Record Group 94, National Archives, Washington DC.

Newhall, Walter S. Correspondence and Diary, 1863. Historical Society of Pennsylvania, Philadelphia.

Pleasonton, Alfred. Correspondence. Historical Society of Pennsylvania, Philadelphia.

———. Correspondence. Library of Congress, Washington DC.

———. Dispatch Book, 1862, and Papers. Alderman Library, University of Virginia, Charlottesville.

Preston, Noble D. Letter of February 18, 1903. Munford-Ellis Papers, William R. Perkins Library, Duke University, Durham NC.

Rawle, William Brooke. Correspondence. Historical Society of Pennsylvania, Philadelphia.

Records of Cavalry Corps, Army of the Potomac, and Predecessor and Subsidiary Organizations, 1861–65. Record Group 393, entries 1439–40, 1449, 1469, 1474, 1532–35, 1538, 1548, National Archives, Washington D C.

Records of Department of the Pacific, 1854–1858. Record Group 393, entry 3584, box 12, National Archives, Washington D C.

Records of the Office of the Secretary of War, Telegrams Collected. Record Group 107, microcopy 504, National Archives, Washington D C.

Sheridan, Philip H. Papers. Library of Congress, Washington D C.

Smith, C. Ross. Correspondence. U.S. Army Heritage and Education Center, Carlisle Barracks P A.

Smith, Thomas W. Correspondence. Historical Society of Pennsylvania, Philadelphia.

Stoneman, George. Correspondence. Simon Gratz Collection. Historical Society of Pennsylvania, Philadelphia.

Taylor, John P. Correspondence. Historical Society of Pennsylvania, Philadelphia.

Webb, Nathan B. Diary, 1863. William L. Clements Library, University of Michigan, Ann Arbor.

Wilson, James H. Correspondence. Library of Congress, Washington D C.

Published Works

Adams, Charles F. *A Cycle of Adams Letters, 1861–1865.* Edited by Worthington Chauncey Ford. 2 vols. Boston: Houghton Mifflin, 1920.

Adams, Francis Colburn. *The Story of a Trooper* [...]. New York: Dick & Fitzgerald, 1865.

Africa, J. Simpson. *History of Huntingdon and Blair Counties, Pennsylvania.* Philadelphia: Louis H. Everts, 1883.

Arnold, James R. *Jeff Davis's Own: Cavalry, Comanches, and the Battle for the Texas Frontier.* New York: John Wiley & Sons, 2000.

Averell, William W. *Ten Years in the Saddle: The Memoir of William Woods Averell, 1851–1862.* Edited by Edward K. Eckert and Nicholas J. Amato. San Rafael C A: Presidio, 1978.

———. "With the Cavalry on the Peninsula." In Robert Underwood Johnson and Clarence Clough Buel, eds., *Battles and Leaders of the Civil War.* 4 vols. New York: Century, 1887–88, 2:429–33.

Bates, Samuel P. *History of Pennsylvania Volunteers, 1861–5.* 5 vols. Harrisburg P A: B. Singerly, 1869–71.

Bauer, K. Jack. *The Mexican War, 1846–1848.* New York: Macmillan, 1974.

Bayard, Samuel J. *The Life of George Dashiell Bayard* [...]. New York: Putnam's, 1874.

Beck, Elias W. H. "Letters of a Civil War Surgeon." *Indiana Magazine of History* 27 (1931): 132–63.

Brackett, Albert G. *History of the United States Cavalry, from the Formation of the Federal Government to the 1st of June, 1863.* New York: Harper & Brothers, 1865.

A Brief History of the Fourth Pennsylvania Veteran Cavalry [...]. Pittsburgh: Ewens & Eberle, 1891.

Burgess, Milton V. *David Gregg, Pennsylvania Cavalryman.* State College P A: privately issued, 1984.

Burr, Frank A., and Richard J. Hinton. *"Little Phil" and His Troopers: The Life of Gen. Philip H. Sheridan* [. . .]. Providence RI: J. A. & R. A. Reid, 1888.

Carhart, Tom. *Lost Triumph: Lee's Real Plan at Gettysburg—and Why It Failed*. New York: Putnam's, 2005.

Carpenter, J. Edward. "Gregg's Cavalry in the Gettysburg Campaign." In Alexander K. McClure, ed., *Annals of the War: Written by Leading Participants North and South*. Philadelphia: Times, 1879, 527–35.

——, comp. *A List of the Battles, Engagements, Actions and Important Skirmishes in Which the Eighth Pennsylvania Cavalry Participated* . . . Philadelphia: Allen, Lane & Scott, 1886.

Carpenter, Louis H. "Sheridan's Expedition around Richmond, May 9–25, 1864." *Journal of the United States Cavalry Association* 1 (1888): 300–24.

Carter, William Harding. *From Yorktown to Santiago with the Sixth U.S. Cavalry*. Baltimore: Lord Baltimore, 1900.

Catton, Bruce. *Grant Takes Command*. Boston: Little, Brown, 1969.

Cleaves, Freeman. *Meade of Gettysburg*. Norman: University of Oklahoma Press, 1960.

Coddington, Edwin B. *The Gettysburg Campaign: A Study in Command*. New York: Scribner's, 1968.

Coffman, Edward M. *The Old Army: A Portrait of the American Army in Peacetime, 1784–1898*. New York: Oxford University Press, 1986.

Collins, John L. "A Prisoner's March from Gettysburg to Staunton." In Robert Underwood Johnson and Clarence Clough Buel, eds., *Battles and Leaders of the Civil War*. 4 vols. New York: Century, 1887–88, 3:429–33.

Comstock, Cyrus Ballou. *The Diary of Cyrus B. Comstock*. Edited by Merlin E. Sumner. Dayton OH: Morningside, 1987.

Comte de Paris [Louis Philippe Albert d'Orleans]. *History of the Civil War in America*. 4 vols. Philadelphia: Porter & Coates, 1876–88.

Cormany, Samuel E., and Rachel B. Cormany. *The Cormany Diaries: A Northern Family in the Civil War*. Edited by James C. Mohr and Richard E. Winslow III. Pittsburgh: University of Pittsburgh Press, 1982.

Cozzens, Peter. *The Shipwreck of Their Hopes: The Battles for Chattanooga*. Urbana: University of Illinois Press, 1996.

——. *This Terrible Sound: The Battle of Chickamauga*. Urbana: University of Illinois Press, 1992.

Crackel, Theodore J. *The Illustrated History of West Point*. New York: Abrams, 1991.

Crowninshield, Benjamin W., and D. H. L. Gleason. *A History of the First Regiment of Massachusetts Cavalry Volunteers*. Boston: Houghton, Mifflin, 1891.

Cullum, George W., comp. *Biographical Register of the Officers and Graduates of the U.S. Military Academy* [. . .]. 2 vols. Boston: Houghton, Mifflin, 1891.

Custer, George Armstrong, and Elizabeth Bacon Custer. *The Custer Story: The Life and Intimate Letters of General George A. Custer and His Wife Elizabeth*. Edited by Marguerite Merington. New York: Devin-Adair, 1950.

Davies, Henry E. *General Sheridan*. New York: D. Appleton, 1899.

Davis, George B. "The Stoneman Raid." *Journal of the United States Cavalry Association* 24 (1914): 533–52.

Davis, Sidney Morris. *Common Soldier, Uncommon War: Life as a Cavalryman in the Civil War.* Edited by Charles F. Cooney. Bethesda MD: J. H. Davis, Jr., 1994.

Doster, William E. *Lincoln and Episodes of the Civil War.* New York: Putnam's, 1915.

Downey, Fairfax. *Clash of Cavalry: The Battle of Brandy Station, June 9, 1863.* New York: David McKay, 1959.

Early, Jubal A. *Autobiographical Sketch and Narrative of the War between the States.* Philadelphia: J. B. Lippincott, 1912.

Edwards, William B. *Civil War Guns: The Complete Story of Federal and Confederate Small Arms* [. . .]. Gettysburg PA: Thomas, 1997.

Fordney, Ben F. *Stoneman at Chancellorsville: The Coming of Age of Union Cavalry.* Shippensburg PA: White Mane, 1998.

Forty-Eighth Annual Report of the Association of the Graduates of the United States Military Academy, at West Point, New York, June 12th, 1917. Saginaw MI: Seemann & Peters, 1917.

Frazer, Robert W. *Forts of the West: Military Forts* [. . .] *West of the Mississippi River to 1898.* Norman: University of Oklahoma Press, 1965.

"Further Recollections of Gettysburg by Major-General Daniel E. Sickles, Major-General D. M. Gregg, Major-General John Newton and Major-General Daniel Butterfield." *North American Review* 152 (1891): 257–86.

Gilmore, D. M. "With General Gregg at Gettysburg." *Glimpses of the Nation's Struggle: A Series of Papers Read before the Minnesota Commandery of the Military Order of the Loyal Legion of the United States* 4. n.p., 1898, 93–111.

Glazier, Willard. *Three Years in the Federal Cavalry.* New York: H. Ferguson, 1870.

Gracey, S. L. *Annals of the Sixth Pennsylvania Cavalry.* Philadelphia: E. H. Butler, 1868.

Greene, A. Wilson. *Breaking the Backbone of the Rebellion: The Final Battles of the Petersburg Campaign.* Mason City IA: Savas, 2000.

———. *Civil War Petersburg: Confederate City in the Crucible of War.* Charlottesville: University of Virginia Press, 2006.

Gregg, David McMurtrie. *The Second Cavalry Division of the Army of the Potomac in the Gettysburg Campaign.* Philadelphia: privately issued, 1907.

———. "The Union Cavalry at Gettysburg." In Alexander K. McClure, ed., *Annals of the War: Written by Leading Participants North and South.* Philadelphia: Times, 1879, 372–79.

"The Gregg Monument." *Historical Review of Berks County* 27 (1962): 95.

Hartley, Chris J. *Stuart's Tarheels: James B. Gordon and His North Carolina Cavalry.* Baltimore: Butternut & Blue, 1996.

Heermance, W. L. "The Cavalry at Gettysburg." *Personal Recollections of the War of the Rebellion: Addresses Delivered before the Commandery of the State of New York, Military Order of the Loyal Legion of the United States* 3. n.p., 1907, 196–206.

Heitman, Francis B. *Historical Register and Dictionary of the United States Army* [. . .]. 2 vols. Washington DC: Government Printing Office, 1903.

Henderson, William D. *The Road to Bristoe Station: Campaigning with Lee and Meade, August 1–October 20, 1863*. Lynchburg VA: H. E. Howard, 1987.

Hennessy, John J. *Return to Bull Run: The Campaign and Battle of Second Manassas*. New York: Simon & Schuster, 1993.

Hewett, Janet, Noah Andre Trudeau, and Bryce Suderow, eds. *Supplement to the Official Records of the Union and Confederate Armies*. 3 series, 99 vols. Wilmington NC: Broadfoot, 1994–2001.

Huey, Pennock, J. Edward Carpenter, and Andrew B. Wells. "The Charge of the Eighth Pennsylvania Cavalry [at Chancellorsville]." In *Battles and Leaders of the Civil War*. 4 vols. New York: Century, 1887–88, 3:186–88.

Humphreys, Andrew A. *The Virginia Campaign of '64 and '65: The Army of the Potomac and the Army of the James*. New York: Scribner's, 1883.

Humphreys, Henry H. *Andrew Atkinson Humphreys: A Biography*. Philadelphia: John C. Winston, 1924.

——. *A Critical Explanation of Pennypacker's Life of Major General George G. Meade*. Tivoli NY: Frank O. Green, 1901.

Huntington, T. T. *Hall's Breechloaders: John H. Hall's Invention and Development of a Breechloading Rifle* [. . .]. York PA: George Shumway, 1972.

Johanson, Dorothy O., and Charles M. Gates. *Empire of the Columbia: A History of the Pacific Northwest*. New York: Harper & Row, 1967.

Johnson, Timothy D. *Winfield Scott: The Quest for Military Glory*. Lawrence: University Press of Kansas, 1998.

Johnston, Angus J., II. *Virginia Railroads in the Civil War*. Chapel Hill: University of North Carolina Press, 1961.

Jordan, David M. *Winfield Scott Hancock: A Soldier's Life*. Bloomington: Indiana University Press, 1988.

Kelsey, Charles C. *To the Knife: The Biography of Major Peter Keenan, 8th Pennsylvania Cavalry*. Ann Arbor MI: privately issued, 1964.

Kempster, Walter. "The Cavalry at Gettysburg." *War Papers: Read before the Commandery of the State of Wisconsin, Military Order of the Loyal Legion of the United States* 4. n.p., 1914, 397–429.

——. "The Early Days of Our Cavalry, in the Army of the Potomac." *War Papers: Read before the Commandery of the State of Wisconsin, Military Order of the Loyal Legion of the United States* 3. n.p., 1903, 60–89.

Kidd, James H. *Personal Recollections of a Cavalryman with Custer's Michigan Cavalry Brigade in the Civil War*. Ionia MI: Sentinel, 1908.

Krick, Robert K. *Lee's Colonels: A Biographical Register of the Field Officers of the Army of Northern Virginia*. Dayton OH: Morningside, 1992.

Linn, John Blair. *History of Centre & Clinton Counties*. Philadelphia: Lippincott, 1883.

Lloyd, William P., comp. *History of the First Reg't Pennsylvania Reserve Cavalry* [. . .]. Philadelphia: King & Baird, 1864.

Long, E. B., and Barbara Long. *The Civil War Day by Day: An Almanac, 1861–1865*. Garden City NY: Doubleday, 1971.

Longacre, Edward G. "Alfred Pleasonton, 'The Knight of Romance.'" *Civil War Times Illustrated* 13 (December 1974): 10–23.

———. *Army of Amateurs: General Benjamin F. Butler and the Army of the James, 1863–1865.* Mechanicsburg PA: Stackpole, 1997.

———. "The Battle of Reams' Station: 'The Blackest of All Days.'" *Civil War Times Illustrated* 25 (March 1986): 12–19.

———. *The Cavalry at Appomattox: A Tactical Study of Mounted Operations during the Civil War's Climactic Campaign, March 27–April 9, 1865.* Mechanicsburg PA: Stackpole, 2003.

———. *The Cavalry at Gettysburg: A Tactical Study of Mounted Operations during the Civil War's Pivotal Campaign, 9 June–14 July 1863.* Rutherford NJ: Fairleigh Dickinson University Press, 1986.

———. "Cavalry Clash at Todd's Tavern." *Civil War Times Illustrated* 16 (October 1977):12–21.

———. *General William Dorsey Pender: A Military Biography.* Conshohocken PA: Combined, 2001.

———. *Lincoln's Cavalrymen: A History of the Mounted Forces of the Army of the Potomac, 1861–1865.* Mechanicsburg PA: Stackpole, 2000.

———. *Mounted Raids of the Civil War.* South Brunswick NJ: A. S. Barnes, 1975.

Luvaas, Jay, and Wilbur S. Nye. "The Campaign That History Forgot." *Civil War Times Illustrated* 8 (November 1969): 12–37.

Lyman, Theodore. *Meade's Headquarters, 1863–1865: Letters of Colonel Theodore Lyman from the Wilderness to Appomattox.* Edited by George R. Agassiz. Boston: Atlantic Monthly Press, 1922.

Lytle, Milton S. *History of Huntingdon County.* Lancaster PA: William H. Roy, 1876.

Manring, B. F. *Conquest of the Coeur D'Alenes, Spokanes and Palouses.* Spokane WA: Inland, 1912.

Marvel, William. *Burnside.* Chapel Hill: University of North Carolina Press, 1991.

McClellan, H. B. *The Life and Campaigns of Major-General J. E. B. Stuart, Commander of the Cavalry of the Army of Northern Virginia.* Boston: Houghton, Mifflin, 1885.

McClernand, Edward J. "Cavalry Operations: The Wilderness to the James River." *Journal of the Military Service Institution of the United States* 30 (1902): 321–43.

McClure, Alexander K. *Old Time Notes of Pennsylvania: A Connected and Chronological Record.* 2 vols. Philadelphia: John C. Winston, 1905.

McWhiney, Grady, and Perry D. Jamieson. *Attack and Die: Civil War Military Tactics and the Southern Heritage.* Tuscaloosa: University of Alabama Press, 1982.

Merrill, Samuel H. *The Campaigns of the First Maine and First District of Columbia Cavalry.* Portland ME: Bailey & Noyes, 1866.

Meyer, Henry C. *Civil War Experiences under Bayard, Gregg, Kilpatrick, Raulston, and Newberry, 1862, 1863, 1864.* New York: Knickerbocker, 1911.

Miller, William E. "The Cavalry Battle near Gettysburg." In Robert Underwood Johnson and Clarence Clough Buel, eds., *Battles and Leaders of the Civil War.* 4 vols. New York: Century, 1887 88, 3:397–406.

————. *War History: Operations of the Union Cavalry on the Peninsula* […]. Carlisle PA: Hamilton Library Association, 1908.

Mitchell, John H. *Within an Invisible Circle: The Mystery of Brevet Major General David McMurtrie Gregg*. n.p.: privately issued, 2011.

Montgomery, Morton L. *History of Berks County in Pennsylvania*. Philadelphia: Everts, Peck & Richards, 1886.

Moore, Frank, ed. *The Rebellion Record: A Diary of American Events*. 12 vols. New York: various publishers, 1861–68.

Moore, James. *Kilpatrick and Our Cavalry*. New York: W. J. Widdleton, 1865.

Morrison, James L., Jr. *"The Best School in the World": West Point, the Pre-Civil War Years, 1833–1866*. Kent OH: Kent State University Press, 1986.

National Cyclopaedia of American Biography. 63 vols. New York and Clifton NJ: James T. White, 1893–1984.

Nye, Wilbur Sturtevant. *Here Come the Rebels!* Baton Rouge: Louisiana State University Press, 1965.

Official Records of the Union and Confederate Navies in the War of the Rebellion. 30 vols. Washington DC: Government Printing Office, 1894–1922.

Official Register of the Officers and Cadets of the U.S. Military Academy, West Point, N. Y. West Point NY: privately issued, 1852–55.

O'Neill, Robert F., Jr. *The Cavalry Battles of Aldie, Middleburg and Upperville: "Small but Important Riots," June 10–27, 1863*. Lynchburg VA: H. E. Howard, 1993.

————. "Col. Benjamin 'Grimes' Davis at Barbee's Cross Roads." https:// smallbutimportantriots.com/2016/08/4.

————. "'What Men We Have Got Are Good Soldiers and Brave Ones Too': Federal Cavalry Operations in the Peninsula Campaign." In William J. Miller, ed., *The Peninsula Campaign: Yorktown to Seven Pines*. 3 vols. Campbell CA: Savas, 1997, 3:79–142.

O'Reilly, Francis Augustin. *The Fredericksburg Campaign: Winter War on the Rappahannock*. Baton Rouge: Louisiana State University Press, 2006.

Oslin, Dallas H., Jr. *New Kent County Virginia in 1863: Land Geography* […]. Sandston VA: privately issued, 2008.

Patterson, Gerard A. "Friends More Than Enemies." *Civil War Times Illustrated* 36 (June 1997): 30–33.

Pleasonton, Alfred. "The Campaign of Gettysburg." In Alexander K. McClure, ed., *Annals of the War: Written by Leading Participants North and South*. Philadelphia: Times, 1879, 447–59.

————. "The Successes and Failures of Chancellorsville." In Robert Underwood Johnson and Clarence Clough Buel, eds., *Battles and Leaders of the Civil War*. 4 vols. New York: Century, 1887–88, 3:172–82.

Preston, N. D. *History of the Tenth Regiment of Cavalry, New York State Volunteers, August, 1861, to August, 1865*. New York: D. Appleton, 1892.

Rawle, William Brooke. "Further Remarks on the Cavalry Fight on the Right Flank at Gettysburg." *Journal of the United States Cavalry Association* 4 (1891): 157–60.

———. "Gregg's Cavalry Fight at Gettysburg, July 3, 1863." *Journal of the United States Cavalry Association* 4 (1891): 257–75.

———. "The Right Flank at Gettysburg," In Alexander K. McClure, ed., *Annals of the War: Written by Leading Participants North and South*. Philadelphia: Times, 1879, 467–84.

———. *The Right Flank at Gettysburg: An Account of the Operations of General Gregg's Cavalry Command* [. . .]. Philadelphia: Allen, Lane & Scott, 1878.

———. *With Gregg in the Gettysburg Campaign*. Philadelphia: McLaughlin Brothers, 1884.

Regimental History Committee. *History of the Third Pennsylvania Cavalry, Sixtieth Regiment Pennsylvania Volunteers, in the American Civil War, 1861–1865*. Philadelphia: Franklin, 1902.

Regulations for the U.S. Military Academy at West Point, New York. New York: John F. Trow, 1853.

Report of the Joint Committee on the Conduct of the War. 8 vols. Washington DC: Government Printing Office, 1863–68.

Rhea, Gordon C. *The Battle of the Wilderness, May 5–6, 1864*. Baton Rouge: Louisiana State University Press, 1994.

———. *The Battles for Spotsylvania Court House and the Road to Yellow Tavern, May 7–12, 1864*. Baton Rouge: Louisiana State University Press, 1997.

———. *Cold Harbor: Grant and Lee, May 26–June 3, 1864*. Baton Rouge: Louisiana State University Press, 2002.

———. *To the North Anna River: Grant and Lee, May 13–25, 1864*. Baton Rouge: Louisiana State University Press, 2000.

Rhodes, Charles D. *History of the Cavalry of the Army of the Potomac*. Kansas City MO: Hudson-Kimberley, 1900.

Robbins, James S. *Last in Their Class: Custer, Pickett and the Goats of West Point*. New York: Encounter, 2006.

Robbins, Walter R. *War Record and Personal Experiences of Walter Raleigh Robbins from April 22, 1861, to August 4, 1865*. Edited by Lilian Rea. Chicago: privately issued, 1923.

Robertson, John, comp. *Michigan in the War*. Lansing MI: W. S. George, 1882.

Rockwell, Alphonso D. *Rambling Recollections: An Autobiography*. New York: Paul B. Hober, 1920.

Rodenbough, Theophilus F., comp. *From Everglade to Cañon with the Second Dragoons* [. . .]. New York: D. Van Nostrand, 1875.

———. "Sheridan's Richmond Raid." In Robert Underwood Johnson and Clarence Clough Buel, eds., *Battles and Leaders of the Civil War*. 4 vols. New York: Century, 1887–88, 4:188–93.

———. "Sheridan's Trevilian Raid." In Robert Underwood Johnson and Clarence Clough Buel, eds., *Battles and Leaders of the Civil War*. 4 vols. New York: Century, 1887–88, 4:233–36.

Rodenbough, Theophilus F., and William L. Haskin, eds. *The Army of the United States: Historical Sketches of Staff and Line* [. . .]. New York: Maynard, Merrill, 1896.

Rosebush, Waldo E. *Frontier Steel: The Men and Their Weapons*. Appleton WI: C. C. Nelson, 1958.

Royer, R. D. *The McMurtrie Family*. Huntingdon PA: Huntingdon County Historical Society, 1964.

Scott, H. L., comp. *Military Dictionary, Comprising Technical Definitions* [. . .]. New York: D. Van Nostrand, 1861.

Scott, Robert Garth. *Into the Wilderness with the Army of the Potomac*. Bloomington: Indiana University Press, 1985.

Sears, Stephen W. *Chancellorsville*. Boston: Houghton Mifflin, 1996.

———. *Controversies and Commanders: Dispatches from the Army of the Potomac*. Boston: Houghton Mifflin, 1999.

———. *Landscape Turned Red: The Battle of Antietam*. New Haven CT: Ticknor & Fields, 1983.

———. *To the Gates of Richmond: The Peninsula Campaign*. New York: Ticknor & Fields, 1992.

Sheridan, Philip H. *Personal Memoirs of P. H. Sheridan*. 2 vols. New York: Charles L. Webster, 1888.

———. *Report of the Operations of the Cavalry Corps, Army of the Potomac, from April 6, to August 4, 1864*. New Orleans: Headquarters Military Division of the Gulf, 1866.

Sommers, Richard J. *Richmond Redeemed: The Siege of Petersburg*. Garden City NY: Doubleday, 1981.

Steffen, Randy. *The Horse Soldier, 1776–1943: The United States Cavalryman—His Uniforms, Arms, Accoutrements, and Equipments*. 4 vols. Norman: University of Oklahoma Press, 1977–80.

"Stoneman's Raid in the Chancellorsville Campaign." In Robert Underwood Johnson and Clarence Clough Buel, eds., *Battles and Leaders of the Civil War*. 4 vols. New York: Century, 1887–88, 3:152–53.

Stonesifer, Roy P., Jr. "The Union Cavalry Comes of Age." *Civil War History* 11 (1965): 274–83.

Styple, William B., ed. *Generals in Bronze: Interviewing the Commanders of the Civil War*. Kearny NJ: Belle Grove, 2005.

Third Annual Message of Charles F. Warwick, Mayor of the City of Philadelphia, with Annual Reports of the Departments of Law, Education and Charities, and Correction for the Year Ending December 31, 1897, vol. 4. Philadelphia: Dunlap, 1898.

Thomas, Hampton S. *Some Personal Reminiscences of Service in the Cavalry of the Army of the Potomac*. Philadelphia: L. R. Hammersly, 1889.

Tobie, Edward P. *History of the First Maine Cavalry, 1861–1865*. Boston: Emery & Hughes, 1887.

———. *Service of the Cavalry in the Army of the Potomac*. Providence RI: Snow & Farnham, 1882.

Trowbridge, Luther S. *The Operations of the Cavalry in the Gettysburg Campaign*. Detroit: privately issued, 1888.

Trudeau, Noah A. *The Last Citadel: Petersburg, Virginia, June 1864–April 1865*. Boston: Little, Brown, 1991.

Utley, Robert M. *Frontiersmen in Blue: The United States Army and the Indian, 1848–1865*. New York: Macmillan, 1967.

Venter, Bruce M. *Kill Jeff Davis: The Union Raid on Richmond, 1864*. Norman: University of Oklahoma Press, 2016.

The War of the Rebellion: A Compilation of the Official Records of the Union and Confederate Armies. 4 series, 70 vols. in 128 books. Washington DC: Government Printing Office, 1880–1901.

Warner, Ezra J. *Generals in Blue: Lives of the Union Commanders*. Baton Rouge: Louisiana State University Press, 1964.

———. *Generals in Gray: Lives of the Confederate Commanders*. Baton Rouge: Louisiana State University Press, 1959.

Weigley, Russell F. "David McMurtrie Gregg: A Personality Profile." *Civil War Times Illustrated* 1 (November 1962): 11–13, 28–30.

———. "The Twilight of Mounted Cavalry: Gregg's Division in the Petersburg Campaign." *Historical Review of Berks County* 27 (1962): 81–86, 89, 91, 93, 95.

Welsh, Jack D. *Medical Histories of the Union Generals*. Kent OH: Kent State University Press, 1996.

Wert, Jeffry D. *Cavalryman of the Lost Cause: A Biography of J. E. B. Stuart*. New York: Simon & Schuster, 2008.

———. *From Winchester to Cedar Creek: The Shenandoah Campaign of 1864*. Carlisle PA: South Mountain, 1987.

Whittaker, Frederick. *A Complete Life of Gen. George A. Custer* [. . .]. New York: Sheldon, 1876.

Williams, Robert A. "Haw's Shop: A 'Storm of Shot and Shell.'" *Civil War Times Illustrated* 9 (January 1971): 12–19.

Williams, W. W. "Letter from W. W. Williams, Co. D, Tenth New York Cavalry, and Orderly for General Gregg" *Maine Bugle* 2 (April 1891): 53–55.

Wilson, James Harrison. *Under the Old Flag: Recollections of Military Operations in the War for the Union, the Spanish War, the Boxer Rebellion, etc.* 2 vols. New York: D. Appleton, 1912.

Wister, Sarah Butler. *Walter S. Newhall: A Memoir* [. . .]. Philadelphia: C. Sherman, 1864.

Wittenberg, Eric J. *Glory Enough for All: Sheridan's Second Raid and the Battle of Trevilian Station*. Washington DC: Brassey's, 2001.

———. *Protecting the Flank at Gettysburg: The Battles for Brinkerhoff's Ridge and East Cavalry Field, July 2–3, 1863*. Rev. ed. El Dorado Hills CA: Savas Beatie, 2013.

INDEX